Yellowstone Command

1. Colonel Nelson A. Miles, Fifth Infantry, taken in 1877 by photographer Stanley J. Morrow after the successful conclusion of the Wolf Mountains campaign. Here Miles wears a beaver or sealskin hat and a nonregulation caped overcoat trimmed in bear fur, the braid on the arms denoting his rank. (Brian C. Pohanka)

Yellowstone Command

Colonel Nelson A. Miles and the Great Sioux War, 1876-1877

JEROME A. GREENE

University of Nebraska Press
Lincoln and London

First Bison Book printing: 1994
Most recent printing indicated by the last digit below:
10   9   8   7   6   5   4   3   2   1

The paper in this book meets the mimimum
requirements of American National Standard for
Information Sciences—Permanence of Paper for
Printed Library Materials, ANSI Z39.48–1984.

Library of Congress Cataloging-in-Publication Data
Greene, Jerome A.
Yellowstone command: Colonel Nelson A. Miles and the Great Sioux
War, 1876–1877 / Jerome A. Greene.
p.   cm.
Includes bibliographical references and index.
ISBN 0-8032-2142-8 (cl)
ISBN 0-8032-7046-1 (pa)
1. Dakota Indians—Wars, 1876.   2. Miles, Nelson Appleton,
1839–1925.   3. United States. Army.—Biography.   4. Generals—
Montana—Biography.   I. Title.
E83.876.M5G74   1992
973.8'2—dc20
91-2269   CIP

Dedicated to the Memory of
Lura G. Camery, 1901–1980
Teacher, Mentor, Friend

Contents

Illustrations
and Maps

Maps

Preface

On a winter day in February 1876, a contingent of blue-clad cavalry and infantry troops under Major James S. Brisbin left Fort Ellis, in southwestern Montana Territory, en route to relieve the trading post of Fort Pease, approximately 175 miles to the east, near the mouth of the Bighorn River. The soldiers reached the stockaded post on March 4, rescuing nineteen citizens threatened by Sioux Indians who had succeeded in killing six and wounding eight of their number. Thirteen others of the trading party had managed to escape earlier.

The action of Brisbin's relief column, which consisted of officers and men of the Second Cavalry and Seventh Infantry, was the first of a series of military events that spanned the next sixteen months and became known collectively as the Great Sioux War. The conflict climaxed in June with the defeat of Lieutenant Colonel George Armstrong Custer's command by allied Sioux and Northern Cheyenne Indians at the Little Bighorn River. Throughout the summer of 1876, the military campaign languished under successive delays and uncertainties while the Commanders awaited reinforcements and direction. It was finally rejuvenated with the arrival of Colonel Nelson A. Miles, Fifth Infantry, who subsequently concluded the war.

The Great Sioux War has long interested historians and students of the post-bellum American West. Comprising the first large military undertaking after the close of the Civil War, and featuring the famous battle that became known as Custer's Last Stand, the war has come to symbolize all of the Indian conflicts on the trans-Mississippi frontier after 1865. Yet the struggle against the Teton Sioux and their Cheyenne compatriots in 1876 and 1877 did not start or end with Custer's defeat. In a previous study I considered the post–Little Bighorn campaign of Brigadier General George Crook. In the present work I offer a history of the role of Colonel Miles and his troops—the so-called Yellowstone Command—in ending the conflict. Miles and his men remained in the war zone through the winter of 1876–77 and fought vigorously against the tribesmen at Spring Creek, Cedar Creek, Bark Creek, Ash Creek, Wolf Mountains, and Muddy Creek, heretofore little-known engagements that dashed all hopes the Indians might have held for reasserting their dominance in the region.

Some of Miles's campaigning has been treated previously in articles dealing with one or more facets of the war. My work, will, I hope, provide a broad context for assessing Miles's contribution as well as offer a new perspective on the Great Sioux War and other Indian conflicts of that period. The study is, foremost, a military history of Miles's campaigns and battles in 1876 and 1877 that is based on documentary research as well as on on-site field investigation. I confess a consuming fascination for the tactical details explaining the courses of engagements between army troops and Indians. I hope the fruits of this interest are conveyed herein to others of similar bent. (My greatest pleasure, perhaps, has been the discovery of the site of Colonel Miles's battle with Sitting Bull's Sioux on October 21, 1876, at Cedar Creek. The discovery was made following a search that entailed numerous visits to eastern Montana between 1981 and 1988, when the location was established beyond doubt.) Although I have relied heavily on army records in determining the courses of these encounters between U.S. troops and the Sioux and Cheyennes, I have made every attempt to incorporate Indian testimony into my study to increase its objectivity. Although I have strived for accuracy in fact and interpretation throughout, I accept responsibility for any errors that remain.

This study has benefited enormously from my associations with a great many generous people and institutions throughout its preparation. I would be remiss if I failed to acknowledge the following: the staff of the National Archives, Washington, D.C., and especially Richard Cox and the late Sara D. Jackson; Richard J. Sommers, David Keough, John Slonaker, and Michael Winey, U.S. Army Military History Institute, Army War College, Carlisle, Pennsylvania; Douglas C. McChristian, Custer Battlefield National Monument, Crow Agency, Montana; John P. Langellier, Gene Autry Western Heritage Center, Los Angeles; Douglas D. Scott, National Park Service, Lincoln, Nebraska; Neil C. Mangum, National Park Service, Santa Fe; Nancy Tystad Koupal, South Dakota State Historical Society,

Pierre; Kenneth E. Hornback, National Park Service, Denver; Robert C. Carriker, Gonzaga University, Spokane, Washington; James H. Gordon, Post Falls, Idaho; L. Clifford Soubier, National Park Service, Harpers Ferry, West Virginia; Paul A. Hutton, University of New Mexico, Albuquerque; Gordon S. Chappell, National Park Service, San Francisco; Dick Harmon, U.S. Geological Survey, Lincoln, Nebraska; Joan Huff, National Park Service, Denver; Robert M. Utley, Dripping Springs, Texas; Erwin N. Thompson, Golden, Colorado; Robert G. Pilk, National Park Service, Denver; Don C. Rickey, Evergreen, Colorado; Brian C. Pohanka, Alexandria, Virginia; Leo J. Revell, Victor, Montana; Gerald Keenan, Boulder, Colorado; Brett Boedecker, Glendive, Montana; Robert G. Palmer, Lakewood, Colorado; John D. McDermott, Sheridan, Wyoming; Paul Harbaugh, Denver, Colorado; the late John M. Carroll, Bryan, Texas; Pauline Wischmann, Circle, Montana; Margot Liberty, Sheridan, Wyoming; Edward Baker, Terry, Montana; David Kasten, Brockway, Montana; the Kansas State Historical Society, Topeka; the Boot Hill Museum, Inc., Dodge City, Kansas; the Library of Congress, Washington, D.C.; the Western History Department, Denver Public Library; the Archives and Manuscripts Division, Harold B. Lee Library, Brigham Young University, Provo, Utah; the Nebraska State Historical Society, Lincoln; the Western Historical Collections, Norlin Library, University of Colorado, Boulder; the Colorado Historical Society, Denver; the Bureau of Land Management, Terry, Montana; the Montana Historical Society, Helena; Azusa, Denver, Colorado; the Henry E. Huntington Library, San Marino, California; the Prairie County Historical Society, Terry, Montana; the U.S. Military Academy Library, West Point, New York; the South Dakota State Historical Society, Pierre; the U.S. Geological Survey Library, Denver; The Newberry Library, Chicago; and the Wyoming State Archives and Historical Department, Cheyenne.

Finally, I wish to thank two special people: Paul L. Hedren, Superintendent, Fort Union Trading Post National Historic Site, North Dakota, my Sioux War trails companion, for his interest, counsel, and persistence in urging me to undertake this study; and Linda Wedel Greene, my wife, who was always ready to assist, who gave unstintingly of her time and knowledge, and without whose understanding and steadfast encouragement this study could not have been accomplished.

CHAPTER ONE

Off for the Great Sioux War

Fort Leavenworth, Kansas, had never in re-
cent memory experienced as much activity as on the afternoon
of Wednesday, the twelfth day of July, 1876. The martial atmosphere that pervaded the garrison had spilled over into the
neighboring metropolis of Leavenworth, causing throngs of
people to assemble at the post. The area around the railroad
depot was alive with activity, as soldiers busily loaded baggage
and equipment onto sixteen Missouri Pacific freight cars
hauled out from the city and arranged on a side track overlooking the Missouri River. Officers consulted one another on the
platform as the men struggled to get mules, tents, and camp
furniture aboard and secured for the journey ahead. Sergeants
barked orders, and the groans and curses of soldiers struggling
with gear pierced the humid heat of the day. Despite their excitement at their imminent departure, the bluecoated enlisted
men accomplished the work in an orderly manner.

Loaded freight cars pulled away from the platform to make
room for passenger coaches. The majority of the six companies
of soldiers affected by the transfer, all members of the Fifth
U.S. Infantry Regiment, had remained at the parade ground
undergoing a final review. That over, they proceeded to the
depot, stepping off smartly behind the regimental flag, with
arms shouldered and haversacks slung, fully equipped for campaigning. The regimental band headed the procession, playing
the rousing air "Sherman's March to the Sea," a nostalgic tune
with deep meaning for the veterans among the men. Near the
depot, the troops halted and broke formation to bid goodby to
loved ones. Their youthful commander, Colonel Nelson A.
Miles, and his wife, Mary, drew up in an ambulance near the

train and held court for farewells from friends from the fort and the city.

Soon the soldiers clambered on the train. When the cars filled, Miles embraced his wife, then leaped aboard himself to wild cheers from the watching throng of citizens and officers. As the cars slowly pulled ahead, the departing soldiers waved from the windows, flourishing hats, bouquets, and handkerchiefs. The bandsmen, who did not accompany the troops, stood on the platform and serenaded their departing comrades until the receding train was lost to sight amid heavy foliage beyond the depot sometime around six o'clock in the evening. They played the old Civil War favorite "The Girl I Left Behind Me."[1] The irony of the selection was probably lost on everyone present: scarcely two months earlier, accompanied by those same strains, Lieutenant Colonel George A. Custer had led his Seventh Cavalry forth from Fort Abraham Lincoln, Dakota Territory, toward a fateful destiny at the Battle of the Little Bighorn.

News of the Little Bighorn tragedy had reached Fort Leavenworth a week earlier, on July 5, when officers and enlisted men had awakened to read the stunning particulars of the disaster in the pages of the *Leavenworth Daily Times*. The topic of Custer's fall had dominated all thought and conversation, for many friends and former comrades-in-arms had perished in far-off Montana Territory at the hands of the Sioux and Cheyenne Indians. Shocked citizens of Leavenworth had gathered on street corners to share their disbelief; that many officers of Custer's regiment had served at the fort only made the news more difficult to bear. The daily tabloids described the prevailing atmosphere in both city and garrison as "nearly the same as if a large portion of our immediate community had been visited by some dread calamity."[2] Two days after learning of the debacle on the Little Bighorn, Miles had received orders directing the available companies of the Fifth Infantry to the war zone. At his request, he was permitted to head the contingent.

The following five days had been active ones, with much to do in little time. Miles would field only six companies immediately (Companies B, E, F, G, H, and K), with the expectation that the remaining six units of the regiment would follow. Over the ensuing days, preparations for departure proceeded amid excitement, sometimes conflicting orders, and ever-startling rumors. The papers on July 10 had refuted one hysterical report that Brigadier General George Crook, commanding one of the principal armies in the field, had been killed and part of his command annihilated by the same Sioux and Cheyennes that had wiped out Custer.[3]

On the evening preceding the departure, Miles permitted his soldiers one last night on the town. Large numbers of them visited the city, "paying their old haunts a farewell." The troops were to travel north via the Missouri Pacific cars as far as Atchison, where they would board a Kansas City, St. Joseph, and Council Bluffs train for the first leg of their journey north.[4]

The orders sending Miles and the Fifth Infantry to the Sioux country in the wake of the worst military catastrophe since the Civil War were designed partly to restore confidence in a foundering army operation that had dragged on for nearly four months. The campaign against the Teton Sioux and their allies had historical roots dating back a century. The interests of the Tetons, or Lakotas (commonly known as the Western Sioux) in expanding their territory, coupled with aggression from their neighbors, had caused those Indians to begin a migration west from the Great Lakes region during the closing decades of the eighteenth century. Ultimately gaining control of a vast area stretching from the Yellowstone to the Platte and from the Missouri River to the Big Horn Mountains, they forced out smaller tribes and entered into loose albeit durable alliances with the Northern Cheyennes and Northern Arapahoes.

By 1851, the Tetons stood in the way of American expansion and in that year the U.S. government negotiated, at Fort Laramie, a treaty to control the northern plains tribes that all but conceded the supremacy of Sioux power among them. Thereafter, the lines were drawn between the Sioux and the government and collision between the mutually expanding powers became inevitable. Warfare erupted in 1854, when Tetons wiped out a small army detachment near Fort Laramie. Troops from Fort Leavenworth, under Brigadier General William S. Harney, retaliated in a slaughter of many Sioux noncombatants at Ash Hollow, Nebraska. Those episodes set the course of Sioux-white relations over the next two decades.[5]

In the second Treaty of Fort Laramie, signed in 1868, following a protracted two-year military conflict between the Sioux and the army, the Indians reluctantly agreed to remain within prescribed boundaries approximating those of the present state of South Dakota west of the Missouri River. The government established several agencies on the Great Sioux Reservation to administer Indian affairs, although the Indians retained hunting privileges in Wyoming Territory west to the Big Horn Mountains and south to the North Platte River. Within this vaguely defined area, Indians who refused to reside on the reservation enjoyed unrestricted movement, and whites were not allowed. It remained unclear whether the "unceded Indian territory" extended north to the Yellowstone River, although the Teton Sioux, who had earlier appropriated the tract from the Crow tribe, continued to occupy it at will.[6]

Enforcement of the provisions of the Fort Laramie Treaty coincided with the Grant administration's formulation of procedures to deal effectively with Indians on and off the reservations. At the heart of the so-called Peace Policy was the government's intention to place all tribes on reservations away from centers of white settlement and the main arteries west. In theory, the Indians would be treated kindly there and taught to farm, with the idea that eventually they would become acculturated and would adopt the ways of the whites. Education and adequate feeding, it was hoped, would prevent such outbreaks as had occurred in the past. Under Grant's program, representatives of different Christian religious denominations were appointed to the agencies to implement the policy. Many Indians openly resisted these attempts to settle them on reservations.

Within a few years most of the army leaders came to oppose Grant's Peace Policy as idealistic and unworkable; many key officers, Lieutenant General Philip H. Sheridan among them, believed certain of its objectives might be realized only after the Indians felt the brunt of military power. Throughout Grant's administration and after, a conflict of varying intensity persisted between the army and the Indian Bureau over who should control Indian affairs. Despite occasional crises that dictated a need for military control, civilian direction prevailed at the agencies. Significantly, most of the Indian wars of the late 1860s, 1870s, and 1880s, including that with the Sioux and Northern Cheyennes in 1876, resulted from the tribes' resistance to the cultural asphyxiation that awaited them on the reservations.[7]

Growing Sioux resentment over attempts to isolate them on reservations and the inexorable movement west by whites combined to thwart the peaceful design of the Fort Laramie Treaty of 1868. The tide of white emigration that spread across the continent after the Civil War hardly touched the newly defined Sioux lands until the early 1870s. Then gold was found in substantial deposits in the Black Hills of Dakota Territory. A government expedition headed by Lieutenant Colonel Custer confirmed the reports, and U.S. authorities were unable to stem the tide of white trespassers on Sioux lands.

The Black Hills gold rush infuriated the Sioux. Many of them struck back along the trails leading to and from the gold camps. Some miners were killed; others faced constant threat of attack by parties of warriors bent on stealing livestock and goods. Troops sent to evict the miners vigorously performed their duty at first, but, after failing to stem the influx, practically conceded the area to them. Even leading military officials sensed the inevitability of white occupation of the Black Hills. Lieutenant General Sheridan, commanding the Military Division of the Missouri, within whose administrative unit the Black Hills lay, did not enthusiastically support the treaty provisions excluding whites. Even more, he desired white emigration into the unceded territory to the north and west—the Bighorn and Yellowstone country, believing it would finally lead to extinction of the Indians' treaty right.[8]

The Tetons who roamed the Yellowstone country in the 1870s comprised members of all the tribal bands, including the large Hunkpapa and Oglala groups under such leaders as Sitting Bull, Gall, and Crazy Horse, as well as representatives of the smaller groups known as Brules, Sans Arcs, Blackfeet, Two Kettles, and Minneconjous. Each of those smaller bands included civil and war leaders of stature more or less comparable to those of the Hunkpapas and Oglalas. Generally, the bands ranged over the region of the Powder, Bighorn, and Yellowstone rivers, hunting buffalo and operating relatively independently of each other. Occasionally, two or more bands merged temporarily for ceremonial or familial reasons; sometimes the tribal cohesion was prompted by security. Because of cultural similarities and intermarriage, the Sioux continued their longstanding alliance with the Northern Cheyennes and Northern Arapahoes.

All three tribes, and especially the Sioux, repeatedly attacked and raided the Crows, who had occupied the region for several generations and who regarded the newcomers as trespassers. Consequently, the once populous and powerful Crows, reduced by smallpox and cholera in years past and numbering only a few thousand people by the 1870s, readily allied themselves with the whites and lost few opportunities to strike against the Sioux. Thus, the government's intended pursuit of the "hostiles" (as the nonreservation Tetons were formally designated by the War Department) was looked upon with certain approval by the Crows and other tribes of the upper Missouri.[9]

For some twenty-five thousand kinsmen of the so-called wild Tetons, the government maintained six agencies on the Great Sioux Reservation: Standing Rock, Cheyenne River, Crow Creek, and Lower Brule, all along the Missouri River, and Red Cloud and Spotted Tail—named for the principal headmen of the reservation factions of Oglalas and Brules—in extreme northwestern Nebraska (actually outside the reservation boundary).

During the warmer months some reservation Indians quietly slipped away from the agencies to hunt and raid with the followers of Sitting Bull and Crazy Horse, only to return to the security of the government ration before the snows fell. Those sojourners greatly troubled the white agents, for they fomented rebellion at the agencies, posed a physical threat to the authorities, and, from the government's standpoint, countered the Indians' progress toward acculturation. Moreover, when away from the reservation, those same people joined the nonagency bands in conducting raids against settlers and other Indians throughout the region to the north and west. "The northern, or hostile, or non-treaty Sioux," surmised the Commissioner of Indian Affairs in recounting the beginning of the conflict,

> are in no sense a recognized band or branch of the great Sioux Nation, but consist of representatives from all the bands, who have rallied around one [Sitting Bull] as their leader who claims never to have been party to any treaty with the United States, and who styles himself chief of the followers whom his personal power and avowed hostility to civilization and the United States Government have attracted around him. This camp at last became a rallying-point for malcontents from the various agencies; a paradise for those who, tired of Government beef and restless under agency restraint, were venturesome enough to resort

again to their old life by the chase; a field of glory for the young braves whose reputation for prowess was yet to be made; and an asylum for outlaws among the Indians themselves, who, fleeing thither might escape retribution for crime.[10]

Thus, the government's eventual targeting of the "northern Indians" for relocation was designed to solve several related problems.

Sheridan's hope of establishing a government presence within the Indians' domain in the form of one or more military posts recalled similar past efforts. As early as 1864, Brigadier General Alfred Sully, operating in the Yellowstone country, sought to build a fort from which soldiers might oversee the Sioux and their allies. Low waters on the Yellowstone River prevented the delivery of supplies, however, and Sully was forced instead to establish a military reservation and supply depot farther downstream, at the confluence of that river with the Missouri River, near the old fur-trading post of Fort Union. Two years later that station was designated Fort Buford. In 1865, Brigadier General Patrick E. Connor led another effort to build a fort in the region. Despite Connor's disastrous campaign, beset by freezing temperatures and mass starvation among his troops, he built Fort Connor, subsequently renamed Fort Reno, along the headwaters of the Powder River in present-day Wyoming.

The establishment of Fort Reno and two other posts, Fort Philip Kearny and Fort C. F. Smith, both erected in 1866 along the Bozeman Trail leading to the Montana goldfields, enraged the Indians. In the resulting all-out warfare between 1866 and 1868, eighty soldiers were killed in the noted Fort Kearny "massacre" of 1866 and there were many other casualties as well. The forts were abandoned by the United States as a provision of the Fort Laramie Treaty in 1868. By the early 1870s numerous military posts bordered the Sioux country, but none had yet been established in the core of the Sioux lands.[11]

The projected route of the Northern Pacific Railroad along the Yellowstone River further encouraged military leaders to consider placing a permanent post somewhere along that stream. The need for protection of the railroad construction crews was a justification for the building of winter quarters. In 1873 Sheridan and Commanding General William T. Sherman called on Congress to appropriate funds for two forts in the region of the Yellowstone. An economy-minded legislature demurred, however, not only in 1873 but over the two succeeding years as well. Undaunted, Sheridan sent an aide to examine the lower Yellowstone and select a site for a supply base for troops escorting the railroad surveyors. A spot was chosen on the river opposite the mouth of Glendive Creek, at the point where the Northern Pacific would enter the Yellowstone Valley. Part of Custer's mission to the Black Hills in 1874 was to locate a site for a post from which the army could watch over the Sioux. Yet Sheridan's major goal remained the establishment of the Yellowstone forts.[12]

By late 1875, the U.S. government believed that, as the crisis over ownership of the Black Hills intensified, a military presence was urgently needed. At a White House meeting on November 3, President Grant had ordered that the army no longer be responsible for keeping miners out of the Great Sioux Reservation, although he hoped that the integrity of its boundaries would be respected. But his directive only encouraged invasion by whites. Furthermore, since it was largely the nonagency Sioux—those who continued to reside in the Yellowstone country—who influenced their reservation kinsmen to oppose the sale of the Black Hills, Grant and Sheridan agreed (with Sherman's concurrence) to force the dissidents onto the reservation, where they might be more effectively controlled. This became the immediate cause of the government's war with the Sioux.[13]

The geographical area inhabited by the affected tribes fell under General Sheridan's administrative control. The Military Division of the Missouri, largest of the army's management spheres, encompassed practically all of the Great Plains and included the territories of Dakota, Montana, and Wyoming, and the state of Nebraska. From his headquarters in Chicago, Sheridan monitored the progress of all Indian campaigns within his jurisdiction. In 1876 operations against the Sioux proceeded in two of the five military departments in the division: the Department of Dakota, headed by Brigadier General Alfred H. Terry from offices in St. Paul, and the Department of the Platte, under Brigadier General Crook, headquartered in Omaha. The Department of Dakota consisted of the state of Minnesota and the territories of Dakota and Montana, and the Department of

2. Commanding General William T. Sherman supported Miles's successes but urged prudence in his handling of Sitting Bull's Sioux after they crossed into Canada. Sherman later credited Miles with ending the Indian war. (Jerome A. Greene)

the Platte embraced the states of Iowa and Nebraska, and the Territory of Wyoming and part of the Territory of Idaho.[14]

In December 1875, the Bureau of Indian Affairs of the Department of the Interior, in rare concert with the War Department, sent word from the agencies to the dissidents in the Yellowstone country that they must come in by the end of January or face the army. Whether because of severe weather or because of a disinclination to obey the summons, or for other reasons, the affected bands did not respond. When the specified date passed, the Interior Department, as expected, turned the matter over to the military authorities, who formulated plans for an army offensive to forcibly round up the Indians. The army campaign that followed over the next seventeen or so months consisted of a number of disjointed movements that constituted the Great Sioux War—in actuality a government action to drive Sitting Bull, Crazy Horse, and their followers onto the Great Sioux Reservation.[15]

The campaign foundered from the beginning. A fierce, freezing winter kept troops from taking the field for several weeks, a period during which the impatient Sheridan renewed his lobbying for a congressional appropriation for building the desired posts in the Yellowstone Basin. Anxious to get his command moving, Sheridan would not be deterred by the weather, preferring to move on the Indians much as he had against those on the southern plains in 1868 and 1874. He devised a plan to trap the Indians between converging columns of troops coming from the east, south, and west. Under this design, Custer would march west from Fort Lincoln with one column, while Crook and Colonel John Gibbon would approach the Yellowstone from Wyoming and western Montana, respectively. Although Sheridan doubtless hoped that cooperation among his army commands would promote a smooth and efficient field operation, he issued no directive emphasizing such concert.[16]

Sheridan's strategy against the Sioux in the winter of 1875–76 won endorsement from Commanding General Sherman. The technique of striking Indian encampments in the dead of winter, when their chief means of mobilization—their ponies—lacked nourishment, had previously proved successful against the Cheyennes on the southern plains. A precursor of the military strategy of "total war," in which entire populations suffered the physical and psychological effects of armed on-

3. Lieutenant General Philip H. Sheridan commanded the Military Division of the Missouri in 1876–77. He conceived the principal strategy for ending hostilities with the Sioux and Northern Cheyennes. Miles's subsequent operations ensured Sheridan's success. (Jerome A. Greene)

slaught, Sheridan's plan represented a continuation of a similar strategy implemented by him and Sherman in the South during the Civil War, most notably in Sheridan's Shenandoah Valley Campaign of 1864 and Sherman's march through Georgia the following year.

The "total war" concept, though never formally instilled among the officer corps, nevertheless extended from the Civil War into the Indian wars, where it became the mainstay of otherwise standard army operations against the ever-elusive western tribes.[17] In the West, under Sheridan's influence, it was coupled with the ancient tactic of surprise; army columns scored their most successful victories between 1865 and 1890 by swooping down on Indian villages at daybreak, driving the occupants from their lodges and capturing their horses before the warriors could effectively counter the assault. The tactic proved immensely costly to villages in the loss of ponies and material goods, and families were often forced to surrender or take refuge in neighboring camps. Often, too, women and children died in the army attacks. The army justified this form of aggression as decisive and—in the long run—humane, a tactic that worked against tribes that seldom stayed in one place and generally avoided direct confrontation. Other than using the frequently practiced surprise and "total war" elements, the army followed mostly conservative and conventional procedures in fighting Indians, especially in logistics, with its winding columns of troops and wagons.[18]

In accordance with Sheridan's directive, the army's action against the Sioux began in March 1876, with a column under General Crook striking north from Fort Fetterman in northern Wyoming. The troops endured days of subzero temperatures while moving toward the Powder River region of southeastern Montana. On March 17, soldiers from Crook's command led by Colonel Joseph J. Reynolds struck an encampment of Indians on the Little Powder at dawn, capturing the pony herd and abundant supplies, while driving the occupants into the snow-covered hills. Reynolds, a former Union commander of great prominence, somehow lost the initiative at Powder River and failed to hold the herd against the tribesmen's repeated efforts to regain their horses. Furthermore, Reynolds ordered the destruction of supplies in the camp on which Crook had planned to sustain his field operation.

Perhaps even worse in the long run, Reynolds's attack was not on Teton Sioux villagers, but on Northern Cheyennes under Chief Two Moon, a factor that no doubt further solidified the alliance between the Cheyennes and the Tetons. Crook became incensed at Reynolds for his failure at Powder River as well as for the negative publicity that the campaign generated in the press. Back at Fort Fetterman, where he had withdrawn his troops because of plummeting temperatures and logistical disarray, Crook brought formal charges against Reynolds that resulted in that officer's eventual court-martial and resignation from the service.[19] If the Crook-Reynolds Powder River campaign accomplished anything, it was to further antagonize the Sioux and bring the Northern Cheyennes directly into the fray, thereby enlarging the scope of the problem facing the army.

The failure of the Powder River expedition necessitated another attempt, one involving more field commands. Adhering to his previous plan, Sheridan once again directed the three columns to close on the Yellowstone region. Colonel Gibbon, who commanded the District of Montana, in Terry's department, moved east from Forts Ellis and Shaw in April, descending the Yellowstone with a contingent of Seventh Infantrymen and Second Cavalrymen, who guarded against the Indians' attempts to ford the stream and head toward Canada. Complementing Gibbon's containment maneuver, Crook's troops were to again drive north and act in concert with the third column, that from Fort Lincoln, commanded by General Terry and including Custer's Seventh Cavalry regiment.

As Terry's command journeyed west from Fort Lincoln during the latter part of May, Crook pulled out of Fort Fetterman and headed back into Montana, accompanied by units of the Fourth and Ninth Infantry and the Second and Third Cavalry. He soon encountered Indians. On June 9, warriors fired on his camp along the Tongue River in northern Wyoming but did little damage. The incident was a portent, for eight days later, Sioux and Cheyennes staged a massive attack on Crook along the headwaters of Rosebud Creek, Montana. It was an engagement notable not only for its fierceness and duration, but also for the fact that it was instigated by the Indians—something almost unheard of in Indian warfare. Crook's command, ably assisted by Crow and Shoshone scouts, fought practically all day over a large and rugged area before the Indians withdrew. Weary from the encounter and weighted down with his wounded, Crook turned about and headed south to recuperate his command and await reinforcements, in effect conceding a strategic defeat that prevented his meeting with Terry and Custer.[20]

The Battle of Rosebud Creek, of which Terry and Custer knew nothing, set the stage for the Little Bighorn disaster one week later. With Crook's location uncertain, on June 21 Terry directed Custer to march from the Yellowstone and reconnoiter the upper Rosebud for a Sioux village suspected to be in the vicinity. En route, Custer encountered a large trail leading west into the adjacent Little Bighorn Valley. On June 25 he located a village of undetermined size and, forsaking the traditional dawn attack, Custer divided his troops and attacked at midday. Those factors, coupled with Custer's insufficient knowledge of the terrain and the size of the village that lay before him, brought resounding catastrophe. Of twelve companies of the Seventh Cavalry, the five with Custer were destroyed. The remaining units suffered heavy casualties and only the timely arrival of General Terry with Colonel Gibbon's command prevented their complete annihilation. The total dead numbered 268, including several soldiers who died later from their wounds. On June 27 the surviving soldiers joined to bury their comrades in makeshift graves scraped out of the ashy soil of the Little Bighorn Valley.[21]

News of Custer's defeat and death jolted the country in early July, all but eclipsing the celebration of the nation's centennial. As shocked citizens pondered the military implications, Sherman, Sheridan, and their immediate subordinates were left to assess the real and psychological damage wrought by the battle and to get the Sioux campaign back on track. Their first response was to reinforce the commands of Terry, Gibbon, and Crook in the Yellowstone region, and within days of the wire stories about Custer's calamity, Sheridan ordered Miles and the Fifth Infantry companies to the front. At the same time he directed six companies of the Twenty-second Infantry, commanded by Lieutenant Colonel Elwell S. Otis, to take the field in Dakota Territory from their stations along the Great Lakes. The entire Fifth Cavalry, under Colonel Wesley Merritt, hastened to join Crook in Wyoming before Crook resumed the offensive. Elsewhere, army recruiting stations began a lively business to fill the vacancies in the Seventh Cavalry left by the

4. Lieutenant Colonel George A. Custer sat for this image two months before his death at the Little Bighorn. Custer's defeat set in motion the events that culminated in Miles's aggressive campaigning to end the Great Sioux War. (Custer Battlefield National Monument)

Little Bighorn carnage; in August Congress approved the enlistment of twenty-five hundred cavalrymen.[22]

Sending fresh troops into the field was only part of Sheridan's reaction to the Sioux crisis. Within two days of learning of Custer's defeat, he addressed a letter to Sherman in which he again called for a congressional appropriation for construction of posts in the region of the hostilities. To his mind, only those manifestations of government jurisdiction, placed in the heart of the area occupied by the northern bands, would destroy tribal freedom, promote white settlement of the region, and end the Sioux problem. Prompted by the recent events, Congress on July 22 passed the desired legislation, authorizing two hundred thousand dollars for the erection of two forts on the Bighorn and Tongue rivers, at or near their confluences with the Yellowstone. Four days later, in another belated victory for Sheridan, who had urged such action since May, the Interior Department turned over to the military authorities control of the Teton agencies in Dakota Territory and Nebraska.[23]

Even as these developments unfolded, and as Colonel Miles and the Fifth Infantry headed north from Fort Leavenworth, the pace of the war briefly quickened. On July 17, Colonel Merritt's Fifth Cavalrymen encountered a large body of Cheyennes en route from the Red Cloud Agency to the Powder River country. In an engagement important because it prevented the union of these Indians with those of Sitting Bull and Crazy Horse, Merritt succeeded, with minimal opposition, in turning the Cheyennes back to the agency. The affair at Hat, or Warbonnet, Creek, in extreme northwest Nebraska, simultaneously symbolized the determination of the government forces to subdue the Indians and restored a measure of confidence to flagging field commands still reeling from the Little Bighorn catastrophe.[24]

By the time the Warbonnet episode took place, Miles and the Fifth Infantry were already five days into their journey. Their arrival in the north country could only further improve the morale of the troops, for the Fifth possessed a long tradition of excellence going back to the early days of the republic. Although it was initially organized in 1798, its service was at first intermittent, the unit being variously disbanded, reorganized, or consolidated with other regiments through the aftermath of the War of 1812. After that it served continuously, fighting in

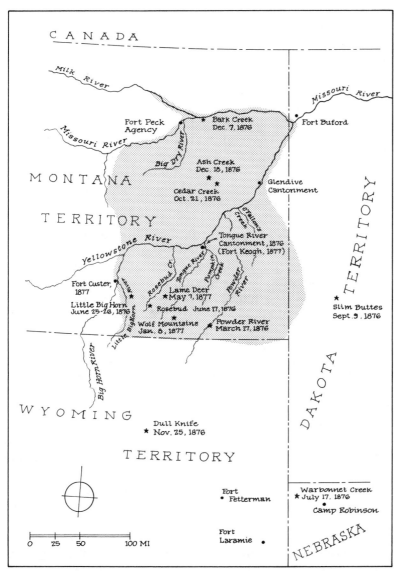

1. The Great Sioux War, 1876–77, showing area of Miles's operations

the Black Hawk War (1841–42), and in the Mexican War (1845–48). Early in the latter conflict the regiment performed meritoriously at the battles of Resaca de la Palma and Monterey under the command of Major General Zachary Taylor. Later, composing part of the command of Major General Winfield Scott, the Fifth fought at Churubusco and Molino del Rey and participated in the storming of the palace of Chapultepec, which precipitated the capitulation of Mexico City. After the Mexican War, the regiment was posted variously in Arkansas, the Indian Territory (present Oklahoma), and Texas. It was transferred to Florida in 1857 to deal with one of the Seminole uprisings, and within three years was back on the frontier, playing a role in the government's war against the Mormons in Utah Territory.

In 1860 the Fifth Infantry transferred to New Mexico Territory. When the Civil War erupted a short time later, the regiment remained in the West, where it effectively countered Confederate incursions. As at other times in the unit's history, the companies of the Fifth did not stay together, but occupied several different garrisons. Parts of the regiment fought in numerous forays against the Confederates, notably at Apache Canyon and Peralta in 1862.

In the Indian wars that followed the Civil War, the Fifth Infantry garnered an illustrious reputation. In 1866 the regiment was reassigned to the Department of the Missouri, and two years later it garrisoned Forts Riley, Wallace, Lyon, Hays, and Reynolds, and Camps Davidson and Cottonwood Creek, Kansas. The Fifth distinguished itself in the sporadic warfare with the Cheyennes in the western part of the state during the late 1860s.

In 1869, the regiment consolidated with the Thirty-seventh Infantry. The reorganized Fifth acquired a new commander, the vigorous Colonel Nelson Appleton Miles, under whose training and leadership it became one of the premier Indian-fighting units of the army. During the Red River War (1874–75) Miles headed a successful drive against a large body of Kiowas, Comanches, and Southern Cheyennes, using parts of the Fifth that were aided by complements of cavalry and artillery. The troops fought a succession of engagements. A signal episode was the rescue at McClellan Creek, Texas, of two white girls, the Germaine sisters, who had been taken captive by the Cheyennes. At the conclusion of the war, most of the Cheyennes surrendered as prisoners; the resistance of the other tribes was practically destroyed by the campaigning of Miles and Colonel Ranald S. Mackenzie.[25]

Miles benefited personally from his success in the Red River War. His reputation as an Indian fighter gradually supplanted the laurels he had won during the Civil War and ensured him a place of prominence in latter–nineteenth-century American military history. A proud man, he was also hard working and dedicated to his profession. In 1876 his career still had more than two decades to run, but at age thirty-six, he had already attained a rank and responsibility matched by few of his army associates. Ever one to seize opportunity and make the most of it, Miles became a superb performer, and by the end of the Sioux War his value to his military superiors would be compounded tenfold.

Such a record as Miles was to make for himself in the Sioux War in particular and the Indian wars in general had much to do with the man's origins. He was not a West Point graduate, and, in fact, had little formal education and no training in the military arts. Indeed, his accomplishments in the army might well be attributed to overcompensation for his perceived educational deficiencies, although his family could boast a military tradition dating from the colonial Indian wars and the Revolutionary War.

Born on a farm near Westminster, Massachusetts, on August 8, 1839, this youngest child of Daniel and Mary Miles attended local schools before emigrating to Boston at age seventeen to work in a crockery shop. He continued his education at night school and became interested in military precepts informally taught him by a former French army officer. After the outbreak of the Civil War, Miles assembled a company of seventy volunteers and received a commission of first lieutenant in the Twenty-second Massachusetts Infantry. Because of his youth, he at first held only staff positions, but in May and June of 1862, as the newly appointed lieutenant colonel of the Sixty-first New York Infantry, Miles led troops at the Battle of Fair Oaks, Virginia, an engagement in which he was wounded. His superiors commended his performance, and within four months he had been advanced to colonel for his service at Antietam. At Fredericksburg, on December 13, 1862, he was seriously wounded in the throat, his neck scarred for life, and at Chancellorsville the following May, he received yet another wound, being shot off his horse "while holding with his command a line of abattis and rifle pits against a strong force of the enemy."[26] For that service Miles received a brevet of brigadier general of volunteers plus, years later, a Medal of Honor. He won further plaudits for subsequent performances in the Wilderness, Spotsylvania, and Reams's Station battles, and at Petersburg, where he was again wounded. He received promotion to brigadier general of volunteers in May 1864, commanding the First Division, II Corps, Army of the Potomac, through most of the campaign leading to Appomattox and the conclusion of the war. On October 21, 1865, Miles, at age twenty-six, was promoted to major general of volunteers, commanding twenty-six thousand officers and men of the II Corps.

Following Appomattox, Miles was appointed custodian of former Confederate States president Jefferson Davis, incarcerated at Fort Monroe. He endured prolonged, bitter, and unwarranted censure from Southerners over the physical treatment of the confined Davis, but was later vindicated for his management of the situation. In the reduction in size of the postwar army, Miles garnered the colonelcy of the Fortieth Infantry and was mustered out of the volunteers in July 1866. On June 30, 1868, he married Mary Hoyt Sherman. The wellchosen bride was the niece of Senator John Sherman of Ohio and his brother, Lieutenant General William T. Sherman, who was soon to command the entire army. Miles shamelessly exploited this relationship, often promoting his unsolicited views, as well as his personal ambitions, to General Sherman, thus circumventing the normal chain of command.

With the reorganization of the army in 1869, Miles was sent to the Fifth Infantry and began his Indian-fighting career. His skilled performance as a field commander in the Red River War marked him as a reliable and resourceful leader (if somewhat prone to self-aggrandizement), who could be trusted to carry out the dictums of authority with precision and dispatch. He quickly became one of a select handful of army officers whose successes against the Indians ensured their long-standing assignment in the West. Dark-haired, mustachioed, and handsome, Miles cut a dashing figure in military circles and was often compared to Custer, his friend. In personality and temperament he was a perfectionist who strove to deliver what the army hierarchy desired, an overachiever who accepted in himself and others nothing short of excellence. Often abrupt and demanding in his relations with others, he nonetheless possessed leadership instincts that brought out the best qualities in his troops. As early as June 15 he had written Sherman requesting to be sent with his regiment to the Indian country and to remain there until the Indians were "worn out or subjected." Based on his enthusiasm and past record, Miles's superiors' confidence could only be reinforced by his performance in the Great Sioux War.[27]

CHAPTER TWO

In Custer's Wake

The six companies of the Fifth Infantry traveled by rail along the Missouri River to Yankton, Dakota Territory, arriving there on July 14 at 2 A.M. The route north from Fort Leavenworth passed through numerous towns draped in black to mourn Custer's fallen command. Citizens gathered at the depots to cheer and shout encouragement to the soldiers, evoking to Miles "the time when the troops were going to the war for the Union in the days of 1861 and '62."[1] Three days after reaching Yankton, amid rumors and fears that the Sioux would long be gone by the time the troops reached the front, the command boarded the chartered steamer *E. H. Durfee* and, at 3:30 A.M. on the seventeenth, continued their journey up the Missouri. On the river, shoreline demonstrations were common at each community passed, and the men, confident in their purpose, reciprocated with shouts of approval. As the steamboat ploughed past one army post, officers and their ladies lined the bank; an officer drew his handkerchief to signal a word of encouragement to the men: "success." One of Miles's men signaled back: "You bet."[2]

Such reminders of the mission of the Fifth Infantry companies occurred frequently during the ascent of the river. Passing the Standing Rock Agency, Miles learned that on the previous day several Sioux warriors had come in, one bearing wounds purportedly received at the Little Bighorn, to urge their kin at that place to stay put and not consider joining Sitting Bull. To his incredulity, Miles also learned from an officer commanding the Sixth Infantrymen at Standing Rock that traders there had delivered nearly one hundred thousand rounds of ammunition to the nonagency Indians. Here, too, he read in a newspaper that, once the four remaining companies arrived, his regiment was expected to garrison the two posts now contemplated for the Yellowstone region. To Miles this was an unrealistic proposition at best because he believed this arrangement would exhaust his men and allow the Indians to place themselves between the two forces.[3]

The *Durfee* docked at Fort Abraham Lincoln, on the west bank, across and downstream from Bismarck, around 8:30 A.M. on Sunday, July 23. Less than three weeks earlier, a steamboat carrying the wounded from Custer's battlefield had moored there. Since that time a gloom had settled over Fort Lincoln, where twenty-seven widows and many orphans of the Little Bighorn victims attempted to adjust to the tragedy. Following an onshore inspection of his command by Lieutenant Colonel Absalom Baird, assistant inspector general of the army, to ensure that the men were properly equipped for campaigning, Miles sought out Elizabeth Custer to offer his condolences. "I never saw anything like it," he wrote his wife. "Mrs. Custer is not strong and I would not be surprised if she did not improve. She seemed so depressed and in such despair."[4]

The inspection completed, the soldiers climbed back on the *Durfee* and at 3 A.M. the following morning started north again.[5] A sister vessel, the *Josephine*, trailed behind, bearing recruits and provisions for Terry's operation. The next day, the command received instructions to crate all articles of equipage deemed inappropriate for the campaign. The men accordingly boxed for shipment back downstream such items as bayonets and their scabbards, knapsacks, kepis, and officers' sabres. "In place of cartridge boxes," recalled Miles, "they gladly buckled about their waists the more useful equipment of cartridge belts, with the cartridges carefully polished for immediate and serious action." That done, the men passed the days drilling, reading, cleaning their rifles and equipment, and writing letters home. Evenings aboard the *Durfee* were often spent in group singing or in listening to talented vocalists among the infantrymen. The journey to the mouth of the Yellowstone passed without incident, except for the frequent times when the steamer went aground on sandbars. "When an accident of this kind occurred," wrote Miles, "the great shafts in the bow of the boat were lowered, and with the engines the bow was partially lifted off, while the stern wheel was reversed and then another effort made to find the main current of the waters."[6]

On Wednesday, July 26, Miles and his soldiers stopped briefly at Fort Stevenson, Dakota, before moving on to Fort Buford on the Missouri at the mouth of the Yellowstone, which was reached the next evening about 10 P.M. Compared to the other days, July 27 was eventful. Miles had learned from a passing steamer, the *Meade*, that a large party of Indians had crossed the Yellowstone downstream from Fort Buford. Although the prevailing thought was that these were mainly women and children bound for an agency, Miles decided that they were probably Sioux warriors and determined to take action. Captain Samuel J. Ovenshine reported that Miles planned to take five companies and surround the Indians, while one company was to stay on the boat to keep them from crossing. When the lodges came into sight and the troops debarked, Miles's men badly scared a band of peaceful Yanktonais bearing agency passes.[7]

At Fort Buford the mood of the garrison was quiet and gloomy, offering a striking contrast to the ebullience of Miles's men. The troops passed the night and reembarked the following morning, the *Durfee* at last steaming up the Yellowstone on the final leg of its journey. The trip was slow, the steamboat able to ascend the river only from daybreak, about 3 A.M., to 6 P.M., when the crew moored the vessel and collected wood along the bank. On the first evening out from Fort Buford, while the boatmen sought timber for their boilers and the army horses grazed nearby, Miles ordered his companies ashore for a skirmish drill. Soon after, campfires dotted the riverbank as the soldiers enjoyed their nightly songfest before retiring.[8]

The advance up the Yellowstone was slowed by the presence of huge buffalo herds that occasionally crossed the stream in front of the boat. Too, the river was falling rapidly, and Miles feared that the *Durfee* might not reach his objective, the mouth of Rosebud Creek, forcing the soldiers to march overland to meet General Terry's command. In his frustration, Miles wrote lengthy missives to his wife, to be forwarded from Fort Buford, in which he complained of Sheridan's excessive devotion to the cavalry arm, Sherman's lack of interest in organizational matters, and Crook's lack of decisiveness.[9]

The lands the Fifth Infantrymen passed through in July 1876, which other columns of soldiers had traversed that summer, represented a mixture of barrenness and richness. Before the

present activity, hunters and trappers had exploited the region's fur resources for decades. In 1855–57 Sir George Gore
led a hunting expedition to the Yellowstone Basin and actually
spent the better part of a winter quartered on the Tongue
River. Six years after Gore's explorations, a group of citizens
from Bannack City trekked eastward along the river, seeking
prospective goldfields. Near the mouth of the Bighorn River,
Indians attacked the party, forcing the men to abandon the
country.

In 1874 yet another citizen expedition organized at Bozeman
for the dual purpose of establishing a wagon road between that
community in south-central Montana and the western terminus
of the Northern Pacific and investigating rumors of valuable
gold deposits on the south bank of the Yellowstone, particularly
in the area of Rosebud Creek and the Powder River. "The Yellowstone Wagon Road and Prospecting Expedition" included
as many as 147 men and more than 200 horses and mules, in
addition to 22 ox-drawn wagons and a complement of artillery.
The project was short-lived. After traveling down the north
bank of the Yellowstone, the men were attacked by warriors
near Big Porcupine Creek and they fled cross-country back to
Bozeman. Nonetheless, the expedition noted the "magnificent
country" south of the Yellowstone in the valleys of the Tongue
and Powder rivers.[10]

Besides these civilian endeavors, several previous government expeditions had acquired knowledge of the lower Yellowstone country. In the summer of 1856 a party headed by Second
Lieutenant Gouverneur K. Warren explored the banks of the
river as far west as the mouth of Powder River. Three years later
a War Department expedition led by Captain William F. Raynolds of the Corps of Topographical Engineers, following Warren's initiative, began an exhaustive survey of the Yellowstone
and Bighorn region that involved extensive peregrinations
through Wyoming (then part of Dakota Territory) as well.
Guided by the renowned frontiersman Jim Bridger, Raynolds
and his companions succeeded in gathering sufficient astro-
nomical and geological data to facilitate preparation of the first
comprehensive charts of the Yellowstone Basin. The activities
of Warren and Raynolds and their associates fueled speculation
that gold in paying quantities existed along the lower Yellowstone. Later military expeditions also penetrated the area, par-

ticularly that of Brigadier General Alfred Sully, which, in
August 1864, pursued parties of Sioux to a point on the Yellowstone below Glendive Creek.[11]

The advent of the railroads, however, spurred far-ranging
interest in the country. In 1872 and 1873 surveying crews for
the Northern Pacific Railroad, escorted by soldiers, entered the
Yellowstone Valley; company entrepreneurs, anticipating the
extension of track through the area, mounted a campaign to
promote its attractions. Steamboat navigation of the Yellowstone coincided with the railroad projects. In 1873, Captain
Grant Marsh piloted the *Josephine* up the stream to the mouth
of Powder River; two years later Marsh took the craft almost
five hundred miles up the Yellowstone. Soon promotional publications encouraged travel into the region via steamboat when
the river was deep from melting mountain snows that flooded
its tributaries. The "June rise" became known as the best time
to ascend the stream; after mid-July, channel conditions were
unpredictable. The Yellowstone, named for the sandstone out-
cropping along its banks as well as for the yellowish muddy
water at its confluence with the Missouri, could promise a pre-
carious journey for its travelers, although the beauty of its surrounding landforms clearly made the trip worthwhile.[12]

The presence of Indians inhibited the population of the
lower Yellowstone by whites. In 1876, military officials and railroad promoters, as well as a host of others with economic interests, counted on the army to clear the region for settlement.
Army officers who were familiar with the lower Yellowstone offered differing opinions as to its value for farming. Some, like
Colonel William B. Hazen, commanding at Fort Buford, de-
nounced it as part of the worthless desert most Americans believed composed the trans-Mississippi West. Others declared
that the Yellowstone country offered splendid opportunities for
farming and ranching. Wrote Colonel John Gibbon:

> There is, of course, a great deal of barren, worthless land, but there is
> also much land in the valley susceptible of cultivation, and an immense
> region of good grazing country which will in time be available for stock-
> raising. Even where from the valleys the appearance of the so-called
> "bad lands" was most forbidding, we found on the plateau above ex-
> cellent grass in the greatest abundance covering the country for great
> distances.[13]

5. Brigadier General Alfred H. Terry, commander of the Department of Dakota from 1866 until his retirement in 1888 and Miles's superior officer in 1876–77. A lawyer by education, Terry boasted a proud Civil War record. As a field commander during the Great Sioux War, however, he proved an uninspired leader. (Custer Battlefield National Monument)

Gibbon's assessment, written in 1876, was particularly credible, for he and his troops had trekked vast distances along the river and its tributaries since leaving their home station in the spring.

In the wake of the Little Bighorn disaster, Gibbon had ample time to observe and contemplate as he and General Terry awaited the arrival of the reinforcements. Both men were accomplished veteran commanders. Terry, an administrative officer with little actual field time during the Indian campaigns, was clearly uncomfortable in his role, especially following the recent disaster to his cavalry arm. A Yale-educated lawyer from Connecticut, he had risen quickly during the Civil War as a commander of volunteers participating in numerous engagements in the South. His everlasting fame came as a result of his successful assault against the Confederate bastion of Fort Fisher, North Carolina, early in 1865; an admiring press tagged him the "Hero of Fort Fisher," and he won a regular army brigadier's star, soon followed by a major general's commission in the volunteers. Terry's postwar service was strictly administrative, though he was not without experience in dealing with Indians. He had been a member of several treaty commissions, most ironically, in light of his present mission, as a delegate to the Fort Laramie proceedings of 1868. Yet he lacked field experience with the Indians and his difficulties during the Sioux campaign stemmed from that fact. High-ranking subordinates with extensive campaign service found Terry's low-key management style, which often exhibited confusion, particularly irritating. His amiable disposition, however, made him a nonthreatening entity in a postwar army rife with egoists, and his high rank continued to serve him well. Wrote one newsman: "The fact that he is open and unreserved operates to his prejudice. Terry is a patriarchal . . . general, loving, caring for, and understanding the men placed under him."[14] Despite his faults, Terry held the confidence of Sheridan and Sherman and his career would continue to profit from his relationship with his superiors.[15] Terry's personal appearance in the summer of 1876 was described by a cavalry officer as possessing "the general air of a scholar as well as a soldier. His figure [was] tall and commanding; his face, gentle yet decided; eyes, blue-gray and kindly; complexion, bronzed by wind and rain and sun, to the color of an old sheep-skin covered Bible."[16]

Like Terry, Gibbon was a Civil War veteran of wide accomplishment. But he was also a West Point graduate (1847) and had accumulated some experience with Indians when he fought the Seminoles in Florida. An artillery instructor at the military

6. Brigadier General George Crook sat for photographer D. S. Mitchell in January 1877, at Cheyenne, Wyoming Territory. In 1876 Crook presided over the controversial battle at Rosebud Creek in June. After weeks of inaction following the Custer fight, Crook oversaw successful operations at Slim Buttes in September and at Mackenzie's fight on the Red Fork of the Powder River in November. Miles and Crook remained rivals until the latter's death in 1890. (Paul L. Hedren)

7. Colonel John Gibbon, Seventh Infantry, who with Terry, Crook, and Miles waged a fruitless campaign through the Yellowstone country in the weeks after the Little Bighorn disaster. Gibbon withdrew from the campaign in September 1876 and returned to his post in west-central Montana. Photograph by David F. Barry. (Denver Public Library, Western History Department)

academy (he authored *The Artillerist's Manual*, published in 1863), Gibbon, at the war's outset, served in that arm, but became a brigadier general in May 1862. He led the famous Iron

Brigade at South Mountain and Antietam and, as either divisional or corps commander, fought at Fredericksburg and Gettysburg, sustaining wounds in both battles. Gibbon was promoted to major general in 1864 and emerged from the Civil War with an enviable reputation as a brave and resourceful combat leader, attributes that accompanied him to the frontier during the years following Appomattox.[17]

After burying Custer's dead and transporting his wounded to the steamboat *Far West*, which ultimately carried them back to Fort Lincoln, Terry and Gibbon, with the remnant units of the Seventh Cavalry and with Gibbon's six companies of the Seventh Infantry and four of the Second Cavalry, on July 2 crossed to the north bank of the Yellowstone via the steamer to await orders and fresh troops. On July 15, word arrived from Sheridan that reinforcements were coming. Meantime, Terry sent forth successive couriers to find Crook, hoping to learn of his location and that of the Sioux and Cheyennes, most of whom had passed into the Big Horn Mountains following their victory over Custer. Terry contemplated moving after the Indians via the Bighorn River Valley or Tullock's Creek, but finally settled on Rosebud Valley. Not only did the former options pose topographical difficulties that would have impeded any movement to join Crook, but the falling waters of the Yellowstone threatened to disrupt navigation of the supply steamers above the Rosebud. He therefore set his command marching for Rosebud Creek. On July 22 the soldiers moved from their camp below the mouth of the Bighorn to a new site not far below the abandoned fur-trading establishment of Fort Pease. To augment his force, Terry directed that the depot he previously had established at the mouth of Powder River, guarded by Major Orlando H. Moore with three companies of the Sixth Infantry and two of the Seventeenth, be moved to a point on the north side of the Yellowstone opposite the mouth of the Rosebud.[18]

For the next several days the command remained in camp fighting mosquitos, which one officer described as "almost intolerable," while awaiting directions from Terry, who had gone down the Yellowstone to select the site of the new camp and determine the location of his reinforcements under Miles and Otis. On the morning of the twenty-fifth the Seventh Cavalry lost another trooper from its decimated ranks when a private drowned while crossing a rain-swollen slough. That evening the long-awaited couriers from Crook arrived with the first word of that officer's whereabouts. He was still at Goose Creek, Wyoming, where he had withdrawn following the Rosebud fight, and was anxious to join forces with Terry. Recorded one captain with Gibbon: "Offensive operations are to be begun as soon as twelve companies of infantry arrive from the East."[19]

The next day Terry returned aboard the *Far West* and prepared his command to move downstream to Rosebud Creek, which move was accomplished by July 30. There, on the north bank of the Yellowstone, "in a flat sandy bottom interspersed with groves of trees," Gibbon's men joined two companies of the Seventeenth Infantry and four of the Sixth Infantry (three had arrived from the Powder River depot and one from duty as boat guard on the *Far West*), and one of the Seventh Cavalry, besides 131 transport wagons.[20]

As Terry's command prepared to reopen the campaign, the anticipated reinforcements were almost at hand. Miles and the Fifth Infantry companies continued their ascent of the Yellowstone only a day behind Lieutenant Colonel Otis and Companies E, F, G, H, I, and K of the Twenty-second Infantry, also traveling from Bismarck. On July 29, as the steamer *Carroll* advanced with the latter unit and the recruit replacements for the Seventh Cavalry, a party of approximately two hundred Indians, camped on the south bank of the Yellowstone while they looted the forage left behind from the depot, fired on the vessel as it passed the mouth of Powder River. The *Carroll* pulled to shore and a company debarked, took up skirmish formation, and briefly engaged the Indians, supported by troops still on the boat. When the Indians withdrew, the soldiers burned the camp, reboarded the steamer with only one man slightly wounded, and continued upstream toward Terry's command. The day after this episode, Miles's men aboard the *Durfee* and *Josephine* saw Indians in the same vicinity and the smoldering ruins of an army wagon that had been tossed into the river, but the tribesmen did not shoot at the boats.[21]

Based on intelligence reports from his Crow scouts and, most recently, from General Crook, Terry believed that the majority of the Sioux and Cheyennes roamed far to the south, even though the incidents at Powder River pointed up the likelihood that the huge concentration of tribesmen that overwhelmed

Custer had begun to fragment and go their separate ways. Indeed, following the Battle of the Little Bighorn, as the Indians
had traveled south toward the Big Horn Mountains, the first
signs of scattering appeared as small parties departed for the
Black Hills and the agencies, creating a veritable terror in that
mining region as they passed. The majority of the Indians, however, stayed more or less together, enjoying their traditional
pursuits while the grass and game remained abundant. In early
July some of the Indians encountered a scouting party from
Crook's Goose Creek camp and a brief but lively fight occurred.
Most of the Indians by that time had headed north again, secure
in their numbers but desirous of avoiding future clashes with
the soldiers. As they moved, they fired the grass behind them in
an annual rite that would ensure an early growth the next
spring. Some army men thought that the fires were meant to
restrict movements of the buffalo herds and keep them north
of the Yellowstone. The burning spread far afield, and throughout the late summer and autumn a smoky haze from the fires
hung over the entire region.

Through the balance of July and into August the Indians
drifted down Rosebud Creek, hunting on that stream and on
the Little Bighorn before moving northeast to the Tongue
River. Despite the seeming casualness of the journey, a certain
urgency kept the people moving and wary as to the location of
Crook's and Terry's commands. From camps on the Tongue
River some of the Indians went to investigate the army forage
and food supplies at the mouth of the Powder, and one warrior
had been killed there by Otis's infantrymen. Soon after this, by
mutual agreement of the leaders, the major fragmentation of
the Sioux and Cheyennes began, due mostly to economic con-
siderations. The unwieldly size of the group precluded the
availability of ample grass to sustain the ponies and it frightened off buffalo and other game. The tribesmen traveled east
across Pumpkin Creek, with the primary division occurring
along a tributary of the Powder River. Many of the Indians continued east, fording Beaver Creek and the Little Missouri River
as they drove for the agencies. Most of the Northern Cheyennes
followed their chief, Dull Knife, south into the Big Horn Mountains, while others camped with Crazy Horse's Oglalas, preparing to join that chief in his annual peregrination through eastern Montana and western Dakota. Sitting Bull prepared to lead

his Hunkpapas to the relative security of the buffalo grounds north of the Yellowstone. As far as the tribes were concerned, the fighting was over.[22]

That feeling was not shared by the army high command, which had sent the Fifth and Twenty-second Infantry contingents to support Terry and Crook in avenging the loss of Custer and his men and in finally subduing the Indians. Following their engagement with the Indians at the mouth of the Powder, Colonel Otis's soldiers arrived at Terry's camp to rousing cheers on the afternoon of August 1.[23] At 3 P.M. that same day, a force commanded by Major Moore started on the *Far West* from Terry's camp to salvage the forage left at Powder River. Moore's command consisted of Companies D and I, Sixth Infantry, and Company C of the Seventeenth, besides a twelve-pounder Napoleon gun and a Gatling gun in the charge of Second Lieutenant Charles A. Woodruff. En route, the soldiers steamed past the *Durfee* and the *Josephine* bearing Miles and his men upstream, then put in for the night near the Tongue River.

As they approached the mouth of Powder River at about nine o'clock on the stifling morning of August 2, Moore made the steamboat, its engines backed, float slowly by that stream and enter the Wolf Rapids so that he might reconnoiter the country before landing his soldiers. Although no Indians could be seen, the smoke from numerous campfires wafted above the distant ravines south of the Yellowstone, indicating their presence. What followed was the first substantive contact since June between warriors who had destroyed Custer and members of Terry's column. Entering the rapids, Moore directed the steamboat to turn back upstream and put in at the smoke-blackened and abandoned depot, a distance below the mouth of the Powder. There the soldiers found a great heap of oats, which the Sioux ponies could not ingest, unsacked but otherwise largely untouched. Nearby they discovered that the body of Seventh Cavalryman William George had been removed from its grave. George, wounded at the Little Bighorn, had died after being transported to the depot aboard the steamer *Josephine*. His remains had been interred there on July 4. Quickly, the major posted part of his command defensively a short distance from the Yellowstone, on a gently rising ridge that enclosed the depot site, and assigned ten soldiers to guard the *Far West*. The rest of the command began resacking the forage. When warriors soon appeared in his front, Moore at first tried to entice them forward while concealing the majority of his troops. Failing at this, he directed Lieutenant Woodruff to shell a party on his distant right, near the Powder River. These Indians fled as the projectile exploded. As the soldiers watched gleefully, the Napoleon gun emitted successive discharges to the left, clearing the distant terrain and driving the warriors back to the bluffs. The infantrymen then started loading the forage onto the steamer.

More tribesmen appeared on the left, near Wolf Rapids, at approximately 11 A.M. Again, the Napoleon was called into play and effectively dispersed them. The men continued their labor in the day's torrid heat. At around one o'clock two scouts and the pilot of the vessel rode downstream, attempting to locate the warriors. They soon encountered them and began a mad scramble back toward the command. Fearing an attack on the boat from the opposite direction, Moore refused to order his infantry forward. Instead, several well-directed rounds from the artillery scattered the Indians, most of whom fled into the timber. One scout named Wesley ("Yank") Brockmeyer took a fatal bullet in the chest before a detachment from Moore's command reached him, reportedly in defiance of the commander's orders. One warrior was killed in the fight, and some of the soldiers, angered over Brockmeyer's death, slashed the corpse with their knives. "His head was cut off and used for a football in camp for several days," recorded a witness.[24] The Indians did not return. At 4 A.M. the next morning the *Far West* started back upstream with seventy-five tons of forage. Two hours later she encountered the *Carroll* descending the river to Fort Buford. The company of Seventeenth Infantrymen transferred to that boat and proceeded to their home station. At noon the *Far West* stopped for wood and Major Moore read a Masonic service as the scout was buried. The nighttime passage back to the Rosebud camp occurred without mishap, although each time the vessel stopped, a force of pickets was cautiously thrown forward.[25]

While Terry's troops made ready to renew the campaign, the general conferred with Sheridan's military secretary, Lieutenant Colonel James W. Forsyth, sent out by the division commander to assess the field situation and direct his lieutenants regarding the proposed erection of the two posts lately approved by Congress. Sheridan advised Terry that the forts were

to be "in accordance with the general plan of the post of Fort
Abraham Lincoln," each to accommodate six companies of cavalry and five of infantry. The projected cost for each post stood
at one hundred thousand dollars. The plan to build the forts
immediately clearly bothered Terry, who had hoped to continue
the campaign after joining Crook. He impressed Forsyth with
the impossibility of navigating the Yellowstone much longer, so
that construction activities would have to await the spring of
1877. He further told Forsyth that when the forts were erected
they should be placed at the mouth of Tongue River and at the
confluence of the Little Bighorn River with the Bighorn. Forsyth carried these views back downstream aboard the *Carroll* on
August 2 and relayed them via telegraph to Sheridan four days
later. The boat also transported out of the war zone twenty
soldiers afflicted with typhoid fever and scurvy.[26]

Terry grasped the situation well. The falling waters of the
Yellowstone were already beginning to hamper the arrival of
supplies and reinforcements for his campaign. On August 1 the
boats bearing the Fifth Infantry ran into trouble as they entered Buffalo Rapids between the Powder and Tongue rivers,
forcing the soldiers to debark and march up the riverbank for
a mile, during which time Miles had them perform target practice and skirmish drill. Passing the mouth of the Tongue that
afternoon, the *Durfee* again landed the men so that the steamer
could negotiate a sandbar. That night Miles and his troops
camped fifty miles from Terry's command. Resuming the trip
the next morning, the *Durfee* and the *Josephine* reached the
camp at about 2 P.M. Officers of Terry's command greeted old
friends among the arrivals. That evening, as the *Josephine*
landed her cargo of 150 cavalry recruits, some 60 horses, 2 Rodman guns, and the gear of the Fifth Infantry troops, Miles's
roughly 400 men located a campsite adjoining the men of the
Twenty-second Regiment at the rear of the depot. It was "the
worst spot I ever saw," remarked Captain Simon Snyder. Besides the doughboys of Otis and Miles, the camp included what
was left of the Seventh Cavalry, Gibbon's Seventh Infantry, and
parts of the Second Cavalry and the Sixth and Seventeenth Infantry Regiments. The soldiers labeled the place where Terry
quartered his command "Fort Beans."[27]

The day after Miles arrived, preparations began in earnest
for resuming the pursuit. On Thursday, August 3, Gibbon's sol-

diers and their train boarded the *Durfee* and *Josephine* and were
ferried to the south side of the Yellowstone, reestablishing their
camp on a rising benchland encircled by high hills. Over the
following days, as the balance of the army was ferried across,
the men spent long hours swimming or soaking in the river to
escape the heat. Officers fished and, in the evenings, renewed
old acquaintances, joined in songfests, or enjoyed selections by
the Seventh Cavalry band. Some talked of the battle at the Little
Bighorn; Captain Ovenshine commented on Lieutenant
Charles DeRudio of the Seventh Cavalry: "He does not hesitate
to express his satisfaction at Genl. Custer's death." Others
caught up on newspaper stories of the campaign; First Lieutenant Edward S. Godfrey of the Seventh Cavalry pondered critical
editorials and concluded that the press knew little of the reali-
ties of Indian warfare. "They seem to think the same grand
tactics are employed in it that is used in 'civilized' warfare, or
battles."[28]

Terry's plan was to move his command south up the Rosebud
and toward the Big Horn Mountains, to connect with Crook
and to mutually determine a course for tracking the Indians.
Miles noted the uncertainty of the situation and the demoralization of officers he had conversed with en route upstream, and
expected that his arrival with fresh troops would help revive
Terry's campaign. Even before he reached the Rosebud camp,
Miles had leveled criticism at the Terry-Crook operation. "I
think it almost a military crime," he wrote, "that these two commands are not under one head and governed by the simplest
principles of warfare." He believed the presence of his men
would turn things around and reinstill confidence among the
soldiers: "One little success would change the whole feeling in
regard to those Indians." His own troops, he believed, were
more than ready for the test, having drilled extensively during
debarkments on the trip up the Yellowstone.[29]

He found Terry's force disunified and in a quandary over the
operations. Worse, Terry, while friendly, seemed remote and
uncertain of himself. On August 4 Miles wrote Mary: "I never
saw a command so completely stampeded as this. . . . [Terry]
does not seem very enthusiastic or to have much heart in the
enterprise." Miles's battalion adjutant, First Lieutenant Frank
D. Baldwin, echoed these sentiments. Terry's troops, he wrote,
"don't move with that vigor and life that would foretell success

and it is rather discouraging to us who have had Indian experience . . . under an active commander." Within days of Miles's arrival, he learned that he would likely be responsible for raising the posts funded by Congress. He evinced frustration with the assignment, feeling that his resolve as well as his regiment would be wasted and lasting accomplishments would be few. "I do not wish to stop on this river and build posts unless I am allowed to continue active operations this winter. I certainly have no desire to go back to Leavenworth without doing anything."[30]

The tedious and time-consuming work of transporting men, horses, and equipment across the Yellowstone continued. On Friday, August 4, the *Far West* returned with its cargo of oats from the Powder River depot. Many hours on that and succeeding evenings were spent puzzling over the discovery in the brush at the mouth of the Rosebud of a dead Seventh Cavalry horse, complete with saddle, bridle, and carbine, that had been shot between the eyes. The discovery encouraged speculation that one of Custer's troopers had somehow escaped the Little Bighorn slaughter and had made his way to that point before being waylaid by Indians or drowning while attempting to swim the heady currents. "His fate," observed one officer, "is the absorbing topic of conversation in the camp, and every one is trying to arrive at a conclusion satisfactory, at least to themselves."[31]

The ferrying of troops continued. Early on Saturday companies of the Twenty-second Infantry boarded the steamers for the trip across the river, and at 1 P.M., amid wind and rain, the transporting of the Fifth Infantry commenced. Equipped with a Springfield rifle, ammunition, shelter half, blanket, and extra underwear and shoes, each man also carried ten days' rations, although Terry's wagons carried supplies for thirty-five days. Several soldiers, unable to march for various reasons, remained behind. The day also saw the departure downstream on the *Durfee* of several Seventh Cavalry troopers whose enlistments were up. Their regiment forded the Yellowstone the next morning, August 6, and made camp about one mile up Rosebud Creek. Major Moore's Sixth Infantrymen followed, preceding a field battery of a Napoleon gun and two three-inch rifles plus the Indian scouts. Company G of the Seventeenth Infantry and 120 dismounted cavalry recruits stayed on the north bank in the charge of Captain Louis H. Sanger of the Seventeenth to guard livestock, tents, baggage, and the several Gatling guns Terry had decided to leave behind. The camp was secured with earthen entrenchments and abatis.[32]

Still Miles chafed at the delays in getting his regiment into the field. As late as the seventh, men and equipment were being forded over the Yellowstone, while temperatures shot above 110°.[33] "We are still at this point, sweltering in the sun, doing nothing," bemoaned Miles. His criticism of Terry's management mounted, and he blamed the commander for having "retreated after Custer's battle," an action that Miles believed only infused "demoralization and timidity" among his officers. Lieutenant Baldwin was "very much disappointed in Genl Terry," describing him as "a farmer stile" of man who "enjoys his ease and [is] very cautious." The news on August 7 that the Fifth Infantry would constitute part of a brigade headed by Gibbon disheartened Miles further. "It looks like an organization for a walkaround," he complained to his wife. He added, "If this kind of campaigning is continual it will last a year or two without much credit to the army."[34] However, he remained optimistic that the opportunity would come when he could head up an active and, he hoped, independent command.

The order of march specified a new organization for field operations. Basically, the command was halved into cavalry and infantry components. The former consisted of seven companies of the Seventh Cavalry and four of the Second, with the whole commanded by Major James S. Brisbin of the Second. The latter, under Gibbon, consisted of the present battalions of the Fifth, Sixth, Seventh, and Twenty-second Infantry Regiments. The right wing of the infantry component was commanded by Miles and Captain Moore, while the left was under Lieutenant Colonel Otis, of the Twenty-second, and Captain Henry B. Freeman, of the Seventh. Second Lieutenant William H. Low, attached from the Twentieth Infantry, commanded the battery of one twelve-pounder and two three-inch rifled guns.[35]

Reveille at 3 A.M. on August 8 announced final preparations for leaving the Yellowstone. The *Far West* was to remain on the river at Terry's disposal while the *Josephine* started for Bismarck for more provisions. At five o'clock the command pulled out, moving ponderously across the terrain bordering the west bank of the lower Rosebud, which at that season amounted to nothing more than a disconnected series of water holes—"a miserable little creek about 15 feet wide, with muddy banks, and a soft bottom," recorded Lieutenant Edward J. McClernand of the Second Cavalry. Engineer Officer Lieutenant Edward Maguire reported that "the valley consists of alternations of bad lands and narrow reaches of bottom-lands covered with grass, rose-bushes, juniper, and cottonwood. Great quantities of dead timber were found strewn over the ground."[36] The creek snaked tortuously across the valley floor, ultimately forcing several crossings that required grading by pioneer details to ease the passage of 240 heavily loaded wagons bearing forage and enough rations to last thirty-five days.

Terry's command comprised 83 officers and 1,611 enlisted men, plus approximately 75 Crow, Arikara (Ree), and white scouts. On the march, the Indians assumed the lead, followed by a battalion of cavalry and the artillery pieces, followed by another unit of cavalry. Next came the ambulances, wagons, and beef herd, and yet another mounted unit brought up the rear. The infantrymen marched in route step along either flank, guarding the train and the cattle. All the troops were in light marching order, with few encumbrances beyond their weapons and what necessities they carried in their saddlebags and haversacks. The day grew torrid and the men suffered from thirst, unable to drink the alkaline creek water. "My belt plate was so hot," wrote Captain Ovenshine, "that I could scarcely touch it." Some soldiers, prostrated by the heat, were placed in the ambulances for the duration of the march. As a result of the many stream crossings of such a large body of men, animals, and wagons, the day's journey was short, only 9.8 miles by odometer measurement. The men began to make camp at two o'clock that afternoon so that bridges for fording the stream might be completed before dark. The site, just a mile below Custer's campground of June 22, lay in a grove of cottonwood trees and afforded cold springs. Miles's men straggled in about four o'clock and three companies were immediately sent forward to help build the bridges. During the night a party of Crow scouts, sent by Terry the evening of August 7 to find Crook, returned without establishing contact. Another group with dispatches shortly departed on the same mission. Neither the scouts nor the soldiers encountered signs of the Indians during the march of August 8.[37]

That night the temperature plummeted, the scorching heat supplanted by freezing drizzle driven by a north wind that continued throughout the ninth. In the morning, soldiers who had been on picket duty discovered their beards and blankets covered with frost. "Shivering bodies and chattering teeth was the order," noted Captain Walter Clifford. Donning greatcoats, the men took up the march at 5 A.M., although the going was slow because the wagons proved exceedingly hard to negotiate across the rough landscape of the lower Rosebud. Numerous crossings were made, many of them unnecessary and ill-advised.

At 2 P.M. some of the Crows who had gone out the night before returned, singing, as was their fashion, to announce the sighting of the Sioux some forty miles ahead. The other Crows had gone on toward Crook's camp. Miles misinterpreted the arrival of the Indians and he notified Colonel Otis that the Crows had been "run in." At this, the left wing of the Seventh Infantry, under Captain Henry B. Freeman, was directed to move to higher ground and deploy in skirmish formation. No Sioux were seen, although the white scouts acknowledged their presence in the area. Later, the Crows who had gone toward Crook's camp returned, reporting a large body of Sioux moving toward the Rosebud from the Tongue River. At 5 P.M. the thoroughly drenched command bivouacked, having traveled less than eleven miles in twelve hours. The wooded campground was on land formerly occupied in May and June by the Indians before they left for the Little Bighorn Valley. Nosing about, Terry's scouts found the burial site of an infant, which they promptly defiled. Despite the cold, the reported sightings of the Sioux inspired the soldiers. "We are beginning to 'burn,' as the children say in one of their games," wrote an officer.[38]

The anticipation lingered on the morning of August 10. The scouts refused another attempt to carry dispatches to Crook, although most of them agreed to push ahead and try to determine the strength of the Sioux in front. Terry's command broke camp early, between 4:30 and 5:00 A.M., and started up the valley. The day grew warm and sunny. Moving tentatively, mindful of what the scouts had reported the night before, the soldiers and straggling train had traveled only nine miles by noon, when the Crows and Rees suddenly withdrew from their advanced positions and raced back to the command. As they approached in groups they were screaming, occasionally running their ponies in circles to notify the troops that the enemy had been sighted. They pointed to a large dust cloud rising in the distant southwest and cried "Sioux!" as they tore through the columns to the rear, where they stripped to breechcloths, daubed paint over their faces, and mounted fresh ponies, readying themselves for the coming fray. Once outfitted in their war finery, the scouts dashed back to the front, anxious to battle their enemies.

At the seeming emergency, the command went into action. Believing they were about to come under attack by the same Indians who had destroyed Custer, the Seventh Cavalry in the van, with the Second Cavalry directly behind, quickly fanned out in skirmish formation, arrayed from the bluffs on the left to the timber bordering Rosebud Creek on the right. The infantrymen meantime continued on the flanks, the two wings forming a protective rectangle about the train. As Captain Clifford described the action, the Seventh Infantry of the left wing "was drawn up in column of fours by company, the wagons . . . moving with redoubled speed, and corraling as fast as they could move in. The right wing, under Col. Miles, was forming in column of companies as fast as the wagons, which they were guarding, joined the corral."[39]

Up ahead, Terry's force halted and waited. Soon Indians were seen a mile away. The artillery pieces were dragged to a promontory and unlimbered. Tense moments passed until finally two more scouts emerged into view, galloping across the bottom towards the deployed cavalry skirmishers. "Maschetee, maschetee!" they screamed, and at once the identity of the foe was learned: soldiers. "General Crook and not Sitting Bull was approaching," wrote Gibbon. "In a moment," remembered First Lieutenant Henry Romeyn, of the Fifth Infantry, "our picture of anticipated battle faded away." The Indians in the distance proved to be Shoshone scouts. Soon after, an official emissary in the form of Crook's longhaired chief scout, William F. ("Buffalo Bill") Cody, galloped up to Major Marcus A. Reno to confirm the proximity of that command. On recognizing the famous Cody, the soldiers with Terry erupted with welcoming cheers.

Crook's command momentarily reacted to the event, believing that Terry's column constituted the Indians whose broad trail they had been pursuing for several days. Leading from the

Big Horn Mountains in a gentle northerly direction, the trace of tipi poles had crossed the upper Tongue to parallel Rosebud Creek before turning east toward the Tongue and Powder river valleys, almost at the precise spot where the commands met. Terry learned that Crook's command was making camp six miles ahead, and he directed his own troops forward. That evening the respective forces assembled, constituting a huge bivouac that encompassed seventy companies of cavalry and infantry troops, besides the scouts and other auxiliaries of both commands. Crook's column included twenty-one companies of the Third and Fifth Cavalry Regiments, plus sixteen companies of the Fourth, Ninth, and Fourteenth Infantry Regiments.[40]

The two forces contrasted greatly. As First Lieutenant Charles King of the Fifth Cavalry remembered:

> General Terry, as became a brigadier, was attired in the handsome uniform of his rank; his staff and his line officers, though looking eminently serviceable, were all in neat regimentals, so that shoulder-straps were to be seen in every direction. General Crook, as became an old campaigner and frontiersman, was in a rough hunting rig, and in all his staff and line there was not a complete suit of uniform. . . . In the Fifth Cavalry, you could not have told officer from private. It may have been suitable as regarded Indian campaigning, but was undeniably slouchy and border-ruffianish.[41]

Crook had no wagons with him. Instead, his scant supplies were borne by a contingent of pack mules, so that his troops might be less restricted in tracking the Indians. Unlike Terry, Crook was a seasoned active field commander who, through years of practice, had developed an operational procedure for Indian combat that was only starting to be emulated by other commanders. Cody recalled that Terry's officers ensconced themselves in large wall tents complete with portable beds, and that hospital tents were used for dining. Crook brought only a tiny fly-tent for his headquarters, and his culinary hardware consisted of a quart-sized cup and "a sharp stick on which he broiled his bacon." In comparing the two camps, Cody concluded that Crook "was a real Indian fighter."[42]

The two commanders met in the afternoon to determine what to do. The news of the Indian trail had immediate import for Terry, especially in light of the recent episodes at the mouth of Powder River. Both commanders now feared that the Sioux might cross the Yellowstone and elude them altogether. Yet

Crook and Terry concluded to follow the Indian trail east—and away from the river—the next day. The latter, seeing the impossibility of getting his wagons across the precipitous divide between the Rosebud and the Tongue, decided to send them back to the Yellowstone depot and, emulating Crook, strike forth with pack animals and provisions for fifteen days.[43] More significantly for Colonel Miles, Terry directed him to accompany the train with his Fifth Infantry companies back to the Yellowstone, to commandeer any steamboats, and to begin patrolling the river to thwart attempts by the Sioux and Cheyennes to ford it and push toward Canada. He was to station detachments of troops on the north bank at points opposite the mouths of the Tongue and the Powder. Miles was also to forward provisions for Terry and Crook from the Rosebud depot to the mouth of Powder River.

The orders to Miles were significant and presently changed the complexion of the Sioux War. Thus far, for him, the war had lacked direction, and the field movements he had witnessed amounted to an embarrassing exercise in gross mismanagement and military inefficiency. Consequently, he did not hesitate to leave Terry and Crook, starting for the Yellowstone just hours after the junction, leaving Captain Snyder and two companies to follow with the train and the Napoleon gun on the morrow.[44] Henceforth, Miles and his independent command would gradually dominate the policy of containment and pursuit that came to characterize the latter stages of the conflict with the Sioux and Cheyennes.

Armed with the two three-inch Rodman guns, Miles marched his weary soldiers through the night, stopping only once to rest and reaching the Yellowstone on the afternoon of the 11th, after covering thirty-four miles. There the *Far West* transported them over to the Rosebud depot. Never one to minimize his accomplishments, Miles termed the march "extraordinary," and "as hard as any I ever knew or have read of. The dust was perfectly blinding, and we must have left a cloud of dust equal to that made . . . by a corps." First Lieutenant Romeyn described the movement:

> It was one to be long remembered. Outside the trail made by the wagons on the outward march, cactus of large growth and ferocious species made any night travel impossible, and, deeply worn by hoof and wheel, the improvised roadway was ankle deep with sand; and often I could

not see through the dust the third man in my rear, though the moon was at the full. . . . At 4 A.M. when the trail passed near the stream and the ground was free from cactus, a halt was ordered for breakfast. Stacking arms, the tired men dropped where they stood, and in a moment were locked in slumber; too exhausted even to eat when roused. An hour later the march was resumed. Mounted officers gave up their horses to wearied men and carried rifles for others, urged up and cheered the raw recruits, and at 2 P.M., footsore and exhausted, . . . the gallant little command halted and dropped down to rest on the banks of the Yellowstone.

An enlisted man, Trumpeter Edwin M. Brown, reported that the dust and sand nearly suffocated the troops. "I assure you that there was more than one sore and blistered foot," he wrote, and this included many officers who were afoot. "I take notice [that] they provided themselves with horses soon as they got in the Post," said Brown, "so as not to be caught afoot again."[45]

At the Yellowstone, Miles arranged for a flatboat to transport the wagons across the river when they arrived. He also directed newly arrived First Lieutenant William P. Clark to take a contingent of 250 Crow scouts and some recruits and patrol the north bank down to the Powder River, while another force commanded by First Lieutenant William L. Reed, Seventh Infantry, proceeded downstream toward the Tongue and Powder in Mackinaw boats. Miles and Companies B, E, G, and H shortly boarded the *Far West* and started for the Tongue, in the midst of a driving rain. Captain Marsh skillfully negotiated islands and low water, and two miles below the mouth of that stream, Company B, with one of the Gatling guns, under Captain Andrew S. Bennett, debarked on the west bank and began throwing up entrenchments. The next day, a short distance below the mouth of Powder River and opposite the site of Moore's August 2 encounter, Company H, under Captain Samuel Ovenshine, erected fieldworks. One three-inch rifled gun guarded their camp. A few hours after establishing this post, the soldiers were fired on by warriors, who quickly dispersed. "I am of the opinion that some [Indians] have already gone north," Miles wrote his wife. "But this movement has been very rapid, and is in time for intercepting any force in front of Terry and Crook."[46]

At Marsh's warning that shallow water below the Powder might prevent the steamboat from returning upstream, Miles turned back toward the Tongue River, reaching that point after nightfall on the fourteenth. He did, however, send couriers with Terry's report to Fort Buford, along with instructions to Colonel Hazen to provide another steamboat to guard the lower Yellowstone. Miles later moved Company B from near the Tongue to a site some twelve miles farther downstream, at Buffalo Rapids. (According to Trumpeter Brown of Company B, the unit had scarcely withdrawn before several hundred Indians successfully crossed below the Tongue.) Increased sightings of Indians spurred Miles to direct the *Far West* downstream to the mouth of O'Fallon's Creek. There another company of Fifth Infantrymen under First Lieutenant Edmund Rice occupied the west bank with a field gun after soldiers aboard the steamer spotted war parties on the east bank and smoke columns rising in the distance. Believing these observations to be of utmost importance, Miles and the balance of his command continued patrolling the Yellowstone by steamer, alert for attempts by the Sioux and Cheyennes to cross at the fords.[47]

CHAPTER THREE

Yellowstone Blues

While the Fifth Infantry troops assumed their strategic positions along the river, Terry and Crook started on the Indian trail. Their combined force numbered nearly four thousand men—the largest such command ever assembled on the northern plains. After getting supplies from Terry's wagons, which shortly set out for the Yellowstone, the soldiers, now supported by pack mules, broke camp on the Rosebud at 11 A.M. They trekked due eastward, up the sharply rising divide between that stream and the Tongue, with the Fifth Cavalry in the van. On the summit they found rolling, burned-over pastures, dotted by pineries and outcroppings of red sandstone. The dust grew thick and the smell of sulphur from a seam of burning coal laced the air. A light rain fell. Ten miles farther the soldiers descended into the timbered bottom of Tongue Valley, turned downstream for two more miles, and went into camp by 6 P.M. on the east bank, among "lofty and corpulent old cottonwoods."

Searching about, the men of Crook's command discovered that they were camped on a recently occupied Indian-village site—and one showing evidence of perennial usage. Trees stripped of bark carried petroglyphs attesting to the participation of the tribesmen in the late fighting. Nearby lay the putrid remains of a white man who had died from gunshot wounds at least a year before. Other skeletal matter located in the vicinity suggested that another man had been burned alive by the Indians. During the evening, Crook's scouts came in to report that the main trail continued down the Tongue before turning east toward the Powder River; minor offshoots headed in opposite directions along the course of the Tongue. Terry and Crook determined to stay on the main trail. That night it rained heavily, a deluge that thoroughly drenched the soldiers, unprotected but for greatcoats, ponchos, and gum blankets.[1]

The rain continued the next day, delaying the soldiers' departure until afternoon. Then progress was slow, the advance requiring three or four crossings of the stream. The valley opened on either side of the stream, affording room to maneuver the sizeable column, and the broken hills evinced deep hues of pink, gray, and brown that darkened as the rainfall increased. The men passed through two more Indian campgrounds and saw a number of Indian burial sites.

Good progress was made August 13, the command trekking nearly twenty-five miles down the Tongue. More Indian campsites were passed. Scouts dispatched to the Yellowstone made contact with Miles's Fifth Infantrymen stationed opposite the mouth of the Tongue. They returned to report that the Indian trail headed east and that some pony tracks were but a few days old. The abundance of grass at the bivouac, moreover, suggested that the Indians had begun to scatter.[2]

The continually falling rain only aggravated the growing despair of the men, and they spent part of the following morning trying to wring out their blankets and overcoats before starting again. Terry and Crook passed farther down the Tongue to Pumpkin Creek, then turned east in the direction of the Powder River. Scouts returned to report that the contingent of Crows at the Rosebud depot were en route to the Tongue, and a courier from Miles brought word that the Sioux and Cheyennes still had not crossed the Yellowstone. That afternoon the exhausted men bivouacked along the banks of Pumpkin Creek, having gone about sixteen miles. "And now once more, as the rain comes down in torrents," wrote Lieutenant King, "we unsaddle, turn our horses out to graze, . . . and we wonder what is going to be done." Officers groused over the perceived lack of leadership. Noted Lieutenant Godfrey: "Something must be wrong about Genl Terry that he cannot hold control of Cavalry & Infty without having merely nominal command."[3]

On Tuesday the troops plodded another twenty miles after the Indians, crossing the rugged, snake-infested divide between the Tongue and Powder valleys and striking Mizpah Creek, a tributary of the latter stream, in their descent. In the afternoon they forded the Powder River, turned north once again, and followed the Indian trail toward the Yellowstone, stopping at 4

P.M. to camp. The weariness increased that day, amid still more heavy rain, and diarrhea and signs of scurvy appeared among the men. That evening hardtack, pork, and coffee were once more the staple, as stragglers from among the infantry battalions gradually reached camp.[4]

The terrain bordering the Powder River was blackened from fires set by the passing Indians, and the lack of grass forced the cavalry companies to fan out to find sufficient grazing for the animals. On the sixteenth the command was off again after downing soaked rations. Another abandoned camp was found, but the scouts could not agree as to the age of the trail, their estimates varying between days and weeks. After consulting with Crook, Terry decided not to follow the trail because the course would lead him away from his Yellowstone supply base. In the afternoon, having gone nineteen miles, the armies halted in yet another rain squall, near the site of Terry's old camp of the previous June. Twenty or more miles away lay the Yellowstone and succor. That evening the men threw caution to the wind, building large fires along the timbered bottom as they sought to dry out blankets and overcoats.[5]

Thursday broke clear and grew hot as the soldiers continued down the Powder. Soon what was left of the Indians' trail traced off to the east, and Terry sent his Ree scouts off to determine its course. The columns kept on to the Yellowstone, following Terry's old wagon trail, reaching its sandy banks in the afternoon. There they found a company of Miles's regiment and some recruits stationed on the north side, but few rations and little forage. As Lieutenant King put it, "no news from home, no mail, no supplies—nothing but dirt and discomfort." The men went into bivouac along the south bank, the cavalry units seeking what few grassy areas were available on the bleak, burned-over ground, a circumstance that forced some to occupy sites farther back up the west bank of the Powder.[6]

Near sundown the *Far West* appeared from upstream with Miles aboard. The colonel gave Terry a full accounting of his movements and the proximity of the provisions. Already the wagon train with supplies had departed the Rosebud en route to the Powder. It had taken three arduous days to ferry some 240 wagons to the north bank of the Yellowstone, and at 5 A.M. on the seventeenth the mules had begun pulling their loads downstream, escorted by two companies of Miles's regiment.

He had bad news concerning the contingent of Crows; their participation in the campaign was increasingly uncertain. He also reported that he had taken every precaution to ensure that the Sioux and Cheyennes remained south of the river. He had withdrawn the Tongue River guard post and dispatched scouts to O'Fallon's Creek, thirty-one miles below the Powder, to check for signs of their crossing. In addition, he had stationed Lieutenant Rice and Company H opposite O'Fallon's as added assurance against the Indians' slipping north. Nonetheless, Terry directed the steamer, with Miles aboard, beyond that point, to the mouth of Glendive Creek, to determine whether the Indians had yet forded. (While providing an enervating discomfiture among the military command, the constant rainfall had caused the Yellowstone to rise nearly a foot, temporarily facilitating its navigation in noted troublesome areas like Wolf Rapids, below the mouth of the Powder.) Also, on August 16, Colonel Hazen at Fort Buford dispatched the steamer *Carroll* to patrol the Yellowstone between Glendive Creek and Wolf Rapids. Terry's fears of the Indians escaping were justified; just two days earlier tribesmen on the south bank had fired on the *Carroll* near the post, withdrawing after troops on board fired back. The incident pointed up the reality of Terry's concern.[7]

For the next six days the commands of Terry and Crook occupied the south bank of Yellowstone River near the Powder while awaiting the arrival of the wagons from Rosebud Creek. On August 18 Terry moved his headquarters and the infantry camp a mile downstream. Also on the eighteenth, the first of several sutlers appeared, charging outrageous prices for fresh produce and canned goods brought down on a Mackinaw boat from Fort Ellis. Many soldiers were forced to buy clothing to replace uniform items worn ragged over the course of the campaign. Terry sent couriers to Miles, directing that the *Far West* return to the Powder River. Some major excitement occurred when a blustery wind from the north whipped up a terrific prairie fire that forced the prompt removal of the horse herds toward the river. Soldiers who were bivouacked west of the Powder fought the blaze, and a party succeeded in outrunning it and establishing a backfire that finally quelled the flames, but not before most of the surrounding grassland was lost. The burn subsequently forced the relocation of the Fifth Cavalry to a site farther up the Yellowstone.

En route down the river, Miles brought Rice's company on
board at O'Fallon's Creek and debarked it on the west bank
opposite the mouth of Glendive Creek before turning back on
the nineteenth. Seeking knowledge of attempted crossings by
the Indians, Scout Cody, who had accompanied Miles aboard
the *Far West*, made a daring eighty-mile night ride, looking for
evidence of such activities along the east bank. He reached Terry's camp the next morning, having encountered no trails.[8]

On Saturday the rest of the command remained in bivouac.
Wrote Lieutenant Godfrey, "We did not move as we expected
with our 14 day rations towards [Fort] Lincoln and those we
love." He continued, "The Plan now seems to be for all to follow the trail toward Lincoln and if necessary Crook can get
rations there or from there." Amid such rumors, the soldiers
kept up a lively business with the sutler's store, buying onions,
potatoes, and new underwear. Late that day the *Far West* returned. At Crook's request, Terry directed the vessel up to the
Rosebud to retrieve forage and provisions. Meantime, Miles
and most of his men got off the *Far West* on the north bank
where they set up camp.[9]

All the while the soldiers awaited supplies and pondered
their course, a restlessness settled on the camps clustered
around the mouth of Powder River. Early on Sunday, August
20, the Shoshone scouts under Chief Washakie decided to pull
out of the expedition. Their lead was shortly followed by the
Crows, who started upriver after voicing frustration over management indecision. In addition, it was ration time at the agencies and both bodies of Indian allies wanted to go home. En
route up the Yellowstone, the Crows encountered some of their
kinsmen coming down from the Rosebud depot; those tribesmen, despite entreaties from Crook, turned about also, leaving
him and Terry with only the Rees. Other than this event, the
troops passed a lazy day in bivouac, most of them going without
reveille or the customary inspection. Searching about the area
of Moore's fight with the Indians, the men found the bodies of
five warriors and shrapnel from the rounds fired on August 2.
Late in the day mail reached the camp in a small boat sent up
from Fort Buford. Miles fretted over the inaction. He wrote
Mary:

> After six days march on the trail, the two commands came in here for
> rest and supplies without seeing an Indian or exchanging a shot, and

this is what is called Indian campaigning! The truth is there is not a man
here who has . . . paid enough attention to his profession to conduct an
Indian campaign. Terry . . . has had little experience and is too much
under the influence of those slow, ineffective men like Gibbon to reap
good results.[10]

Despite Miles's impatience at the course of events, the logistical reality of such an enterprise dictated that supplies be obtained before proceeding. Crook's horses were exhausted and
needed rest and something besides grass to eat. His infantrymen, moreover, needed new shoes that were stockpiled at the
depot. On top of all this, rumors circulated that General Sheridan's arrival was imminent. Thus, through the twentieth and
twenty-first the soldiers could do nothing but wait. The rain
returned, mixed with hail and accompanied by thunder and
lightning, which only made matters worse. Still without shelter,
save for some crude wickiups, officers and men endured the
discomfort, but with much complaint. "It rained so hard Tuesday and Wednesday nights," remembered Lieutenant King,
"that the men gave up all idea of sleep, built great fires along
the banks, and clustered round them for warmth."[11]

The frequent storms exacted a toll among the troops. The
surgeons examined some cases and determined whether the invalids were too sick to remain in the field. Several, including the
partially paralyzed Captain Archibald H. Goodloe, Twenty-
second Infantry, and the accidentally wounded Second Lieutenant George O. Eaton, Fifth Cavalry, prepared to go downstream on the boats. Some of the newspaper reporters who had
accompanied the troops, concluding that the warfare was past,
also departed, having grown weary of following Terry and
Crook through the Yellowstone wilderness. At 5 P.M. on the
twenty-first the *Carroll* finally appeared, having surmounted the
rapids. The boat brought more mail and more rumors regarding Indian movements. Later, the long-awaited wagon train finally came in sight, its passage from Rosebud Creek marked by
laborious exertions of the men as they guided the vehicles over
excruciatingly rough terrain. At one point on the twentieth the
soldiers accompanying the train had thought they were about
to come under attack by Indians. To their relief, the tribesmen
proved to be Terry's Crow scouts en route home. Miles's
nephew, who came in with the train, later wrote that on the

evening of August 21, General Terry and his staff crossed the Yellowstone to dine with the colonel.[12]

The next morning, Terry directed forty of the wagons to prepare to accompany his command during the ensuing march. By now it had been determined that both forces would follow on the weeks-old Indian trail, although Terry decided this time not to emulate Crook and to instead carry twenty days' rations in the wagons for his own troops. The *Carroll*, meantime, moved below Wolf Rapids to ferry the wagons to the south side of the Yellowstone. Rapidly falling waters made it imperative that the commands continue eastward. Promoting that view, word came that the *Far West* had been grounded at Buffalo Rapids, necessitating the removal of its Rosebud cargo before it could be freed.

Events quickened on Wednesday as Crook and Terry finally prepared to move out. *The Far West* arrived and Crook's command received rations. Word came from Lieutenant Rice at Glendive that on the twenty-second a large force of Indians had reached the north bank of the river, but Terry attached little significance to the report. He would later learn, however, that on this day warriors had fired on the steamer *Yellowstone*, bringing provisions from Bismarck, at a point some forty miles below Glendive. One soldier took a bullet in the chest, dying in the exchange, but the Indians withdrew when fired on and the troops on the vessel did not pursue. On the night of August 23 a driving rain pelted the men in the Powder River encampment without abatement, knocking down tents and shelters and turning the ground to mud.[13]

Early the next morning Crook pulled away up the Powder to retake the Indian trail, his rain-soaked cavalry troopers leading their exhausted mounts ten miles along the slick banks of the stream. Terry remained encamped along the Yellowstone, intending to follow on the next day. The Dakota column spent the day preparing for the march, readying animals and supplies and attempting to dry their clothing. The weather finally cleared, then turned cold. Miles chafed to get going, desiring to head down the Yellowstone, where Rice had reported seeing warriors, instead of following Crook. "I believe it is much better to go directly where we know the Indians are than to hunt up an old trail that has been made nearly a month. . . . There is too much demoralization in these commands, and everyone is

anxious to get home." Meantime, the *Carroll* took on supplies
for Rice's men and nearly one hundred invalids from the various units to move them to Fort Buford, while the *Far West*
crossed four companies of Miles's infantrymen to the south
bank of the Yellowstone. Captain Bennett, with Company B,
Fifth Infantry, stayed to man the new depot. The wagons remaining on the north side were scheduled to depart for Fort
Buford on August 30, in the charge of Captain Sanger's soldiers of the Seventeenth Infantry. In Terry's absence, the *Far
West* was to keep above Wolf Rapids. The *Carroll*, meantime, was
to resume patrolling the lower river after debarking the evacuees.[14]

At dawn on the twenty-fifth, Terry's troops began moving up
the Powder after Crook. They marched seventeen miles before
halting along the stream. While the soldiers made camp that
afternoon, Cody brought important news that changed the
course of the campaign. En route down the Yellowstone aboard
the *Carroll*, near the junction of O'Fallon's Creek, Cody had
encountered the *Josephine* and the *Yellowstone* ascending with
construction supplies. The *Josephine* carried Lieutenant Colonel Joseph N. G. Whistler and two additional companies of the
Fifth Infantry. Whistler carried further dispatches from Sheridan concerning the proposed forts and directing the construction of a cantonment at the mouth of Tongue River.

Learning that Terry had gone up the Powder, Whistler had
implored Cody to carry the dispatches to him cross-country.
Cody also informed Terry of further Indian activity near the
Glendive post, including accounts of the tribesmen shooting at
the steamboats and even crossing the river. Perhaps Cody related to him the ordeal of two deserters from the Powder River
camp who had been attacked by Indians along the Yellowstone.
One had been killed, while the other, wounded, managed to
reach the *Josephine* and safety. The news of the continued Indian presence around Glendive, added to earlier reports of similar activity, provoked new fears that the Sioux and Cheyennes
were, in fact, breaking north. That evening Terry rode seven
miles ahead to consult with Crook, and the decision was
reached that Crook would continue following the trail while
Terry would hurry back to the Yellowstone to halt attempts by
the Indians to cross that stream. Terry's rationale was that the
Indians could not travel east indefinitely without being driven

into the agencies, and that Crook could deal with that probability alone. Meantime, if they traveled north they might seek asylum in Canada, and Terry wanted to block any trails leading
from the Yellowstone to the Missouri River trading post of Fort
Peck, where sympathetic agency tribes offered sustenance.[15]

Terry believed that the Indians attempting to cross the river
constituted the followers of Sitting Bull, to him "the heart and
soul of the Indian mutiny." Crook, who longed for independence from Terry's influence, countered that Crazy Horse represented the "disaffected people belonging to the Southern
Agencies" and was "about equal in strength to Sitting Bull, who
similarly represent[ed] the Northern Sioux." Crook cited his
duty to protect settlements in his department as a reason for
his desire to continue on the trail, but told Terry, should the
trail scatter or turn north, "you can calculate on my remaining
with you until the unpleasantness ends."[16]

The exchange between Terry and Crook marked the end of
their cooperative venture. Crook pushed on east and was soon
gone from the Yellowstone country. His campaign to pursue
the scattering bands and to protect the Black Hills settlements
became fraught with disunity, despair, and general disgust
among his command. Running short on supplies, Crook opted
to strike for the Black Hills rather than seek relief at the Glendive depot, where Terry had promised to deliver stores, and his
men suffered as a result. Forced to kill and butcher their flagging cavalry steeds, the men struggled into western Dakota Territory, where on September 9 a portion of Crook's Bighorn and
Yellowstone Expedition, under Captain Anson Mills, fell on a
Minneconjou village at Slim Buttes. Most of the Indians fled,
leaving the village and its foodstuffs to the army. At Slim Buttes,
Crook earned the first substantive army victory of the Sioux
War, then drove his exhausted force on to Deadwood before
finally terminating his campaign at Camp Robinson on October
24.[17]

Following his decision to prevent the Indians from heading
north, Terry dispatched Cody back to Whistler, ordering that
officer to hold all available river craft ready for the troops when
they reached the Yellowstone. Early the next day Colonel Gibbon moved most of the men twenty-three miles obliquely across
the plateau east of the Powder and on to the Yellowstone,
reaching the river at 3:30 that afternoon, near the junction with

O'Fallon's Creek. Terry, meantime, hurried back to the mouth of the Powder, accompanied by his staff and one company of the Second Cavalry. The wagons followed. On the way, another courier overtook the general with further instructions regarding the Tongue River post. As anticipated, because of the lateness of the season and the problem getting supplies and building materials up the Yellowstone, Sheridan now directed him to post fifteen hundred men at a cantonment to be raised there, the troops "obliged to hut themselves the best way they can." Miles and the Fifth Infantry were to garrison the place, along with Otis and the battalion of the Twenty-second Infantry, plus a regiment of cavalry. Gibbon's men were to return to western Montana at the conclusion of the campaign. The Seventh Cavalry was to go to Fort Lincoln, while the detachments of the Sixth and Seventeenth Infantry regiments joined the garrisons of posts in the Yellowstone-Missouri country. Terry received orders to return to his St. Paul headquarters by October 15.[18]

Sheridan's orders represented a substantive change in direction in the management of the Sioux War. Sheridan had won military control of the Sioux agencies and now needed troops to disarm and dismount returning Indians. But he also needed to hold the Yellowstone Valley through the winter against the followers of Sitting Bull and Crazy Horse—those "northern" Indians who assuredly would not come in to the agencies and whose presence in the unceded territory might continue to entice their reservation kin. Simultaneously, the orders to Terry establishing the cantonment provided an infusion of new leadership where it was sorely needed, for the vigorous Miles would at last have his way in dealing with the Indians, and seemingly with minimal interference from higher authority. The step further conceded the failure of the summer expedition. General Sherman, in approving Sheridan's plan, expected that the very promulgation of the orders to begin building the cantonment would negatively affect Crook, with whose performance he was dissatisfied and who he feared might construe the orders "as a warrant for him ceasing to pursue the hostile Indians to the bitter end."[19]

Terry reached the Yellowstone on the afternoon of the twenty-sixth. He found several vessels waiting to serve him: the *Far West*, the *Carroll*, the *Daphne*, and the *Josephine*. The latter three were moored at the foot of Wolf Rapids, below the Powder. The *Josephine* had arrived on the twenty-fifth, along with the *Yellowstone*, and was loaded with stores, besides Whistler's two companies of the Fifth. On Terry's direction, the *Josephine* discharged some cargo and then ascended the stream to the Tongue River to debark the soldiers before returning to the mouth of the Powder. The *Yellowstone*, meantime, had turned back downriver. The remaining boats refused to chance the rapids, the water having fallen to an extremely low level. Terry ordered their cargoes removed and hauled by wagon to the waiting *Far West* for delivery to Tongue River. On the twenty-seventh the *Far West* conveyed Major Moore's wagons to the north side before starting upstream. The wagon train shortly made ready to start for Fort Buford, escorted by the four Sixth Infantry companies.[20]

Whistler reached the Tongue the next afternoon, with Companies C and I of Miles's regiment and some fifty recent cavalry enlistees. The men immediately erected an entrenchment on the west side of the Tongue, near the stream's junction with the Yellowstone. After Whistler had selected a site somewhat sheltered from the weather by cottonwood trees and the river bluffs, they began erecting barracks, supply buildings, and officers' quarters out of logs cut in the vicinity and with tools and materials brought from the Powder. Already tons of supplies and equipment were en route to the new station, including six months' worth of medical stores, at least 250 tons of subsistence goods, and 25 tons of quartermaster provisions. In addition, hundreds of tons of hay and thousands of cords of firewood were coming. The government contracted for more steamboats to transport this materiel to the head of navigation, and up until August 21 the *Yellowstone* and *Josephine* had borne quantities of beef cattle and ordnance supplies (including three Gatling guns) upriver for use at the cantonment. Over the ensuing year the new post was to be known variously in military correspondence as Cantonment at Tongue River, Post on Tongue River, Tongue River Barracks, New Post on the Yellowstone, and Yellowstone Command, Post No. 1, M.T.[21]

August 27 saw the start of Terry's maneuver to the north that attempted to curb the movements of any Indians who might have crossed the Yellowstone. First the general traveled downstream to meet Colonel Gibbon, who was waiting below O'Fallon's Creek. Then the steamers *Yellowstone* and *Carroll* spent the balance of the day ferrying the command to the north bank before continuing with the evacuees to Fort Buford. At dusk Terry's infantry and cavalry, freshly provisioned with beef and accompanied only by pack mules, traveled six miles up a dry creek bed and camped without wood and scant water along an immense buffalo trail. The country set upon was unknown to the commanders and the civilian guides, and over the following days the column was forced to move between water holes as it fingered its way northwestwardly toward the barren divide rising between the Yellowstone and Missouri rivers. "Occasionally," remembered one enlisted man years later, "we followed a buffalo trail which would lead to their wallows, only to find the alkali water covered with nauseating green scum and spiders." Many of the soldiers sated their frequent thirst by nursing small pebbles in their mouths.[22]

On August 28 the command moved on, halting briefly for breakfast when water was encountered. Near the headwaters of Bad Route Creek, the command was besieged by buffalo gnats, which, wrote Colonel Gibbon, "swarmed around us like bees, stinging men and horses in a way which rendered both almost frantic with pain." Because of the horses, the "winged ants," as officer Maguire called them, were drawn only to the cavalrymen, and the infantry troops went largely unscathed. Late in the afternoon the command found water, and the troops went into bivouac along Bad Route Creek, after having traveled more than twenty-one miles. Here Terry dispatched Cody and scout George Herendeen to the Glendive post to retrieve messages.[23]

Early Tuesday morning the soldiers made their way to the imposing divide separating the tributaries of the Yellowstone River from those of the Missouri. Terry sent Captain Edward Ball's battalion of four companies of the Second Cavalry to reconnoiter for Indian trails beyond the divide, while the remainder of the command turned east to scout the base of the ridge for water. Ball returned the next day, having found no fresh signs. In fact, Indians were nearby. The presence of the troops in the divide country frightened at least one tiny village of Hunkpapas under Long Dog, whose inhabitants fled so precipitately that the lodges were left standing. These Indians had been drawn to the area by the buffalo and managed to avoid detection by Terry's soldiers.[24]

The country passed over during the next few days after leaving the divide was pleasant, except for a brief stretch of badlands. Finally, on August 30, the command headed for Deer Creek, down which Terry intended to march to the Yellowstone. During the day the soldiers found good water in pools before the terrain degenerated into an alkaline wasteland near Deer Creek. At dusk Cody and Herendeen arrived from Glendive to report no further Indian activity around Rice's post. Dismayed, Terry wrote another note to Crook, doubtless reporting his lack of success, and sent it off with a Ree courier. The Yellowstone lay less than fourteen miles away.[25]

On the morning of August 31, Terry received word of a strong trail having been located near Glendive, along with information regarding an attempted crossing of the Missouri near Fort Berthold by some of Sitting Bull's Hunkpapas. Responding to the latter news, Terry ordered Major Reno and the Seventh Cavalry, accompanied by the scouts, to continue searching east. The balance of the command, including Gibbon and Miles and their regiments, trudged through the worst part of the circuit, the badlands bordering Deer Creek, which led southeastwardly all the way to the river. At 3 P.M. the troops reached the Yellowstone and went into camp just below the Glendive post.[26]

Back at the river, Terry found to his disappointment that the water level had dropped even lower in his absence and that the *Silver Lake*, then at Glendive, loaded with provisions for Tongue River, could proceed no farther. He subsequently learned that three more steamboats lay aground eighteen miles downstream and required partial unloading to reach Glendive. Even Captain Grant Marsh's *Far West* had deserted the upper river on the thirty-first, after leaving supplies and a company of Seventeenth Infantrymen below Buffalo Rapids. The difficulty in river transport made it imperative that Terry find an alternative means of supplying the new cantonment. The obvious solution lay in retaining Colonel Otis and six companies of the Twenty-second Infantry at Glendive to guard supplies and to serve as an escort to wagon trains bearing them to Tongue River.[27]

That evening Terry issued orders returning Gibbon's Seventh Infantry home, the troops to march on September 6. Colonel Miles completed the monthly muster of the Fifth Infantry. The last two companies of the regiment to reach Mon-

8. Glendive Cantonment, winter of 1876–77. Christian Barthelmess photographed this sketch of the camp of the battalion of Twenty-second Infantry along the north side of the Yellowstone River. The drawing, presumably executed by an officer stationed at the post, clearly shows the log buildings and the line of epaulement protecting the rear. The view is to the south, toward the bluffs across the river. (Jerome A. Greene)

tana remained twenty miles below Glendive aboard the *Benton,* which had blown a steam chest and could not proceed. Terry directed the *Silver Lake* to retrieve those troops, but that vessel soon ran aground. Meantime, Miles, anticipating his independent command, submitted a request to hire twenty-five white and fifty Indian scouts and an interpreter to serve him at Tongue River over the winter. He further asked that he be provided with a sum of money to give as payment to "any Scouts or Indians who shall inform me of the locality of any hostile Indian camp."[28]

Logistical matters occupied the various commanders over the next several days, as Terry prepared to dismantle the expedition in accordance with Sheridan's instructions. On Friday, September 1, the wagon train from Powder River, escorted by Colonel Moore's Sixth Infantrymen, arrived opposite the Deer Creek bivouac, named Camp Canby to honor Brigadier Gen-

eral Edward R. S. Canby, who had died during the Modoc Indian War in California three years earlier. That same day, Companies A and D, Fifth Infantry, marched from the stricken
Benton, in the charge of Captain Henry B. Bristol, reaching the
encampment on Saturday and giving Miles ten companies of his
regiment with which to operate. On the second, Terry endured
one more frustration when a party of his soldiers failed to locate a crossing by which he might ford his command to seek out
Indians or productively cooperate with Crook. Meantime,
along with the *Far West*, the *Silver Lake* once freed from its sandbar, proceeded downstream, while the *Josephine* went down to
assist the *Benton*. A private in Moore's command recounted Saturday's happenings: "Lay in camp all day. Washed our cloathes
and [spent the time] sleeping and mending. Bean soup for din-
ner. Tried it. It was burnt awful bad. All kinds of rumors where
we are going."[29]

Major Reno's Seventh Cavalrymen came in from their reconnaissance late on Sunday, having encountered no Indians.
Along the Yellowstone, members of this command had seen the
Carroll going up to the Tongue River, loaded with machinery
and followed by the *Yellowstone*, from which they obtained forage. After learning from his scouts that no signs of Indians had
been located near the Missouri, Reno had started back to
Terry.[30]

The arrival of Reno's troopers followed the departure of
Miles and most of the Fifth Infantry for the Tongue River earlier the same day. Together with Companies A, D, E, G, K, and
L, and a small supply train, the restless Miles left the Glendive
Cantonment on September 3 and started upstream on his assignment, at last independent, physically if not figuratively,
from the army hierarchy. Company F followed three days later.
Two companies of the Twenty-second Infantry would proceed
to join Miles on September 11, closing the Powder River depot
on the way.[31]

Terry also made ready to leave Glendive. "The expedition
has 'busted,' " wrote Lieutenant Godfrey as the command components began to disperse. On the fifth Terry formally ended
the campaign. While not admitting defeat, he nonetheless had
been bested as much by the forces of nature as by the Indians.
"The Yellowstone has fallen so rapidly within the past few days
that no boat can go to Powder River," he wrote. To economize

9. The supply steamer *Rosebud* was typical of the vessels that plied the Yellowstone River, carrying troops and supplies to combat the Indians in 1876–77. Photograph by David F. Barry. (Paul Harbaugh and the Denver Public Library)

on the available stores, it was mandatory to diminish the number of troops they would have to sustain. "I shall send the Montana troops home at once and shall use our wagon train to get forward the supplies to Tongue River. . . . The immediate organization of a very large wagon train at Buford is an absolute necessity." Terry directed Otis and four companies of the Twenty-second Infantry to erect huts at Glendive. Captain Sanger and two companies of the Seventeenth Infantry would be posted at Powder River to help forward supplies to the Tongue River cantonment. Reno's Seventh Cavalry and Major Moore's battalion of the Sixth Infantry were to march leisurely for Fort Buford in a maneuver designed both to guard the river and to repel any Indians that Crook might yet drive toward the Yellowstone. In the afternoon of the fifth several officers took leave and, along with Scout Cody, started downriver aboard the *Yellowstone*. That evening, reported Captain Snyder, "a large party of officers gathered at Genl Terries Hdqtrs, and after several hours spent in singing & talk bade each other good bye."[32]

On the morning of September 6, Gibbon's soldiers, accompanied by thirty wagons bearing their provisions as well as materials for the new post, began the six-hundred-mile trek back to their stations in western Montana. Likewise, the troops from the east headed home. Terry and his staff proceeded downstream by steamboat, arriving at Fort Buford the next day. The Seventh Cavalry and Moore's battalion, moving in accordance with Terry's wishes, deviated to Wolf Point on the Missouri in a last futile attempt to strike a party of Sioux seen crossing there, and did not reach Fort Buford until September 18. Four days later the cavalrymen arrived at Fort Berthold on the Missouri, and reached Fort Stevenson on the twenty-third. Three days after that the weary troopers rode into Fort Lincoln.[33]

Thus far, the events in the wake of the Custer fight had only compounded the army's embarrassment over that disaster. Terry's movement had foundered, frustrated time and again by delay and indecision; whatever opportunities had existed for the armies of Crook and Terry to catch the Indians in July had vanished altogether by September. The reality was that the tribes had scattered. As Gibbon proclaimed: "Our stern chase had thus proved a long and fruitless one, and we had no longer even a shifting objective point to move against." The failure was a sore topic in all army quarters. At the higher offices the subject

10. Scout William F. ("Buffalo Bill") Cody brought the drama of
the Great Sioux War to the eastern stage following his departure from
the front in early September, 1876. Cody had taken the "first scalp
for Custer" at Warbonnet Creek in July, but became frustrated with
the army's subsequent ponderous movements seeking out the Indians. Photograph by Rockwood. (Denver Public Library, Western History Department)

was generally avoided or the military deficiencies rationalized away, while in places like Fort Lincoln or Fort Buford criticism and ridicule of the operation was common.[34] Presumably, if success against the Sioux and Cheyennes was to happen, it would follow during the next spring and summer. In the meantime, Colonel Miles and his force, ensconced through the winter at Tongue River, were expected to assume a stationary presence that would signal the determination of the government to hold the region and quell further disturbances by the Indians. Given its static character, it was a plan that the agile and ambitious Miles would find difficult to honor in the months ahead.

CHAPTER FOUR

The Road
to Tongue River

September in eastern Montana Territory occasioned an annual transformation of color accompanied by climatic extremes. The leaves of the cottonwoods abounding along the Yellowstone and its tributaries turned bright yellow, their tips curled from repeated nighttime frosts. Daytime temperatures infrequently soared, while evening chills increasingly neutralized their effect. Biting winds and rainstorms continued to plague the military operations. By September, summer's lush verdure had assumed a straw-colored monotony that mirrored the tedium of the frustrated army. As the disbandment of Terry's campaign indicated, the Indians were no longer together and the prospect that they would be brought to account quickly now proved fleeting.

The tribes had continued to go their separate ways, more or less following their traditional seasonal inclinations, in spite of the military presence in the region. Crook, as mentioned, had encountered some of them at Slim Buttes, within the confines of the Great Sioux Reservation. In fact, Crook's assault on American Horse's village likely disrupted plans of many of those Indians to surrender. Following that engagement, the Indians who did not go to the agencies began filtering back to the Yellowstone country to start their fall hunt, hoping to avoid further contact with the soldiers.[1] The Sioux followers of Crazy Horse gravitated to their Powder River haunts, ultimately camping in the smoke-blackened valleys of the Tongue River and Prairie Dog Creek, where they found game scarce. Indicative of the growing dissension among the Indians, some families traveling with Crazy Horse reportedly desired to go into the agencies, but Oglala warriors intimidated them by killing their ponies and destroying their tipis. Most of the Northern Cheyennes had long since gone into Wyoming to camp along the Powder River and search for game west of the Big Horn Mountains. In the weeks that followed, the Cheyennes would be joined by numerous kinsmen slipping away from the agencies after the army took charge.

Meantime, the followers of Sitting Bull tarried for a time at Twin Buttes, along the Grand River in Dakota, before striking for the buffalo lands north of the lower Yellowstone. Some military reports stated Sitting Bull was going to the Yellowstone country to disrupt army transportation along the river and force the troops to abandon the region altogether. His real objective, however, was to capitalize on lucrative game prospects. As noted, several parties of Sioux had earlier forded the stream, and during September the number of crossings increased, a few observed by scouts and couriers who reported them to Colonel Miles. Also, rumors came from the mounted police in Canada that parties of Sioux were congregating along Porcupine Creek, ten miles south of the international border. Scouts from Fort Benton went to verify those movements. From all indications, both major groups of nonagency Sioux—those associated with Sitting Bull and those accompanying Crazy Horse—disdained further confrontation.[2]

Besides the military response of the Terry-Crook campaign, the government invoked civil recourse in its attempt to contain the crisis with the Indians after the battle at the Little Bighorn. The army disaster clearly embarrassed the administration because of its implications of confusion and failure of Grant's peace policy toward the western tribes. On the frontier, communities expressed alarm that the faltering "Quaker" policy had left them needlessly exposed to the Indian threat, while in the East political sentiment generally determined the tone and extent of the criticism. By September, earlier calls in Congress for raising units of volunteers to go after the Sioux had been tempered, and, as the 1876 presidential election campaign got underway, both sides concluded it was probably best to let the regular army do its job. Nonetheless, Indian policy, while not part of either party's platform, remained a hot topic in the West. That autumn Commissioner of Indian Affairs John Q. Smith asserted confidently, possibly as a Republican panacea, that dwindling hunting grounds made inevitable "the civilization or the utter destruction of the Indians."[3]

The immediate manifestation of the government's civil response to the Sioux came in the reopening of negotiations at the Nebraska and Dakota agencies for cession of the Black Hills, roughly one-third of the reservation laid out for the Indians in 1868. On August 15, in its appropriation for fiscal year 1877, the Congress, while allotting funds for feeding the agency Sioux, decreed that unless those Indians ceded the Hills and the Powder River hunting grounds and moved the Spotted Tail and Red Cloud agencies to the Missouri River, further provision for their welfare would be denied. The threat was accompanied by the appointment of another commission—this of seven individuals prominent in Indian affairs—to induce the Sioux to surrender their treaty lands.

In early September the delegation convened at the Spotted Tail and Red Cloud agencies among "friendly" but suspicious Brules, Oglalas, Northern Cheyennes, and Northern Arapahoes, all members of tribes party to the Fort Laramie treaty. For the balance of September and October the commissioners lectured, finessed, and cajoled the adult males of the various agencies, comprising, in addition, members of the Hunkpapa, Yanktonais, Sans Arc, Blackfeet Sioux, Two Kettle, and Minneconjou tribes. Eventually the commissioners obtained approval of an agreement that the Indians would turn over the coveted gold region encompassing the Black Hills, and prominent Sioux leaders, such as Red Cloud, Spotted Tail, Man-Afraid-of-His-Horses, and John Grass, affixed their marks to the document. In securing approval by these Indians, the commission ignored a proviso of the 1868 treaty stipulating that such changes must be ratified by three-fourths of all adult males residing on the reservation. Threatened with the loss of foodstuffs that would affect their physical survival, the agency people had no recourse but to accept the terms imposed on them.[4]

Compounding the situation for the reservation people was Sheridan's military seizure of the agencies, an act sanctioned by the Interior Department. In late July troops went into Red Cloud and Spotted Tail agencies, and Terry's cavalry and infantry took over the Missouri River agencies in September and October. Seeking to confirm reports that many of the off-reservation bands were not only being aided and abetted by the agency Indians, but also were returning from afield to seek winter abode among them, Sheridan ordered a census by his officers. At Standing Rock, figures revealed that the population of two thousand had recently doubled over two weeks. Fully one thousand of the returnees were suspected of having traveled with the nonagency bands during the summer. Similar reports came from the other agencies.[5] To thwart this trend, troops from Terry's command confiscated all arms and ponies at the Missouri River agencies. Similarly, Crook and Colonel Ranald S. Mackenzie seized weapons and ponies from tribesmen at Red Cloud and Spotted Tail. Sheridan firmly believed that the difficulties with the Sioux and Cheyennes would end if the army controlled the agencies and prevented the comings and goings of the so-called hostiles to those stations.

The counterpoint to Sheridan's agency strategy was, of course, his design to establish a permanent military presence in the heart of Sitting Bull's domain. The success of that plan lay with the placement of strong garrisons on the Tongue and Big Horn rivers as well as in the country west of the Black Hills. The latter post, founded east of the Big Horn Mountains in October 1876, became Cantonment Reno (later Fort McKinney) and stood in northern Wyoming. It was a few miles from the site of Fort Reno, which had been abandoned by the government in 1868. Completion of the other two posts, delayed by the seasonal drop in water level of the Yellowstone River, promised final military control over the unceded hunting grounds accorded the Indians since 1868.[6]

At the mouth of the Tongue River, Colonel Miles and the Fifth Infantry began their labors as the various companies reached the site of the new cantonment. Companies E, G, and H arrived with Miles on September 10, joining Companies C and I already there with Whistler. The command had seen no Indians during its march, and the trip from Glendive Creek had been accompanied only by rain and light snow that capped the distant hills. En route, Companies A and D had been detached at Custer Creek to guard government property; those units did not reach the cantonment until September 22, after being relieved by Companies E and F of the Twenty-second, also soon to come to the Tongue River. On September 12, two days after Miles arrived, Company F, briefly attached to Gibbon's command, joined with Captain Snyder. Company K also arrived. Company B, meantime, occupied a camp at Buffalo Rapids until September 19, at which time it marched to the new cantonment. At the Tongue, Miles's effective force in addition to the Fifth and Twenty-second, included a complement of white and Indian scouts, several interpreters, and a few artillery pieces. In all, his command as of early September totaled about five hundred officers and men, about one-third the force he had expected to operate with. Miles's request that the regimental headquarters and band personnel at Fort Leavenworth join him was granted, over the objections of Brigadier General John Pope, commanding the Department of the Missouri, who believed their presence in the war zone would be "merely ornamental." Meantime, the other four companies of the Twenty-second and two companies of the Seventeenth Infantry were posted to Glendive under Colonel Otis. During the first weeks of September those troops alternated duty with troops of the Fifth and Sixth Infantry, escorting trains of foodstuffs and provisions from the mouth of the Yellowstone to the Tongue. Other supplies continued to Glendive via steamer. The only other troops in the vicinity consisted of six companies of the Sixth Infantry in the charge of Colonel Hazen at Fort Buford. Because low water precluded delivery of most building materials until spring, those items were generally stockpiled at Buford after coming by steamboats up the Missouri.[7]

An activist commander, Miles hoped to avoid the lethargy that would result from simply garrisoning the cantonment until spring. Instead, he anticipated what his adjutant called "a systematic campaign"—moving his troops against the Indians despite the seasonal restrictions. Even as Miles labored to prepare his command for the coming winter at Tongue River, he began formulating the strategy that became his hallmark in dealing with the Sioux and Northern Cheyennes during the months ahead. Employing an assortment of scouts and guides who knew both the territory and the army's quarry, Miles inaugurated an intelligence system to carefully monitor the whereabouts of the tribes.

Cognizant of the separation of the two main Sioux groups that stayed in the Yellowstone country, he determined to pursue the followers of Sitting Bull, principally composed of Hunkpapas, Minneconjous, and Sans Arcs, while observing the location and activities of Crazy Horse's Oglalas as they traversed the upper Powder, Tongue, and Rosebud. His goal was to keep the two groups separated and prevent their joining together again.[8] The previous movement of some Indians to the buffalo lands across the Yellowstone likely gave further incentive for the implementation of Miles's strategy because it dashed chances that the diverse tribal groups could quickly reassemble.

Although Terry had reportedly tried to dissuade him of conducting winter operations, especially after Crook's disastrous campaign of early 1876, Miles remained confident of success and planned accordingly. As he later recollected:

> I felt sure that simply to hibernate and allow the Indians to occupy the country meant a harassing and unendurable existence for the winter; besides giving great encouragement to the Indians by permitting them to believe themselves masters of the situation while we were simply tolerated upon the ground we occupied. My opinion was that the only way to make the country tenable for us was to render it untenable for the Indians. . . . I was satisfied that if the Indians could live in that country in skin tents in winter, . . . we, with all our better appliances could be so equipped as to not only exist in tents, but also to move under all circumstances.[9]

Other officers, although in the minority, agreed with that concept. Indeed, Colonel Gibbon himself, possessing wide field experience in the Indian country, endorsed winter campaigning as a valid tool against the enemy because it allowed the army to strike "when their [the Sioux] movements are restricted, their watchfulness less efficient, and any 'signs' left in the snow as plainly read by a white man as by an Indian." Perhaps most important, Sheridan himself staunchly advocated winter campaigning and had pursued such operations on the southern plains. To ready his men, Miles immediately began stockpiling quantities of heavy fur and woolen clothing. Moreover, by keeping his men moving in the field through September, October, and November, he would acclimate them to the increasing cold, making it easier for them to withstand even lower temperatures.[10]

While preparing for active campaigning, Miles kept up steady communication with the force at Glendive, which provided troops to guard the wagon trains bearing supplies from the mouth of the Yellowstone. Since its establishment during Terry's campaign, the "Glendive Cantonment," as it came to be called, had proved to be of increasing value as the water level of the Yellowstone dropped. As the head of navigation on the stream, it became the supply depot nearest the Tongue River post; through the autumn, forces from Glendive escorted about three trains per month to and from the Tongue. Each train averaged one hundred wagons full of building materials, tools, and provisions.

The Glendive Cantonment stood along the north bank of the Yellowstone on land sloping gently back from the river and commanding a broad view upstream and down. It was nearly opposite the mouth of Glendive Creek and was separated from it by several wide sandbars supporting small growths of cottonwoods. The log huts constituting the quarters followed the line of entrenchments laid down in August by the Fifth Infantrymen under First Lieutenant Edmund Rice, utilizing that officer's patented invention of a trowel-shaped bayonet. The earthworks fronted a line paralleling the river for about 600 feet, then arched back 250 feet to encircle the camp. Log-and-earthen barracks stood inside the works on either end, angling toward the rear, and officer cabins and storehouses were nearer the front of the cantonment.

There Lieutenant Colonel Elwell S. Otis commanded the four companies of the Twenty-second Infantry and two of the Seventeenth. Otis had served in the New York volunteers during the Civil War, emerging from the conflict with the brevet of brigadier general. He joined the Twenty-second Infantry in 1866. In the early 1880s Otis would help organize and superintend the famous school for infantry and cavalry at Fort Leavenworth. A regular army brigadier general during the 1890s, in the Spanish-American War he would become military governor of the Philippines.[11]

The infantry troops with Otis at Glendive Cantonment consisted of Companies G, H, I, and K of the Twenty-second Regiment and Companies C and G of the Seventeenth. Besides Otis, there were 16 officers and about 220 enlisted men. The 2 scouts assigned to Glendive were Robert Jackson, a mixed-blood Blackfoot, and one John C. Smith. During the second week of September, Companies E and F of the Twenty-second, assigned to Miles, marched up the Yellowstone to the mouth of Custer Creek, almost twenty miles below the Tongue River, to guard property unloaded by the steamboats. The remaining four units spent the balance of the month escorting wagons trains to and from that point and the site of the Tongue River Cantonment.

The slow-moving wagons normally took from ten days to two weeks to complete the roughly 140-mile trip from Glendive to Tongue River and back. The winding route was difficult, with two of the lengthy daily marches being over a timberless plateau. Numerous streams entering the Yellowstone from the north through foliaged ravines had to be forded by the teams and wagons. Designated road camps were located at Spring Creek (fourteen miles above Glendive), Clear Creek (twenty-one miles), Bad Route Creek (thirty-two miles), Cherry Creek (forty-seven miles), and Custer Creek (sixty-two miles). "All of it had to be made with constant vigilance to avoid being surprised by Indians," recalled an officer. "There was no rest for my men. It was a continuous tramp day after day."[12]

At Tongue River, Miles put his soldiers to work on the post, assisting the troops of Colonel Whistler in erecting stockade-like supply houses and quarters of cottonwood logs chinked with mud and set on end in trenches. The huts went up hurriedly but solidly, with roofs of wood poles and mud. Miles's headquarters building, of square-hewn logs laid horizontally, differed from the rest. On September 12, a detachment under Captain Edmond Butler departed for the mouth of Custer Creek to lay out a shorter route from Glendive.

In the meantime, provisions that had been landed across from the mouth of the Tongue were ferried to the new station, while twenty-nine wagons continued bearing supplies to the post from steamer drop points at Buffalo and Wolf rapids. In addition to the government train coming from Glendive, a civilian outfit, the Diamond R train, bore goods by that route. Supplies earmarked for the cantonment as of late September included two hundred buffalo overcoats and one thousand pairs of buffalo-hide overshoes. The Sibley tents Miles had requested could not be obtained, and twenty hospital tents were sent instead. Miles was permitted forty wagons and a like number of six-mule teams at the post. Once sufficient supplies were on hand, he was to send all excess trains back to Buford.[13]

Meanwhile, Miles remained sanguine that the frequent rains would permit the steamboats to continue navigating upstream, and the *Far West*'s ascension to Wolf Rapids on September 10 unreasonably heightened that prospect. He requested authority to purchase horses on which to mount his scouts and asked for additional mules and wagons, promising to "go as far with

Infantry as possible." Miles announced plans to search the region between the Missouri and the Yellowstone and "to make it uncomfortable for any hostile party." He called for at least fifty Indian scouts to help facilitate his project.[14]

Miles had already been authorized to employ as many as twelve scouts or guides, and by mid-September he had recruited a dozen whites and mixed-bloods, some of whom had served him during the summer. One newcomer was Luther S. "Yellowstone" Kelly, a ruggedly handsome man with long black hair, who had come to Miles offering the large paw of a recently slain cinnamon bear as his calling card. An educated man and former army enlistee, Kelly had come to the region in the late 1860s as a hunter and trapper and in 1873 had assisted in an army exploration of the Yellowstone.[15] Miles spent much time with Kelly, inquiring of the young man about the character of the largely unknown country between the Yellowstone and the Missouri and its susceptibility for campaigning. Kelly told Miles that he knew little of the region in question, but provided information on that area north of the Missouri running to the international border. "Before our interview came to a close," Kelly remembered years later, "I was impressed with the fact that General Miles had in view considerable fall and winter campaigning." Miles was likewise impressed, providing the scout with two fine horses with which to conduct his missions. Of Kelly he later wrote: "I felt convinced that he was a person who could be put to a very useful purpose at that juncture of affairs."[16]

Besides the civilian guides, Miles hoped to employ a contingent of fifty Crows, who knew the country and who possessed experience tracking the Sioux and Cheyennes. Soon after reaching the Tongue he sent an officer up the Yellowstone to persuade the Crows to join him. And late that month Terry notified him that the famed battalion of Pawnee scouts and their commander, Major Frank North, would be coming to the cantonment, ostensibly in place of the contingent of cavalry originally promised but now needed at the Missouri agencies. Reduced military appropriations, moreover, forced Miles to limit the civilian scout hirings to four rather than twelve, although he was empowered to enlist up to seventy-five Crow scouts if he wished.[17]

11. Luther S. ("Yellowstone") Kelly, a principal scout for Miles. A native of upstate New York, Kelly proved a constant and dependable asset in the operations of 1876–77. His varied career later included stints as a Washington, D.C., bureaucrat, Alaska guide, captain of volunteers in the Philippines, Indian agent in Arizona, and California fruit grower. Kelly died in 1928. Photograph by Brund. (Denver Public Library, Western History Department)

Miles also intended to utilize artillery in his pursuit of the Sioux and Cheyennes. Long an advocate of the use of ordnance in support of infantry operations, Miles had suggested early in 1876 that the mountain howitzers employed on the plains be replaced by field guns of under five hundred pounds, preferably rifled pieces with an effective range of fifteen hundred yards. From the cantonment at Tongue River, Miles wrote that his ordnance on hand consisted of "one Rodman Rifle Gun, with sight for 12 lb. Napoleon Gun (smooth bore) and ammunition made some fifteen (15) years ago, unreliable and ineffective." He also had available one twelve-pounder Napoleon gun and eight .50-caliber Gatling guns.

Those weapons, he wrote the Department of Dakota, were impractical to maneuver "over this country where Indians would be likely to leave a trail" and thus were deemed "almost worthless." He continued: "The chief objections to our Field Guns is their great weight, and to the Gatling Guns their weight and small calibre. I have used both in Indian fights, and it is impossible to determine the range of the latter at twelve or fifteen hundred yards." Citing his imminent movement against the tribes and the likelihood that he would eventually have to divide his force or post a guard over his supply train, Miles asked that one or two light guns be sent to him as soon as possible. It was not until the following summer, however, that a newly designed gun arrived—too late for its use in any major operations against the Sioux.[18]

Thus, Miles was left with rather derelict artillery, principally the so-called Rodman rifle gun and the twelve-pounder Napoleon. The former in reality was a Model 1861 three-inch Ordnance Rifle that only physically resembled the larger cast-iron Rodman smoothbore cannon used during the Civil War and after, primarily at seacoast fortifications. Fashioned of wrought iron, this field gun proved useful on the frontier after the war; a number of them were converted to breechloaders with the addition of steel breechblocks and boring of their barrels to a diameter of 3.2 inches. The piece fired iron shells charged with gunpowder and had a maximum effective range of around fifteen hundred yards. The bronze twelve-pounder Napoleon was also a prominent fixture on the frontier. Named after Emperor Louis Napoleon, who had promoted its development in France, the medium-weight gun was capable of delivering shot, shell, or spherical case against targets nearly seventeen hundred yards away. During the Civil War the piece was considered an exceptional antipersonnel weapon over quarter-mile distances. Mounted on a wooden carriage and dragged by a team of draught animals, the Napoleon nonetheless proved a cumbersome battle component when employed in Indian warfare.[19]

Miles pushed ahead with his work, despite the deficiencies he perceived with his artillery complement. Through the balance of September the men labored on their winter quarters and assisted in building a new road from the mouth of Custer Creek to expedite the trip from Glendive. On September 19, Miles wrote Terry that the new route had shortened the wagon journey to under one hundred miles. Yet supplies were still slow in arriving, and he admonished the department commander that the accumulation he needed to last his command until the following June would take time to acquire. To service his field force, Miles proposed that one month's supplies be placed under guard at Fort Peck, on the Missouri River, and also near the site of old Fort Pease, across from the mouth of the Bighorn, on the Yellowstone. "These would be available in case any movement was made in the direction of those points." A blockhouse served by infantrymen would guard the forage and provisions placed at the latter point.

Miles reported that as of September 18 there were on hand at Tongue River 32,000 pounds of hard bread, 11,500 pounds of flour, 10,000 pounds of bacon, and 35,520 pounds of beef— barely enough food to last the men twenty days. The beef ration consisted of a herd of seventy-eight cattle, with the arrival of many more expected. Wood for burning was to be furnished on contract from among the numerous citizens congregating at the site. As for the cantonment, Miles wrote:

> The work of building huts is in rapid progress, and, if the present weather continues, I think the command will be in comfortable shelter in four (4) weeks. We are laboring under many disadvantages from the fact that such articles as Broad-axes, Iron wedges, spikes, coal for welding iron, Crow-bars, have not been received. The location for the Cantonment is excellent and there is an abundance of timber for the entire command.[20]

Miles further informed Terry that he hoped to obtain enough Mackinaw boats to erect a pontoon bridge across the Yellowstone near the station.[21]

On the twenty-fifth, Miles, with two officers, fifty soldiers, and several civilian scouts, proceeded under clear skies along the north bank of the Yellowstone to Fort Buford, attending to the new road and scouting the area en route. Miles arrived five days after leaving the Tongue, amid reports of Indians being sighted in the vicinity of the fort.[22] In many ways, Fort Buford symbolized military permanence on the edge of the war zone. Established in 1866 on the left bank of the Missouri, below the juncture of that stream with the Yellowstone and less than three miles below the old trading post of Fort Union, the one-company station guarded the emigrant route from the east to the Montana goldfields against attack from Indians. Built on a site selected by General Terry, the stockaded station was named for deceased Major General John Buford of Civil War fame. Enlarged to accommodate five companies over ensuing years, the fort served as a vanguard of settlement of the upper Missouri and Yellowstone basins.

When new, its adobe and wood structures composed one of the finest outposts on the northern plains, but as time passed, living conditions at Fort Buford deteriorated and troops who garrisoned the place during the winter months endured legendary hardships. Never directly attacked by Indians, its soldiers were nonetheless harrassed constantly during the early years, with several men killed. In 1876 the post, by its strategic posture, assumed significance as a depot site and conveyance point for materiel sent from below. Because of its proximity to tribes of Assiniboines, Yanktonais, Mandans, and Hidatsas, all of whom were friendly to the U.S. government, Fort Buford also functioned as an important observatory for all Indian movements along the Montana-Dakota frontier.[23]

The post's commander, Colonel William B. Hazen, had been assigned there since 1872. Like those of many other army officers, Hazen's career was marked by controversy and unfulfilled ambition. A brave and capable officer, with considerable experience in matters of Indian administration, Hazen regularly managed to offend his seniors and established few lasting friendships with them. He graduated from West Point in 1855, served in the West until the Civil War, and during that conflict rose to the rank of major general, commanding volunteer troops at Shiloh, Chickamauga, Chattanooga, and Atlanta, among other places. Reverting to the rank of colonel in the

12. Colonel William B. Hazen commanded the Sixth Infantry troops at Fort Buford. A man of integrity who possessed wide experience fighting Indians, Hazen lacked tact and judgement in his relationships with his superiors, alienating many and hurting his career. Consequently, in 1876–77 he played only a peripheral role in pursuing the Sioux and Cheyennes. In 1880 Hazen became chief signal officer of the army, serving a stormy tenure marked by the disastrous Greely Arctic Expedition, for which he was court-martialed. Hazen died in 1887. (U.S. Army Military History Institute)

regular army after the war, Hazen served with the Thirty-eighth and Sixth Infantry Regiments on the frontier, notably in Dakota and in the Indian Territory, where, as protector of the Kiowas, he incurred Sheridan's anger. His assignment, or exile, to Fort Buford allegedly occurred after he implicated Secretary of War William W. Belknap in the sale of post traderships in the Indian Territory.

From that outpost, Hazen wrote lengthy and controversial letters critical of government policy, army organization, and the thoughts and writings of many of his military contemporaries, including Custer, whom he despised. As a result, his seniority, conscientious service, and valuable expertise were mostly ignored during the Indian operations in the Yellowstone country during the 1870s. Hazen's involvement in controversy continued later in his life. Appointed chief signal officer in 1880, he leveled harsh criticism against Secretary of War Robert Lincoln over his handling of the Greely arctic expedition, for which Hazen was court-martialed in 1885.[24]

At Fort Buford, Miles conferred with Hazen and the Sixth Infantry officers before returning to the Tongue. He stopped briefly at Glendive, then pushed on, and within several hours encountered a courier from one of the agencies, who informed him of the latest movements of the Indians. Miles heard in particular that the Hunkpapas, Minneconjous, and Sans Arcs might soon be expected north of the Yellowstone, while the group with Crazy Horse, mostly composed of Oglalas, was reported to be roaming the upper reaches of the Tongue and Rosebud. A few days after the troops had left Buford, near midnight, a small number of Sioux hunters attacked Miles's camp, driving in a picket guard composed of recruits before being repelled by heavy fire from the other pickets. Bullets ripped through the colonel's tent in the darkness but did little damage. The warriors fled and did not return, inflicting no casualties among the soldiers. If nothing else, the incident pointed up the ubiquitous presence of the tribesmen and undoubtedly made Miles impatient to launch his offensive in earnest. Two days after this attack Miles and his party reached the Tongue.[25]

The increased knowledge about the whereabouts of the Indians, coupled with the recent attack on his reconnoitering party, led Miles to seek additional firsthand intelligence. Early in October he sent Kelly and scout Victor Smith to search and report on the country north of Milk River. They scouted along the Big Dry River to the Fort Peck Indian Agency, returning to the Tongue with no news of permanent camps in that region. At the Tongue, meanwhile, the companies continued working on their quarters, erecting a hospital and stocking supplies from the Custer Creek depot site. On October 1, the Diamond R train came in, along with the paymaster, and the following day the two companies of the Twenty-second reached the cantonment from their Custer Creek station. Miles notified Terry that the huts would be ready for the men by the sixteenth and that the stores remaining at Glendive would be at the new cantonment by the twenty-sixth, precluding the need to let further freighting contracts.[26]

Similar activity occurred over the next fortnight. On the third, another detachment of Fifth Infantrymen left for Glendive to continue laying out the new road and to escort the train back to the lower post. Through ensuing days more steamers arrived at Buford with building supplies and provisions. The boats served as a vital communications link with army stations down the Missouri and ultimately with the highest authorities directing the war. Officers from the Yellowstone posts frequently shuttled between Buford and the downriver posts as they labored to coordinate activities at the front.

All the time, wagon trains from the Glendive cantonment made frequent trips to and from Fort Buford to get goods and foodstuffs to sustain the garrisons upstream. Those designated for the Tongue River post were transferred to wagons on reaching Glendive, for relay on to Miles's command. Occasionally, too, civilian trains from the Tongue River made the trip directly to Buford.[27] It was the passage of the wagon trains between Glendive and the Tongue River that provoked the first important action between the army and the Indians since Terry's operation had closed. The clash instigated the beginning of Miles's offensive against the Indians, which would last until the following summer.

A routine train of ninety-four wagons and one ambulance started from the Glendive depot at 10:30 A.M. on October 10, escorted by three companies of the Twenty-second Infantry and one of the Seventeenth, approximately 160 men. Captain Charles W. Miner of the Twenty-second commanded the escort. The other officers were: First Lieutenant Benjamin C. Lock-

wood, Company G, Twenty-second; First Lieutenant William
Conway and Second Lieutenant Alfred C. Sharpe, Company H,
Twenty-second; Captain Mott Hooton and Second Lieutenant
William H. Kell, Company K, Twenty-second; and Captain Mal-
colm McArthur and Second Lieutenant James D. Nickerson,
Company C, Seventeenth.

As the wagons proceeded along the trail, the men witnessed
columns of smoke ahead in the distance, which they supposed
came from Indian signal fires. The train covered fourteen
miles, stopping at about five o'clock at Spring Creek (present
Sand Creek) at a site known as Fourteen-mile Camp, approximately two miles from the Yellowstone. Captain Miner described his situation as follows:

> The camp is in the bed of a creek, and commanded by hills at short
> range on all sides but the south, where it is open toward the Yellowstone
> River. There is a good deal of brush, and some timber along the banks
> of the creek. The corrals were made as compactly as possible for the
> night, and secured with ropes; the companies were camped close to
> them, two on each side; thirty-six men and four non-commissioned of-
> ficers were detailed for guard; two reserves were formed and placed on
> the flanks not protected by the companies.[28]

At around eleven o'clock a lone shot rang out as one of Miner's
pickets challenged an approaching figure who then escaped
into the darkness. The men retired uneasily.

Scattered shots and yells aroused the troops near 3:00 A.M.
Warriors posted several hundred yards away fired on the camp,
their rounds whistling through the air and kicking up the earth
as the muzzles of their weapons were seen flashing in the distance. The soldiers did not respond in the darkness. When the
firing stopped, they realized that the shooting had targeted on
the corral; a number of mules were wounded and forty-seven
more had run off. As daylight increased, the men made breakfast, packed their tents and bedding, and prepared to move
ahead.

As the train and escort pulled out of camp Wednesday morning, Captain McArthur's unit of the Seventeenth Infantry, acting
as rear guard, suddenly came under attack by Indians hidden
among trees and bushes in a ravine two hundred yards away. "A
large body of Indians," reported Miner, "estimated at from two
to three hundred, came over the foothills between the camp and

the Yellowstone River on the east side of camp."[29] McArthur and Lieutenant Nickerson reacted quickly, deploying the company in skirmish order, charging forward, and driving the Indians beyond the hills. In this action, Company H of the Twenty-second assumed a position of support on McArthur's right. As the train slowly continued down the trail, the tribesmen struck again. This time warriors ensconced in a ravine on the right fired at the troops before they had gone five hundred yards. The soldiers shot back, but the train kept moving.

As the hours passed, the number of warriors increased to several hundred and the attacks mounted. Keeping their distance, the Indians hung on the rear, flanks, and front, pouring disruptive fire among the soldiers and wagons. Finally, after going almost eight miles, his advance slowed by the previous loss of mules and with dangerous prospects ahead, Miner turned the train about and headed it back to Glendive. He moved up Clear Creek to a higher trail on open ground with a commanding view. As he withdrew east, the Indian gunfire slackened and ceased. The escort and wagons gained the Glendive Cantonment at around nine that evening.[30]

The attack on Miner's train was not unexpected, in light of reports that the Sioux were heading north to hunt. Indeed, the warriors belonged to the several Teton bands known to be allied with Sitting Bull's Hunkpapas, who were moving through the country from their sojourn in western Dakota. Leaders of this assemblage of Hunkpapas, Sans Arcs, and Minneconjous included Gall, Bull Eagle, No Neck, Pretty Bear, and Red Skirt; most of them effected their crossing of the Yellowstone between Glendive Creek and the Powder River. The tribesmen intended to enjoy their annual buffalo hunt before moving on to Fort Peck to trade with members of the Yanktonais Sioux and various mixed-bloods residing at the agency.[31] They viewed the continued presence of the army as an obstruction to their normal activities, one that challenged their customary freedom and, most immediately, threatened prospects for good hunting. In the attack on the wagon train, the Indians vented their anger and frustration at the apparently permanent occupation of their territory by whites.

At Glendive, Colonel Otis faced the problem of getting the supplies through to Tongue River. Following his encounter with the Sioux, Captain Miner urged that more soldiers be as-

13. Lieutenant Colonel Elwell S. Otis commanded the battalion of Twenty-second Infantry and Seventeenth Infantry during the Spring Creek encounters. Wounded in the Civil War, Otis was an intellectual whose contributions to military training during the late nineteenth century were profound. He retired from the service a major general in 1902. (U.S. Army Military History Institute)

signed to the escorts, at least two dozen of them mounted; that plenty of water kegs be carried; and that a Gatling gun or other artillery piece be brought along. With those recommendations in mind, Otis reorganized the escort to include another infantry unit and three Gatling guns. He dispatched a courier to Hazen at Fort Buford, informing him of his projected movement. On Friday, October 13, Otis notified departmental headquarters that he was starting for the Tongue the next day, writing, "I think we can pass through the country with the force I am taking."[32]

Otis departed the depot with eighty-six wagons at 10 A.M. on October 14, leaving the post in the charge of Captain Francis Clarke and Company I, Twenty-second Infantry, plus details from the other companies that gave Clarke a command totaling 4 officers and 97 enlisted men. Otis's force numbered 185 soldiers, but because of the scarcity of horses at Glendive, only 3 or 4 men were mounted. Besides the units previously composing Miner's escort, Company G of the Seventeenth, under Captain Louis H. Sanger, accompanied Otis. Also accompanying the troops were First Lieutenant Oskaloosa M. Smith, Twenty-second Infantry, as battalion adjutant, and Acting Assistant Surgeon Charles T. Gibson.

Another change was the replacement with enlisted men the forty-one civilian teamsters who had become demoralized over the attack on Miner's train. The first day's march proceeded without incident, and the train with its strengthened escort camped in the Yellowstone bottom twelve miles out of Glendive without sighting the Indians. Warriors ranged close by, however, for in the evening several approached the bivouac, but fled at a picket's fire.

At 7 A.M. Sunday, the fifteenth, Otis directed the train forward in four lines and it shortly reached Spring Creek, three miles away. The escort enclosed the wagons, with Company H, Twenty-second, serving as advance guard; Company C, Seventeenth, composing the advance right and left flankers; Company G, Twenty-second, guarding the right flank rear; Company G, Seventeenth, guarding the left flank rear; and Company K, Twenty-second, composing the rear guard. At Spring Creek, Otis sent two men, Scout Robert Jackson and Sergeant Patrick Kelly of Company F of the Twenty-second, to a bluff beyond the stream to watch for Indians as the train forded. Jackson and

Kelly rode toward the summit of the appointed hill, but were suddenly set upon by warriors, who fired at them and chased them back toward the train. They arrived safely, but their clothing had been riddled by numerous shots. At the appearance of the Sioux, Otis sent skirmishers forward on each flank; those on the left composed Company H of the Twenty-second. Lieutenant Sharpe and ten men of this unit were detached with instructions to take a high hill in front of the company's advance, while the main force, led by Lieutenant Conway, surged forward up the bluffs. They forced out as many as fifty warriors. While the soldiers took the bluffs on either side, the train passed safely through the defile and ascended a broad plateau.

Shortly, three scouts from Miles's command made their appearance. Four had been sent out to find Captain Miner's train after it failed to arrive on schedule at Tongue River. They had encountered the Indians the previous evening and one scout had been killed. The others had lost their horses but managed to flee after dark to the timber along the Yellowstone, where they stayed hidden through the night. Otis's soldiers helped bury the fallen scout, then the train moved on, protected by skirmishers deployed on all sides. The Sioux, meantime, increased their numbers in front while keeping their distance. Few shots came from either party as the train approached Clear Creek at about 2:00 P.M., preparing to pass into and through its deep and tortuous ravine. Otis noticed upwards of two hundred warriors on a bluff to his left, commanding the approach to the stream, and he reported seeing the smoke of many signal fires rising in all directions.[33]

Otis determined to drive the warriors from the bluffs and quickly dispatched Company H of the Twenty-second and Company G of the Seventeenth for that duty. The soldiers raced forward and scaled the heights, yelling as they advanced, and forced the Indians to reassemble along a ridge farther back. Meantime, the warriors had ignited the grasslands ahead of the train, creating a blinding smoke screen. Lieutenant Sharpe recorded details of the encounter:

> We had but 180 muskets in line. One of the Gatling guns was placed in position, and under its cover my Company H, being the advance guard, made a rush for the valley; as we filed through it along the stream the Indians devoted their best shots to us. Sergeant H[athaway?] of my company was marching about two paces from me when he was struck

with a thump in the breast by a spent ball, which fell, harmless, at his feet. They soon got the range and bullets came hissing about our heads and [were] tearing up the ground all around and about us. Finally, we reached the foot of the opposite side, and with a cry, we charged up the hill. The Indians then set fire to the tall grass which was dry as tinder. The smoke was blinding and the heat intolerable, but rushing onward and upward, we gained the crest and again drove the villains before us. Panting and exhausted, the men sank down, completely overcome. But we had cleared the way, and we soon saw the long, white train of wagons climbing the hill.[34]

The train now proceeded rapidly to Clear Creek, took on water for the livestock and replenished the soldiers' supply, then lumbered up the bluffs through treacherously difficult ravines. All the while, the number of warriors increased. Atop the bluffs, the train was again split into four components, the whole completely surrounded by skirmishers before advancing. The Indians persisted in attacking all sides, particularly the rear, guarded by Company K, Twenty-second, under Captain Hooton and Lieutenant Kell. Those men expended so much ammunition shooting at the Sioux that a thousand additional rounds had to be sent back to them. "The roar of musketry was terrific," wrote Lieutenant Smith. At one point, the Gatling guns were brought forward, but their range proved to be so limited that they were of no use.

Gradually, the soldiers succeeded in extending their flanks for almost one thousand yards and, through frequent sallies in front, were able to keep the road open for the train to advance. Fearing that Hooton's unit was about to be cut off from the command, Captain Sanger led Company G of the Seventeenth to his relief. The Sioux repeatedly succeeded in halting the train, necessitating a fight for the road so that it could proceed. In one instance, wrote Sharpe,

Lt. Conway with ten men from the right of Company H was detached to go ahead and clear the way, while I was left with the remainder of the company on the left. Company G, 22nd Infantry, was advancing to our support; when about ten paces from us, I saw a man in its lines drop like a log; he was shot in the knee. After a half-hour halt, we again prevailed and wound onward. The prairie was ablaze all around us, rendering our passage in the road at certain places quite difficult.[35]

After a few more miles, Otis stopped for the night at a broad depression, on ground with a commanding view in all direc-

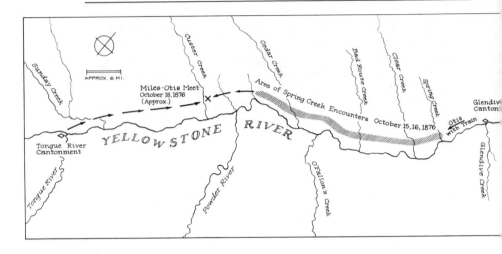

2. Area of the Spring Creek encounters, October 15 and 16, 1876

tions. It was almost five o'clock. Random shots were exchanged with the tribesmen for another two hours until night fell. Otis ordered rifle pits dug along a perimeter five hundred yards from the train corral, and all available troops went on picket duty through the night. Although the Sioux had fired on the soldiers and wagons for many hours, Otis sustained casualties of only three men wounded. The Indians, he reported, "met with considerable loss. A good number of their saddles were emptied and several ponies wounded."[36]

Early the next day Otis directed the train forward in four columns, the whole encompassed by skirmishers deployed as on the previous afternoon. The Indians kept their distance, observing the soldiers from the nearby hills and firing randomly on them. Before long, as the train approached Cedar Creek, Otis and his officers spied a warrior approaching. The Indian placed a note written on a piece of white cloth on a stake atop the hill in front, then ran off. Scout Robert Jackson rode forward, retrieved the note, and brought it to Otis. It read:

YELLOWSTONE.

I want to know what you are doing traveling on this road. You scare all the buffalo away. I want to hunt on the place. I want you to turn back from here. If you don't I will fight you again. I want you to leave what you have got here, and turn back from here.

I am your friend,
SITTING BULL.
I mean all the rations you have got and some powder. Wish you would
write as soon as you can.[37]

The note, evidently dictated by Sitting Bull to a mixed-blood
hunter named John Bruguier, who resided in the Hunkpapa
village, was the first physical manifestation of the Sioux leader's
presence in the area since early summer. Otis sent Jackson to
tell the Indians that he planned to move the train forward to
Tongue River "and that we should be pleased to accommodate
them at any time with a fight."[38] The wagons pressed on, and
by 8 A.M. it was obvious to Otis that the warriors were once
more massing to attack him. Near the next stream scattered
gunfire erupted, but the troops were able to gather wood and
water the livestock while the skirmish line stood guard. Ascending from the bottom, the train moved on. The warriors surrounded the command but maintained a wide margin and
shooting occurred only sporadically. Otis estimated the number of tribesmen to be between three hundred and five
hundred.

Soon two Indian men appeared on the left, one bearing a
white flag and the other wearing a white rag on his head. Otis
permitted them to enter his lines. They identified themselves as
Long Feather and Bear's Face, Hunkpapa scouts from Standing
Rock Agency who had been dispatched to seek out Sitting Bull
and convince him to surrender. They bore messages from the
officer commanding the agency, Lieutenant Colonel William P.
Carlin, and they told Otis that they had that morning visited
Sitting Bull's camp near the confluence of Cabin Creek with the
Yellowstone. Further, the scouts brought a request from the
Hunkpapa chief that Otis agree to meet with him outside the
lines. The colonel sent the Indians back to Sitting Bull with his
declination, but promised to see the chief inside the army lines.

Shortly, three of Sitting Bull's lieutenants rode forward, accompanied by the two scouts, and reiterated through interpreters the concerns made in the note—that the trains were driving
off game and that the Indians wanted food and ammunition.
They also stated that they were weary of fighting and wanted
peace. Otis denied their request for ammunition and told the
Indians that he lacked authority to offer or accept terms of surrender. He urged them to go to Tongue River and gave assur-

ances for their security at that place. The three Sioux told Otis that the Indians would go directly to Fort Peck on the Missouri to trade, then proceed to the Tongue River cantonment. As a sign of good faith, Otis deposited two sides of bacon and 150 pounds of hard bread on the road for the tribesmen.[39] Then the train and escort continued down the trail, unmolested, as the warriors pulled back, soon to leave altogether.

Army casualties in the two days of skirmishing numbered but three men wounded. One of those, Private John Donahoe of Company G, Twenty-second Infantry, had been previously wounded on July 29 in the skirmish at the mouth of Powder River. The others were Sergeant Robert Anderson, also of Company G, Twenty-second, and Private Francis Marriaggi, Company G, Seventeenth Infantry. The Indian casualties apparently totaled one killed and three wounded.[40]

The Spring Creek affairs signaled the determination of the Sioux to carry on their traditional activities in spite of the presence of the military. Just as determined, however, was Colonel Miles in his conviction that the Sioux were not to be left alone in their age-old pursuits. Through his scouts he tried to ascertain the location and tendencies of the people on both sides of the Yellowstone. Even before Miner and Otis had started for the cantonment, Miles had attempted to track the Indians with scouting detachments sent out from the post to explore the countryside. One of those detachments was commanded by Second Lieutenant Frank S. Hinkle, who returned to the Tongue from a scouting trip on the thirteenth. Two days later Hinkle was sent with six men to search the upper reaches of the Powder River, Mizpah Creek, and the Tongue, in the hope that they would find an Indian encampment reported to be on the Powder.[41]

Miles, meantime, grew apprehensive over the nonappearance of the train, which was scheduled to arrive on the evening of October 16. His scouts, also attacked by the Indians, had not reported back. At 2:30 A.M. on the seventeenth, he outfitted a command with fourteen days' rations and started for Glendive, the companies of the Fifth Infantry fording the Yellowstone at daybreak and moving northeast along the road while the two units of the Twenty-second manned the nearly finished garrison. The command under Miles consisted of 15 officers and 434 men of Companies A, B, C, D, E, F, G, H, I, and K, besides 10 civilian and 2 Indian scouts. It was the first time in eighteen years—since the operations against the Mormons in 1857–58—that the Fifth Infantry had marched as a complete unit.

Miles took his ordnance rifle along, as he did throughout his subsequent Sioux expeditions. Trumpeter Brown remembered the journey: "[We] marched all day through clouds of dust and burning sand which nearly choked and blinded us; we stopped at sundown, made a cup of coffee and again took up the line of march." The command halted at 1:00 A.M., after traveling nearly thirty miles. The next day the men moved up Custer Creek, and approximately forty-four miles and twenty-four hours after leaving the cantonment, Colonel Miles found Otis and the train wending their way towards the Tongue. Captain Snyder placed the occurrence of the October 18 meeting with Otis about five miles above the mouth of Custer Creek and some fourteen miles from the Fifth Infantry's previous night's bivouac. Assured that the men and supplies were safe, Miles determined to keep after the Indians the next day, hoping to intercept them at some point nearby and punish them for their actions. Otis steered the wagons on to Tongue River, arriving two days later. On October 21 he started the train back to Glendive, reaching that point without incident on the twenty-sixth.[42]

CHAPTER FIVE

Cedar Creek

On Thursday, October 19, at 9 A.M., Miles and the Fifth Infantry pulled out of their bivouac and headed northeast. Otis had told Miles that the Sioux would likely be found encamped near the mouth of Cabin Creek or en route overland to Fort Peck. During the day's march, hunting parties of soldiers forged ahead, seeking buffalo. Late that afternoon, after traveling about sixteen miles, the troops encamped along the timbered banks of Cherry Creek. Acting on Otis's information, Miles dispatched Yellowstone Kelly with two other scouts, Vic Smith and Billy Cross, to find out if the Indians had left their river camps. During this reconnaissance, which evidently lasted two days, Kelly's men came on the site of a recently abandoned village and the next day trailed the Indians north toward the divide separating the Yellowstone drainage from that of the Missouri. In fact, the skirmishing with Otis's infantrymen had frightened the bison herds away from the Yellowstone, and Sitting Bull and his followers had gone after them.[1]

In the biting cold of early Friday morning, the Fifth Infantrymen resumed their march to the northeast. As the column proceeded beneath sullen skies, tribesmen appeared on distant ridges, signifying to Miles the proximity of Sitting Bull's village. When the command halted in a valley to rest, several hundred Indians gradually positioned themselves on the hills and ridges facing the regiment. Miles ordered his troops deployed in line of battle and moved forward.

Late that morning, several miles east of Cedar Creek, the command spotted riders with a white flag approaching from among a large body of tribesmen arrayed along a bluff to the left. Two Indians advanced and identified themselves as Long Feather and Bear's Face, the same men sent from Standing

Rock Agency who had previously contacted Otis. They informed Miles that Sitting Bull desired to meet with him to discuss surrendering his people.[2] Relishing the chance to learn something of the strength and condition of the Indians and the location of their camp, Miles immediately agreed to the proposal. In the near distance, a group of Sioux numbering between 150 and 300 took position atop a hill to watch the proceedings. His interpreter absent, Miles directed his aide-de-camp, Second Lieutenant Hobart K. Bailey, to accompany the two Indians back to the waiting group, where the mixed-blood John Bruguier was enlisted to translate.

After extensive negotiations, during which Miles permitted the suspicious Indians liberal preliminary concessions, a meeting was arranged on the prairie midway between the soldiers and the tribesmen.[3] Guarding against treachery, the Fifth Infantry spread along the summit of a ridge facing that occupied by the Indians. Company I, under Captain Wyllys Lyman, supported the ordnance rifle, which peered down on the proceedings from a hill on the north of the line, while First Lieutenant Mason Carter's Company K similarly occupied a knoll on the south. A line of skirmishers took station behind the train. Miles, Lieutenant Bailey, scout Robert Jackson, and five enlisted men advanced several hundred yards to the designated spot and stood their horses. After nearly an hour, and following protracted exchanges between the Indians and Lieutenant Bailey, twelve unarmed and dismounted Sioux leaders, including Sitting Bull, paraded forward in line, followed by armed warriors on horseback. Thirty yards from where Miles waited, the party stopped and requested that the officers dismount. Then four of the Indians followed Sitting Bull into a circle.

The crisp air was charged with a tension accelerated by the wind whipping over the prairie with increasing velocity. Soon the mounted warriors advanced and surrounded the group, randomly coming and going, evoking memories in the watching troops of the death of General Canby at the hands of the Modocs under similar circumstances three years earlier. Sioux accounts state that Miles was wearing a fur cap and a long overcoat trimmed on collar and cuffs with bear fur, hence he was dubbed "Man with the Bear Coat" by the Indians. Sitting Bull wore only his leggings, moccasins, and breechcloth wrapped about with a buffalo robe; he wore no feathers or ornamentation. After shaking hands all around, Sitting Bull spread out a large buffalo robe and invited Miles to sit down. The colonel initially demurred, but soon took a place opposite the chief, while the interpreter Bruguier sat between them. Then Sitting Bull commenced to smoke and to pass the traditional pipe of peace. On the Hunkpapa's left sat White Bull, a nephew, while on his right was High Bear, a Brule; Jumping Bull, a Hunkpapa; and Fire-What-Man, a Sans Arc.[4] Despite the agreement precluding weapons, Miles and his soldiers had concealed revolvers beneath their coats.

Sitting Bull exuded a commanding presence that momentarily absorbed the attention of all. In 1876 he was approximately forty-four years old. Already his stewardship of the Tetons was legendary. Emerging in the 1860s as a warrior of wide repute among his people, Sitting Bull had risen through the years to a position of respect and authority by virtue of his brave deeds and adamant resistance to whites. As leader of the "Northern Sioux"—a coalition of tribes resolved to preserve the ancient lifeways—Sitting Bull's stature grew in the public eye with increasing media coverage of the Sioux War. Among whites he was viewed as the man who had almost single-handedly orchestrated Custer's defeat. In reality, however, he possessed a keen acumen for unifying the objectives of his large Hunkpapa following with those of the several other Teton tribes, therefore serving more as a political than war leader among the Sioux. Indeed, Colonel Gibbon described him as "a leader who possessed the tact, courage, and ability to concentrate and keep together so large a force." As a result of his activities in 1875 and 1876, Sitting Bull would remain an important and pervasive figure in Teton society until his death in 1890.[5]

Sitting Bull's meeting with Miles marked the first occasion in the Sioux War that a federal representative had confronted a major leader of the nonagency bands. Miles later recollected his adversary's physical appearance and mannerisms during the council:

> He was a strong, hardy, sturdy looking man of about five feet eleven inches in height, well-built, with strongly-marked features, high cheek bones, prominent nose, straight, thin lips, and strong under jaw, indicating determination and force. He had a wide, large, well-developed head and low forehead. He was a man of few words and cautious in his expressions, evidently thinking twice before speaking. He was very de-

14. Sitting Bull, a Hunkpapa Lakota, posed for photographer David F. Barry about 1883, approximately two years after his surrender at Fort Buford. His meetings with Miles in October 1876 precipitated the skirmish at Cedar Creek, resulting in the first capitulations of the Indians a few days later. Sitting Bull's authority waned thereafter. (Paul Harbaugh and the Denver Public Library)

liberate in his movements and somewhat reserved in his manner. At first
he was courteous, but evidently void of any genuine respect for the
white race. Although the feeling was disguised, his manner indicated
his animosity toward those whom he had to meet. During the conversation his manner was civil and to some extent one of calm repose.[6]

The council was both lengthy and tumultuous. The various
accounts of the proceedings do not altogether agree on what
was discussed or the degree of emphasis accorded the topics.
Moreover, it seems apparent that in his memoirs Miles confused parts of this meeting with that which occurred the next
day. It is clear that the Hunkpapa chief was the unrivaled
spokesman for the Sioux. Despite indications from several of
the chiefs that they wished to yield in their conflict with the
army, Sitting Bull demanded that all troops leave the Yellowstone promptly and permanently. Miles reported that Sitting
Bull "desired to hunt buffalo, to trade (particularly for ammunition), and agreed that the Indians would not fire upon soldiers if they were not disturbed."[7]

Miles anticipated this attempt by the Hunkpapa to secure
peace through the winter months, when their movements were
most difficult. He told the tribesmen that they must yield immediately to the authority of the United States government and
go in to the Tongue River Cantonment. The Indians, however,
wished to follow their traditional practices and to continue
hunting without restriction. Sitting Bull told the colonel that
"God Almighty made him an Indian and did not make him an
agency Indian." At one point, Miles became fearful that the
Indians were intent on killing him and kept his gun hidden but
accessible: "The young Indians continued their line until they
had nearly formed a circle around us. I told Sitting Bull he must
send them back, or the council would end at once. After that
warning and my caution I was interested to learn from his interpreter [Bruguier] that Sitting Bull had designed to kill me, or
at least to make the attempt, but that he was persuaded from it
by others."[8] Miles himself briefly entertained notions of killing
Sitting Bull during the meeting. He later wrote Mary: "I could
have . . . destroyed him and his party when they were within
range or under our guns. But that would have been violating a
flag of truce and the whole civilized world would have de-
nounced it."[9]

15. Artist Frederic Remington's fanciful treatment of the meeting between Miles and Sitting Bull near Cedar Creek, October 21, 1876. In reality, the day was cold and the respective parties were afoot. (Miles, *Personal Recollections*)

During the proceedings Miles angered Sitting Bull by telling him that he had learned of his intended movement to the Big Dry River to hunt buffalo. "This fact enraged him. . . . You could see his eyes glistening with the fire of savage hatred." Several hours passed, with little change in position on either side, and, with no agreement imminent, both parties consented to reconvene the next day. Miles later wrote his wife that he believed Sitting Bull had been tired and depressed, "suffering from nervous excitement and the loss of power." He continued, "I endeavored to explain to him the requirements of the Government. . . . At times he was almost inclined to accept the situation, but I think partly from fear and partly through the belief that he might do better, he did not accept. I think that many of his people were desirous to make peace." This assessment compares favorably with a statement of Long Feather and Bear's Face, wherein they related that Sitting Bull indeed wanted to make peace, but was afraid that the soldiers would not keep it. Further, the chief desired to continue hunting and demanded trading privileges and assurances that the troops would leave the Yellowstone country. Miles evidently requested a number of hostages in return for allowing the buffalo hunting to continue.[10]

It became clear that the talks had resolved nothing and Miles determined to break them off, telling the Hunkpapa leader to consider his remarks overnight. "I was convinced that something more than talk would be required." Some time after 3 P.M. the Fifth Infantry turned and, escorted part way by several mounted Sioux warriors, marched about five miles back to Cedar Creek for the night, "in position," wrote Miles, "to move easily to intercept [the Indians'] movement north."[11]

That evening Sitting Bull convened the Hunkpapa, Minneconjou, and Sans Arc leaders. Having agreed to meet Miles again in the morning, he accepted the consensus that the Sioux would abide by whatever result came out of their discussion. During the night some of the Indian ponies got loose and the men sent after them saw soldiers watching the village. Some tribesmen suggested that the Sioux initiate an attack on Miles after dawn, but the proposal found few adherents among the chiefs and was dropped. Instead, the Indian leaders agreed to prepare for an assault by the troops.[12]

In that presumption the Indians were correct. Shortly past dawn on Saturday, the soldiers started up Cedar Creek in order of battle. Near 10 A.M. the column encountered some Sioux moving downstream and arraying themselves on a high knoll in front, whereupon Miles ordered his men to halt and prepare for action. The soldiers discerned in the distance what they took to be the inhabitants of Sitting Bull's village moving away "like a vast herd of buffalo."[13] Skirmishers took position on either side of the train and the advance proceeded, the men finally stopping along a lofty ridge that overlooked the east fork of Cedar Creek, near the Sioux position. From that vantage a breathtaking panorama of jutting ridges, hillocks, and successively rising eminences stretching away to the horizon contained hundreds of Indians, seemingly more than had appeared the day before. When the nearest warriors on the knoll withdrew, the ordnance rifle was hauled up the rise and placed in position, and Captain James S. Casey and Company A occupied another knoll in front. Once more the Indians brought out a white flag, and the soldiers closest to them soon found the warriors mingling among them, having been mollified by the preceding day's council.

As before, preparations consumed much time, with Sitting Bull expressing great alarm over the placement of the gun. Presently the two sides agreed to meet atop a small rock-covered promontory that stood midway between them. Accompanying the Hunkpapa leader were White Bull and several men who had not attended Friday's meeting, or who had at least not been present in the inner circle: Bull Eagle, Black Eagle, Rising Sun, Small Bear, Standing Bear, Gall, Spotted Elk, Red Skirt, Pretty Bear, Yellow Eagle, and John Sans Arc. They came forward afoot, walking abreast to the designated site. Miles was accompanied by several officers. According to the account of a Sioux participant, Spotted Elk, the formalities were like those of the previous day, only in reverse. This time it was Miles who spread out a buffalo robe, and this time it was Sitting Bull who refused to sit on it. A few of the other chiefs, evidently to Sitting Bull's dismay, accepted the colonel's invitation and were seated, and Sitting Bull soon followed their lead.[14]

The council differed little from the earlier one in content, too. The Hunkpapa leader remained intransigent, his demands the same as before, while Miles reiterated his position on the Indians' surrender. Much of the talk centered on Sitting Bull's desire to have trading facilities nearby. When Miles told him he would find a trading store at the Tongue River cantonment, the Hunkpapa insisted on going to Fort Peck to trade. Miles nonetheless made headway with certain of the other chiefs, especially with the Minneconjous Bull Eagle and Red Skirt, both of whom, he reported later, were prepared to yield. One man went so far as to offer himself as a hostage for his band's compliance.

During the proceedings, mounted Sioux warriors again gravitated toward the circle, but this time Miles had planned an appropriate response. Each time an Indian approached the gathering, a soldier from the line likewise advanced and stationed himself on the periphery. When the warrior withdrew, so did the soldier. Thus, the numbers from each side rose and fell. If anything, the meeting created more tension than the preceding one, and Miles once more felt he was targeted for death. Several accounts state that one of the arriving Indians tried to slip a carbine beneath Sitting Bull's robe. "Even the accidental discharge of a firearm," remembered one officer, "would have precipitated an attack in which all between the lines would have fallen."[15]

After lengthy haranguing by both sides, Miles told Sitting Bull that he must accept his terms or prepare for immediate military consequences. At that point the Hunkpapa, frustrated and doubtless angered by the lack of unity exhibited by his companions, precipitately rose and walked out of the meeting, leaving the other chiefs to follow. Miles and his men returned to the command to await the Indians' next move.[16]

After an hour it was apparent that the Indians were not disposed to surrender. At about one o'clock Miles ordered the command forward in battle formation. The main body of Sioux, meantime, had assembled on high ground several miles to the front, while numerous other warriors continued to occupy closer ridges to observe the army movements. The terrain held by the Indians in fact comprised part of the divide rising between the watersheds of the Yellowstone and Missouri rivers. In front of the army command, the field stretched northeast in a succession of small plateaus and ridges that gradually ascended from the broad valley bottom to the divide escarpment rising on the left, the forward end of which fairly towered above the plain. At its base, the twisted ravines of several tributaries intersected, forming the source of the east fork of Cedar Creek, which zigzagged to the east and south, offering brushy and thorny obstacles to a military advance. The ground fronting the divide presented a profusion of treeless ridges, knolls, and hills, behind which warriors might easily hide to frustrate the troops. "The plan of Sitting Bull," wrote one witness, "was to yield in front, and then while the troops pressed forward and became entangled in the ravines to pour his warriors around the flanks and rear, and play his magazine guns upon the disordered mass." Miles believed the Indians' intentions were to draw them "on to a position they had selected, and then . . . make another [Little] Bighorn affair of it."[17]

Advancing a few hundred yards, the Fifth Infantry suddenly fanned out in skirmish order across the valley floor. Miles assembled his officers and issued his orders. John Bruguier, who had gone with Sitting Bull, reappeared to ask Miles why the soldiers were following the Indians, to which Miles responded

16. View to the northeast of Cedar Creek battlefield, showing the wooded ravines and ascending terrain traversed by Miles's infantrymen passing left to right. The high ridge at top left was cleared by a movement of Company H, under Lieutenant David Q. Rousseau. (Paul L. Hedren)

that the chief's nonacceptance of the government's terms constituted an act of hostility. Immediately, companies stepped off from either flank to clear Indians from the ridges. On the left, Company A, under Captain Casey, found little resistance as the warriors melted away. Some fifty or sixty Indians stood fast atop a knoll on the right until First Lieutenant Mason Carter mounted the slope with Company K, when, without a shot being fired, the tribesmen took flight.

The dual maneuvering succeeded in momentarily outflanking the Sioux, most of whom continued massing on the high central ridge in front of the steadily advancing blue-clad skirmishers. The line of soldiers pressed ahead, negotiating the first ravine and starting up the slope in good order, arrayed left to right as follows: Company A, Captain Casey; Company B, Captain Andrew S. Bennett; Company C, Captain Edmond Butler; Company I, Captain Wyllys Lyman; and Company K, Lieutenant Carter. Three more companies composed a reserve force advancing behind the main line: Company H, Second Lieutenant David Q. Rousseau; Company G, First Lieutenant Theodore F. Forbes; and Company E, Second Lieutenant James W. Pope. Company F, Captain Simon Snyder, supported the ordnance rifle, while Company D, First Lieutenant Robert McDonald, served as rear guard protecting the train. (The wagons were in the charge of Second Lieutenant William H. C. Bowen, and the pack animals were under Second Lieutenant James H. Whitten.)[18]

Thus far, the confrontation was a purely tactical exercise, as no shots had yet been fired. While the soldiers pressed ahead, Snyder's artillery piece was unlimbered atop a high knoll-like ridge toward the right and trained on the Sioux a mile away. As the troops gained the height and closed on the warriors, some of the Indians began a remonstrance, dashing their ponies in circles, while others retreated before the command. Then the first shooting erupted, directed by several of Miles's scouts against Indians who were caught igniting the grass in the ravines surrounding the soldiers. Many of the Sioux who had retired from the center now joined these warriors on the periphery of the command; a large number also claimed the towering ridge on the left. In all, the Indian force totaled between eight hundred and one thousand warriors.

From its vantage, the ordnance rifle belched forth its first round, eliciting cheers from the men below. As the gunfire quickened, two of the reserve companies went into action, Lieutenant Pope's Company E responding to clear out warriors who were shooting at his men from ravines in the rear, while Lieutenant Rousseau endeavored to lead Company H against the Indians atop the prominent ridge on the left. "The latter movement was beautifully performed," reported an observer, "the little company looking like a slender thread as it fearlessly pressed up the almost perpendicular height—while the Indians poured a rapid but harmless fire over their heads, and the key to the field was soon won."[19] Concurrently, Lieutenant Carter and Captain Lyman led their units in clearing the ravines on the right.

The skirmishers on the main line forged ahead, now discharging their Springfields at the Sioux who raced about on their ponies firing at the men and alternately advanced and sought cover behind the hills. "It was only our best marksmen [who were] able to make them bite the dust," noted a soldier, "but occasionally they were seen to throw up their hands and tumble from their ponies." Meanwhile, the wind whipped the grass fire, driving its flames higher, creating a smoky, suffocating inferno that encompassed the whole moving scene, described by one participant as "awfully grand, . . . sublimely terrible." Trumpeter Edwin M. Brown graphically depicted the advance: "Bullets whistled lively over our heads and around us for a short time; many a strong heart grew weak as our thoughts flew back to the Custer massacre; we began to think our case as hopeless, for indeed the odds were against us; no doubt had we been cavalry they would have killed every one of us, but as we were enabled to fight them on their own principles it was much to our advantage."[20]

The infantrymen passed up and over the smoldering ridges, Companies I and K on the right of the line finally gaining the abandoned Sioux encampment nestled along the winding east fork of Cedar Creek, where they found dried meat and utensils. There the Indians mounted another attempt to stop the troops, but the soldiers drove on through the fire and smoke and forced the tribesmen to withdraw. A man of Company I was wounded in the skirmish near the village site. All during the advance Snyder's artillery piece hammered the Sioux positions, doing "excellent service, as it appeared to completely demoralize the enemy and kept them at a respectful distance." Recalled an enlisted man: "The big gun broke loose on them [and] scattered them in all directions; had it not been for the cannon, they might have done much greater damage."[21]

During the fighting, Yellowstone Kelly, Billy Cross, and Vic Smith joined the command, having returned from their two-day scouting mission. Vic Smith recollected that the scouts had camped in a thicket the night of October 20. The next day they spotted Miles's command eight miles away, engaging the Indians. At Kelly's urging, the scouts darted forward. "The Indians had set fire to the prairie, and the smoke had shut off our view; but every time the wind lifted the screen, we got our bearings." On approaching the troops, they were mistaken for Indians and fired on. "We found shelter in a convenient washout until a sergeant, with a small detail, came down to scalp the dead. The soldiers were certain they had seen a number of Indians fall . . . but it was only us."[22]

While this action was proceeding, Company E completed clearing the ravines at the base of the divide and remained behind to protect the supply train as it passed over the tortuous ground. As the company moved forward, Sioux posted on surrounding hills and ridges once more fired at the troops, but then they, too, fell back, leaving only a few warriors around some water holes in the rear. Lieutenant Pope with Company E was ordered to clear out these Indians and secure the water source. A sergeant was injured in this action. Following a lengthy pursuit that lasted until dark, the remaining companies of the Fifth Infantry moved back to the lofty ridge taken by Rousseau's men and bivouacked for the night, "all hands being completely tired out," recorded Captain Snyder. "We marched and fought over about 18 miles of country today." Miles's casualties numbered only two men and several horses wounded in the contest, the slight losses likely attributable to the fact that the warriors were aiming from the ridges at targets much lower than themselves. Indian losses were higher, with at least five bodies counted on the field. Despite low Indian casualties, Miles was satisfied with the encounter, citing it as "a good thing for the regiment as it was all engaged, every company, and the fact of whipping and routing Sitting Bull's body of Sioux has inspired them with great confidence and spirit."[23]

The prairie fire glowed through the night, and the yells of distant warriors punctuated by shots from the pickets combined to disrupt the soldiers' rest. Of that night Trumpeter Brown wrote: "A fellow was almost afraid to go to sleep for fear he might never waken. . . . I heard more than one remark that they wished we were back in camp at Tongue River." In the night Miles consulted with his officers and scouts about pursuit of the Indians. "The night was clear and cold," remembered scout Kelly. "While all around the ground was covered with sleeping bodies, the commander was awake and taking measures for the coming day's work." Brief action occurred the

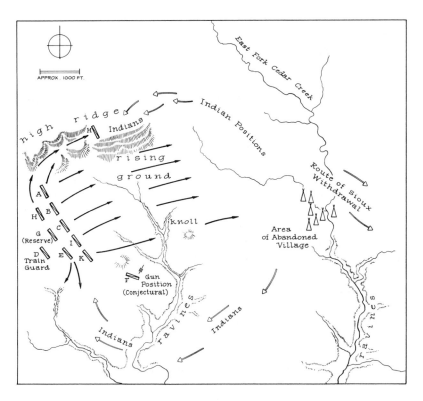

3. The Battle of Cedar Creek, October 21, 1876

next morning when about twenty Sioux were driven off by the gunfire of Company E.[24]

The command headed east, soon encountering the Indian trail, scattered with lodgepoles, abandoned ponies and mules, and refuse from the village, including a number of articles bearing the imprint of the Seventh Cavalry—evidence that at least some of these people had likely participated in the Little Bighorn battle. The debris revealed the course of Sitting Bull's people down Bad Route Creek, southeasterly toward the Yellowstone. In their retreat, the tribesmen repeatedly burned the prairie to impede the soldiers and keep them from gaining on the noncombatants, in which enterprise they succeeded. At one point the fire grew so intense that Miles halted and ordered his men to build backfires. When the Sioux attacked again, the infantrymen drove them away, the sound of their muskets rattling through the wilderness. Miles's men kept up the pursuit over eighteen miles, finally stopping at dark.

On Monday, October 23, the soldiers saw no Indians. In anticipation of their presence, however, Miles reformed his command into a hollow square, with four companies of skirmishers in front deployed five paces apart, two companies on each side, and two at the rear. The latter units were configured so as to enable them to deploy left and right, thereby extending the sides. Yet another company brought up the rear of the train, which was itself partially enclosed by the square, and still another accompanied the ordnance rifle. "Such a line, like vertebrae, can be bent in any direction without disorder and without any change of order, and cannot be broken by any irregular cavalry," boasted an officer. "Such a formation presented a magnificent and formidable picture as it swept over the prairies."[25]

The command reached the Yellowstone late that day, after a punishing chase of nearly twenty-seven miles. The Indians had already crossed the stream and encamped on the south side. Miles's adjutant examined the ford a short distance downstream and nearly opposite the mouth of Cabin Creek on the south bank. There Yellowstone Kelly waded into the middle of the river and found the cold water only waist deep. The next day, as the command approached the ford, a small party of Sioux were pursued into the hills by some of Miles's scouts, who engaged them for a time at long range. The Indians finally retreated, but shortly afterwards attacked a lone herder from the command. Although pursued vigorously by the warriors, the herder escaped, spurring his mule furiously back toward safety. As the scouts and infantrymen dashed ahead to save him, the artillery dropped a bursting shell in front of the onrushing tribesmen, who precipitately turned their mounts toward the hills.[26]

From his camp on the Yellowstone, Miles wrote a note to Terry, detailing his movements before, during, and after the Cedar Creek fight. He reported, "[The Indians] are in great want of food, their stock is nearly worn down, and they cannot have a large amount of ammunition. What they have has been taken from citizens in the Black Hills, from troops in the Custer massacre, or from friendly Indians." Some of the recent arrivals from the agencies had brought ammunition, too, and Miles told Terry of other reports suggesting that the Sioux were getting ammunition from traders at Fort Peck. "I believe that Fort Peck should be occupied," he said, with "all ammunition in that vicinity seized by the government." He suggested that if Sitting Bull's people did not yield, his command might next pursue them to the Bighorn country, where grass and game were plentiful.[27]

Miles hoped to continue pressing the main body of the Indians, although dwindling provisions made him reassess his position. As the warriors watched the army from across the stream and tried to divine Miles's intentions, the colonel settled on a ploy to buy time to replenish his supplies. Having observed from his conferences with Sitting Bull that several subordinate leaders had been inclined to accept the government terms, he sent a proposal across the Yellowstone, suggesting that another council be held the next day. When the Indians assented, sending forth a white flag, Miles directed his supply train to proceed after dark to the Glendive cantonment, twenty-four miles downstream.

On October 25, a warm, sunny day, the chiefs crossed the stream and met Miles. Kelly remembered that a number of Indians attended the session, in which Miles, his officers, and the principal Sioux leaders sat on the ground in a semicircle. Some of the Indians, he wrote, "circled around like wild creatures suspicious of a trap."[28] One in attendance was Gall, the heavyset Hunkpapa war chief who had played a leading role in the Custer fight and who opposed surrendering.

At the meeting, Miles learned that Sitting Bull and thirty lodges of Hunkpapas had diverged from the trail during the flight down Bad Route Creek and, circumventing the troops, had gone north toward the Missouri to continue hunting. Yet another body had fled in the direction of Dakota's Standing Rock Agency. Red Skirt and the other Sioux leaders evinced bitterness over Sitting Bull's departure. In fact, Sitting Bull would shortly be joined by Gall, Pretty Bear, and other chiefs and their partisans, until his following totaled about four hundred people. While most of the chiefs in council with Miles expressed no eagerness to yield immediately, they nonetheless agreed to continue talking with him the next day. One leader, Bull Eagle, indicated to Miles that he was indeed ready to sur-

render.[29] Miles had met Bull Eagle in the councils preceding
Cedar Creek and believed this Indian sincerely wanted peace.

On the following morning, the train returned from Glendive
with enough rations to enable the regiment to resume the chase
for twenty more days if required. When the council opened,
Red Skirt, Bull Eagle, and Small Bear, all Minneconjous, told
Miles that the Sioux with them planned eventually to go in to
an agency, that the people lacked clothing and their ponies
were worn out, and that the Indians did not want to fight any
longer. They wanted to hunt bison and requested that the soldiers return to the Tongue River and leave them alone. Miles
fed the Indians and then responded with his standard line: if
the Indians desired peace they must accept the government's
terms. He further explained that his provisions were ample and
that he was prepared to follow them if necessary. At that disclo-
sure, the chiefs, clearly tired of running, showed a readiness to
submit.

Miles realized that his attempt to find Sitting Bull would be
thwarted if his command had to escort these Sioux to the distant Cheyenne River Agency. Knowing, on the other hand, that
ensconcing them at the Tongue River Cantonment would jeopardize his command's provisions, he proposed that the Indians
turn themselves in at the agency and that five chiefs or headmen
be delivered to St. Paul to guarantee the surrender. Miles
agreed to provide sufficient rations for the journey to the Cheyenne River Agency and allowed the Indians thirty-five days to
reach it, including five days at their current encampment to
hunt buffalo. Red Skirt consented to serve as one of the hostages. The others were the older White Bull (a Minneconjou
and the father of Small Bear) and Black Eagle, Sun Rise, and
Foolish Thunder, all Sans Arcs. They were to be sent east by
steamer and escorted by a ten-man detachment of the Fifth Infantry commanded by First Lieutenant Theodore F. Forbes.[30]
Bull Eagle and Small Bear, along with the Sans Arc headman,
Bull, agreed to accompany the rest of the tribesmen to the
agency. Other leaders among those who surrendered included
Yellow Eagle, Spotted Elk, Tall Bull, Poor Bear, Two Elk, and
Foolish Bear.

On the twenty-seventh, in accordance with the terms offered
by Miles, the five hostages began their journey to Terry's headquarters. Roughly two thousand freshly provisioned Hunkpa-

pas, Minneconjous, and Sans Arcs—three hundred or four hundred lodges as estimated by Miles—prepared to start for the Cheyenne River Agency. "I consider this the beginning of the end," Miles jubilantly wrote Terry. The Indians, he informed the department commander the next day, "are very suspicious, and of course [are] afraid that some terrible punishment will be inflicted upon them." He exhibited compassion over the tribes' fate on reaching the reservation: "While we have fought and routed these people, and driven them away from their ancient homes, I cannot but feel regret that they are compelled to submit to starvation, for I fear they will be reduced to that condition as were the southern tribes in 1874."[31] Nevertheless, pleased with their military success, Miles and the Fifth Infantry marched for Tongue River, shortly to renew the campaign with a search for Sitting Bull and any other disparate elements still afield. "I will endeavor to keep them divided, and take them in detail," he wrote.[32]

In reality, Miles's design only partly succeeded. Spotted Elk later reported that most of the Indians had planned a ruse to obtain needed rations. The hostages, with the exception of Red Skirt, were all lesser headmen who had lived at Cheyenne River and who had left there earlier so they could keep their ponies.[33] On November 16, Lieutenant Forbes delivered four of the hostages to Lieutenant Colonel George P. Buell at Cheyenne River for transport to St. Paul. Fearing he was to be executed, Red Skirt had managed to jump from the boat and escape before it reached the agency.

Meantime, despite the surrender, many of the Indians, those who had recently fled from the Cheyenne River Agency to avoid losing their arms and ponies, were reluctant to return for the same reason. Few of the Indians made it to Cheyenne River by the end of November—only about forty lodges rather than the larger number Miles had projected. Bull Eagle, one of his favorites, did not go in after all but stayed in the field with his followers, supposedly to try and convince some of the Sioux in the Bighorn country to go to the agency. While others drifted south to the Spotted Tail Agency, most of the remainder found haven with the Oglalas under Crazy Horse, south of the Yellowstone. The surrender orchestrated by Miles, lamented Commissioner of Indian Affairs E. A. Hayt, seemed "to have been made in good faith by some of the leading men taking part in it; but

17. Red Skirt, the Minneconjou leader (left), and John Sans Arc. Red Skirt surrendered to Miles following the Battle of Cedar Creek and started as a hostage to the Cheyenne River Agency. He fled, however, before reaching that point and returned to his people in the Yellowstone country. From a stereopticon card by C. H. Newcombe, 1884. (Smithsonian Institution, National Anthropological Archives)

their influence over the others was not great enough to prevent any but the immediate relatives of the hostages from again joining the hostile camp."[34]

It appears that the surrender Miles negotiated was somewhat tainted with promises that he had neither the authority to make nor the power to deliver. Indian accounts substantially confirm that throughout Miles's discussions with them, the colonel, sensing their growing destitution, allowed that provision would be made either for establishing an agency at the confluence of the Cheyenne and Belle Fourche rivers, near the Black Hills, or for moving the existing Cheyenne River Agency to that location, traditionally cherished by the Indians. This offer proved extremely palatable to many of the leaders, with the notable exception of Sitting Bull, and may have been the catalyst for the initially large surrender on October 27 as well as for subsequent submissions the following year. In any event, word of Miles's assurance seems to have pervaded the tribal groups of Sioux and Northern Cheyennes still scattered through the Yellowstone region.[35]

The elusive Sitting Bull posed Miles no small problem, yet the colonel remained confident following the surrender of Red Skirt's people. "If we can keep them divided and destroy Sitting Bull's influence," he told Terry, "I think we can end this trouble. . . . I believe Sitting Bull would be glad to make a peace, . . . but he is afraid he has committed an unpardonable offense."[36] After eluding the soldiers during the pursuit down Bad Route Creek, Sitting Bull continued north, crossed the divide, and led his Hunkpapas to a fording spot on the Missouri at the mouth of Porcupine Creek. With him were the Hunkpapa bands of Four Horns, Black Moon, and Iron Dog.

On October 23, Sitting Bull sent runners ahead to Fort Peck with notice that he was coming in for food and ammunition and that his intentions were peaceful. Indian Agent Thomas J. Mitchell sent an interpreter to tell him that he would get no ammunition. A few days later, Colonel Hazen departed Fort Buford for Fort Peck with four companies of the Sixth Infantry and an artillery piece, all borne up the Missouri aboard the steamer *Peninah*. Hazen hoped to head off the Hunkpapas and he proposed that Miles drive his force north to work with him. Nothing immediately came of Hazen's proposal, however. Reaching Fort Peck too late to intercept Sitting Bull, the colonel interrogated Sioux headmen from camps along the Milk River. Unable to convince these tribesmen to give up, Hazen posted one company at the agency and returned to Buford.[37]

The activity generated in the aftermath of the Cedar Creek events pointed up the significance of that action in turning the course of the Sioux War from a stalemated conflict toward a resolution favoring the government. Miles's vigorous movement north of the Yellowstone displayed both his propensity to go after the Indians on their own terrain and his willingness to react diplomatically, if not altogether honestly, to their peaceful overtures. Whereas Terry's campaign had foundered along the base of the Yellowstone-Missouri divide because of the weariness of his command and the inability to locate the tribes, Miles's succeeded because the now plentiful Indians were becoming increasingly impoverished and found themselves unable to present a united front to prolong the warfare.

The Cedar Creek councils and the fighting that ensued aggravated the tribal fragmentation among the followers of Sitting Bull. After the events at Cedar Creek, the Hunkpapa, whose influence had appeared to be waning, was clearly out of favor with a majority of the Minneconjous and Sans Arcs who had been traveling with him. These incidents had long-lasting effects, too, as word of the encounters with Miles and the subsequent surrender on the Yellowstone filtered back to the people under Crazy Horse and other chiefs hunting and preparing for the winter on the lands below the river. Even though those surrendering on October 27 ultimately numbered less than anticipated, the message that Miles meant business doubtless encouraged the move toward the agencies that occurred over the next few months.

From a military point of view, the performance of the Fifth Infantry at Cedar Creek in doggedly chasing the Sioux over the rugged terrain of the divide and down to the Yellowstone finally pointed up the value of infantry in field operations, heretofore almost exclusively dominated by the use of cavalry. In this respect, the engagement represented the beginning of a sustained army presence that promised hope for final termination of the Sioux War. Miles could justifiably glow in his accomplishments, made despite limited time and exposure to the problem. "From the reports of the disgraceful failures of late," he boasted, "I judge that the country sooner or later will understand the difference between doing something and doing nothing."[38]

CHAPTER SIX

The Fort Peck
Expedition

The Fifth Infantry returned to the Tongue River Cantonment amid rumors that Miles did not intend to tarry there long before continuing his offensive. The colonel and his staff reached the post October 31, followed the next day by Companies A, C, D, E, F, H, and I. Companies B, G, and K came in November 3. The Cedar Creek encounters and their aftermath had encouraged Miles that his presence on the Yellowstone could end the warfare. Although his attention had been directed to the area north of the river, he did not neglect that to the south. On October 21, the same day Miles fought Sitting Bull, six men under Second Lieutenant Frank S. Hinkle returned to the cantonment from patrolling the Powder River country, having traveled a distance of 166 miles without sighting Indians.[1]

Meantime, the strength of the regiment was augmented with the arrival from Fort Leavenworth of the band, additional staff, and remaining enlisted men of the Fifth, all in the charge of First Lieutenant Frank D. Baldwin. Baldwin was a veteran officer who had gained respectable credentials as an Indian fighter during Miles's campaigns on the southern plains. He had served as Miles's battalion adjutant during the August maneuver under Terry, following which he had been on detached service at Fort Leavenworth and had missed the engagement at Cedar Creek. The newcomers had traveled via Yankton up the Missouri aboard the *General Meade*, debarking October 22 opposite Fort Buford and continuing on foot to the mouth of Tongue River, which they reached November 3.[2]

Miles's successes were viewed as a hopeful sign at army headquarters. Sheridan wired a glowing report to General Sherman and noted that his plans for continuing operations through the winter included a movement of Crook's command from Fort Reno in Wyoming to strike Crazy Horse. Ecstatic over these developments, Sherman wired back: "I congratulate you and all concerned on the prospect of closing this Sioux war. . . . Genl Miles has displayed his usual earnestness & energy and I hope he will crown his success by capturing or killing Sitting Bull and his remnant of outlaws." He registered his optimism in a newspaper interview, stating, "We shall push things as rapidly as possible . . . [and] we will dog them till they succumb." Both Sherman and Sheridan envisioned placing the disarmed, dismounted, and defeated Indians on a tract along the Missouri River between Standing Rock Agency and Fort Randall, where they might be effectively controlled. Earlier plans to relocate the surrendered people in the Indian Territory were dropped as impractical.[3]

Such optimism was premature, for, as of early November, most of the nonagency Indians still remained at large, their movements only negligibly affected by the military presence in the Yellowstone Valley. Although it was too soon for senior officials to learn that the body of Indians delivered by Miles was in fact less than promised, the whereabouts of all the other tribes was only vaguely known to them. Following the surrender to Miles, many of the Indians who decided against turning themselves in at Cheyenne River went over to Powder River, where several hundred lodges of Oglalas and Cheyennes joined them. Later these people moved to a point on the Yellowstone below the mouth of the Tongue, from which they watched the winter activities of the nearby soldiers. During November the Indians learned the disturbing news of the sale of the Black Hills. In response, the followers of Crazy Horse and other Oglala, Brule, and Northern Cheyenne leaders reaffirmed their opposition to the whites. (Possibly indicative of their growing desperation, one incredible report stated that the Indians expected ammunition from several thousand Mexicans said to be en route.)[4]

As for Sitting Bull, on November 2 Hazen sent word to Miles that the Hunkpapa, with thirty lodges, was still in the vicinity of the Fort Peck Agency, on Big Dry River, twenty miles below the Missouri, where he had been joined by one hundred additional lodges under Iron Dog. The entire group had fled Fort Peck on Hazen's approach, abandoning in their haste some jaded Sev-

18. Tongue River Cantonment, 1876–77, with its quarters of cottonwood logs chinked with mud. This photograph shows glass-paned windows and, at lower right, the three-inch ordnance rifle. (National Archives)

enth Cavalry horses. "Their own animals are also racks of bones," observed Hazen, who termed the Indians "entirely destitute." "I don't think they can stand the winter if kept stirred up." He vowed to concentrate on prohibiting Sitting Bull's warriors from receiving ammunition by seizing unauthorized quantities from mixed-bloods and citizens before it reached the Indians' hands.[5]

Miles spent the next few days at the cantonment, readying his command to retake the offensive. A small herd of cattle, purchased on contract and constituting ten thousand rations of beef, was to go with the expedition, accompanied by two herders. Meanwhile, troops of the Twenty-second Infantry marched to the mouth of the Bighorn to escort a vegetable train back to the Tongue. Other companies of that regiment, posted near the mouth of Cedar Creek, continued their work of guarding supply trains between the Tongue River and Glendive Creek. Miles also dealt with other administrative concerns. He had earlier opposed a departmental directive that the number of his white scouts be reduced, citing their importance to his operations: "They are all excellent and valuable men, and as I have no other mounted men, I recommend that they be retained."[6] With his recent success, Miles's confidence soared; he could be comfortably direct in stating his opinions as to the course the field operations should take without fearing intimidation by his superiors.

At Tongue River, Miles learned that Major Alfred L. Hough had arrived to replace Otis in commanding the four companies of the Seventeenth Infantry at Glendive. Ascending the Missouri to Fort Buford aboard the same steamer that brought the Fifth Infantry band forward, Hough had pronounced the passage over countless sand bars difficult and tedious. He had reached Glendive on October 26. Cognizant of the personalities with which he was to work, he lamented his position, "midway between two ambitious men, Hazen and Miles, who [were] making plans to effect their own advancement." His troops, he observed, were "hewers of wood and drawers of water for both of them, but more especially Col. Miles."[7] Hough formally replaced Otis on October 28, when the latter returned from the Tongue and took passage downriver.

Hough's principal concern with the onset of cold weather was to provide sufficient cover for his men. He described the Seventeenth Infantry as "a shabby looking set, having been out from their proper posts since April last." "I have several wounded men and several sick . . . and it looks like old war times to see the poor fellows lying on poles covered with sage brush for a bed for we have no cots or mattresses." Otis had constructed a number of huts to temporarily house the soldiers, but more were needed if the command was to garrison the place through the winter, which now appeared likely. Hough instituted a procedure wherein half his force alternated with the other half in erecting huts and in escorting the trains. "My provision for staying at Glendive proved wise," he recounted, "for we did not get away. . . . Genl. Miles . . . directed me to remain till Spring."[8]

Miles himself evinced concern over the growing cold weather. Although he fully expected his troops to continue their expeditions through the winter, he realized the need for special provisions to ensure their effectiveness and safety under climatic extremes. Convinced that the winter season offered the best chance of subduing the Indians because of their immobility during that time, Miles requested for his men clothing and equipment sufficient to withstand the blizzards and deep snows of eastern Montana Territory. "I was satisfied that if the Indians could live there the white men could also, if properly equipped with all the advantages we could give them, which were certainly superior to those obtainable by the Indians."[9]

Quartermaster General Montgomery C. Meigs had anticipated Miles's concerns, and early in October had written Sherman about winter clothing. The Yellowstone country, said Meigs, was one where "the climate is cold at best, and the elevated plains are subject to fierce storms of wind and drifting snow during which the thermometer sinks far below zero, and the exposure is like that of the Arctic regions." He cited the survival of recent polar expeditions as having been due to their adoption of the fur attire of Eskimos. For troops campaigning in the Indian country, Meigs recommended their "being clothed in furs," particularly "buffalo coats, overalls and shoes." He predicted, however, that the troops would resist burdening themselves with this extra heavy clothing on mild days, and would have problems with the bulky attire interfering with their movements.[10]

In November, in accordance with Miles's wishes and with the acquiescence of the Quartermaster Department, many of Colonel Hazen's troops at Fort Buford began to fashion overcoats, leggings, and mittens from tanned buffalo robes that had been acquired in the vicinity of the Yellowstone. The soldiers cut out the coats and either stitched them themselves or let the company tailors finish them. Instructions called for inspecting all robes before they were cut to eliminate defective ones. Miles specified that the coats be made "of large sizes, long, coming below the knees, double breasted, and [with] high rolling collar, such as can be turned up about the ears." Leggings were "to come above the knees, sewed at the sides, to buckle or tie over the instep and buffalo overshoes, and to be sustained at the sides and top by a strap attached to the waist belt." Parties of

Hazen's men journeyed to the Fort Peck agency to obtain additional robes for making the clothing.[11]

Many of Miles's soldiers had endured severe winter weather during their campaigning on the southern plains during the Red River War and they benefited from that experience along the Yellowstone. Besides the buffalo coats and leggings, Miles's men fashioned underwear from woolen blankets. A soldier stationed with the Twenty-second Infantry at Glendive recollected that the men of his unit also had caps and gloves made from bison robes. Regular Quartermaster Department supplies included woolen mittens, buffalo overshoes, sealskin gauntlets and visored sealskin caps with earflaps (precursors of the muskrat caps and gauntlets that were issued beginning in 1879), and arctics, the vulcanized rubber footwear that was introduced sparingly to the troops. Blankets were also cut into woolen face masks and grain sacks were ripped apart and worn about the feet to help prevent frostbite. Miles later reported that his command, when fitted out in winter campaign dress, "looked more like a large body of Esquimaux than like white men and United States soldiers."[12] Presumably, much of this clothing, particularly the buffalo overcoats, was unavailable for Miles's first winter expedition from the Tongue River Cantonment in November and December, 1876.

Without benefit of the special attire, Miles would have been forced to remain in the cantonment during the winter of 1876–77, something Terry had expected him to do, but a course contrary to his nature. Winter in Montana promised a meteorological dichotomy ranging from fairly balmy days with minimal precipitation to sharply freezing periods that sent temperatures plunging. Snowfall varied from a few inches to several feet in depth; rain intermixed with snow often turned the ground into a slushy quagmire. Mercurial thermometers frequently froze solid, so that temperature readings were sometimes inaccurate or had to be estimated. Wind chill was neither recorded nor factored into determinations of temperature, but it was ever present. A temperature of minus twenty degrees Fahrenheit accompanied by a relatively moderate wind velocity of twenty miles per hour would have produced a temperature equivalent to minus sixty-eight degrees without wind. That same temperature accompanied by winds of thirty miles per hour would have registered an equivalent of minus seventy-nine degrees. Thus,

an account of early November specifying a reading of minus
ten degrees during a "keen norther," which might be interpreted as a wind ranging anywhere between twenty-five and
thirty-eight miles per hour, likely produced a corresponding
wind chill effect of from minus fifty-eight to minus sixty-eight
degrees. During November the below-zero temperatures recorded by Miles's command seem to have coalesced around minus ten degrees, and although references to the wind did not
occur often, the impression remains that it blew almost constantly during daylight at velocities ranging between ten and
thirty-five miles per hour. Occasionally there were calm days
when the thermometer stayed below zero. Miles described the
frigidity as "simply appalling. Even when the air was perfectly
still and all the moisture of the atmosphere was frozen, the air
was filled with frozen jets, or little shining crystals."[13]

Miles learned that the Sibley tents he had requisitioned had
not arrived, making the need for suitable winter garments more
urgent. In addition, one-third of the horses delivered by the
departmental quartermaster proved unfit for the rigors of service. Both horses and draft animals were fed corn and hay to
heat their bodies against prolonged periods of cold; in the field
the beasts were to substitute cured native grass for hay when
the latter became unavailable.[14]

On November 5, ferries began moving the wagon train that
would accompany the next expedition across the Yellowstone.
Outfitted for a month, Miles and his command crossed the
stream early the next day, "a cold frosty morning," and began
their trek in three-inch-deep snow to seek out the Indians over
a vast, largely unknown, barren scape roughly framed by the
Missouri River on the north and the Redwater and Musselshell
rivers on the east and west. "I shall endeavor to follow the Indians as long as possible, even to their retreats where they think
we can not go," Miles wrote his wife. "It is only in that way that
we can convince them of our power to subjugate them finally."[15]

Two companies of the Twenty-second Infantry stayed to garrison the cantonment. Miles's command included 15 officers
and 434 soldiers of companies A, B, C, D, E, F, G, H, I, and K,
besides the artillery detachment of the three-inch ordnance rifle and the twelve-pounder Napoleon gun, 10 civilians, 2 Indian
scouts, a wagon train, 2 ambulances, pack mules, and the cattle

herd. The wagons hauled 250 rounds of ammunition for each man. Descending from the tableland north of the Yellowstone and passing along Sunday Creek, the route was checkered with myriad ravines that required great labor to bridge for the wagons. After marching nine miles, the infantrymen made camp in the afternoon at a spot where wood and water were accessible. On the seventh—Election Day, noted Lieutenant Baldwin—they trudged twelve miles through slush and cactus along Sunday Creek, crossing the stream eleven times in less than five hours. On the eighth they covered nineteen miles in a day-long tramp over the game-rich high ground of the divide, before camping on an alkaline tributary of Sunday Creek. The troops used buffalo chips to fuel their cooking fires. The daily marches generally proceeded before dawn, "under a bright northern moon, and a heaven studded with brilliant stars."[16]

Miles usually rode two or three miles ahead of the column, accompanied by several officers, soldiers, and scouts, as he watched from high ground for signs of Indians. On November 9, the command proceeded nearly twenty more miles before reaching and camping along a branch of the Big Dry River early in the afternoon. The next day they explored canyons adjoining the stream, halting shortly past 2 P.M. amid cottonwoods on the east bank of the Big Dry. As the soldiers made camp, scouts arrived and reported a fresh Indian trail ahead. On November 11 the troops awoke to a snowstorm, "a blinding, thin, misty snowstorm, driven by a keen norther," that stayed with them all day. During the march they located a lodgepole trail and some bison carcasses, but the falling snow soon obliterated all signs of the trail. Still, the exhausted men managed fourteen miles and bivouacked on ground used by the Indians only a few days earlier. That night the thermometers registered minus ten degrees. Miles later postulated that he was following Iron Dog's Sioux, 119 lodges strong, and that these Indians had crossed the Missouri to go to Fort Peck for supplies.[17]

The command pressed on down the frozen bottom of the Big Dry, the wagons and mules occasionally breaking through the ice. On the twelveth, profound ravines retarded the march and the weather became increasingly cold. One diarist observed that although the bed of the Big Dry stretched nearly one-fifth of a mile from bank to bank, the river channel was but twenty feet across. "The country on either side is very broken, much of it being bad land, and high, precipitous, sterile bluffs meet the river at many points along its course."[18] After going twelve miles through snow four inches deep and a driving northeast wind, the men took shelter in a cottonwood grove below the mouth of the east branch of the river. During the night the temperature fell to minus twelve degrees. Still fighting the cold wind, the soldiers stayed in camp the following day to rest the livestock, and the mercury rose to only 16 degrees. Companies E and H went with Lieutenant Baldwin to seek Indian trails, but returned that afternoon, having reconnoitered thirteen miles of the Big Dry Valley without success. From the camp, Miles sent out couriers with dispatches telling Hazen of his movements.

On Tuesday, November 14, the command moved down the Big Dry twenty-three miles before halting along its east bank. More wagons cracked through the ice and became lodged in quicksand, causing repeated delays and further tiring the men, who had to extricate them. As the soldiers approached the Missouri River, the topography became refreshingly diverse, the stark barrenness graduating into rolling grasslands and timbered bottoms. The next morning, while Miles's column neared the Missouri, the scouts raised an alarm that there were Indians in front. The soldiers deployed in skirmish order and continued their advance. It was soon discovered that the quarry consisted of agency Indians who were on the north bank of the Missouri near Fort Peck. "Our fond expectations of a good fight vanished," wrote Baldwin. Miles bivouacked his men under the bluffs of the Missouri, west of its confluence with the Big Dry and scarcely a mile below the Fort Peck Indian Agency on the opposite bank. The "King of Rivers," wrote one observer, was "no longer dark and muddy, but clear as crystal, rolling rapidly under a surface frozen over completely."[19]

At Fort Peck, Miles found Second Lieutenant Russell H. Day and thirty-one soldiers of Hazen's Sixth Infantry in control. Originally a fur-trading post, the fort was now an agency for the Yanktonais, Assiniboines, and Gros Ventres, and formerly for assorted groups of Tetons. It consisted of numerous log buildings encircled by a stockade and stood beside the river under bluffs towering more than one hundred feet high. It provided annuities for about seven thousand Indians, but now additionally harbored a number of Indians who had lately been with Sitting Bull. From stocks at the agency, Miles was able to replenish his supplies for the expedition. The goods were "snaked" across the river with a rope and pulley concocted by the soldiers because the river ice was deemed not strong enough to support the wagons. Miles's officers saw a number of the nonagency Sioux chiefs at the agency, including Iron Dog, who was recognized from the councils at Cedar Creek. One account reported that Iron Dog's 119 lodges had come in to Fort Peck following the engagement of October 21. Some of these people were observed carrying arms and receiving government rations, an incongruity not lost on the command.[20]

The command passed three days at the bivouac across from Fort Peck. On Friday, Miles and Baldwin crossed the ice to the agency, where they encountered John Bruguier, the mixed-blood who had interpreted for Miles and Sitting Bull at Cedar Creek. Bruguier was a wanted man, having fled a murder indictment in Dakota Territory to live with the Indians. At Fort Peck he agreed to use his resources to attain Sitting Bull's surrender at Tongue River; in return, Miles promised to do what he could to help Bruguier settle his legal difficulties. Perhaps from Bruguier, Miles learned that some Indians reported as being camped along the Porcupine Creek were not those he sought, but belonged to the agency. He therefore called off a previously contemplated movement with four companies to that place.[21]

On the eighteenth Miles met with the agency Indians, attempting to learn particulars about the Tetons' condition and more precise data of Sitting Bull's whereabouts. He forwarded a letter to General Sherman, writing with confidence, "We have divided Sitting Bull's people and . . . his strength and influence is fast breaking down." Ever looking to his own advancement, Miles further proposed, "Give me command of this whole region and I will soon end this Sioux war," adding as an afterthought, "I would be very glad to govern them [the Indians] afterwards."[22]

On Sunday morning, November 19, Miles divided his command to cover more territory. From information obtained at the agency, Miles had learned that Sitting Bull's camp lay to the southwest, in an area called Black Buttes, about forty miles below the Missouri. He would personally lead Companies A, B, E, G, H, and I, along with a twelve-pounder Napoleon gun, and go after the Hunkpapa. Meantime, Captain Snyder and the remaining four companies, C, D, F, and K, prepared to march back up the Big Dry, intending to meet Miles near Black Buttes in eight to ten days. Snyder's movement south and then west was intended to reconnoiter the drainage of the Big Dry and possibly drive the Indians north of the Missouri where Miles would attempt to detain them. In the forenoon, Miles sent his battalion across the river and rationed it, in preparation for moving the next morning. Snyder and his command stayed in camp on the south bank.[23]

Miles was off early on the next day, leading his troops up the ridge behind Fort Peck and along the freight road to Carroll before turning southwest through sterile lands devoid of nearly all growth save cactus and sagebrush. Steep-walled banks held up the column at Willow Creek, where tree branches were used to construct artificial fords. For the next two days, Miles's battalion ascended this stream. "A more desolate . . . country I never saw," Lieutenant Baldwin wrote, remarking that the terrain was "as barren as a barn floor." Another chronicler described the region: "[It is] a sterile desert. No living thing is seen; even vegetation dies for want of nourishment."[24] On Wednesday, fog enshrouded the command, forcing officers to steer their course west along Willow Creek by compass. Near the head of the stream, Baldwin climbed a high butte and etched " '5th' Inf., Nov. 22, 1876" into a slab of sandstone. After traveling nineteen miles, the troops camped on a tributary referred to by its Indian-derived name, "the creek on which the women were killed." The next day, which was warm and pleasant, they moved south to the valley of Fourchette, or Frenchman's, Creek, a richly grassed area that afforded grazing for numerous antelope and bison. There word spread among the troops that Indians had been spotted on their flanks, but this went unconfirmed. On the twenty-fourth the temperature ranged between twelve degrees in the morning and fifty-eight degrees at 2 P.M. The companies passed along the west branch of Fourchette, heading generally southwest for twelve miles.

On November 25, nearly 110 miles west of Fort Peck, Miles detached fifty-two men of Company B under Captain Andrew S. Bennett, directing them to Carroll City, on the Missouri, about twenty miles above the mouth of the Musselshell River, to seize any ammunition reportedly being delivered to the Indians by the trader there. Accompanied by mule-drawn supply wagons, Bennett marched west and reached Carroll City four days later. Meantime, the balance of the soldiers arrived at the Missouri River opposite Squaw Creek, a short distance below the mouth of the Musselshell, camping at a site with sufficient grass and a variety of game nearby, including buffalo, elk, and deer.

At that point the Missouri was not frozen; large ice floes swept along with the swift current. Anticipating crossing the stream, the troops covered a wagon box with canvas to make a boat and fashioned crude oars. Baldwin directed the construction of a log raft, eighty feet long by twelve feet wide, and early the following morning the men launched it, with Miles, Baldwin, Lieutenant Pope, and a dozen soldiers aboard. The twenty-foot-long cottonwood poles the men used proved worthless against the raging current, which practically knocked them overboard. Midway across the river, the craft abruptly snagged, jarring its occupants and stranding them until late afternoon, when it was cut loose. During the interim, a line was run from the raft to the south shore and a wagon-boat carried several men across. Efforts to run a rope from the north shore to the raft failed, however, and eventually the wagon-boat with line was sent to the north shore, and the raft, at last freed, was pulled to safety.[25] A witness described the dangerously complicated maneuvering to rescue Miles's party:

> The canvas covered wagon bed succeeded in reaching the raft, the men using spades for paddles. The rope which was to be stretched across the river was on the raft and the central position was of advantage as one point of fastening. The wagon bed was now sent over to the opposite shore with the rope, and this was secured to the opposite shore by private [Thomas] Kelly of Company "I," boldly venturing over the frail ice. The object next was to reach the other bank, and the attempt was made first to reach this, and then to reach another snag half way, but it was discovered that there was not sufficient rope. Another wagon-bed boat was constructed and sent out with additional rope attached to the desired bank. . . . The desired juncture was actually effected when the swift current bore down so rapidly that it near capsized the boats. . . . The second boat, however, succeeded in reaching the second snag, thus connecting two-thirds of the river. Once more a wagon-bed boat was constructed, but [it] could not be made to reach over the nearer snag. . . .

To add to the scene now, . . . immense ice floes began to sweep down, striking the raft and boat with terrific force, until one immense field of solid ice, covering a third of the river, came booming down the raging current. The outer edge alone struck the raft, while the main body bore down directly upon the men in the boat. The cry to cut the rope arose, but Private [Richard] Bellews [Bellows], of Company "E," calmly untied it, and holding the end until hopeless of longer resisting such force, let go and [the boat] was borne down without injury by the ice field and this crew soon paddled in to the shore. The huge blocks warned those on the raft that it was high time to do likewise, and drawing in the rope from the opposite bank, the raft was loosened from its snag, the first boat manned, and given one end of this rope, paddled for the shore, while the poles on the raft were vigorously plied. The boat got in to the shore, and the old raft with its thoroughly tired human freight, was hauled in about a quarter of a mile below the scene of their long imprisonment.[26]

Apparently, the enlisted men relished the humor of Miles's predicament, dubbing the commander "our shipwrecked General." As one of them reported:

While the Gen. was on the raft a herd of elk ran into camp and the picket commenced firing into them; the Gen. yelled out, "What is the meaning of that firing?" Some rogue responded, "Indians coming!" As the Gen. was down below the bank out of sight and could not see what was going on, he began to cry "Fall in! Fall in!," giving orders in a true military style deserving of credit. After the true state of affairs were communicated to him his appearance became more calm, but I would not have been in the fellow's boots that shouted "Indians" for a mint of money.[27]

In the morning of November 27, Baldwin succeeded in getting the line to the south side and with great difficulty prepared to move the battalion across the stream. In one instance, a huge block of ice struck the raft, nearly sinking it and the men aboard. Baldwin's frustration grew, compounded by Miles's constant interference. "Just about as I would be ready to do a thing, he would come along and want to change it in some way. . . . We would get a thing all ready to operate and pretty sure of succeeding, but before [we] could . . . complete the trial he would want to do something else and in this way we have not as yet accomplished anything."[28]

On Tuesday it snowed. At dawn the temperature registered three degrees above zero, though it rose above freezing in the

course of the day. A new raft, built according to Miles's speci-
fications, prepared to transport men to the south shore. The
river was now swelling rapidly and filling with broken ice, which
raised fears that the sharp edges would cut the lines intended
to draw the craft across. During the day, Miles managed to get
four soldiers over the stream to scout up Squaw Creek; he also
sent two mounted men to contact Captain Bennett at Carroll
City. On the twenty-ninth the raft ferried two loads across, but
the cascading ice made the crossings extremely dangerous.[29]

On November 30, Lieutenant Baldwin wrote in his diary:
"The National Thanksgiving Day of our Country and here we
are 1000 miles from civilization on the banks of a turbulent
river which we have for 5 days endeavored to cross, but [have]
not yet overcome." Exasperated at the delays and the danger
posed by the plunging ice floes, Miles determined to move to a
place where the stream was frozen so they might ford. In the
morning he sent a scout with more dispatches for Captain Bennett. At noon the two riders previously sent to Bennett returned with word that the captain would start for the command
the next day. From his scouts Miles learned that the Missouri
was solid ice eighteen miles above, at the abandoned fur-trading establishment of Fort Hawley. Accordingly, he directed his
column to that place.[30]

While Miles struggled to cross the Missouri River, the battalion under Captain Snyder was moving toward the appointed
rendezvous near Black Buttes. Leaving the bivouac opposite
the Fort Peck agency on the twentieth, with Companies C, D, F,
and K of the Fifth Infantry, Snyder had marched his command,
which included supply wagons, the short distance to the mouth
of the Big Dry, where he camped for the night. Over the next
three days his battalion traveled forty-seven miles up the bed of
the stream. On Friday, the twenty-fourth, the troops diverted
from the Big Dry, following a tributary, which Snyder dubbed
Baldwin's Creek, that led to the northwest. In the afternoon,
after bivouacking, the captain was notified that sounds of distant artillery firing had been heard, but he dismissed the reports. As night fell, Yellowstone Kelly and a number of scouts
arrived in camp. Acting on orders from Miles, they had explored east from Fort Peck along the south bank of the Missouri
for several days, looking for Indians who might be planning to
join Sitting Bull. A short distance beyond Wolf Point, Kelly's

19. First Lieutenant Frank D. Baldwin, shown here in a Civil War photograph. One of Miles's most reliable subordinates, Baldwin proved his worth in encounters with the Sioux and Cheyennes in 1876 and 1877, and in several postwar skirmishes. Baldwin retired from the army a brigadier general in 1906, after forty years of service. He died in 1923. (Colorado Historical Society)

20. Captain Simon Snyder, whose diaries composed an important source for this study, served in the Fifth Infantry almost continuously from 1861 until 1888. During the Cedar Creek encounter, Snyder commanded Company F in support of the artillery piece. He participated in the Fort Peck expedition and later headed the mounted infantry detachment organized toward the end of the Sioux War. After a career spanning the Civil, Indian, and Spanish-American wars, Snyder retired as a brigadier general in 1902. (Miles, *Personal Recollections*)

21. First Lieutenant George W. Baird was regimental adjutant of the Fifth Infantry from 1871 to 1879. Baird published a useful account of Miles's campaign that incorporated the recollections of several officers. He fought and was wounded at Bear Paw Mountain in the Nez Perce War (for which he won a Medal of Honor) before transferring in 1879 to the Pay Department. He retired in 1903. (Miles, *Personal Recollections*)

men had found evidence of a small camp. But snow had obliterated any trail, and the scouts had headed cross-country to find Snyder. Three days after this union, Snyder's command reached Black Buttes, south of the fork of the Big Dry. On November 28, Companies F and K remained in camp to guard the wagons while Captain Butler took C and D to patrol ten miles up the fork. The detachment returned in a snowstorm, having found no sign of the Sioux. After a short trek the next morning, Snyder halted to await contact with Miles. That evening and the following morning he directed Kelly and his scouts forward to locate Miles's battalion while his men stayed in camp. Hoping to attract the colonel, Snyder fired signal guns and sent up smoke signals.[31]

Unaware of Miles's predicament at the Missouri, Snyder waited until December 2, when, his forage running low, he left the Black Buttes camp and headed for Tongue River. Guided by Kelly, he moved to the Big Dry, where he abandoned a wagon. Three days into the march and anxious over his dwindling supplies, Snyder sent the scout and a companion ahead to the cantonment. On the sixth, his "animals growing very weak from lack of grain," he cast off three of them before camping atop the divide between the Big Dry and Sunday Creek. Relief came two days later when Crow Indians from Tongue River arrived with corn for Snyder's livestock. (They also brought news, later determined inaccurate, that the Democratic contender in the recent election, Samuel J. Tilden, had been elected President of the United States.) Early the next day Kelly and two scouts started back on the trail in an effort to locate Miles. Snyder's battalion dragged into the cantonment the morning of December 10, having logged 330 miles in their fruitless pursuit of the Sioux.[32]

Conditions at the river had thwarted Miles's design of reuniting his battalion with Snyder's. Further disrupting his plan was the report that had reached him November 29—that Sitting Bull had gone east, intending to cross the Missouri somewhere below Fort Peck. This news came from Lieutenant Day at the agency, where word among the Yanktonais held that the Hunkpapa, with 160 to 170 lodges, was thirty miles from Peck. The report proved at once disconcerting and frustrating for Miles; if it were true, it not only meant that Sitting Bull had evaded his dragnet operation—in fact, was not even in the immediate

area—but it challenged Miles's strategy of isolating Sitting
Bull's Sioux from those of Crazy Horse, should the Hunkpapa
succeed in returning across the Yellowstone. In order to check
the Indians before they attempted that maneuver, Miles detached Lieutenant Baldwin with three companies to again reconnoiter the country to the east. On December 1, with the
remaining companies and gun, Miles set off upstream to cross
the Missouri at Fort Hawley and then examine the upper
reaches of the Big Dry before returning to the Tongue River
Cantonment to resupply.[33]

Miles hiked his battalion for seven hours, through the rugged
breaks north of the Missouri, his train repeatedly bogging down
in the quicksands of a small creek they were following. At 9 P.M.
the tired soldiers camped along another stream, after having
gone nineteen miles. In the morning they skirted the hills near
the Missouri and cut a road through the heavy underbrush to
facilitate the wagons' approach to the river. They forded the
frozen stream without incident and arrived at the site of Fort
Hawley, abandoned since 1869. "A few pieces of burnt timber
scattered about, the remnants of an iron stove, and several
graves marked by wooden headboards, are all that is left."[34]

At half past six o'clock the next morning the column moved
on, soon reaching Crooked Creek and passing along its sinuous
valley lined with cedar and pine. The many crossings of this
creek took time, and the exertions in getting the wagons up the
dangerous precipices were great. On the third and fourth,
Miles's troops made little more than nineteen miles filing along
the lofty heights. Captain Bennett, with Company B, rejoined
them on the latter day. Deer abounded, and the men feasted on
venison at each bivouac. On December 5 the command crossed
the Musselshell on the ice, near its confluence with the Missouri, but interposing bluffs again delayed the wagons. Yet another road had to be carved, part of which climbed up a perpendicular bank. The vehicles were then unhitched, unloaded,
and pulled up the incline by the men. After traveling but seven
miles, the command halted on the south bank of the Missouri
near Squaw Creek, opposite the site of their former attempts to
cross the river. On December 6 the soldiers moved southeast
along solid terrain adjoining Squaw Creek. Forage for the animals began to run out and fears grew that the weather might
turn bad. Finally, on the seventh, Miles's battalion sighted Black

Buttes beyond the timbered valley of the Big Dry. It became evident, however, that Snyder had gone toward the cantonment, and Miles followed closely on his trail.[35]

The soldiers spent the ensuing days traversing the jagged ground about the Big Dry and its tributaries. Progress was slow. Miles's animals suffered because of the sparsely grassed terrain that offered only alkaline water, so the colonel detached scouts to follow Snyder's trail and obtain forage. Temperatures again began to fall. On Monday, the eleventh, Kelly and his scouts arrived as the battalion broke camp. They confirmed Snyder's return to the cantonment and reported the presence there of eighty Crow scouts from the agency up the Yellowstone who had enlisted. Miles further learned that Sioux and Northern Cheyenne warriors had recently driven off a herd of civilian-owned cattle grazing in the vicinity of the Tongue River post. He also received a dispatch from Baldwin, who had reached Fort Peck. The letters had been brought by John Bruguier and Billy Cross, and before going on, Miles sent these scouts back to Baldwin. He expressed encouragement to that officer and told him: "If you meet with ill-success I can take the responsibility of the movement; if you are successful it will be very creditable to you." He urged Baldwin to alert him of the direction Sitting Bull's people were headed, promising, "If I get the information in time [I] will endeavor to intercept them."[36]

As the troops proceeded on December 12, they became enveloped by a formidable snowstorm that kept up through the day. Nonetheless, in the afternoon they located Snyder's trail, most obvious from the dead animals scattered along it. The battalion labored on to Sunday Creek, where it camped at 8 P.M., after a march of twenty-four miles under exceedingly difficult conditions. An enlisted man later remembered the last portion of the march of the twelfth: "As it was a very dark night we could scarcely keep the trail; such feeling with hands and striking matches I never heard of. The scouts went ahead and fired their guns in the air. All we could see was a flash, then all was darkness; we would go in the direction of the flash till we came to the scouts and they would then go ahead again." Colonel Miles recollected the technique employed by his men in passing through the deep snow: "They frequently marched in single file, the leading man breaking the road until weary, then falling out for another to take his place and returning to the rear of the column while the fresh man continued to beat the pathway through the snow." The soldiers could scarcely see beyond thirty feet as the blizzard swept around them, and they found their way mostly by compass.[37]

With forage supplies exhausted and rations running low, Miles's battalion faced desperate conditions. "Our mules grew so thin," lamented one soldier, "that you could almost read a newspaper through them." On the morning of December 13, the situation was alleviated with the arrival of Captain Charles J. Dickey and Companies D and I, Twenty-second Infantry, with food for the animals. The command continued southeastwardly down Sunday Creek, along the trail it had embarked on more than a month earlier. At noon the following day, the troops pulled up on the north bank of the Yellowstone opposite the cantonment. Between November 6 and December 14, Miles and his battalion had campaigned 558 miles.[38]

Only Baldwin's infantrymen remained in the field. News borne by the lieutenant's scouts, to the effect that Sitting Bull was fleeing in the direction of the Yellowstone, reached Miles the day after he gained the cantonment. Miles sent scouts to the Powder River to verify Sitting Bull's approach and readied his troops to take the field once more if the reports proved true. In fact, the country of the Big Dry remained the primary attraction for Sitting Bull and his followers, for game, especially buffalo, was plentiful there during the winter months, a reality that had been corroborated by the army during its presence in that area. More recent intelligence indicated that Sitting Bull and several other Sioux leaders, including Black Moon, Four Horns, Yellow Liver, Drag, and Red Horn, along with a hundred lodges, had forded the Missouri opposite Bark Creek on December 3 and had encamped on Milk River, along the wagon road to Fort Buford. Reportedly, too, a fugitive named White Horse, with five lodges and sixty ponies, had joined them the next day from Standing Rock Agency. Sitting Bull sent word to Colonel Hazen that he did not want to fight any more that winter, and that he hoped to go into Peck to trade after the soldiers departed.[39]

Although Sitting Bull anticipated that the fighting was over for the time being, Miles believed differently. A strong indication of the colonel's conviction was evident in his instructions to Lieutenant Baldwin after he heard the news on November

29 that the Hunkpapa leader was in the vicinity of Fort Peck. Miles had sent the lieutenant with Companies G (Second Lieutenant David Q. Rousseau), H (Second Lieutenant Frank S. Hinkle), and I (Second Lieutenant James H. Whitten), along with two orderlies, four mounted soldiers, and thirteen six-mule teams to search the country between the agency and Fort Buford, paying particular attention to the area around the Big Dry and the Redwater River farther east. As he had on the southern plains, Miles trusted Baldwin to use discretion and judgment in carrying out these instructions and gave him no written orders.[40]

An energetic, talented, and dependable subaltern, Baldwin possessed Miles's full confidence to complete this mission. Only thirty-four years old in 1876, the Michigan-born former lightning-rod salesman, now acting assistant adjutant general of the Yellowstone Command, was a battle-tested veteran of Sherman's southern campaigns during the Civil War. His wartime experiences included a stint as a captive of the Confederates in the notorious Libby Prison at Richmond. Later, on the plains, Baldwin became one of Miles's favorite junior officers, accompanying the colonel during the Red River Expedition of 1874 and distinguishing himself in no less than five successive engagements with Indians. Baldwin's gallantry and bravery were widely recognized. During the 1890s he was awarded two Medals of Honor—one for his 1864 performance at the Battle of Peach Tree Creek, Georgia, and another for his attack on a village of Southern Cheyennes at McClellan Creek, Texas, in November, 1874, during which he succeeded in rescuing two white girls held captive by the Indians.[41] Like Miles, Baldwin was a non–West Pointer, a factor that doubtless increased their camaraderie and contributed to the confidence that the colonel felt in his lieutenant.

Aided by the light of a full moon, Baldwin had set off on the trail back to Fort Peck before dawn on December 2. The trip was uneventful. The men sloshed through thawing ice, snow, and mud, generally following the road Miles had used previously in his march up the Missouri. The mules grew weak, but after four days the battalion arrived at Fort Peck unscathed. There Baldwin learned from John Bruguier, who had left Sitting Bull three days earlier, that the Hunkpapa, with a hundred lodges, was again north of the Missouri, encamped fifteen miles

from the agency on Porcupine Creek. While Bruguier prepared
to carry this word to Miles, Baldwin readied his command to
find the Sioux. In a dispatch to the colonel, Baldwin wrote: "If
I thought you could arrive here in time I would wait, . . . but [I]
am afraid the chance will be lost. . . . I shall start this evening
and endeavor to reach the main camp in time to pitch in early
in the morning."[42]

Thus rationed for two days, and with eighteen thousand
rounds of ammunition borne by a mule pack train, in addition
to a hundred rounds carried by each of Baldwin's 112 men, the
lieutenant marched east from Fort Peck at 8 P.M., hoping to
strike Sitting Bull at dawn. Seven miles from the agency, on the
Buford Road, the battalion encountered several groups of Indians reportedly frightened by Sitting Bull's presence in the
area and en route to Fort Peck. They told Baldwin's scouts that
the Sioux had moved their camp to the Missouri. Noted Baldwin in his diary: "I felt very much elated at the prospects of
finding his camp on this [north] side of the Mo. R. where I
could get at him."[43]

Soon after this meeting, the troops came on the abandoned
village site on the Porcupine, near that stream's confluence
with the Milk River. The ground was strewn with litter. Still-
blazing campfires indicated that Sitting Bull had withdrawn has-
tily, evidently after learning of Baldwin's movement. The Indians' trail, some thirty yards wide, led toward the Missouri River.
Guided by eighteen-year-old Joseph Culbertson, who had
signed on with Miles at Fort Peck, and another scout named
Edward Lambert, Baldwin's men pressed forward, now moving
easily across the previously trampled snow. At 3 A.M. they
stopped at the Milk River and prepared a meal, then moved on.
Near dawn, warriors attempted to stampede their mules, but
were driven away, with one of their number killed. In the bitter
cold of the morning of December 7, Baldwin halted in the timber a short distance from the Missouri to await daylight. Fearing
discovery by the Sioux, he allowed the soldiers no fires. Learning that several bands of Yanktonais from the agency were
camped in various places along the north side of the river, Baldwin issued strict orders against firing at any Indians on that
bank.

Anticipating a fight, Baldwin directed his scouts and
mounted men to advance to the river. They returned shortly,

reporting no signs of the Sioux. Baldwin, meantime, deployed his troops in skirmish order, with Companies G and I in line and H as rear guard. Finally, daybreak revealed glimpses of Indians in front and on the right. Baldwin moved his skirmishers downstream along the north bank, following the trail, which led across the frozen stream. About one mile below the crossing, near the mouth of Bark Creek, Baldwin halted and watched as the last Indians retreated over the ice. "Their long caravans of women, children & ponies with packs rushing in frightened haste could be seen winding their way through the timbered foothills to the south." While Culbertson and two of the mounted men crossed the river to reconnoiter the Indians, Baldwin watched and waited. He allowed his men some rest, even permitting them to start breakfast. The scouts hardly gained the south bank, however, before shooting erupted and they fled back toward the battalion, which once more fanned out in skirmish formation.[44]

At Baldwin's direction, Company H started across the ice to drive the Indians from the timber. Under fire from warriors ensconced on the bank, the unit nonetheless forged ahead, gained the shore, and advanced, Springfields barking, to clear the trees and underbrush up to the hills. Before long, however, larger numbers of warriors appeared in front, having removed their noncombatants a safe distance from the troops. Meanwhile, Company I deployed along the bank on the north side to oversee the action, while Company G acted as a reserve force. Complicating matters, as the shooting went on, a large body of agency Yanktonais assembled in Baldwin's rear, causing the lieutenant to withdraw his reserve unit from in front and place it behind, "with orders to open fire on the Yanktonnais if they did not leave at once."[45] The Yanktonais pulled back.

Fearing an ambush by Sitting Bull's force, which he now estimated at six hundred strong, and lacking artillery support, Baldwin declined to commit his undermanned force further. "All of the officers were in doubt as to the chances of success and advised that no attack be made."[46] Further, Baldwin worried that the thin ice of the Missouri might break up, spelling disaster by barring his withdrawal to Peck should Sitting Bull defeat him on the south bank. At two o'clock, after holding the south bank for several hours, he withdrew Company H to the north side. Beyond one mule killed in the action, no casualties had occurred. The Bark Creek encounter, by its location, suggested certain premeditation on Sitting Bull's part; later intelligence confirmed that Sitting Bull had intentionally removed his followers to that relatively impregnable position, which provided the best protection for his women and children and the most advantageous position for fighting the soldiers.

Baldwin marched his battalion slowly downstream, along the north side of the Missouri to Little Porcupine Creek, where he camped behind a barricade of cottonwood logs, hoping yet to entice Sitting Bull into instigating an encounter on open ground. The Hunkpapa did not respond, although warriors occasionally appeared to exchange gunfire with the pickets. Baldwin's men built fires, ate, and got some sleep. At dusk, a sudden raging norther swept down on the men, dropping the temperature to minus thirty-five degrees and causing Baldwin to forsake his expedition for the safety of his command. At 9 P.M., the men having consumed all remaining food, he started for Fort Peck in a blizzard, driving the soldiers through a fearfully cold wind that froze ears, noses, and fingers. "If we had remained in camp, many of the men would have frozen to death; all along the march every officer was constantly busy watching that some man should not lay down from stupification caused by cold and then die."[47] Baldwin placed the pack mules at the head of the column to break the way across the snowy ground. To keep the column moving, a long rope was strung from one of the mules and the men required to cling to it, the animal occasionally being forced to trot to quicken the soldiers' blood circulation.

Years later Baldwin recalled that long night: "[The] men [were] so fatigued and [the] weather so cold I had to put 3 old sergeants in [the] rear with fixed bayonets and strict orders to prick any man who tried to lag or lie down. I myself got to sleep and fell off my horse, and I carry the marks of the wound until this day where one of them prodded me to wake me up, and for this I recommended the man for a medal, which he got." Members of Baldwin's command later told of being so weary that they experienced hallucinations on the march back to Fort Peck. "Some thought they were riding in steam cars, . . . others thought they saw parks, lakes and cities when there was nothing but the vast snow-covered prairie before them." Upon learning of the agony of his fellows, an enlisted man at Tongue River wrote: "I hope I may never have the pleasure of taking a trip under Lieut. Baldwin. Gen. Miles marches us hard enough, but then he is reasonable and permits us to rest a moment when he sees we are tired."[48]

Baldwin reached Fort Peck in the early afternoon of December 8, with nearly a quarter of his men suffering from frostbite and lack of sleep. In little more than two days they had traveled seventy-three miles. "I never experienced such suffering," wrote Baldwin. Yet he was satisfied that the incredible hardship sustained by his soldiers was no match for that experienced by the Indians because of the uprooting of their winter encampment. He sent news of his encounter with Sitting Bull to department headquarters and dashed off a report of the skirmish to Miles. He told Miles that the Hunkpapa had sent word that he would attack Baldwin when that officer started for Tongue River and then would strike Fort Peck. Baldwin proposed that the colonel march for the headwaters of Bark Creek and coordinate with his own force in trapping the Sioux between them. He further told Miles that he planned to enlist several Indian scouts at the agency, and that he would start for Fort Buford in three days unless Miles should direct otherwise.[49]

Following their ordeal, Baldwin's infantrymen stuffed themselves with bison meat before sleeping away the rest of the afternoon at Fort Peck. The next day Baldwin began planning his future movements. He sent an Indian scout, Left Hand, to check on Sitting Bull's camp. Seeking artillery, he located an old howitzer with a broken wheel and no limber, and set the agency carpenter to work fixing the wheel and attaching the gun to the front truck of a wagon. Baldwin further readied twenty-two wagons, pulled by six-mule teams, to transport his soldiers. On December 10 he learned from Indian Agent Thomas J. Mitchell, who had arrived from Wolf Point with fifty Assiniboines, that Sitting Bull had left Bark Creek and gone east to Redwater Creek. Faced with an urgency should the Hunkpapas evade his command and head toward the Yellowstone, Baldwin decided to embark in the morning even though his soldiers still showed fatigue and needed clothing. He again dispatched couriers to notify Miles of his plans, apologetically explaining his decision not to attack full force at Bark Creek and promoting his intention of driving Sitting Bull's people south of the Missouri, where Miles might finally corner them.[50]

Leaving the agency early Monday morning with most of his
jaded troops aboard the wagons, Baldwin picked his way east
over the thawing road along the Missouri. Besides Lieutenants
Rousseau, Hinkle, and Whitten, Second Lieutenant William H.
Wheeler, Eleventh Infantry, from the agency, went along.
Many soldiers, their shoes failing, contrived new foot coverings
from buffalo skins. The lieutenant went one-half mile beyond
the Sioux crossing place of the seventh and camped. On December 12 the way grew muddy as temperatures rose. Reaching
Wolf Point Agency, Baldwin stopped and obtained flour, oats,
and some hams for his command. A nineteen-year-old Assini-
boine leader named White Dog promised warriors to assist the
troops in the quest for Sitting Bull, but failed to deliver any.
The Assiniboines nevertheless told Baldwin that Sitting Bull
had left the Redwater and headed toward the Yellowstone with
intentions of uniting with other Indians, presumably Sioux.
Spurred by this news, Baldwin on the morning of December 14
began moving his men over the thin ice of the Missouri; the
wagons were unhitched, tied to long ropes, and pulled across
by the soldiers while the mules were brought over individ-
ually.[51]

Once across, the column proceeded several miles up a small
tributary before leaving the bottoms and crossing a small divide, ultimately emerging in the valley of the Redwater River,
which led generally south. Deep snowdrifts stalled the movement, forcing the fatigued infantrymen to clear paths for the
wagons and animals. Nonetheless, the column accomplished
sixteen miles on the fourteenth before stopping and building
fires to offset a rising cold wind. On the fifteenth a fierce
norther beset the soldiers, who struggled fourteen miles farther
up the sparsely wooded stream. Baldwin noted in his diary that
rations were again running low and that the unshod animals
were tiring quickly. "The country is covered with ice and the
mules slip down and cannot travel easily." Two days later the
command encountered a week-old Indian trail, but continuing
subzero temperatures, the worsening state of the mules, and
dwindling rations with little game in sight now concerned Baldwin.[52]

Baldwin believed his chances were favorable for striking an
Indian camp somewhere in the Yellowstone-Missouri divide
country. On Monday morning, December 18, he kept his com-

mand tightly together as he probed the snowy bottoms of Ash
Creek, a southeastwardly leading tributary of the Redwater.
The troops began the march shortly past 7 A.M., striking east
and then south as they crossed branches of the stream, all the
while attempting to conceal their presence from any Sioux.
Around 1 P.M. a mounted warrior appeared in the distance in
front of the column, and soon the soldiers spied smoke wafting
in the sky ahead, clear evidence of a village nearby. Baldwin
advanced, saw the camp, then returned to his battalion and prepared it for an immediate assault.

The village that Baldwin targeted with Companies G, H, and
I of the Fifth Infantry at midday December 18 represented the
principal assemblage of Indians still with Sitting Bull—122
lodges sheltered beneath a bluff along the east side of Ash
Creek, only about two miles north of the divide. The size of the
camp suggested that the Hunkpapa's following had recently increased.

Baldwin approached the camp from the northwest, bearing
down the creek bottom quickly, his force arranged much as it
had been two years earlier during his successful attack on the
Southern Cheyennes at McClellan Creek. One company advanced in skirmish order in front of the wagons, which were
drawn up in four columns and flanked on either side by another
company. The entire formation was followed by a small rear
guard. The Indians remained unaware of the presence of the
soldiers until it was too late to mount any effective defense.
Most of the men were out hunting. When they saw the troops
coming, those present made a feeble stand on the right, perhaps to distract the soldiers so the women and children might
get away.

Baldwin opened the contest with three rounds of solid shot
from his howitzer, causing the Indians—warriors as well as noncombatants—to flee immediately. Each time the gun discharged
it fell off its makeshift carriage and had to be remounted. "It
had only a moral effect," remembered Baldwin, "but that effect
served a good purpose."[53] As the soldiers fired on the village,
the Sioux abandoned their tipis, which contained their clothing, buffalo robes, blankets, agency-issued goods, and winter
foodstuffs, and floundered their ponies through the snow to
escape. The soldiers did not pursue, but captured at least sixty
mules and ponies. Baldwin later told how almost twoscore sick,

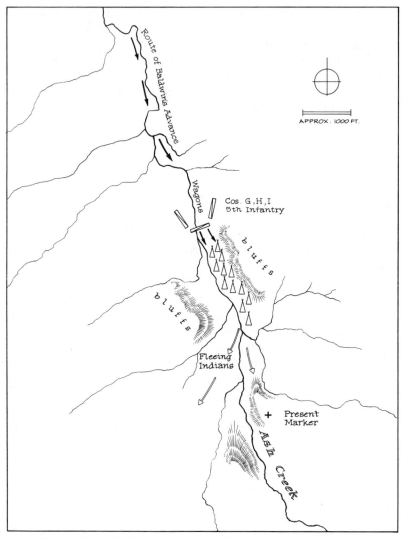

4. The Ash Creek fight, December 18, 1876

badly fatigued, and wagon-borne soldiers left the vehicles to join their comrades in the onslaught. "Victory complete and effective," the lieutenant jotted in his diary. Although there were no immediate casualties on either side (Baldwin later reported one Indian killed), he had succeeded in routing the

22. In August 1920, retired general Frank D. Baldwin visited the site of his December 1876 attack on Sitting Bull at Ash Creek, Montana. The man pointing is former scout Joseph Culbertson. (Custer Battlefield National Monument)

Hunkpapas, leaving them without food and clothing in harsh winter conditions.

Garnering dried buffalo meat and supplies to sustain his men in the coming days, Baldwin loaded the plunder into the wagons and burned what was left, including about ninety lodges still standing. The men marched through the village and toward the divide, camping after dusk at a site without water. Scout Culbertson said that the troops erected breastworks from sacks of corn and hardtack boxes and encircled the livestock with the wagons. Both men and mules were weary from the day's exertions, and with the temperature at minus forty degrees, Baldwin directed that the captured robes and blankets be distributed among the soldiers; others were used to cover the mules. Later, at the cantonment, these items were quickly fashioned into overcoats, caps, and pants for Miles's next campaign.[54]

23. Present marker at the site of Lieutenant Baldwin's attack on Sitting Bull's village, December 18, 1876. The draw of Ash Creek is in the background. (L. Clifford Soubier)

During the night Indians fired on the soldiers' bivouac near the divide, but no injuries occurred. After dawn, and before leaving camp, Baldwin ordered the killing of part of the captured herd. Some animals were shot and others, to preserve ammunition, had their throats slashed. Then the column proceeded over the divide, crossing through a narrow gap that facilitated passage of the wagons, and emerged in the Yellowstone drainage at Cedar Creek. Livened by prospects of relief, the troops followed this stream and on the nineteenth reached the road running from the Tongue to Glendive and Fort Buford.

Throughout the day they observed Sioux warriors following at a distance, and shortly before sundown, as they went into camp, the tribesmen mounted a determined attack that was quickly turned away.

That night Baldwin sent Lieutenant Hinkle and Vic Smith ahead to the cantonment to report the recent developments and to request that Miles forward corn for his mules to Custer Creek. Pushing on in the morning through new snow, the troops camped under a strong wind on the banks of Custer Creek. As they lay in camp the next morning, Sioux warriors approached close enough to harrass Scout Culbertson and a soldier who had gone after some spent mules. The lieutenant quickly marched to their relief.[55]

Hinkle and Smith arrived at the cantonment on the twentieth and informed Miles of Baldwin's success against the Sioux village. The colonel immediately sent forth a forty-man relief column under Captain Ezra P. Ewers with forage for the mules. These troops met the battalion on December 21 along the Yellowstone road. On directions from Miles, Baldwin left his men and rode through the night with an escort, reaching the cantonment at 5 A.M. the next morning. Companies G, H, and I stumbled in the following afternoon. Since leaving the Tongue in early November, Baldwin's men had marched 716 miles over an often bleak and tortuous terrain and under the most extreme climatic conditions. Many still suffered from exposure, some with their feet trundled in gunny sacks taken from the Sioux camp.[56]

The Fort Peck expedition, though an arduous undertaking, proved beneficial to Miles's campaign against the Sioux and Cheyennes from several standpoints. It served them notice that they were not to be forgotten over the winter months, that Miles had made no idle threats when he vowed to persevere in his pursuit of them. Most significantly, Baldwin's engagements seem to have effectively shattered any vestige of pan-Teton influence that Sitting Bull might still have commanded after Cedar Creek. His people devastated and exposed to a merciless climate, the Hunkpapa turned south to find refuge with the Oglalas. Finally, word of Miles's winter offensive may have brought about the later desire in some of Crazy Horse's people to settle the war peacefully.

At Tongue River, Baldwin's men joined the balance of the regiment in gaining some relief from campaigning activities. In the shelter afforded by the hovels of the cantonment, they welcomed Christmas appropriately, with spirits provided by the post traders. Outside temperatures stood at minus thirty degrees and the snow was eight inches deep. While the men savored the warmth and festivities, Colonel Miles and his officers laid plans that would once more lead them far afield and confront them with the frigid Montana elements.

CHAPTER SEVEN

Wolf Mountains

The snows of eastern Montana Territory deepened in late December after Baldwin's return to Tongue River. A numbing cold driven by gusting winds gripped the region, assuring continued frigidity. In the confines of the cantonment, the soldiers back from the Fort Peck expedition found solace in their modest surroundings. Yet, the shelter afforded Miles's infantrymen was but a respite in a season of continuing hardships. Two recent events made an impact on Miles's plans and induced him to retake the field quickly, this time against the Indians wintering with Crazy Horse south of the Yellowstone. One occurrence was the outcome of the Crook-Mackenzie campaign into the Powder River region of Wyoming in November. The other involved the ambush slaying of a number of Sioux chiefs by Crow scouts immediately outside the cantonment on December 16, just two days after Miles's return from the Missouri.

The result of Crook's and Mackenzie's campaign bore significantly on Miles's operations. Hoping to strike the Sioux under Crazy Horse a mortal blow, General Crook had organized an expedition of more than 2,000 infantry-, cavalry-, and artillerymen that left Fort Fetterman on November 14 and assembled at Cantonment Reno, near the site of old Fort Reno, in east-central Wyoming. Five days later this Powder River expedition departed Reno. Learning of the presence of a large Northern Cheyenne village along the North, or Red, Fork of the Powder River, Crook dispatched Colonel Mackenzie west on the twenty-third with 750 men of the Second, Third, Fourth, and Fifth Cavalry Regiments and a contingent of 350 Pawnee and other Indian scouts, including some recently enlisted Sioux and Cheyennes. In the icy dawn of November 25, Mackenzie's troopers stormed the camp, situ-

24. Colonel Ranald S. Mackenzie's strike against Dull Knife's Cheyennes in November 1876 strongly influenced Miles's operations during the subsequent winter. Considered a brilliant cavalry leader whose campaigning was successful on both the northern and southern plains, Mackenzie died at age forty-eight from paresis, or insanity brought on by syphilitic degeneration of the brain. (Nebraska State Historical Society)

ated in a walled canyon, killing at least forty warriors and driving the remaining occupants into the freezing elements. The victory was complete. Besides taking seven hundred ponies, the soldiers captured two hundred lodges containing clothing, ammunition, and winter supplies, then burned them as the routed families watched helplessly from afar. Army casualties in the fighting numbered six men killed, including one officer, and twenty-five wounded. On the twenty-sixth, Mackenzie was unsuccessful in extricating the Indians from their refuge farther up the canyon and fell back to meet Crook and the infantry. In December, after struggling through blizzard conditions in Wyoming and Dakota, the soldiers abandoned the campaign and returned to quarters.

The Indians on the Red Fork had belonged to the bands of Little Wolf and Dull Knife, prominent Northern Cheyennes who had played important roles in the events of 1876 and, according to some sources, had been inclined to surrender if they could get assurances of good treatment from the government. The village contained evidence of the presence of some of its residents at the Little Bighorn in June. As their camp smoldered in ruins following Mackenzie's attack, the refugees fled north seeking shelter with Crazy Horse and his followers. On the night after the battle the temperature dropped to minus thirty degrees, killing eleven Cheyenne infants. More froze to death on succeeding nights, and, reportedly, fourteen warriors who had been wounded died during the flight.[1]

It took the destitute Cheyennes more than two weeks to reach the Tetons. Subsisting on horse meat, they followed the Big Horn Mountains to present Clear Creek, which they then followed to Lake DeSmet. Passing down Prairie Dog Creek, the refugees finally reached Crazy Horse's camp on the Tongue, near Beaver Creek, about December 12. There they found ten lodges of Northern Cheyennes belonging to White Bull, Old Man Chief, and Black Moccasin that had already joined Crazy Horse. Although willing to give food and clothing to the Cheyennes, the Oglalas were themselves growing impoverished, having to eat some of their starved ponies. They provided the newcomers with food, blankets, robes, tobacco, and even ponies. Also, either with Crazy Horse or in close orbit around his village were the Minneconjous and Sans Arcs who had forsworn their agreement to go into the Cheyenne River Agency following their capitulation to Miles in October.

After recuperating several days, the Cheyennes and their hosts moved through drifting snow farther up the Tongue River. The people of Dull Knife and Little Wolf attempted to hunt, with hopes of obtaining hides to build lodges. But bison were scarce, and the combined Sioux-Cheyenne encampment soon became too large to sustain itself.[2] Although later denied by both Sioux and Cheyenne informants, the lengthy imposition of the Cheyennes may have compounded problems for the Oglalas, exacerbating tensions already aggravated by their crisis conditions. Word that Cheyenne scouts had assisted the army in the assault on Dull Knife's village devastated the Northern Cheyennes and fostered suspicions within their group. It spread among the Oglalas, who henceforth welcomed messengers from the agencies with skepticism and distrust. Some Cheyennes later criticized Crazy Horse for limiting the extent of relief to the Dull Knife refugees. Although such criticism may have grown out of frustration that arose later within the village community, the seeds of contention may indeed have been sowed on the arrival of the Cheyennes. Intertribal unrest may also have evolved from the rise of a peace faction within the combined Oglala-Cheyenne hierarchy, which Miles would one day recognize and encourage. Ultimately, the augmentation of Crazy Horse's village with the Dull Knife refugees meant more Indians with whom Miles had to contend.[3]

The pursuit of peace by at least some of the Sioux seems to have been at the root of the tragedy of December 16, wherein five Teton leaders were assassinated by Crow scouts as they approached the cantonment. Indian sources have given at least two reasons for the convergence of the headmen on the garrison. One was that Crazy Horse, He Dog, Lame Deer, and other chiefs, not wanting to present themselves at Red Cloud and Spotted Tail agencies, hoped to assess Miles's disposition towards a peaceful settlement of the war. This hope may have been based on the October 27 surrender of the Minneconjous and Sans Arcs, who had been treated well and not punished. Another reason held that the Indians, wanting to return some horses that had recently been stolen from the cantonment by some of the younger men, hoped also to use the opportunity to trade robes and furs for rations.[4]

Details of the composition of the party, as described by different Sioux, also vary. Spotted Elk reported that it contained Sitting Bull the Good (also known as Young Sitting Bull and Drumpacker), an Oglala headman and peace proponent not to be confused with the Hunkpapa of a similar name. This man, who carried an engraved repeater given him by President Grant the previous year, had grown distraught over the sale of the Black Hills and had recently journeyed from the Red Cloud Agency to join Crazy Horse. He argued forcefully on the futility of continuing to fight, especially in view of the suffering endured by the Cheyennes at the hands of Mackenzie. The other Sioux were The Yearling, Fat Hide, Lame Red Skirt, and Bad Leg. However, whites later recognized four of the five as people they knew as Tall Bull, Red Cloth, Red, and Bull Eagle, all Minneconjou headmen, the latter being the peace advocate that Miles had regarded so highly.

The Indians advanced down the Tongue Saturday morning, accompanied by perhaps two dozen other men leading the stolen horses. En route, they encountered cattle herders from the post and, later, a wood-cutting party, to whom they conveyed intelligence of their peaceful mission. Approaching the cantonment, the Sioux sent in the five chosen leaders with the army horses. These unarmed Indians continued riding ahead, bearing two white flags tied to lances. Shortly after 11 A.M. they came in sight of a number of Crow lodges pitched along the frozen Tongue on their right, at a distance from the cantonment. The Crows, numbering about one hundred, had been recruited at their agency and had arrived on November 25. In pretext of friendship, twelve of the scouts walked forward with hands outstretched. But when the Sioux reached out to shake hands, the Crows yanked their old enemies from their mounts, pulling them to the ground behind the garrison woodpiles, and beating, stabbing, and shooting them without mercy. On hearing the commotion, the entire command turned out under arms, but it was too late. Spotted Elk was among the Sioux who had waited in the distance. At the first sound of firing, he later reported, "we left our pack horses and ran back several hundred yards to a hill where we could get a better view. The firing had stopped, but we could see a great many people moving around in confusion, and [we] could hear the war song of the Crow Indians."[5]

The incident infuriated Miles, who immediately ordered the Crows disarmed, although the instigators fled into the hills and started up the Yellowstone for their agency, followed within two days by most of the rest of the scouts. Likening the tragedy to "unprovoked, cowardly murder," Miles accused the Crows of trying to hide the truce flags and thus conceal the enormity of

their crime. Only the day before he had threatened with hanging any Crow who killed one of his Yanktonais couriers.

Miles was particularly distressed over the loss of Bull Eagle.
The Minneconjou, who had been instrumental in the negotiations of October 27, had received Miles's assurances of continued support as he sought to comply with the surrender agreement. In early November, after Miles had left for Fort Peck,
Bull Eagle had come into the cantonment with several other
Sioux under a white flag to get rations, in accordance with earlier instructions. Wrote Miles:

> I [had] told him if he had any trouble in going in [to the Cheyenne
> River Agency], or [if] his people hesitated, or doubted that the Govern-
> ment would deal fairly and justly with them, to come back to me, and I
> would tell him what to do. . . . I could not but regard him with respect,
> as he appeared in every sense a chief, and seemed to be doing every-
> thing in his power for the good of his people, and endeavoring to bring
> them to a more peaceful condition.[6]

The deaths of Bull Eagle and the other chiefs clouded Miles's
hopes for shortening the war; he saw in their overture the best
chance for securing Minneconjou, Sans Arc, and Oglala submission. "It would have broken and reduced the influence and
power of Sitting Bull, Crazy Horse, and others, who are not yet
disposed to accept the terms of the Government." Confused
and angered by the rebuff, Crazy Horse turned against the discredited peace faction and prepared to prolong the conflict.
When two Sioux messengers arrived from Cheyenne River
about December 22 promoting peace, Crazy Horse, through
the council, spurned their arguments and prevented any of his
people from going off with them by killing their ponies. He
apparently never learned of an offering from Miles: twelve
Crow horses, sugar, coffee, and tobacco, plus a letter explaining the incident, with assurances that no whites had been involved. The two Sioux scouts Miles had sent out the day after
the killings returned in a few days, having been unable—or unwilling—to locate Crazy Horse. Instead, the Oglalas intensified
preparations to attack the soldiers: plans were established to
send a decoy party of fifty Oglalas and Cheyennes to the cantonment to draw the troops out, while the main force of warriors waited up the Tongue to ambush them.[7]

The failure to win a conciliatory end to the conflict nettled
Miles, and his soldiers, tired of campaigning through ice storms

and snowdrifts, saw that the lost opportunity for peace could only mean a resumption of field work. As always, the location of the various congregations of affected Indians was a major concern. A few days after the event, the Cheyennes and Sioux decided to separate because of difficulties in finding enough game to sustain the encampment. The Oglalas with Crazy Horse moved east up Hanging Woman Creek, while the Cheyennes with White Bull and Two Moon continued up the Tongue River. The division was short lived, however; the bands soon reassembled for mutual defense against Miles's soldiers. Following the departure of the decoy party, the Oglalas and Cheyennes moved their camps up the Tongue to a defensive position near the mouth of Prairie Dog Creek. Although the exact size of the assemblage cannot be stated, it is likely that the various bodies of Tetons and Cheyennes loosely arrayed under Crazy Horse and other leaders embraced as many as six hundred lodges—constituting the majority of the Indians who had overrun Custer the previous June. A growing paucity of game kept many of these groups scattered through the region of the upper Powder and Tongue, although the largest segment likely comprised those people with Crazy Horse.[8]

Meantime, Sitting Bull and his Hunkpapas lingered for a time in the country below the Yellowstone. After Baldwin's strike on December 18, the families had fled through the snow, much as the Cheyennes had done, finally regrouping south of the Yellowstone, where they hoped to join Crazy Horse. But it was not to be. Snowdrifts and distances complicated the effort and prevented a union of the two major Sioux bodies. Miles anticipated that the Sioux would meet in the area of the upper Rosebud and later claimed that the presence of his force at the mouth of the Tongue had prevented it. Most likely, however, bad luck, bad weather, and ill timing were to blame. There are indications, however, that Sitting Bull and a small party of Hunkpapas succeeded in making a brief visit to Crazy Horse's camp in about mid-January. Accounts stating that he brought the Oglalas new supplies of ammunition are probably untrue, for in all likelihood he remained destitute so soon after his encounter with Baldwin's soldiers.

It is doubtful that the army ever had a clear idea of the precise whereabouts of Sitting Bull during his time south of the Yellowstone after Baldwin's fight, mainly because it redirected its intelligence-gathering mechanism toward Crazy Horse. But by then the Hunkpapa leader had become an impotent factor, unable to command the dominating influence he had exercised earlier. Reportedly, he camped at the mouth of Little Powder River with 50 lodges in January, and was joined there by perhaps 150 lodges of Minneconjous, Hunkpapas, and Sans Arcs before crossing to the north of the Yellowstone. He traveled to the Missouri, finally passing beyond that stream to hunt and trade with local mixed-bloods not far from the British Possessions. On January 11, 1877, British authorities noted that 109 lodges of Sioux (later increasing to more than 200) had passed into Canada near Wood Mountain and announced their intention to remain there peaceably and permanently. Yet reports of Sitting Bull's continued presence in the Yellowstone-Missouri country persisted until late spring.[9] With the Hunkpapas neutralized geographically as well as politically, Sitting Bull thereafter remained but a remote ingredient in the war.

Late in 1876, following the killing of the Sioux chiefs, Miles turned his attention to the south. When his attempts at diplomacy with the Oglala camp failed, the colonel resorted to his time-tested military response. He sent word to the Crow agent, requesting the arrest of those guilty in the incident and the return of seventy-five Crow scouts to resume their service. Meantime, supply trains continued to arrive from downriver, escorted by men of the Twenty-second Infantry stationed at Glendive, ninety miles away. Through November and December they had brought grain and other provisions, including sutler goods, for use at the cantonment. Through November, wagon trains periodically came from upriver, too. A shipment of potatoes—a luxury item—also reached the garrison from Fort Ellis, above, but they were frozen on arrival. A drove of cattle from that post arrived on December 3, and tons of hay were hauled up the north bank of the Yellowstone from Fort Buford and Glendive to sustain the livestock.[10]

The military presence in the Yellowstone Valley late in 1876 already had stabilized the region and encouraged the introduction there of wholly civilian enterprise. In September, the sheep-raising industry of eastern Montana began on the Tongue, across from the cantonment, with the arrival from California of fourteen hundred head of Merlino-Cotswold mix en route to the Black Hills. Miles's nephew, George M. Miles, later purchased

the herd and, despite initial setbacks, managed to develop it profitably. On December 1, a diarist at the Glendive Cantonment
noted the passage of an ox train from Bozeman. "Truly the Yellowstone Valley is opened to civilization," he marveled. "This
was the first travel not connected with military operations on the
lower Yellowstone."[11]

Throughout the winter, work continued on the buildings at
the cantonment. Logs were raised, roofs nailed on, and exterior
walls plastered. One structure raised by the time Miles's men
returned from the Missouri was the sutler's store, and it soon
became a problem. Liquor was sold without appropriate regu-
lation, and the number of inebriated soldiers multiplied until,
as one man observed, "the Guard House was always full to
overflowing & Genl Miles said the whiskey caused him more
trouble than the Indians."[12] Miles tried several solutions, but in
the spring of 1877 finally closed the bar. Thereupon the traders
moved beyond the east edge of the military reservation and set
up shop, and drinking continued unabated. One trader was
found to be dispensing a lethal moonshine that left some soldiers dead. Over the next year a civilian community called
Milesburg or Milestown—later Miles City—grew up around this
log shantytown nucleus. (By 1879 the community boasted a
courthouse, a school, numerous restaurants and saloons, and
an industrial complex complete with blacksmiths, carpenters,
painters, and other mechanics—all largely dependent on the
military presence for their livelihood.)[13]

On December 20, four days after the slaying of the chiefs and
before his emmissaries to Crazy Horse had returned, Miles informed General Terry of his intended movement: "I shall now
endeavor to strike the large camp of Crazy Horse." To provide
the additional transportation required, he commandeered a civilian bull train of eight wagons, each drawn by a dozen oxen.[14]
While preparations ensued, the unavailability of adequate seasonal clothing again concerned officers and men. Quartermaster supplies were woefully insufficient and the men quickly went
into debt with the traders for such items as gloves, mittens, un-
derclothes, socks, overalls, and arctic overshoes.

Some soldiers fashioned blanket suits that proved comfort-
able, while most protected their heads from the icy blasts with
caps with ear flaps. Some fabricated face masks with openings
for eyes and mouth. Many wore canvas leggings, often blanket

25. Soldiers of the Fifth Infantry at Fort Keogh, ca. 1880, pose in buffalo overcoats and sealskin caps and gauntlets and carry Springfield trap-door rifles with fixed bayonets. Troops similarly attired fought the Sioux and Cheyennes at Wolf Mountains on January 8, 1877. (Custer Battlefield National Monument)

lined, made from shelter tents. Blankets were cut into assorted garb, including underclothing and trousers, while duck overalls safeguarded many soldiers against the cold. Buffalo overcoats, both manufactured locally and shipped in to the cantonment, were popular, despite their great weight, although their sheer bulkiness threatened to compromise the wearers' performance in action. "The problem to be solved," wrote Surgeon (Major) Henry R. Tilton, "is protection from the cold without being so bundled up as to be helpless." On their feet the soldiers wore rubber arctics or buffalo overshoes, although some managed to acquire oil-tanned snow pack boots before leaving the cantonment. In addition to burdensome clothing, each man carried the requisite haversack, canteen, ammunition, and a Springfield breechloading rifle that weighed in excess of eight pounds. "Efficiency was the object aimed at," wrote Lieutenant Baird, "and to this end the army belts and cartridge boxes had given place to canvas belts made by the soldiers, looped with the same to hold a row or two rows of metallic cartridges."[15]

Even as Miles announced his strategy to department headquarters, Teton and Northern Cheyenne warriors, unaware of these developments, began several maneuvers designed to coax the troops from their garrison. On Thursday, December 18, they attacked a mail party from Glendive along the road near Cedar Creek, forcing abandonment of the government animals and the mail. Eight days later, on the Twenty-sixth, the raiders struck close to the cantonment and drove off the beef contractor's herd, consisting of about 150 animals. In response, Miles the next morning directed Captain Charles J. Dickey to scout up the trail with Companies E (Dickey) and F (First Lieutenant Cornelius C. Cusick), Twenty-second Infantry, and D (First Lieutenant Robert McDonald) of the Fifth, accompanied by a supply train of the company wagons plus four of the ox-drawn civilian vehicles. Dickey's command got underway about ten o'clock, "after a good deal of fuss." Within a day, his scouts skirmished with four of the warriors and succeeded in taking back 108 head of the cattle. Apprised of this event, Miles on the twenty-eighth sent out First Lieutenant Mason Carter with his Company K, Fifth Infantry, and the twelve-pounder Napoleon disguised with bows and canvas to look like a wagon.

On the twenty-ninth, an intensely cold and gray day with spitting snow, Miles, now bearded against the weather, took the field with Companies A (Captain James S. Casey), C (Captain Edmond Butler), and E (Captain Ezra P. Ewers) of his regiment. Each company had been increased to fifty-eight men by assigning details of riflemen from the units left behind (Companies B, F, G, and I). Approximately forty of the soldiers, designated as a mounted infantry detachment commanded by Second Lieutenant Charles E. Hargous, rode into the field on the backs of ponies confiscated from the Sioux in October. Miles's entire command, including the detachments of Dickey and Carter, comprised 436 officers and men, besides five white scouts (including Kelly, Thomas Leforge, and "Liver-Eating" Johnson),

Robert Jackson, John Bruguier, two Crows, and one Bannock named Buffalo Horn. Also disguised as a wagon was Miles's other artillery piece, the three-inch ordnance rifle, in the charge of Second Lieutenant James W. Pope. Optimistic over his chances of catching the Sioux, Miles wrote his wife: "I expect to overtake them some sixty or seventy miles up the river, and then we make a fresh start from there."[16]

There is some indication that Miles's troops had not fully recuperated from the Fort Peck march. "Miles is working his men to death," wrote Major Hough. "His men are tired and worn and all men and officers seem dissatisfied. . . . I am afraid if he met with a large body of Indians his men would not be able physically to compete with them." As the troops pulled away from the cantonment, they presented a spectacle, arrayed in their heavy buffalo coats, with many soldiers, in the words of one chronicler, "fur-clad from head to foot; in lieu of a face there was . . . a frost-covered woolen muffler frozen solidly upon an ice-clad beard, 'trimmed with the same' in form of icicles."

Second Lieutenant Oscar F. Long, acting engineer officer, described the first day's march:

> The morning of the 29th of December, 1876, is cold and cheerless, the thermometer indicates 30 below zero. A burden of snow covers the ground, rests on the spreading branches of the trees that line the river's bank, and wreathes every stem and bough with fairy festoons of the most exquisite design. The train starts early from the cantonment, crosses Tongue River twice on the ice, and after a march of 11-1/2 miles, crosses the river again just previous to making camp at 2:05 p.m. The valley is well timbered with cottonwood along the line of the day's march, and high sterile bluffs hem it in on either side. About 6 miles from the cantonment Tongue Buttes stand prominent among the surrounding bad lands on the east bank of the river. The valley averages 1 mile in width.[18]

On the thirtieth, the combined force pushed up the Tongue, crossing the frozen stream ten times in the ascent and fording Pumpkin Creek where it entered from the east. Moving ahead next morning, the column found the Tongue Valley becoming wider, its bordering buttes and ridges topped with pine, its winding stream still demanding frequent passage. The soldiers tramped through snow eight inches deep, occasionally coming upon dead cattle, before overtaking Dickey and Carter, forty-

26. John ("Liver-Eating") Johnson, who scouted for Miles in 1876–77. A huge man, Johnson hunted and trapped through the Yellowstone region and later became a Montana law officer. He died in 1900 in California. Photographer unknown. (Denver Public Library, Western History Department)

27. Miles posed with some of his officers and staff in frigid temperatures just before starting up the Tongue River after Crazy Horse in January 1877. From left to right: Second Lieutenant Oscar F. Long, engineer officer; Surgeon (Major) Henry R. Tilton; Second Lieutenant James W. Pope (wearing an enlisted man's pleated fatigue blouse); Miles (in buffalo overcoat); First Lieutenant Frank D. Baldwin, acting regimental adjutant; Second Lieutenant Charles E. Hargous; and Second Lieutenant Hobart K. Bailey. Headquarters guards and orderlies stand in the rear, and the mounted individual behind Long is scout Luther S. ("Yellowstone") Kelly. (National Archives)

six miles up the Tongue. As the officers at headquarters prepared their bivouac that evening, they discovered that the crates containing their canvas-wall tents had been mislabeled and they would have to endure the freezing journey in tents of linen.[19]

On New Year's Day, reveille sounded at 4:30 A.M. and the journey resumed under the light of the moon. Each day Miles had followed standardized procedures, marching before or shortly after daylight, with a guard unit well in front and flankers along each side of the column. At the close of the day a good defensive site with timber and water was selected, the snow

28. Artillery played an important part in Miles's operations. Here his gun crews pose in the snow near the Tongue River Cantonment in January 1877, with the three-inch ordnance rifle and the twelve-pounder Napoleon gun. Both pieces performed valuable service in the Battle of Wolf Mountains. (National Archives)

cleared away, the picket guard established, and the scouts and flankers withdrawn. The animals grazed until dusk, when they were corralled to feed on cottonwood bark cut for them. As January 1 wore on, the weather moderated. Rain fell and the road turned slushy, slowing progress. In the evening, as the soldiers stopped in a woods below the mouth of Otter Creek to camp, the Crows out in front startled twenty-five or thirty warriors, who fled on horseback. The scouts exchanged gunfire with the Indians and chased them a short distance. Immediately, Miles threw skirmishers across the Tongue Valley and sent troops to take some high bluffs on the right, but by then the warriors could be seen moving off two miles away. "It is useless to pursue them," wrote a diarist, "for we have no cavalry."[20]

Leaving the slow-moving wagons and driving the oxen ahead, the command on January 2 sluggishly advanced only five miles, diverting briefly from the valley to bypass difficult terrain. En route, the soldiers came on an abandoned camp consisting of shelters rudely erected from rocks, poles, and sections of earth, suggesting to Yellowstone Kelly that it had been occupied by the Cheyennes lately rousted by Mackenzie. Regaining the valley, the command crossed the Tongue four times before bivouacking for the night, the animals exhausted.[21]

At dawn on the third, the men proceeded along the valley floor, which gradually increased in altitude. They left behind four mounted soldiers and a civilian guide to round up stray oxen. No sooner had the rear guard gone beyond sight of the bivouac, when fifteen or twenty Indians appeared from the bluffs and attacked the herders, killing one, Private William H. Batty of Company C, Fifth Infantry, and wounding one of the oxen. At the sound of shooting, a company raced back over the trail but arrived too late. The warriors had fled. Dr. Tilton examined the dead soldier. "As I saw him in his long Buffalo overcoat, I realized how perfectly helpless he must have been against a savage stripped for the fight."[22] The body was buried on the road, the gravesite effaced by rolling wagons over it. Pushing ahead, the troops passed Turtle Creek and halted at noon after crossing the Tongue. Noted Lieutenant Long: "The ice, made weak by recent rains, will scarcely support the weight of our heavily-loaded wagons." Hoping to learn something of the distribution of the Indians, Miles sent Kelly and the scouts to find out whether any camps lay in Rosebud Valley to the west. The scouts returned at dawn, having found no confirming signs.[23]

Evidence of the nearing proximity of the Indians increased over the next two days as the column continued southwest. On Thursday, the fourth, the troops marched through "a cold, continuous rain" that complicated their passage and camped in the afternoon across from the mouth of Otter Creek, near the present community of Ashland. By then, almost all the snow had melted, so that on Friday, amid steady rainfall, the men plodded through mud. By then, too, the formerly wide valley had contracted into a serpentine canyon, the imposing shale and sandstone bluffs that approached the river on either side necessitating its frequent crossing. As the low-lying Wolf Mountains heaved into sight, Indian signs appeared everywhere in the form of abandoned war lodges—vestiges of the recent habitation of upper Tongue Valley. The soldiers discovered wandering cattle along with the remains of slaughtered oxen, while great quantities of cottonwood trees had been stripped of their bark by the Indian ponies. The men camped late that day, having marched almost fifteen miles.[24]

On January 6, heavy snow returned, its blinding fury lasting all day and impeding the advance. The Wolf Mountains, a localized range of rugged, pine-topped bluffs of shale, coal, and sandstone bordering the upper Tongue Valley, afforded scenic grandeur in their muted whites, grays, pinks, and purples. In crossing the Tongue, the soldiers had to cut away the earthen banks as well as the ice to accommodate the wagons, a process that consumed many hours. More Indian camps were encountered scattered through the valley; in one, several gaunt ponies still grazed while campfires smoldered. "We infer from this," wrote Lieutenant Long, "that the camp is aware of our presence, has been moving slowly, and is but a short distance in advance of us." The riflemen encamped at 4 P.M. on a grassy site above Hanging Woman Creek, having covered fifteen miles. As night fell, hail and wind joined the snow and the temperature dipped below zero once more.[25]

The movement of Miles's command up the Tongue seems to have aligned perfectly with Crazy Horse's plan. Coincidental or not with that design, the village sites through which the soldiers passed on the fifth and sixth constituted a special enticement for Miles; if in fact the Indian plan was approaching fruition, it was because the military was going eagerly for the bait. Miles was not altogether oblivious to the warriors' intentions, although he believed that the withdrawal was calculated to distance the warriors from him and his command and secure a stronger defensive position in the increasingly rugged fastness of the upper Tongue Valley. By that time the intertribal assemblage occupied a position near Deer Creek, approximately twenty miles above the command. Colonel Miles estimated their number at twelve hundred.

On January 7 an incident occurred that accelerated the warriors' timetable for attacking the soldiers. The march that day was uneventful except for its brevity. New snow had fallen during the night. The troops departed camp at 7:30 A.M. and traveled only two and one-half miles before stopping in a grove of cottonwoods along the east side of the Tongue, having crossed the stream three times in that distance. That afternoon Miles directed Kelly and his scouts forward to look for the Sioux camp.[26] The scouts advanced about three miles to a position on a high bluff. Through field glasses they spotted a group coming down the valley—mostly women, who showed no caution and appeared ignorant as to the location of the village and the nearness of the troops. Kelly told his Indian scouts not to harm them, then moved down a gully and approached the party while making peaceful gestures. The anxious Indians halted and the women started crying, whereupon the Crows took turns touching each with their coup sticks.

The party consisted of one young man about fourteen years old, four women, and three children, and included their ponies, lodges, food, and baggage. "I surmised," remembered Kelly later, "that they were probably members of some prominent Sioux family who had been on a visit to some distant camp, and returning missed their people who were all around us."[27] In fact, the people were Cheyennes. Seven of the group have been identified: Sweet Taste Woman, the oldest; her daughters, Crooked Nose Woman and Fingers Woman; Twin Woman, widow of the Southern Cheyenne leader, Lame White Man, who was killed at the Little Bighorn; that chief's two daughters, Crane Woman (Buffalo Cow) and Red Hat (Red Hood); and Black Horse, the adolescent warrior. Kelly was correct about their reason for traveling. They were en route from a sojourn with Teton relatives near the Belle Fourche River and had been lured by the smoke from Miles's bivouac, which they mistook to be from their people's village. Kelly's scouts signed to them, directing them to the army camp, where they were fed and given shelter.[28]

After accompanying the Cheyennes to the bivouac, the five white scouts returned up the valley, crossing to the west side of the Tongue to see if any warriors were approaching. Besides Kelly, there were Thomas Leforge, Liver-Eating Johnson, George Johnson, and James Parker. At dusk the soldiers heard firing upstream. Immediately they took up arms and deployed around the camp, while Miles assembled three companies, the three-inch gun, and Lieutenant Hargous's mounted detachment and moved out to Kelly's assistance. Warriors on horseback followed along the hills on either side of the relief battalion, while distant gunfire still resounded down the valley. The scouts had stumbled into an ambush and, in the surprise of the moment, had charged the body of Indians waiting behind a ridge. "That is where we made a mistake," remembered Kelly. The Indians fired back at them, driving them into a stand of timber, where they opened a pitched fight with more than one hundred warriors closing on three sides. Kelly recalled their race for the woods: "To reach it we were compelled to jump our horses down a rocky shelf five or six feet to solid ground. All this time the Indians were firing away at us, the bullets striking the rocks and raising little dust patches from the ground. It was miraculous that no one was seriously hurt."[29] The Indian scouts, meantime, had followed Kelly's group and had assumed a line some two to three hundred yards from the besieged party, in the direction of the troop encampment. One of the Indian scouts—the Bannock, Buffalo Horn—joined Kelly in the timber and performed excellent service in keeping the Sioux and Cheyennes at bay.

Three-quarters of a mile above his camp, Miles directed Captain Casey to take position in front, on a hill on the west side of the Tongue. Casey charged ahead with Company A, the field gun, and the mounted unit and crossed the frozen stream. More than two hundred warriors advanced on Casey's line and brisk shooting lasted until darkness, when several artillery rounds hastened the Indians' withdrawal. The Indians had inflicted no casualties other than two horses killed, although one unofficial report indicated that Liver-Eating Johnson had "had a furrow cut through his long hair; he said it was *close.*" The skirmish seems to have occurred after the Indians had learned the fate of the eight Cheyennes and had initiated efforts to rescue them.[30]

The night passed with tension. Anticipating action, the command remained watchful. The Cheyennes, meantime, convened a nighttime council in their camp at the mouth of Deer Creek to determine what do to about the captives. Apparently the headmen of the warrior societies decided to launch an all-out assault the next morning, and sometime after midnight the war party started downstream to the soldier camp. A small group of Cheyennes that had left earlier succeeded in approaching the bivouac and opened communication with one of the captives before they were driven off by pickets. Snow continued to fall through the night.[31]

It was fourteen degrees and still snowing at daybreak, when Miles's soldiers began preparing breakfast. The encampment lay in a cottonwood grove along a jutting bend in the river, across which, to the north, low hills melded with the familiar red bluffs beyond. About four hundred yards southwest of the command stood a long, precipitous ridge, surmounted near the middle by a shaley knob and in front of which a dry creek bed (today called Battle Butte Creek) ran to the river. As a precautionary measure, during the night Miles's men had thrown up breastworks on this knoll. Three hundred yards farther south, a prominent butte, later known as Battle Butte, overlooked the field. Southeast of the troops, timbered hills and bluffs shot up three hundred feet to dominate the scene, while to their north the iced-over Tongue veered sharply south and east, then northeast down the valley floor.

Early that morning, Miles climbed the butte where the breastworks had been dug and peered through a field glass along the river bottom. Through rising mist he saw hundreds of Indians in the distance. In his official report, he estimated that six hundred mounted warriors confronted him, a figure conforming with the recollections of others. Making no pretense at hiding, the Indians suddenly appeared on the heights along the river. Some yelled defiantly to the soldiers that they "would eat no more fat meats," a statement construed by Miles to mean that the men had eaten their last breakfast.[32] Responding in the Lakota tongue, Kelly challenged the warriors to battle and called them women. At 7 A.M., some of the warriors commenced moving toward the soldiers.

Miles reacted quickly, deploying his men to keep from being surrounded. Lieutenant Carter with Company K, Fifth Infantry, crossed the ice and took position below the hills on the west side of the stream; Captain Dickey and Lieutenant Cusick with E and F of the Twenty-second positioned themselves on the east side, facing downstream, the right of their line adjoining the base of a low plateau or bench, below which stood the supply train. Above, on the edge of the plateau, Miles posted his two artillery pieces under Lieutenant Pope. The soldiers of Company A, Fifth Infantry, stood in support, their commander, Captain Casey, ready to assist shelling warriors in the ravines and woods across the Tongue. On Casey's left, atop the long ridge with its conical knoll, were Captain Ezra P. Ewers and Company E.

29. Engraving of the Battle of Wolf Mountains, January 8, 1877, prepared from a sketch furnished by an officer of the expedition. This is a somewhat distorted view to the southwest, showing the prominent butte held by Captain Ewers's company throughout the fighting. In the lower right foreground are the artillery pieces, and on the left, Miles's infantrymen advance against Indian positions in the towering distant hills. (*Frank Leslie's Illustrated Newspaper*, May 5, 1877)

Ewers held this dominating ridge throughout the ensuing battle, and upon its retention or loss hung the balance between military success or failure on the field. Finally, guarding against an assault from the rear, Captain Butler and Lieutenant McDonald placed Companies C and D in skirmish order, facing east and parallel with the bend in the river. The entire line was thinly arrayed, wrote an officer. "Every man must be a hero, for there is no touch of elbow and no rear rank. . . . No one who has not participated in such an engagement . . . can realize how short a line a score or two of men make, springing boldly out in single rank, flanks in air and no support."[33]

At the deployment, the initial Indian attack melted away, the warriors assuming positions along the hills and buttes on either side of the bottom. They did not fire from horseback and used their ponies only to convey themselves from one area of the field to another. Miles reported that they signaled each other with "loud shrill whistles," probably made of eagle bone. The buffalo-coated riflemen labored through the snow as quickly as they could to meet the first gunfire from the Indians west of the river. When within range, the soldiers opened fire, the sounds of their weapons rumbling through the valley beneath the gray sky. Simultaneously, the Napoleon gun was hauled forward, its canvas cover pulled away, and several rounds directed at the Indians. The sounds of exploding projectiles reverberated loudly and momentarily caused great commotion among the Indians, but did them no physical harm.

West of the river, Captain Dickey's men joined in the shooting, and eventually the warriors pulled back. One man at that location recalled having fired his weapon so much that his "gun barrel was sizzling hot."[34] All the while the artillery lobbed exploding shells over the heads of the soldiers to fall among the tribesmen. Shortly the Indians abandoned that flank, having succeeded only in wounding two pack animals. Thereafter they concentrated on the range of high bluffs east of the stream, where the heaviest fighting took place. Carter's infantrymen withdrew across the ice and assumed an exposed position in the valley bottom. On the far left of the command, the warriors mounted the imposing flat-topped bluff (Battle Butte) directly south of the knoll occupied by Ewers's men, from which height they dominated those soldiers. From his position near the artillery, Miles directed Casey with Company A to take the almost perpendicular butte, replacing Casey's unit with Butler's company, summoned from its rear guard position on the valley bottom. McDonald's company was soon brought in on Butler's right. Meantime, to protect the rear flank, Miles sent Company F, Twenty-second Infantry, to ford the river and establish rifle pits on the commanding bluff north of the field.

Captain Casey's assault on the high southeastern bluff became a dangerous mission. As the soldiers stormed across the flat terrain, warriors ensconced in the hills and timber to the right of Battle Butte opened a heavy fire on them. Atop the lofty bluff, a Cheyenne medicine man later identified as Big

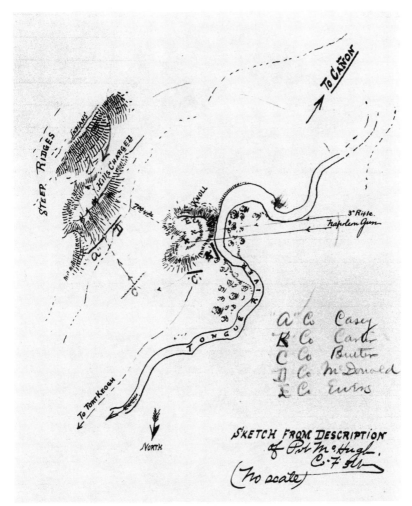

30. John McHugh was a sergeant in charge of the twelve-pounder Napoleon gun at Wolf Mountains. In 1891 he accompanied this sketch map with his recollections of the encounter: "The General told me to shell the Indians over the heads of Cos. 'A' and 'D.' These companies were at that moment engaged in a hot rifle fight with masses of the Indians [on the left]. . . . I continued to shell the Indians until they were driven clear back. The range was not long—700 yds I should say, for I had scarcely any elevation on the gun." (Deposition of John McHugh, August 4, 1891, Baird Papers, Kansas State Historical Society.) (Boot Hill Museum, Inc., Dodge City, Kansas)

31. Second Lieutenant James Worden Pope, West Point class of 1868, commanded Company E, Fifth Infantry, during the Cedar Creek fighting and wrote an important eyewitness account of that encounter. At Wolf Mountains, Pope commanded Miles's two artillery pieces. He later served as commandant of the U.S. Military Prison at Fort Leavenworth and as chief quartermaster of the expeditionary force to the Philippines in 1898. Pope retired as a brigadier general in 1916 and died in Denver in 1919. (Special Collections Division, USMA Library)

Crow sallied out in war regalia, including feathered eagle headdress, and began dancing in full view of the command. Their
bullets missed him for several minutes, until the riflemen approached close enough to take bead on Big Crow and another
Indian. The soldiers advanced under a raking fire from above,
presently gaining the steep bluff and ascending its rocky slope.
One enlisted man, Corporal Augustus Rathman, died instantly
from a bullet wound to the head during the maneuver with
Casey. Two men were wounded. On top, a group of two
hundred dismounted warriors attempted to regain the position,
charging within fifty yards of the company from a neighboring
hill. Casey's troops efficiently repelled them with help from
McDonald's Company D, sent by Miles to prevent the Indians
from turning Casey's left, but which, in fact, drifted to a position on Casey's right. This erroneous placement caused Miles
to send forth Butler's Company C.

Butler focused on the continuing advance of the warriors on
Casey's left. Unchecked, they would outflank the troops and
rake the rear of the line with their fire. "Take your company
and take that hill," Miles told Butler, pointing to the highest
summit at the left. Moving forward in double time across the
bottom to the base of the bluff, Company C drew heavy fire
from Sioux and Cheyennes in the timber and began to swerve
from its course. Lieutenant Baldwin, as acting adjutant, dashed
forward with a crate of rifle ammunition precariously balanced
on the front of his saddle to tell Butler to move farther to the
left in his ascent. As his horse plunged ahead, Baldwin lost control of the box of cartridges and most tumbled into the snow.
Undeterred, the lieutenant kept on, shouting encouragement
to the men as he passed up the slippery grade. Details of the
action were recollected by Butler:

> Facing by the right flank, the company charged up the first rise. The
> left of the company was a little in advance, owing to the nature of the
> initial movement. From ravines, and from behind rocks and fallen trees,
> the force was concentrated on this portion of the line. It seemed to
> those who watched the movement that nothing could save this company
> from decimation. Butler's horse was shot under him as he led the
> charge up the first ascent. The steepest part of the ridge was yet to be
> scaled. Giving the Indians in the ravine a volley, and taking the run, Co.
> C moved up, its commander now on foot. The men behaved admirably,
> dashed up through the snow and over rocks, firing as they advanced—

32. The Fifth Infantry in action against Crazy Horse's warriors at Wolf Mountains, January 8, 1877, as depicted by Frederic Remington. (Miles, *Personal Recollections*)

not a man of the company or the detachments of G and F attached to it, lagging or flinching—and drove the Indians from the hill. Many of these were concealed behind fallen cedars and improvised breastworks of flat stones. From these positions they fired volley after volley. Fully 400 shots were fired at this company from Winchester and Sharps rifles, and, under Providence, only the plunging nature of the fire, which made it too high, the precipitate rapidity with which the Indians worked their magazine guns, which made it uncertain, and the impetuous rush of the men which demoralized their opponents, saved this company from heavy loss.[35]

Aided by several rounds from Pope's three-inch gun, the troops succeeded in driving the Indians back across several lines of bluffs, the men stumbling, sliding, and falling as they scaled the ice-covered cliffs in their heavy garb. Two of Butler's men, Privates Philip Kennedy and Patton G. Whited, were first to mount the crest and face heavy fire from the warriors. Both later received Medals of Honor. Once on top, Baldwin directed a detachment of Company C into position, then moved to the right and instructed McDonald, "by order of General Miles, to move forward with his company and drive the Indians out." Three men with McDonald were wounded in this advance against warriors posted on a hill about 100 yards away. During the action, Dr. Tilton said later, "fires were made by the Indians to make up for lack of clothing, while our men stamped their feet to keep warm."[36]

Meantime, Company K, Fifth Infantry, and Companies E and F, Twenty-second, stayed near the river, protecting the supply wagons, which were arranged in rows with the pack mules in between after several had been killed near the bivouac. These soldiers remained for hours "lying in deep snow . . . and suffering intensely from the cold." In addition to Baldwin, Lieutenant Long, the expedition's engineer officer, acted as an aide to Miles and spent the morning carrying orders among the various field commands. In the wagon park, Drs. Tilton and Louis S. Tesson treated the wounded. Finally, at noon, after five hours of combat, a blowing snowstorm descended, blinding the adversaries and causing the fighting to slow and finally stop. Rebuffed in their attempts to outflank the soldiers, and further demoralized with the loss of Big Crow, the warriors filed back up the valley, bearing their wounded, Miles's guns lofting shells after them. The troops pursued for only three miles. "I concluded," wrote Miles, "that it was useless to try to catch mounted men on the run with foot soldiers."[37]

The accounts of the Sioux and Cheyennes who participated in the fighting on January 8 were not immediately available. A few were made known to whites within weeks, but most such oral renderings stayed within the tribal cultures for years. Nevertheless, a study of Indian testimony regarding Wolf Mountains indicates that the accounts generally conform to the military description of the action while providing particulars of what individual tribesmen experienced. They suggest that the Cheyennes and Sioux planned to ambush the soldiers by using the decoy party to draw them from their camp to a point some two miles upstream, between Battle Butte and the mouth of Wall Creek, where the mass of warriors lingered. But the decoys advanced too quickly, revealing their position and giving away

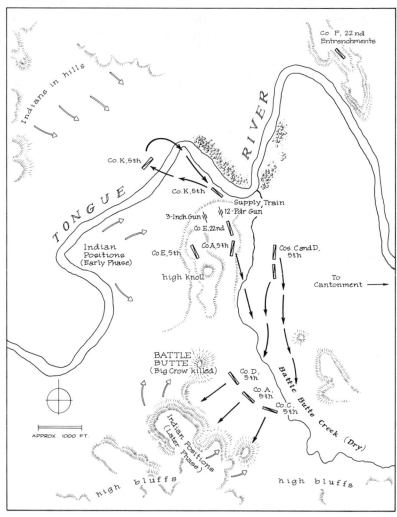

5. The Battle of Wolf Mountains, January 8, 1877

the plan before it could be executed, so that the warriors waiting behind had to come forward.

Armed with Henry and Winchester lever action rifles and with Springfield carbines taken from Custer's men, the Indians first fired on the tents of the soldiers, only to discover that the

men had left them to assemble near the ridge and butte southwest of the camp and had taken the Cheyenne captives with
them. The soldiers, probably those with Captain Ewers, returned fire from that position. Many Oglalas, including Crazy
Horse, posted behind a ridge west of the Tongue, fired bullets
and arrows on Miles's men crossing on the ice. Wooden Leg
remembered: "Many Indians were hidden behind rocks and
were shooting toward the soldiers. I chose for myself a hiding
place and did the same. I had my soldier rifle and plenty of
cartridges. Many soldiers were coming across on the ice, to fight
us. But we had the advantage of them because of our position
on the high and rocky ridge."[38]

Also west of the stream, Sioux warriors drove some of the
soldiers from breastworks they had dug on that side (where the
Indian accounts say a field piece stood), while a charge from
the north led by the Cheyenne chief Medicine Bear skirted the
west bank, then crossed the frozen river in an assault along the
ridge held by Ewers's company. This charge was disrupted by
an artillery shell that struck the chief's horse but failed to explode. A number of Oglala boys watched the action from afar.
Black Elk remembered that the cannon projectiles did not always explode and that one ball "went right above [them] and
one of the boys went out and picked it up and brought it
home."[39]

When the action shifted south, many of the Indians hid in
the rocks on the bluffs to meet Casey's assault. The warriors,
low on ammunition, used their weapons as clubs to help beat
back the advance. Wooden Leg described the loss of Big Crow:

> [He] kept walking back and forth along a ridge on the side toward the
> soldiers. He was wearing a warbonnet. He had a gun taken from the
> soldiers at the Little Bighorn battle. He used up his cartridges and came
> back to us hidden behind the rocks, to ask for more. Cheyennes and
> Sioux here and there each gave him one or two or three. He soon got
> enough to fill his belt. He went out again to walk along the ridge, to
> shoot at the soldiers and to defy them in their efforts to hit him with a
> bullet. . . . Big Crow finally dropped down. He lay there alive, but ap-
> parently in great distress. A Sioux went with me to crawl down to where
> he was and bring him into shelter. Another Sioux came after us. . . .
> The three of us crawled and dragged him along on the snow.[40]

The warriors withdrew from in front of Casey's surging command, and the injured medicine man was carried away in a blan-

ket. At his request, he was wrapped in a buffalo robe and left behind; Wooden Leg and other Cheyennes found his body the next spring, still covered with the robe. After Big Crow was shot, the quickening blizzard cut visibility. That, together with low ammunition, forced the Indians to gradually pull back and stop fighting. Crazy Horse and several other Sioux acted as rear guard in the withdrawal.[41]

Casualties suffered by both sides at Wolf Mountains appear to have been minimal. Miles reported one man killed and nine wounded. Considering all the shooting by the troops, Indian casualties were surprisingly few. "We wasted an awful lot of ammunition," remembered one man.[42] A Northern Cheyenne, Wooden Leg, stated that Big Crow was the only Cheyenne killed, and that only two Sioux had been killed. Another Indian said that three more warriors had been wounded, and that two of these died later; and a Sioux named Eagle Shield remembered only three Indians wounded and one Cheyenne and one Sioux (Runs the Bear) killed. Despite these tallies, Miles's officers noted that as many as twenty-three Indians fell during the fighting (most of them in front of Casey, McDonald, and Butler) and were presumed dead. Miles believed their loss to be "about twelve or fifteen killed and twenty five or thirty wounded." Several warrior positions examined after the battle contained blood on the snow, and blood was seen along the route of the Indians' withdrawal.[43]

The soldiers followed the Indians up the valley, then returned late in the afternoon to move their camp to the bench near the artillery so they might guard against surprise. Before nightfall, the snow turned to rain, which lasted until morning. The army campfires drew a volley from hidden warriors, causing the men to extinguish the flames for the night. Miles was jubilant at his success, having bested the Tetons and their Cheyenne allies in a contest played out on their terms and on their terrain. He cited the performance of his men and officers: "I never saw troops behave better or fight with more coolness or pluck."[44] "Captains Casey and Butler and Lieutenant McDonald are entitled to great praise for the cool and determined manner in which they led and handled their companies under fire, and Lieutenant Baldwin for his gallantry in leading a charge." Years later, Casey, Butler, and McDonald received Medals of Honor for their brave assault up the bluffs.[45]

33. Looking north across the Wolf Mountains battleground from the principal Indian positions in the hills. The distant tree line shows the course of the Tongue River. Company E, Fifth Infantry, held the high butte at center throughout the fighting, while Companies A, D, and C traversed the lower ground at the right in advancing against the Sioux and Cheyennes. During the battle the ground was covered with snow. (L. Clifford Soubier)

At 2 P.M. on January 9, Miles led the scouts, the mounted detachment, and six companies up the valley to see where the Indians had gone. During the advance upstream, pickets held the bluffs that had been fought over the previous day and guarded the wagons. The troops moved forward in skirmish order, their line extending from the hills on the east side all the way across the valley floor to those on the west side. They found the site of one recently abandoned encampment, but returned to their bivouac at dusk without firm knowledge of the Indians' whereabouts. Miles lacked enough supplies to continue the pursuit, and he feared that uncertainties in the weather might jeopardize his men. Consequently, he turned his command about and started for the cantonment.[46]

After the fighting at Wolf Mountains, the Indians wasted little time moving away from the area, to protect their camps.
Some Oglalas and Minneconjous journeyed up Hanging
Woman Creek, while others, including Crazy Horse, returned
with the Cheyennes farther up the Tongue to the large village
at Deer Creek. Accompanying that body were the Northern
Cheyenne chiefs Little Wolf and Dull Knife, among other leaders. Those Indians traveled through the night of the eighth and
all the next day to escape the soldiers. By all accounts, recent
events perplexed the Indians, who were becoming desperate.
Most importantly, they lacked clothing and food, and the winter
climate, coupled with the army pressure, made their existence
miserable. In the upper Tongue Valley, however, they found
buffalo. The Indians eventually moved west to hunt along the
headwaters of the Little Bighorn and Bighorn, remaining in
that region for weeks before Crazy Horse headed east to the
Little Powder River. Hard times returned, and the Indians once
more began to eat their starving ponies. Evidently, because of
the necessity of obtaining sufficient food, the camps began to
fragment and go their separate ways, with some heading in the
direction of the agencies. Several bands, mostly Minneconjous
and Sans Arcs, joined their kin in small camps along the Little
Missouri River north of the Black Hills.[47]

On January 10, Miles's fatigued soldiers marched toward
home. "Our stock is very much exhausted, and the rations are
getting low," wrote Lieutenant Long. They made only seven
miles that day because of the weather, which one enlisted man,
Edwin M. Brown, described as "stormy and cold." The following two days brought little relief, and many men suffered from
frozen limbs while wading through the foot-deep snow. Private
Bernard McCann, wounded at Wolf Mountains, died on the
twelfth. Brown noted in his diary for the thirteenth: "Marched
about 15 miles and camped in one of our old camps. Thermometer at 40° below zero. . . . The marching was very rough owing
to the snow being frozen in crusts." Making things worse, the
alternating freezing and thawing of Tongue River made the frequent crossings of that stream treacherous, with mules and
wagons having to be removed "by sheer force when they broke
through."[48]

The weather now posed a greater threat to the safety of the
command than did the Indians. The intense cold, driven by un-

remitting winds, became practically unbearable, and some cases of frostbite occurred. As Dr. Tilton testified,

> The men got accustomed to the symptoms of frost bite and occasionally one could be seen to drop out of the ranks, take off his shoes and rub his toes with snow. As I was riding along one day in the face of a snow and wind storm, with the thermometer down below zero, I saw a man who was rubbing his nose with snow and relieving his mind at the same time by uttering in the most bitter tone, "G——D D——N it!" "What's the matter, nipped your nose?" I inquired. "Yes, my nose and fingers and everything else. G——D D——N it." The tone of voice spoke volumes.

Tilton noted that "only one man had his face frost bitten. Not many fingers were frost bitten and I am glad to be able to say that no toes will be lost."[49]

The doctor offered appraisals of several articles of winter clothing used by the troops that he believed contributed to the discomfort of the march. Buffalo overcoats, he observed, were "too heavy and long in the skirt" for any service other than guard duty. "It is extremely difficult to march in them." Tilton recommended that their skirts be shortened for field use. Such bulky, burdensome attire, however, seems to have been the norm on the Wolf Mountains expedition. His own campaign apparel exemplified such "bundling up":

> I wore two pair of woolen socks, buffalo mocassins and leggins, and buffalo overshoes; 2 pr drawers, one of them buckskin; 2 pr pants, one made out of blanket; 5 shirts, one of them buckskin and one made out of blanket; a coat and buffalo overcoat; blanket cap, which would cover the face when necessary; a comforter; [and] buck-skin gloves inside of blanket lined buckskin mittens—and yet, on two days when marching in the face of a snow and wind storm, I felt as if there were no blood in my body.[50]

Of the two types of footwear employed by the soldiers, Tilton favored the newly adopted vulcanized rubber arctics over the old pattern buffalo overshoes. "It was painful to see men laboring along in buffalo overshoes, the soles of which becoming slippery, they slid all over the surface and gave the men a tumble at nearly every gully and ravine." At Wolf Mountains, the problems posed by this type of footwear on troops scaling the bluffs above the Tongue must have been particularly acute. Most incidents of frostbite to toes and feet occurred among men wearing buffalo overshoes and plain leather campaign shoes with cable-screwed soles. Speaking of the latter, Tilton complained: "The cable screwed shoes would have a deposit of frost around each piece of metal, on the inside of the sole, every cold morning. Many of the boots and shoes would be coated with a cake of ice inside when they were not dried out in the night."[51] Wet feet became a problem almost daily, especially for those men assigned picket duty each evening, who had no chance to dry their feet.

In sum, Tilton described a command riddled with illness caused by fatigue and exposure. Frequent cases of rheumatism were present, and on "some nights it was impossible for the men to sleep, on account of the cold; coughing could be heard from one end of the Battalion to the other." At each bivouac the men built roaring campfires to keep warm, often standing so close as to badly scorch their clothing. "Shoes, pantaloon legs, and coat skirts were burned in at least 20 per cent of the command."[52]

Under those conditions, the men of Miles's command endured an expedition of recurring privations that led them into largely unknown country, placed them in combat against a determined and desperate foe, and brought them out under equally trying circumstances. On the return march the men followed the trail they had made coming in, camping at their previous bivouacs. On January 14, en route down the Tongue, they exhumed the body of Private Batty to take home, reaching the site of their fifth camp just as a major storm blew in. Polar temperatures persisted through the rest of the journey, and the haggard command, evoking images of "Napoleon's army marching into [sic] Russia," gained the cantonment at noon on the eighteenth, to the rousing strains of the Fifth Infantry band playing "Marching through Georgia." The laborious 190-mile undertaking, during which the soldiers had crossed Tongue River more than one hundred times, had sapped all participants. "The men," recorded Brown, "[are] elated at the prospects of glowing fires in nice snug and warm quarters, shelter from the bleak mountain winds, well cooked meals and a good wash."[53]

Over the next few days the troops who had accompanied Miles rested while resuming their garrison duties. Rumors of Indians nearby filled the air, though most were quickly discounted. Four days after the soldiers returned, an alarm that the cattle herd had been captured sent one hundred of them back into the field. Leaving at 11 P.M., the men came back four hours later to pronounce the report untrue. On the twenty-third, some of the troops and animals that had campaigned with Miles started down the Yellowstone to Glendive. In solemn cadence, others accompanied the muffled remains of Batty, Rathman, and McCann to a spot on the bluffs, where they were interred.[54]

The outcome of the Wolf Mountains expedition created an afterglow that permeated the cantonment. The campaign, said Miles, was "one of the most successful in [the] history of Indian warfare," and in celebration he opened the sutler's bars to his men. Yet the old frustrations reappeared, too. Back at the cantonment, Miles learned that Terry, responding to budgetary cutbacks, had directed the release of all but two of Miles's civilian scouts, along with his packers, guides, teamsters, and blacksmiths, and had ordered him to send most of his wagons down to Fort Buford. This news angered him. In a letter to his wife, he castigated Terry for "the outrageous way I am supported. . . . I do not believe that General Terry ever reads my reports or pays any attention to my requests. [The directive, moreover,] virtually compels me to abandon the campaign" on the verge of total success. He implicitly charged Terry with politically toying with the Sioux War: "There seems to be a determination that this war shall not be ended this winter, or that it shall not be ended by this command."[55] On January 20, Miles wrote General Sherman, venting his feelings and endorsing a more independent command for himself. In his insistent manner, he boldly requested that Sherman establish for him a department embracing the war zone: "If I have not earned a command I never will, and if I have not given proof of my ability to bring my command into a successful encounter with Indians every time I never will. . . . If you will give me this command and one half the troops now in it, I will end this Sioux war once and forever in four months."[56]

Miles's heated petition was momentarily ignored, along with his appeal that his regiment be transferred out of Montana should his request be denied. A few days later Miles made formal recommendations for closing the war with the Sioux and Cheyennes. He urged the establishment of supply camps in the upper Tongue drainage and in the badlands of the Little Missouri, where the remaining Indians still found refuge; at the mouths of the Little Bighorn and Musselshell rivers; and at Fort Peck. He further called for installation of telegraph facilities between Bismarck, Dakota, and Bozeman, Montana, as well as between the Yellowstone and Fort Fetterman, Wyoming. Action on these recommendations, he believed, would bring an end to Indian resistance and promote rapid settlement of the Yellowstone Valley.[57]

In view of the restrictions imposed by his superiors, Miles acquiesced. He would mount no more winter campaigns and his soldiers would henceforth remain in quarters, pending further directions. On January 31, he issued a congratulatory order to his men, acknowledging their "laborious and dangerous service" in the engagements at Cedar Creek, Ash Creek, and Wolf Mountains, as well as in lesser actions, thereby demonstrating "the fact that the American soldier hesitates not at any undertaking however hazardous, and can overcome obstacles apparently insurmountable." He also paid tribute to the work of his officers and to the ultimate dedication of those few "who have laid down their lives in this remote region, battling against a savage foe, for the advancement of civilization."[58]

The Wolf Mountains campaign assured the success of Sheridan's strategy of controlling the Yellowstone corridor by a permanent military presence. Miles's execution of the campaign, coupled with those recently conducted north of the river, fulfilled his particular design of thwarting a union of Indians north and south of the stream and of preventing further assembly of large numbers of the Indians such as had occurred in the spring and summer of 1876. Ignoring weather conditions, over the objections of higher authority, Colonel Miles had reasserted his determination to dog the Indians to the end. Desperate, hungry, and weary of fighting, the rapidly weakening Indian coalition rallied one last time at Wolf Mountains, when the soldiers threatened the sanctity of their homes. But for the Sioux and Cheyennes, offensive warfare was over. Sitting Bull and Crazy Horse never again united. Instead, the disintegration of the massive Indian resistance was finally at hand. As Miles averred, "We . . . had taught the destroyers of Custer that there was one small command that could whip them as long as they dared face it."[59]

CHAPTER EIGHT

Capitulation

The weeks following the Wolf Mountains expedition became a period of consolidation for Miles and his command, a time for relief from the rigors of field work in an inhospitable climate, and a time when the principal objective of the fall and winter campaigns—final defeat of the Sioux and Cheyennes—began to be realized. That Generals Sherman and Sheridan ascribed the state of affairs to Miles's spirited service cannot be doubted, and with Wolf Mountains behind him, the self-reliant colonel became the one senior officer who, in their eyes, was capable of ending the war. Sherman openly regretted that Crook had not conducted similar operations north from Cantonment Reno. In correspondence with Sheridan, the commanding general acknowledged Miles's bold requests for additional authority, and he criticized both Terry and Crook for throwing "off on the other any seeming failure to success." With Congress set to reduce army enlisted strength, Sherman believed it imperative to finish the Sioux operations by July 1877. As he put it, "It becomes our duty to make the utmost possible use of this time." Therefore, he told Sheridan:

> I think Genl. N. A. Miles, 5th Infantry, is in the best position and possessed of [the] most mental and physical vigor to exercise this command. I think you should assign him the exclusive task of hunting down the hostile Sioux to kill them or compel them to take refuge at the several agencies. . . . His command and authority should be clearly defined by you. . . . I believe . . . he will be able before June to destroy Crazy Horse's band and the remnants of Sitting Bull, so that small detachments will thereafter be able to complete the work.[1]

In response, Sheridan made plans in March to establish the District of the Yellowstone to embrace the region of Miles's operations and of the two posts projected there. Additional infantry, plus cavalry, were slated to be sent to bolster Miles's command. "I learn . . . that I may have a large command," he wrote Mary. "I would prefer a small command with the means of placing supplies where I know I will want them . . . than having a large command and having it supplied by the incompetency or indifference of others." While Miles remained poised for further action, the lack of adequate supplies of grain for his livestock continually threatened to immobilize him. For this he blamed the mismanagement of Terry, Otis, Hazen, and others who failed to deliver the provisions he had requested and, in the case of Terry, for not granting him permission to acquire such supplies locally.[2]

The first announcement of reinforcements to the Tongue River garrison came in a late February directive that sent four companies of the Second Cavalry from Fort Ellis down the Yellowstone to Miles. Because of poor road conditions, Companies F, G, H, and L, totaling 8 officers and 315 men, took most of March and April to reach the cantonment, arriving there on April 23. Besides this battalion, on March 4 two more companies of the Twenty-second Infantry at Glendive received orders to report to Miles; Companies G and H arrived on the twelfth, bringing "glorious news," according to Captain Snyder, that Hayes had apparently won the disputed presidential election. They joined Companies E and F of the twenty-second, stationed at Tongue River since October and recent participants in the Wolf Mountains campaign. Also slated for the posts in the proposed District of the Yellowstone were eleven companies of the Seventh Cavalry, which would again march west from its Missouri River stations, and four companies of the First Infantry from Fort Sully, Dakota.[3]

The added forces would give Miles in excess of two thousand men to close the war and secure the region, although he believed that the Fifth Infantry was sufficient to complete the task and that "the Indians could do nothing to stop [them]." Miles did concede a need for enlisting Indian scouts, and he succeeded in reestablishing a relationship with the Crows, although many still feared punishment for their role in the ambush slaying of the Sioux chiefs. A pragmatic officer of the Second Cavalry, First Lieutenant Gustavus C. Doane, managed to convince them otherwise and enlisted a large number that Miles would use profitably in his spring and summer operations.[4]

In addition to Miles's augmented force, other troops scheduled their arrival for the spring to begin construction of the
post at the confluence of the Little Bighorn River with the Bighorn, barely fourteen miles from Custer's battleground. Six
companies of the Eleventh Infantry, reassigned from duty at
Cheyenne River and Standing Rock agencies, would assume
that project under the direction of Lieutenant Colonel George
P. Buell, who would also supervise a contingent of civilian mechanics hired by the Quartermaster Department. To ensure
contact with the new station, Miles ordered construction of a
trail between the Tongue and Bighorn posts, and installed a
signal system incorporating flags and a heliograph that would
permit communication across the hundred-plus-mile distance
in just fifteen minutes. Meantime, plans proceeded for building
more ample quarters for Miles's enlarged command, despite
fears of citizens in the infant community nearby that their projected municipal tract might be usurped by an expansive military reservation. Instead, the site of the new post was laid out
on ground west of the cantonment. Division headquarters instructed Terry and Miles to practice economy in building the
post by using local materials in its construction.[5]

Through the early part of 1877, however, the rude cantonment buildings sufficed as shelter for the army command. Despite the cold weather and the tenuous nature of the dwellings
at the post, army life proceeded much like it did elsewhere,
dominated by routine and tedium except for periods when the
troops were active on campaign. When Miles and his men had
marched up the Tongue River in December, those officers and
men who remained behind were beset by snowstorms and freezing temperatures that kept them confined to their quarters.
Through the balance of the winter, after the infantrymen returned to the cantonment, the regimental band provided mu-
sical diversions that proved immensely popular. Concerts, min-
strel shows, and dramatic fare, held in a large canvas-covered
structure thrown up in the garrison, frequently helped dispel
the monotony that threatened.[6]

Duties that occupied the soldiers included escorting contracted civilian trains, such as the Diamond R outfit, and military supply trains to and from Glendive, Fort Buford, and other
points along the Yellowstone. Often, small parties of twenty
men led by noncommissioned officers accompanied the mail

downstream and back. Some soldiers spent their days cutting ice from the river for storage in ice houses built to help preserve perishable food during warmer months. On at least one occasion the weather grew so cold that the men balked at going out for their daily drill. With improved conditions in April, the regiment held inspection and review—its first formal unit parade in more than fifteen years. Early that month the command hurried to prepare the cantonment huts and shelters to receive the wives and families of the Fifth's officers, who were due to arrive on the first steamboat of the season.[7]

Occasional military reconnaissances of the countryside also lessened the monotony of garrison existence. On February 14, Captain Snyder prepared to take the field with 150 men trained only briefly in cavalry tactics and mounted precariously on mules. "The sight was as good as a circus," said the captain. During their scout, the soldiers examined the terrain between Sunday and Cedar creeks on the north side of the Yellowstone. After two days, having found no evidence of Indians in the area, Snyder headed his force back to Tongue River. Similarly, in April, Lieutenant Bailey led two companies of the Fifth Infantry in a scout up Sunday Creek, to the head of Big Porcupine Creek, then back to the Yellowstone to a point opposite Rosebud Creek.[8]

Life downriver at the Glendive Cantonment differed little from that at Tongue River. Army activities there consisted of delivering mail to Fort Buford, appointing boards of survey to investigate lost or damaged supplies, forwarding materials to the Tongue, and conducting courts-martial. Daily drills included calisthenics, training in the school of the company, and target practice, with officers paying special attention to ascertain "what men, if any, do not understand the use of a musket." On the night of March 20, excitement reigned after the ice floes in the Yellowstone gorged below the post, precipitating a rapid rise in the water level. Fearing that the river would overrun its banks, Major Hough ordered all provisions packed in wagons and escorted by the command to the bluffs, a mile behind the cantonment. Fortunately, extensive damage to the post was averted when the ice jam finally broke. The river had risen some fifteen feet, the last four feet occurring within fifteen minutes.[9]

Routine garrison life at Glendive and Tongue River served as a backdrop for Miles's attempts to solidify his gains after Wolf

Mountains. While he anticipated that yet another field maneuver might be required, in the immediate aftermath of the Wolf
Mountains campaign he directed his resources to ascertain
whether the people with Crazy Horse would finally surrender.
In fact, the time was ripe. Since the action at Wolf Mountains,
the peace faction that had been discredited following the slaying of the Sioux chiefs had reasserted its objective among the
Tetons and Northern Cheyennes. Using the Wolf Mountains
combat to force their point, the peace proponents argued that
the soldiers could not now be beaten and that the arrival of
more of them was but a matter of time. Capitulation was also
promoted by the fact that Sitting Bull was gone from the region, making it impossible for the camps to ever come together
again. Indications persist that Crazy Horse again resisted this
course and once more physically intimidated those who coun-
seled peace.[10]

Miles's interest in promoting the Indians' surrender, while
sincere, was prompted by a personal desire to effect a settlement and gain credit for himself and his command. Further
hastening this objective was his desire to attain a unilateral arrangement before others could. By January, for instance,
Crook was already sending emissaries among Crazy Horse's
people to urge their kin to yield and turn themselves in at the
Nebraska agencies. Crook may have concluded that Miles's victories meant an end to the fighting and that opportunities for
distinction now lay in the negotiation of a final peace. The first
Indians from Red Cloud Agency to reach Crazy Horse as part
of Crook's initiative consisted of a party of thirty men headed
by Sword, an Oglala, who told the chief that the agent at Red
Cloud Agency was aware of their suffering and that they would
receive blankets, food, and clothing if they came in. While the
Indians politely declined, opposition to surrender was clearly
dwindling among them. One of its proponents now was Spotted
Tail, the respected fifty-three-year-old Brule leader who had
earlier refused to undertake a similar mission to his nephew,
Crazy Horse, without some favorable concessions to report. He
now agreed to deliver Crook's promise that, in return for their
surrender, the Oglalas could have an agency somewhere in the
Powder River–Black Hills region rather than face the dreaded
prospect of removal.[11]

On February 13, even as Sword's party remained afield, Spotted Tail left Camp Sheridan near his agency with 250 armed warriors, bound for the Powder River country. An army pack train, its mules laden with gifts, accompanied the Indians over the wintry miles. En route north, the party met several small bands camped in the country south of the Black Hills who agreed to turn themselves in at the agencies. Pushing on, the Brule chief and his entourage arrived in March among the Minneconjou and Sans Arc encampments along the Little Missouri, north of the Black Hills. Those people, led by Roman Nose, Red Bear, High Bear, and Touch the Clouds, numbered as many as fifteen hundred and remained divided over what course to take; although they feared reprisals from the army, many were disposed to yield. Spotted Tail made them promises of safety, telling their chiefs that Crook was a personal friend of President-elect Hayes and could be trusted to treat them well. If they did not come in, more soldiers would be sent to fight them. After considerable debate, the Minneconjous and Sans Arcs agreed to go to the agencies.

Spotted Tail next journeyed west to the Little Powder, where Crazy Horse's people camped. There he related Crook's promise of a northern agency and received assurances that the Oglalas, too, planned to go in when the weather permitted. At that, the Brule chief started back to his agency to report that the majority of the tribes below the Yellowstone would surrender peacefully. The party returned to Camp Sheridan on April 5, following fifty days of travel and intense negotiation.[12]

During the weeks that Crook's overture unfolded, Miles attempted to negotiate the surrender of the Indians at the Tongue River Cantonment. Largely unaware of the prologue from the south, he embarked on a diplomatic course of his own. His chief envoy was John Bruguier. Still sought by Dakota Territory authorities for a killing at the Standing Rock Agency in 1875, Bruguier, in fact, was innocent (and later exonerated) of the crime. In appearance, Bruguier was dark complexioned, heavy bodied, with long hair; the Sioux called him "Big Leggins" because of his propensity for wearing cowboy chaps. The mixed-blood Indian son of a French-Canadian fur trapper, Bruguier had been educated in St. Louis. After his flight from prosecution in Dakota, he employed his dark features to advantage in his relations with the Sioux, and Sitting Bull reportedly

34. Spotted Tail of the Brules, as photographed by Alexander Gardner in 1872. Spotted Tail's peace mission early in 1877 was undertaken at Crook's behest and confounded Miles's own efforts to bring about the surrender of the Sioux and Cheyennes. (Smithsonian Institution, National Anthropological Archives)

35. The venerable Oglala chief Red Cloud, as photographed in 1880 by Charles Bell. Red Cloud did not participate in the Great Sioux War, but in 1877 he worked with Crook to facilitate Crazy Horse's surrender at Camp Robinson. (© Azusa)

36. John Bruguier, a mixed-blood who lived for a time in Sitting Bull's village before joining Miles. As a scout, Bruguier proved invaluable, and Miles later supported dismissal of charges against him in a murder case in Dakota. Bruguier settled at Poplar, Montana, where he was killed by an assailant in 1898. (National Archives)

took kindly to him and adopted him as a brother. It was during this period that Bruguier became fluent in Lakota. In his mid-twenties in early 1877, he had already proven his worth to Miles during the negotiations with Sitting Bull at Cedar Creek as well as during the Fort Peck expedition that followed.[13]

When Miles learned of Sword's presence among Crazy Horse's people he sent Bruguier with his own message of peace. On February 1, Bruguier departed Tongue River, armed with presents and tobacco, accompanied by Sweet Taste Woman, the Northern Cheyenne captured by the scouts on January 7, and escorted by a detachment of infantry to guide the pack mules. The mission was dangerous, and Bruguier feared for his life should he not be recognized and accepted by the Indians. The message he carried called for the Indians' unconditional surrender, failing which the soldiers would be again sent after them. Following a lengthy trek through deep snow, the party found Crazy Horse's camp of about one hundred lodges nestled along the Little Bighorn River, near the mouth of Lodge Grass Creek. The troops turned back to the cantonment when the village was sighted. Bruguier entered the camp successfully with the aid of Sweet Taste Woman and explained Miles's basic proposal, and possibly, at Miles's behest, also offered promises of the coveted northern agency to accelerate their surrender.

As before, Bruguier used his appearance to benefit his mission. He was not well known among the Oglalas and Cheyennes, and some of them thought he was a Hunkpapa, a circumstance that may well have initially saved his life. The presents he brought were welcome commodities and seemed to help sway opinions. Sweet Taste Woman told of good treatment of the Cheyenne prisoners and of Miles's professions of peace and good will towards the Cheyennes. Crazy Horse initially resisted the proposition but appeared to waver. Among the Cheyennes, Standing Elk declared his intention to lead a group into Red Cloud Agency. The other chiefs were clearly interested also and, after several days' discussion, arranged a party of twenty-nine leaders to go back to the cantonment with Bruguier and hear in detail from Miles his plans for their suffering people.[14]

The mixed Oglala-Cheyenne delegation arrived with Bruguier at the mouth of Tongue River on the afternoon of February 19. The group comprised a number of chiefs and headmen, including Hump, a Minneconjou Sioux, and White Bull

37. Hump, the Minneconjou leader who surrendered at the Tongue River Cantonment early in 1877. Hump became a favorite of Miles, thereafter serving as a scout for the army and participating in the combat at Lame Deer's village on May 7. He is shown here with his wives, as photographed by L. A. Huffman, ca. 1879. (Montana Historical Society, Helena)

(Ice), Crazy Head, Brave Wolf, Old Wolf, Little Chief, Roan Bear, and Two Moon, all Cheyennes, along with a few Cheyenne women. At Miles's direction, the Indians dismounted and, dressed in their war finery, entered the post, where the soldiers were arrayed in line formation on the parade ground. Miles, attired in a bearskin coat, quickly dispelled any fears they might have had by riding forward to shake hands with the leaders. He had two large tents raised for the Cheyennes and Oglalas and he directed that they be fed. Late Wednesday morning, the twenty-first, the Indians were conducted to Miles's quarters, where a conference ensued. Suspicions lingered on both sides. Commented one officer: "There was probably a mutual fear of treachery in the councils. Officers had no arms in sight but wore their revolvers beneath their coats, and Indians drew their blankets close about their scowling faces, with Winchesters grasped within." "At first," wrote Miles, "they seemed disposed to talk strong, but they were given to understand that that would be of no use, that there could be but one big chief in this part of the country, and that I proposed to occupy that position."[15]

One tense moment occurred when Little Chief said something interpreted as advising "the young men to put something in their guns," but nothing happened. Miles urged the chiefs to surrender with their people either at the cantonment or at their agencies, and called on them to give up their mounts and arms. According to the Cheyennes, Miles told them: "If you do as I tell you, I will be a good man to you, but if you do not do this, I will be mean to you." Two Moon spoke on behalf of the Cheyennes, acquiescing to these stipulations and asking for volunteers to stay at the cantonment until the rest of the Indians came in. Miles also took the opportunity to solicit scouts from among the Cheyennes for any future campaigns. In return for their help, he reportedly told the Indians, "I will see that you will be allowed to choose your own place for a reservation—anywhere from Yellowstone River south." Four days after their arrival, assured of obtaining provisions for their subsistence, the delegation departed, pledging to bring their people in within a few days.[16]

"If no other benefit results from this," wrote Miles, "it has given me exact . . . information as to the location, numbers and condition of the hostile Indians." During the proceedings, Miles had taken to White Bull, the Northern Cheyenne who, he said, "has never been in any Agency, has never shaken hands with any white man and is a friend of Crazy Horse and Sitting Bull." He also wrote, "I think White Bull was very much impressed with our strength and with the ways of the white man. He had never heard a band play before and was much amused." When the Indians started back to their village, White Bull and two or three others volunteered to remain at the post.[17]

The success of the Indians' visit was briefly marred when, shortly after their departure for their village, one of the remaining Cheyenne women prisoners, young Crooked Nose, evidently distraught because her husband had not come in with the party, shot and killed herself. She was buried near the post. Meantime, Bruguier returned with the Cheyennes and Oglalas to their camp, which was in transit from the Little Bighorn to the forks of the Powder River. They reached the village on March 4 and, following discussions among the Indians, most agreed to accept the terms Miles offered, which included turning themselves in, not only at Tongue River but at the southern agencies if they wished. A large number of Sioux and Cheyennes started for the cantonment. En route down the Tongue, the Indians passed over the battleground of January 8 and found the remains of the fallen Big Crow. They pressed on until they reached the mouth of Otter Creek on the Tongue, where runners from Spotted Tail's party overtook them with word of the Brule leader's approach. The messengers brought gunpowder, too, along with promises of good treatment awaiting the Indians at the Red Cloud and Spotted Tail agencies. The Sioux and Cheyennes decided that the chiefs who had previously dealt with Miles should return to the mouth of the Tongue and exact better terms from him. A large assembly of 160 warriors went with them.[18]

At the cantonment, the news chagrined Miles, especially that pertaining to the powder. Most certainly he regarded Spotted Tail's contact as interference from Crook, although he believed that traders, and not Crook, had sent the gunpowder as an inducement for the Indians to come in where they might readily trade for more. "I think if it had not been for the diversion caused by a runner from the Spotted Tail Agency, a good part of them would have come in here." On the other hand, Miles conceded the Indians the opportunity to obtain the best terms: "It is perfectly understandable that . . . they should want to go where they will be best treated." The Indians had arrived on Saturday, March 18. Miles talked with them again, offering few concessions. He wrote his wife optimistically: "I think we will become sufficiently acquainted to understand each other, although they are very wild. . . . I am playing my last card. Owing to lack of supplies, I am forced to remain quiet, but I will keep up as bold a front as possible." On the twenty-first he met the tribesmen again, but things did not go well, and in the afternoon Miles ordered his officers to prepare the companies to surround the Indians. But that proved unnecessary.[19]

Miles had been feeling concern over what course the Indians might take. Low on provisions for his animals, he could not at that moment muster enough to sustain a five-day march against those people disposed toward continued freedom. Nor did he have sufficient supplies to properly support a surrendered foe. "The management of these people just at this time, considering the condition of my command, is a difficult question," he admitted. Nevertheless, at a meeting held March 23 he told them that they must surrender either at the agencies or to his command or risk renewal of the warfare. They must turn in, as Miles put it, "such ponies and arms as I might require." He further dismissed as inaccurate a representation conveyed by Spotted Tail that the troops at Tongue River were to be removed.[20] In his memoirs, Miles recalled the council:

> At the close of my remarks absolute silence prevailed for at least five minutes. . . . [Then] Little Chief, a noted warrior and their principal orator, came forward with great dignity and deliberation, threw back the rich buffalo robe from his shoulders, like the toga of a Roman senator, letting it drop until it remained suspended from his belt. The Indian orator finally threw off everything above his waist, displaying the scars of the sun-dance on his upper arms and breast. His manner, movements, and gestures were the perfection of dignity and grace. With eloquence and deep feeling he recited the history and misfortunes of his race, their devotion to their country and their efforts to defend and retain it. Finally he said, "Your terms are cruel and harsh, but we are going to accept them."[21]

Miles convinced nine of the chiefs, including Little Chief and Little Hawk, Crazy Horse's uncle, to remain as hostages to ensure the surrender to him of at least some of the Indians. Over the next few weeks Miles developed a fondness for the hostages, especially young Hump, who became a favorite. The Indians delighted in the frequent band recitals, enjoyed the artwork in such tabloids as *The London Graphic*, and marveled over the performance of an acrobatic troupe that visited the post. "They would not believe that the acrobatic feats were real, and insisted that the performers were medicine men or had no bones," wrote Miles.[22]

Meanwhile, following the March councils, the rest of the Indians returned upstream to Otter Creek and the whole body continued on to the mouth of the Little Powder, where the majority of the Oglalas and Cheyennes had encamped. There Spotted Tail appeared, reiterating Crook's liberal proposals and his promises of amnesty as well as for the northern agency; although Crazy Horse was not present and so did not discuss these terms with his uncle, he indicated through an intermediary his desire to conform with the wishes of the other chiefs, most of whom were now disposed to accept Crook's terms. At this camp the final separation occurred between the Northern Cheyennes and the Tetons. Some of the Sioux journeyed down the Powder River, toward the Yellowstone; the others, however, likely swayed by prospects of food and supplies, turned toward Red Cloud Agency.

The Cheyennes moved to near the site of the village that had been attacked by Colonel Reynolds the previous March. After two days of inconclusive discussion among the warrior societies, the chiefs decided that each person could do as he wished. Four divisions appeared: the large Standing Elk faction, which included Dull Knife, Little Wolf, Old Bear, and Charcoal Bear, proceeded east to join Cheyennes residing with Sioux relatives in the Little Missouri country, eventually to turn themselves in at Camp Robinson; another group, which included Black Hairy Dog, Big Horse, and Spotted Elk, traveled south along the Big Horn Mountains to join their kin in the Indian Territory; yet another band headed into central Wyoming to settle with the Arapahoes and Shoshones at Wind River; the followers of Two Moon, Crazy Head, Old Wolf, and Medicine Bear, among others, convinced they would receive fair treatment from Miles and concerned for the condition of the hostages, most of whom were relatives, proceeded down the Tongue to the cantonment. A few small, scattered parties of Northern Cheyennes opted to continue hunting in the upper Tongue and Powder region before surrendering.[23]

The history of the Northern Cheyennes following their surrender is particularly disheartening. Removed to the Indian
Territory, they languished until 1878, when their leaders Dull
Knife and Little Wolf, defying the military authorities, led them
north in an epic trek that ended only after troops cornered Dull
Knife's band in Nebraska and Little Wolf's followers surren-
dered at Fort Keogh. On a freezing January day in 1879, Dull
Knife's people broke out of their prison barracks at Fort Robin-
son, precipitating a bloody encounter that left more than sixty
Indians dead. Survivors were ultimately permitted to stay with
the Sioux at Red Cloud Agency until 1884, when they joined
Little Wolf's people in Montana.[24]

During the first few weeks of April, Bruguier kept up contact
between Miles and the Cheyennes, and small bodies of the Indians continued to trickle in. On April 20, four weeks after the
council at the cantonment, Bruguier escorted in several Sioux,
including the Minneconjou Hump, who had returned briefly to
his people and now surrendered his arms to Miles. The colonel
described Hump as "the finest specimen of an Indian . . . ,
[who is] evidently as bold and enterprising as he is represented
to be." On the twenty-second,"a very raw, disagreeable day
with snow squalls every few hours," some forty-five lodges—
three hundred Cheyennes, the people of Crazy Head, Old
Wolf, and Two Moon—approached the garrison with several
hundred ponies in tow to give themselves up. "They are
wretchedly poor," observed Captain Snyder. Miles immediately
made available a number of cattle to feed them. The next day
the Indians were ushered into the cantonment, where, on the
parade ground, they turned over their guns and horses. Within
days, Miles had enlisted thirty of the tribesmen as scouts, ready
to assist him, if required, in tracking down their own relatives.[25]

Miles's achievement in winning the surrender of the Cheyennes paled in comparison to that of Crook. In April, the results of Spotted Tail's mission began to manifest themselves:
Indians—Sioux and Cheyennes—began straggling into Red
Cloud and Spotted Tail agencies. The first large group, a thousand Minneconjous and Sans Arcs, appeared on the fourteenth. Within two weeks, five hundred bereaved Cheyennes
under Dull Knife, Little Wolf, and Standing Elk came in to
Camp Robinson. Guarding against an impasse that might somehow negate the results of Spotted Tail's mission, Crook sent the

38. Chief Two Moon led Northern Cheyenne warriors in destroying Custer, but surrendered to Miles in March 1877 at Tongue River. He was photographed with trailered warbonnet by L. A. Huffman at Fort Keogh in 1878. (Montana Historical Society, Helena)

prominent Oglala, Red Cloud, to smooth any last-minute problems that might deter Crazy Horse. Furthermore, Red Cloud's party brought foodstuffs so that the Indians need not tarry to hunt, thereby hastening their surrender. On May 6, the previously indomitable war chief gave himself up, along with nearly nine hundred followers, at Camp Robinson.[26]

Crook's accomplishment in bringing about this signal event in the Sioux War overshadowed Miles's own success and received the most publicity. Moreover, it involved the capitulation of Indians who had been on Miles's doorstep, and the event, ascribed by the press to the army victory over Dull Knife the previous November, negated much of the acclaim Miles felt that he deserved. It became an element of the continuing rivalry between him and Crook. In fact, the surrender at Camp Robinson probably was due less to Crook's attractive conditions than to his astute enlistment of Spotted Tail—a Brule leader who held the abiding respect of most of Crazy Horse's people. Some Indians who surrendered at Camp Robinson said that Miles had attempted to counter Crook's terms by agreeing to allow the Indians to keep some of their weapons and by telling them that they would be badly treated by Crook.[27] Whether this was true or not, the submission of Crazy Horse denied to the ambitious Miles the recognition he sought and believed himself justified to receive, and perhaps momentarily delayed the reward he coveted for his winter campaigning—a district command.

CHAPTER NINE

Lame Deer

While Crazy Horse's people drifted toward
the Nebraska agencies, Miles prepared his own Indian charges
for a postwar future. Those who had enlisted as scouts made
ready to assist his command in a final thrust against the Sioux
and Cheyennes who still remained afield. In March, a body of
Minneconjous under Lame Deer had defected from the group
in transit from the Little Missouri to Camp Robinson after
Spotted Tail's visit. Emboldened by the presence of Crazy
Horse in the Powder River country, Lame Deer and about
thirty lodges pulled away near Bear Butte and started west, only
to learn that the Oglalas themselves were bound for the agency.
It is not clear what caused Lame Deer to steer an independent
course thereafter, but he kept moving until he reached the area
of Rosebud Creek. During his course, he drew to him small
parties of disaffected Indians still desiring to hold out. Many
were Sioux from the various camps, and by early May the number of lodges with Lame Deer seems to have at least doubled.
More newcomers composed fifteen lodges of dissident Cheyennes under a minor chief named White Hawk. Lame Deer's
followers roamed through the upper Tongue and Rosebud
country, finally camping along an eastern affluent of the Rosebud known as Muddy Creek.[1]
    Apparently, for a time Miles thought that Lame Deer was en
route to Tongue River to surrender, an impression that vanished with word from the prisoners that, in fact, his presence
constituted an act of defiance to the government as well as to
those who had surrendered and who might be implicitly blamed
for further depredations. White Bull, Two Moon, Hump, and
the others were also subjected to ridicule from the Lame Deer
people, a factor that seems to have encouraged the tribesmen

at Tongue River to join Miles in tracking them down. Seeking to determine Lame Deer's intentions, Miles once more sent John Bruguier afield; he reported back that these Indians, well provisioned and with numerous ponies, refused to surrender. Lame Deer told Bruguier that he kept his scouts alert, that "no white man could get near his camp" and, moreover, that he intended to pursue an unrestricted existence by hunting buffalo in the Rosebud country.[2]

For a while, at least, Lame Deer could roam unmolested. Miles continued to be hampered by a lack of supplies, particularly grain and hay for his animals, which had stayed alive only by eating cottonwood bark and dried winter grass. On Saturday, April 28, all this changed with Lieutenant Baldwin's arrival from Bismarck with a wagon train of grain.With his recent reinforcements, Miles was ready to begin his advance against Lame Deer immediately.

The march began the next day, Company F (Lieutenant Cusick) of the Twenty-second escorting a bull- and mule-drawn supply train a short distance along the east bank of the Tongue. On the thirtieth, eighty-one men of Companies G (Captain Miner and Lieutenant Lockwood) and H (Captain DeWitt C. Poole and Lieutenant Smith) joined under the overall command of Poole, and the entire group proceeded forward. The balance of the command, under Captain Dickey, consisted of Companies B (Captain Bennett and Lieutenant Woodruff) and H (Lieutenant Hargous), Fifth Infantry; Company E (Dickey), Twenty-second; and Companies F (Captain George L. Tyler and Second Lieutenant Alfred M. Fuller), G (Captain James N. Wheelan), H (Captain Ball and Second Lieutenant Lovell H. Jerome), and L (Captain Randolph Norwood, First Lieutenant Samuel T. Hamilton, and Second Lieutenant Charles B. Schofield), Second Cavalry, with Captain Ball commanding the mounted battalion. Attached to this latter unit were Second Lieutenant Samuel R. Douglass, Seventh Infantry, serving as battalion quartermaster; Assistant Surgeon (First Lieutenant) Paul R. Brown; and a civilian contract surgeon, Dr. Van Eman. These troops, plus a complement of Indian and white scouts and a detachment of mounted infantry composed of troops of the Fifth and Twenty-second Regiments (Second Lieutenant Edward W. Casey, Twenty-second Infantry), left the cantonment early on the morning of May 1, with Colonel Miles and his staff following at about 1:00 P.M. With Miles rode his adjutant, First Lieutenant George W. Baird, and his engineer officer, Lieutenant Long. In sum, Miles's command numbered in excess of 21 officers and 450 men.[3]

The troops passed along the trail previously used in the winter march upstream and back, camping fifteen miles up the Tongue the first day out. Four days later and sixty-one miles from the Yellowstone, the command encountered Lame Deer's trail leading west toward Rosebud Valley. At 2:30 P.M., Miles left his wagons in the charge of Companies B and H, Fifth Infantry, and G, Twenty-second Infantry, and struck out on the Indian trail with a small pack train laden with enough ammunition and rations for six days. The Second Cavalry battalion led the way, followed by the mounted infantry detachment and Companies E, F, and H, Twenty-second Infantry. The troops passed into a narrow valley that punctuated the divide between the Tongue River and Rosebud Creek and opened on the latter stream eight and one-half miles away, near the site of the Crook-Terry meeting of August 10, 1876. There the men found water in abundance. They continued up Rosebud Creek three miles, then followed another stream west, amid increasing darkness, until 2:30 A.M., when they bivouacked after marching an estimated forty miles.[4]

The presence of the knowledgeable Indian guides facilitated the army's progress over the difficult terrain at night, during part of which time it rained. The country in which Miles emerged west of Rosebud Creek constituted the divide between that stream and an affluent known as Tullock's Forks that lay farther to the west. Soon after dawn on the sixth the soldiers moved on, this time cautiously following a small stream while the scouts, riding ahead, kept careful watch from the high ground. It was from one of the peaks that they discovered the location of Lame Deer's village "some fifteen miles away in an air line." "When first seen," recalled Miles, "the camp was not recognized by the white men, but the Indians declared that they could see the smoke over the village. . . . The Indians also announced that they could see ponies grazing on the hills. This was discovered to be correct by their [white] companions, but not without using their field glasses."[5] Later, the Northern Cheyennes White Bull and Brave Wolf, along with Bruguier, Robert Jackson, and some other scouts, advanced quite close

39. White Bull, also known as Ice, the Northern Cheyenne who served Miles as a scout in 1877, was about forty years old at the time of the Lame Deer fight. He was photographed by Christian Barthelmess at Fort Keogh, probably in the late 1880s. (Smithsonian Institution, National Anthropological Archives)

to the Indian encampment, on a tributary of the Rosebud then
called Muddy Creek but today called Lame Deer Creek. Although White Bull counted only thirty-eight lodges, the village
in fact harbored sixty-one. When they returned to the troops,
the scouts reported to Miles their intelligence of the location
and size of the camp.

Meantime, the command had labored along the creek bottom until it reached the top of a high, pine-covered ridge from
which the soldiers obtained a panoramic view of the countryside. Between 2:00 and 6:00 P.M. the men rested and ate along
a rivulet on the north side of the ridge, allowing their livestock
to graze. Then Miles and the mounted troops resumed the
march, riding for three more hours over broken ground and
through deep, concealing ravines before camping next to yet
another stream running east to Rosebud Creek. Accompanying
each cavalry company was a pack mule bearing two thousand
rounds of ammunition, and each soldier carried two days' rations in his saddlebags. Captain Dickey followed with the remaining packs, guarded by the three companies of infantrymen. The day's journey totaled sixteen miles, and the soldiers
were exhausted. In bivouac, Miles took safeguards against discovery by hiding his horses and forbidding fires. Near midnight, Scout Jackson came in to report that the village was farther away than earlier thought.[6]

Miles determined to strike the Indians at daybreak. He
stripped his command of needless articles, placing them, along
with surplus ammunition, on the pack mules. He rearranged
canteens, weapons, and other necessary accoutrements so that
their rattle would not alert the villagers of their approach. At
2:00 A.M., the soldiers resaddled and resumed their advance in
a rainstorm, once more moving their horses over demanding
terrain and fording several swollen creeks until, at four o'clock,
they regained the Rosebud. Crossing that stream, they halted
to adjust saddles and girths, then trotted and galloped their
horses up Muddy Creek for almost five miles, the winding bottom of the stream requiring repeated changes in formation as
the men advanced. They reached the proximity of Lame Deer's
sleeping encampment at about 4:30 A.M., just as the rainfall
ceased and the first rays of dawn tinted the eastern horizon. A
veil of smoke hung motionless above the lodges as the soldiers
approached, and the scouts reported to Miles that they could

see cooking fires being prepared in some of the tipis. Years later, an enlisted participant vividly recalled the moment: "The twittering of birds in the trees, the wealth of grass which the Chinook winds spread soft over the sheltered valleys . . . contrast[ed] with wasting snow-drifts still clinging to the northern sides of the hillcrests."[7]

Quickly, in the growing light of dawn, Miles ordered his scouts and officers to reconnoiter the area surrounding the camp and then formulated his attack. Executing the common army tactic of the plains wars, Miles prepared his command to strike the village while most of its occupants still slept. He gathered his officers, "giving them explicit instructions to prevent firing upon women and children, and directed [his] interpreter and Indian scouts to demand the surrender of the hostiles." The camp stood in a loop on the north bank of Muddy Creek. Across the stream and a short distance from it, grassy pine-topped hills jutted from the bottom to a plateau running between Muddy Creek and the Rosebud, approximately five miles due west. Unknown to Miles, about a mile above the Sioux encampment stood one of Cheyennes, containing fifteen tipis. These Indians quickly departed the area when the shooting erupted and apparently played no role in the fighting.[8]

Miles ordered Lieutenant Casey, with twenty scouts and mounted infantrymen, and Lieutenant Jerome with Company H, Second Cavalry, to charge through the camp, continuing upstream to stampede the grazing pony herd approximately one-half mile above the village. These units struck the village first, the horsemen tearing upstream along the north edge of the camp to place themselves between the ponies and the Indians and drive the animals farther away from the village. A few boys tending the herd offered trifling resistance, firing their guns at the onrushing troops before fleeing to the hills. At the commotion, warriors stumbled from their lodges, shooting randomly at the invaders through the murky twilight. Lieutenant Jerome's jaw was grazed by a round during this preliminary encounter, and at least one soldier was killed as he raced by on his horse. Approaching the sizable pony herd, which was on the opposite side of the creek, the soldiers found the banks so steep that they had to ford in single file before resuming their mission. Meantime, at the village, many of the warriors and their families exited tipis and fled afoot through the rain-swollen

40. Second Lieutenant Edward W. Casey, Twenty-second Infantry, shown here as a graduating West Point cadet in 1873. Having a
prominent military lineage, Casey commanded the scouts and
mounted infantry in the attack on Lame Deer's camp on May 7, 1877.
In later years he gained renown in army circles for his work in orga-
nizing and leading a troop of Cheyenne scouts. Casey was killed by
Sioux Indians in January 1891 near Pine Ridge Agency, South Dakota,
a few days after the Wounded Knee conflict. (Special Collections Division, USMA Library)

stream, pursued by Tyler's Company F and Wheelan's Company G. Company L, under Captain Norwood, was held in reserve during the initial attack.

Miles and his aides approached the camp through a bend in the creek. In trying to communicate with the fleeing Indians, the colonel provoked an incident that nearly cost him his life. Although accounts of the episode vary slightly, in its important aspects they agree. Spotting Lame Deer among the refugees, Robert Jackson pointed the chief out to Miles, who ordered his interpreters to speak with him. The Lakota scout Hump rode forward to address him. The headman's nephew, later identified as Iron Star, was with him. Iron Star was restless and angry and strode nervously beside Lame Deer, who wore an eagle-feathered headdress with a long trailer and clutched a white rag in his hand. After talking to the chief, Hump rode back and reported: "That is Lame Deer and he wants to see General Miles." The shooting stopped.

Miles donned a white hat and rode forward, accompanied by eight persons, including White Bull. Four Sioux advanced, one of whom led Lame Deer's pony. Lame Deer, carrying a Spencer carbine, reached out and shook Miles's hand while Iron Star continued his nervous pacing. Then Lieutenant Baird shook hands with Iron Star. Through his interpreter, Miles told Lame Deer to put down his weapon. As the chief complied, he cocked the arm and laid it on the ground, its muzzle facing Miles. Lieutenant Long then dismounted to take the carbine while Miles continued addressing the chief, specifying that after the guns and horses were delivered, the Indians had to accompany him to the cantonment.

But Lame Deer either was not paying attention or was not inclined to yield, according to Miles, "having already meditated treachery or fearing it on our part." At that moment, Scout Jackson rode up and indiscreetly leveled his gun at Lame Deer. Meantime, White Bull, spying the cocked gun on the ground, rode close to Miles, nudged him, and motioned toward the firearm. As Iron Star continued his behavior, White Bull and an aide spurred their mounts forward and tried to coax him to surrender the rifle he waved menacingly. White Bull grabbed the muzzle and tried to twist it from Iron Star's grasp. As they scuffled, the weapon discharged and the bullet passed through the scout's overcoat. Lame Deer, perceiving all this action, sud-

41. Miles's brush with death at the Lame Deer fight in May 7, 1877 is captured in this pen-and-ink rendering first published in his autobiographical *Personal Recollections* in 1896.

denly reclaimed the carbine before him, pointed it directly at Miles, and pulled the trigger. At the sudden movement, the officer instinctively jerked on the reins and his horse veered, the bullet narrowly passing by him and crashing into the chest of his orderly, Private Charles Shrenger, knocking the soldier from his mount and killing him instantly.

In the aftershock, pandemonium erupted. A soldier tried to shoot Lame Deer, but apparently killed another Sioux before being shot himself. In the confusion over Miles's condition and that of the men who had been shot, Lame Deer and Iron Star started away unmolested. But as the shooting continued, they managed only about two hundred yards before Lame Deer was cut down in a hail of gunfire from the soldiers of Company L. Private David L. Brainard of that unit witnessed the moment:

> The head-dress made a very conspicuous target, and many shots were fired at the Indian wearing it. Finally he was seen to totter, and the other Indian . . . placed his hand about the other's waist and supported him up the hill; Lame Deer was seen to take a pistol from his belt and fire backward in our direction. . . . When the old man fell, Iron Star escaped over the hill through our left, and ran into the face of G troop under Wheeland [*sic*], and was shot by Wheeland, who used a pistol.

Later, Scout Jackson examined Lame Deer's corpse; the Minneconjou, scalped by the Cheyenne White Bull, had seventeen bullet holes in him.[9]

Companies F and L, under Lieutenants Tyler and Norwood, respectively, now bore down on the fleeing people, dashing their horses across the Muddy to prevent the Indians' retreat by that route. At Ball's direction, Lieutenant Wheelan with Company G followed the withdrawing Indians and took up a reserve position among the lodges in support of Tyler and Norwood. These companies were not swift enough to prevent the warriors, many mounted on ponies that had been kept near their lodges, from gaining the ridge west of camp. From the draws at its base and from boulders above, the surprised and angered Sioux directed a sweeping fire against the soldiers. As one participant recalled: "Norwood would never have gotten up [the ridge] if Tyler had not first been in position to get in a cross fire and thus occupy the attention of at least a part of the Indians; the hill was so steep that it was as much as the men could do to creep up it without having to fight at the same time."[10] In this exchange, Lieutenant Fuller, of Norwood's company, received a severe gunshot wound in the chest.

Desirous of clearing the high ground, Miles directed his men into skirmish order. Leaving Jerome's Company H to guard the village and the herd, which included ponies as well as government horses and mules, he had the dismounted troopers of F, G, and L forge up and over the steep, timbered ridge while their horses were brought forward up a gentler rise. In this advance, Wheelan's Company G assumed the left of the line, Norwood's Company L the center, and Tyler's F the right. Where the hills fell away on the left, Company G flanked the Indians pursued by the other units and "slaughtered them right

42. Site of Lame Deer's village where Miles attacked it on May 7, 1877, as photographed by L. A. Huffman in 1901. Today a mobile-home park occupies much of the site. (Montana Historical Society, Helena)

and left and did terrible execution in a few moments." An enlisted participant in this action later told of "an old woman struggling up the bluffs . . . in an effort to get away. [A soldier] pursued her, caught up with her and seized her long braids of hair. He jerked her down and dragged her by the hair-hold until he got to a tree. . . . Then he walked away ten or twelve feet, took deliberate aim, and sent a fatal bullet crashing into her head."

By 9:00 A.M. the attack was finished, the warriors and their families having scattered into the wooded ravines beyond the camp and fleeing in the direction of Rosebud Creek, pursued all the way by the cavalrymen.[11]

Fourteen dead Indians, including several women, lay strewn in the area of the village and along the line of the occupants' retreat to the west. The abandoned camp, estimated to have

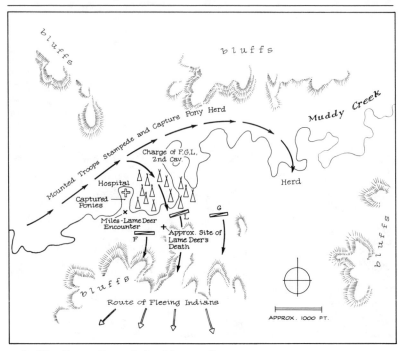

6. The Lame Deer fight, May 7, 1877

contained about three hundred people, bequeathed an untold wealth in robes, dried meat ("at least thirty tons"), and carbines, powder, and ammunition, although the warriors did manage to retain most of their firearms during their desperate rush from the camp. Miles reported that a search of the camp disclosed "many trophies of the Custer battle and several scalps of white men and women." Four hundred fifty horses ("round, fat, sleek and in excellent condition") composed the camp's herd, some bearing the Seventh Cavalry brand.[12] Returning from the chase, the cavalrymen went to work pulling down tipis and placing them and their contents in piles, together with saddles, arms, beadwork, and other retrieved equipment (including curry combs and brushes with Seventh Cavalry markings). Then all was set ablaze, the smoke from the burning camp filling the air for miles about.

In the wake of the fighting, Miles took account of his losses: four men killed and nine wounded, all of the Second Cavalry. The dead were Privates Frank Glackowsky and Charles A. Martindale, Company F; and Privates Peter Louys and Charles Shrenger, Company H. They were buried on the battlefield approximately two hundred yards southwest of Muddy Creek. In addition, eleven cavalry mounts were killed or driven off by the warriors. Other than Lame Deer and Iron Star, the identities of the Indian dead were unknown to the whites, although White Bull later confirmed two as Heart Ghost and Shorty.[13]

Shortly after noon, Companies E, F, and H, Twenty-second Infantry, under Captain Dickey, arrived at the village, too late to participate in the fighting. Having left the packs in camp along Rosebud Creek, Dickey, with Captain Poole and Lieutenants Cusick and Smith, had moved rapidly on the trail of the horsemen after hearing the sound of distant gunfire. Earlier, some warriors had come upon the pack train and the Twenty-second infantrymen and had succeeded in driving off two ammunition-laden mules and killing a civilian packer. Soon after, a cavalry soldier who had lagged behind Miles's command to adjust his saddle found himself surrounded and under attack by some of the fleeing tribesmen. He entrenched himself on a small hillock and miraculously held the warriors off until the advancing infantrymen relieved him.[14]

After the Twenty-second soldiers reached Miles, they joined the cavalrymen in position on the high ridges east and west of the village, to guard against attempts by the warriors to free the ponies. Miles established his headquarters in the loop of the stream immediately west of the tipis, near the place of his close encounter with Lame Deer, while his medical staff treated the wounded in an adjacent area directly to the north. Throughout the balance of the day, groups of Indians intermittently appeared on distant hills to open volleys on the soldiers. A Company H cavalryman was shot in the arm during one of these encounters. Through the night, Indians occasionally fired on the pickets from afar, disrupting the sleep of the command but causing no further casualties.[15]

On the morning of May 8, the innovative Miles decided to mount his infantrymen on some of the captured Sioux ponies, an adventure that brought mishap and hilarity. Cavalryman Havilah Carpenter described the event:

> General Miles had [the foot soldiers] each take a pony, an Indian blanket and saddle, then borrowed a spur from each Cavalryman. . . . The Indian saddle had a high horn on the pommel and the doughboy . . .

tied the gun on with rawhide. His gun [rifle] was much longer than ours so the muzzle hung down and the butt up. The next day they had drill and they saddled up and got in line. The officer instructed them how to lead out and mount, so at the command "prepare to mount" they did a good job. At the command "mount," as many as could get on mounted and the ponies commenced to buck. The long gun on the pommel of the saddle was about even with their eyes and as the ponies bucked the muzzle of the gun would strike them in the faces. . . . Of course, he supposed the spur was to hold on with. He brought them up in the ponies flank which made the pony buck all the harder. Any way you looked, you would see a doughboy tumble. But they soon became good horsemen.[16]

Miles had some of the excess ponies shot to keep them from falling back into the hands of the Sioux. Then, at half past ten o'clock, after completing the destruction of the camp and burying the dead Indians, Miles and his command set off downstream, passing only eight miles because of difficulties managing the captured ponies, before camping in the broader valley of the Rosebud. Grass, wood, and water were abundant. During the night, the Sioux made another effort to retrieve their horses, but were driven away by the troops firing into the darkness.[17]

The command proceeded down Rosebud Creek early the next morning and gained the camp of the Fifth Infantry guard before noon. On the tenth, the soldiers remained in camp and rested, and Captain Ball issued a congratulatory order to his cavalrymen for their participation in "the greatest and most complete victory yet gained over the hostiles during the Sioux campaign." The next morning, leaving Ball's cavalry battalion afield, the infantry troops set off downstream, going but a short distance before diverging through the pass leading to the Tongue. They followed their former trail back to that river and on down to the cantonment, arriving in the forenoon of Monday, May 14, having journeyed approximately 210 miles since setting out two weeks earlier. Leaving nothing to chance, Miles immediately organized Companies B, F, G, and I, Fifth Infantry, as a mounted unit, utilizing the captured ponies, and placed Captain Snyder in charge.[18]

Miles had earlier forwarded to Terry's headquarters dispatches announcing his victory over Lame Deer's band; they apparently became lost in the mail, and for several weeks little news of the engagement reached the outside world. In military circles it became known that Miles had destroyed a camp that in all probability was the last to hold out. Crook attempted to downplay the result by contending that Lame Deer had been in contact with Spotted Tail and had merely gone on a final hunt before surrendering—thus implying that Lame Deer had been killed after consenting to go to an agency.[19]

Following his return to the cantonment, Miles did not remain idle but sent his troops back into the field as soon as they had rested from their campaign. Still wary of Lame Deer's Sioux, on May 17 he sent his mounted infantrymen to camp on the east side of the Tongue, opposite the post. Ball's tired cavalrymen, meantime, were resupplied from the cantonment and ranged south to the Wolf Mountains before being sent to camp along Rosebud Creek with three companies of the Twenty-second Infantry and an artillery piece. The cavalry spent the last week of May casually negotiating the terrain between the Rosebud and Tongue. Other companies of the Fifth Infantry continued to escort supply trains to and from the lower Yellowstone. Miles still planned to use anticipated reinforcements against remaining Indians in the region south of the Yellowstone, and he urged that the mouth of the Little Bighorn rather than the mouth of the Bighorn be selected for the proposed military post.[20]

The soldiers at the Tongue River garrison spent the rest of May welcoming the first steamboats of the season and preparing for any military eventualities the summer might bring. On May 23 the steamer *Josephine* arrived, after almost a month's delay at Glendive awaiting rains to raise the level of the Yellowstone so the vessel might pass Buffalo and Wolf Rapids. Following a five-day deluge, the *Josephine* brought badly needed forage and sutler's wares. Also on board were a new sutler and his family and the returning detachment of Fifth infantrymen who had escorted the Sioux hostages east following the Cedar Creek battle. That evening another vessel, the *Fanchon*, approached the landing, transporting Major Henry M. Lazelle and Companies B, G, H, and K, First Infantry, from Dakota to reinforce Miles. At the post, the newcomers found that the heavy rains had taken a toll on the meager fort structures. "In the band quarters," observed one, "some had 'A' tents to keep their beds dry, some had wall tents, some shelter tents and some tent flies."[21]

Having returned downstream, the *Josephine* came back to the landing four days later, bringing Companies I and K, Twenty-second Infantry, under Major Hough, to participate in summer campaigning. Hough found the Tongue River post so flooded that most of the troops had been sent to camp several miles away. Nor did the weather improve; by early June, Hough's soldiers were forced to seek high ground after their own camp was inundated with water two feet deep. At the cantonment, "the rains worked through the earth roofs, washing the mud down upon the occupants. Some of the huts were flooded a foot deep."[22]

On May 28 the *Josephine* again turned downstream, this time carrying Company G, First Infantry, to the mouth of Cedar Creek, where the soldiers established a supply camp for the contingent of Seventh cavalrymen expected to support Miles's summer movements. Eleven companies of the Seventh, commanded by Colonel Samuel D. Sturgis, had left Fort Lincoln early in the month. The renovated outfit included so many replacements for those men who had fallen at the Little Bighorn that they were popularly known as "Custer Avengers." They traveled overland, with expectations of future combat fueled by rumors that Sitting Bull, bolstered by several hundred Sioux from the Standing Rock Agency, was again operating south of the Missouri.

Gaining Fort Buford on the seventeenth, the regiment camped in the mud during a violent thunderstorm. The soldiers continued along the north bank of the Yellowstone, accompanied by the supply steamer *Far West* and on the twenty-third learned of Miles's victory over Lame Deer. Three days later they camped at Glendive, and during the night the cavalry pickets drove away a party of Indians. Then the horsemen rode west through badlands and alkali flats. Twice dispatches arrived from Miles urging the troops to hurry, and more Indians and their signal fires were sighted ahead of the command. Finally, on May 29, the Seventh Cavalry settled into bivouac along Cedar Creek, having been greeted by Lieutenant Casey of Miles's command. Miles directed Sturgis to stay there rather than proceed to the flooded cantonment. The regiment was to send parties out to watch for Indians appearing from the north. At the Cedar

43. Colonel Samuel D. Sturgis, commander of the Seventh Cavalry, who supported Miles's force in pursuit of scattered bands of the Indians in the spring and summer of 1877 before assuming a major role in the Nez Perce War. This photo shows Sturgis, an 1846 West Point graduate, during his Civil War service. Photograph by Limmerman. (Denver Public Library, Western History Department)

Creek outpost, the "Custer Avengers" camped through the tor-
rential rains and wet snows of early June, awaiting word from
Miles on their ultimate disposition.[23]

In fact, the continuing downpour ruined roads and trails,
delaying Miles's plans to retake the field. Word that Sitting Bull,
with a mixed body of Indians, had been sighted on the Milk
River impelled him to move in that direction once the rains
abated. "A display of a strong force on that side of the Missouri
would in my judgment have a most excellent effect upon those
Indians." It would also, in Miles's opinion, put a halt to the
illicit arms traffic in that region. Anticipating the departure of
the Twenty-second Infantry, which had been reassigned east,
Miles recommended that the regiment's replacement, proposed to be the Sixteenth Infantry, report to Fort Peck to begin
its Montana tour.[24] Having eliminated Lame Deer's lingering
presence in the wake of the large surrenders, Miles now determined to close off the Yellowstone-Missouri hinterland to any
residual presence by Sitting Bull's followers. Implementation
of that strategy would at last end hostilities with the Sioux.

CHAPTER TEN

War's End

The Lame Deer Fight constituted the last significant engagement between the army and the Indians in the Great Sioux War. Some of the refugees from Lame Deer's camp remained away from the agencies, however, and, along with the threatened resurgence of Sitting Bull in the north, continued to occupy Miles's troops into the summer of 1877. Some of the Lame Deer people, particularly Minneconjous, Sans Arcs, and Northern Cheyennes, under a warrior named Fast Bull, fled east into the region of Slim Buttes in Dakota Territory. Destitute and afraid, they committed random depredations in the area of the Black Hills; a few lodges of Hunkpapas traveling with Fast Bull eventually headed for Canada.[1]

In June, Miles turned his attention north. He continued his patrols along the Yellowstone to prevent any union of the Indians. He also organized several hundred Crows and sent them, under Lieutenant Gustavus C. Doane, Second Cavalry, to scout the headwaters of streams between the Little Bighorn and the Tongue. Yet his obsession now became Canada. Miles believed that he should move to the international boundary to keep Sitting Bull from returning to United States soil and to prevent incursions by war parties. When General Sheridan learned of Miles's intentions, he sent word that the colonel should instead concentrate on the construction of new posts and on patrolling the country on either side of the Yellowstone. Despite rumors and reports that Sitting Bull had earlier crossed into Canada, not until June 20 did the dominion's Privy Council notify the United States Government of the presence of the Sioux on British soil.[2]

Miles did concern himself with the erection of the posts, and as the waters of the Yellowstone became increasingly navigable,

more construction materials were routed upstream. A battalion
of four companies of the Eleventh Infantry under Lieutenant
Colonel George P. Buell reached the junction of the Bighorn
and Little Bighorn rivers on June 23 and commenced raising
barracks. Construction of the Bighorn post, 110 miles from that
at Tongue River, lasted into the fall and following winter. On
June 25, the team charged with erecting the new station at
Tongue River reached the cantonment. This fort was to stand
at a site, selected by Miles, almost two miles west of the cantonment. It was built to accommodate eleven companies of cavalry
and infantry in five frame barracks and contain fourteen officers' quarters, three warehouses for commissary and quartermaster goods, and several stables, corrals, and collateral structures.[3]

Meantime, two more companies of the Eleventh Infantry
joined Miles's command at the Tongue. With these plus the reinforcements of the Seventh Cavalry and First Infantry, Miles
was ready for any exigency regarding the Indians. During the
month of June, the troops patrolled both sides of the Yellowstone and guarded supply camps above the stream. Constant
rumors of Indian movements kept them vigilant. Units of the
Second Cavalry, accompanied by Captain Snyder's mounted infantry battalion, scouted the Rosebud country in response to
rumors that Crazy Horse had bolted the agency with three
hundred lodges and was back in the area. Snyder's men also
pursued a body of warriors that ran off a herd of civilian-owned
horses from Miles City. North of the Yellowstone, Seventh Cavalrymen broke the monotony of daily drills at their camp near
Cedar Creek to investigate reported sightings of warriors.[4]

On June 14 Colonel Michael V. Sheridan, brother of the general, arrived at the cantonment. Colonel Sheridan, accompanied by a unit of the Seventh Cavalry, was to retrieve the
remains of Custer and other officers from the Little Bighorn
battlefield and rebury enlisted men killed in that fight. On the
same day, Captain Ewers crossed the Yellowstone with thirty
infantrymen as an escort to seventy Sioux and Cheyenne prisoners who were going north to hunt buffalo. They returned on
the twenty-seventh, having killed 150 buffalo and 100 antelope.
As late as June 17, however, unsurrendered tribesmen still har-
ried the cantonment. In the evening of that day a party of Fifth
Infantry soldiers guarding government transportation on the

north bank of the Yellowstone came under attack by three dozen mounted warriors, who succeeded in capturing two horses.[5]

On June 16, Miles had ordered Major Henry M. Lazelle to scout the Little Missouri country and that toward the Black Hills and to assess the potential for a wagon road at the same time. The veteran officer's command comprised two companies of his own First Infantry battalion, the entire battalion of Twenty-second Infantrymen that was transferring east, one company of Seventh Cavalry, and the scouts under Lieutenant Casey, plus the Napoleon gun, a wagon train, and a beef herd. While Miles journeyed to Fort Buford to discuss upcoming summer operations with Terry, Lazelle's soldiers traveled by steamer down to the mouth of the Powder River, then moved southeast up that stream. On June 24 the cavalry and scouts examined two Indian trails leading to a recently abandoned village along the Little Missouri River that held some two hundred people. Lazelle pursued the Indians, apparently belonging to Fast Bull's band, over the next week, and on July 4 his scouts engaged about fifteen of them near the "big bend" of the stream. Learning that the Indian encampment was at Sentinel Buttes, Lazelle hurried through the night of July 7 with his cavalry, infantry, and scouts, but by dawn the people had escaped. "A careful examination gave convincing proof that the Indians were a remnant of Lame Deer's band," reported the major. Another camp nearby was also deserted, and Lazelle was left with nothing but the problems involved in maneuvering his wagons through the adjacent badlands. The companies of the Twenty-second Infantry marched for Dakota and their new assignment, and Lazelle and his remaining command returned to the Yellowstone to resupply. Lazelle once more turned east, erected a stockade on the Little Missouri for a mounted company of the Fifth Infantry, then trailed the Indians into Dakota Territory before returning to the Yellowstone empty-handed.

Meantime, the battalion of the Second Cavalry, accompanied by Crow Indians, one company of the Seventh Cavalry, and two mounted companies of the Fifth Infantry, opened a wide-ranging scout that took them all the way east to the vicinity of Standing Rock Agency, south to the vicinity of Custer City, and west again into Wyoming before closing the pursuit on August 30, the command having traveled nearly six hundred miles. The

action between Lazelle's scouts and the Sioux along the Little
Missouri on July 4 constituted the final gasp of the war. Within
weeks, Fast Bull's people filed into Camp Sheridan and surrendered.[6]

Miles returned from his conference with Terry on June 29,
having reached no conclusions regarding forthcoming summer
operations. As General Sherman was expected to arrive at the
cantonment, it is likely that Terry and Miles agreed to await that
officer's assessment before settling on a course of action. Miles
had already garnered Terry's personal appreciation for his
management of the campaign and the subsequent surrenders
at the agencies. "It is to be regretted," he told Miles, "that you
will not receive from the public at large credit for the results
which are really due to your efforts."[7]

On July 4 Miles headed a command of nine companies of the
Seventh Cavalry, two of the Second, and six of the mounted
Fifth Infantry, besides a contingent of Indian scouts, a supply
train, a herd of cattle, and the usual artillery component, to
examine the country between the Yellowstone and Missouri rivers and to interpose his force between Sitting Bull's camp to
the north and the remnants of Lame Deer's band. This inspection ranged between Sunday and East Cedar creeks, and several
days were spent in bivouac on the site of Miles's battle of October 21, 1876, at the headwaters of the latter stream. From this
location, small units were dispatched to scout the country
towards the Glendive post and towards the Big Dry and Redwater, beyond the divide. After twelve days, the soldiers returned to the Tongue River Cantonment, while Miles proceeded to Glendive to meet the steamer *Rosebud*, bringing
General Sherman on an inspection tour of military posts.[8]

While the troops had been away, the *Josephine* had reached
the landing at the cantonment on July 11 with a welcome cargo:
Colonel Miles's wife Mary, his daughter Cecelia, and Elizabeth
Sherman, niece of the general, in addition to a number of wives
of the junior officers. Most had left Fort Leavenworth on May
10 aboard the *J. Donald Cameron*, accompanied by the *General
Sherman*, which had carried the remaining freight and baggage
of the Fifth Infantry up the Missouri. Below Sioux City the
Cameron snagged and sank in eighteen feet of water, but not
before its passengers were heroically rescued by the crew of the
Sherman. Much of the regimental property, however, went

down with the steamer. Mrs. Miles and party joined the other travelers at Bismarck and transferred to the *Josephine* at Glendive.[9]

Miles returned to the cantonment on July 16 aboard the *Rosebud*, along with General Sherman's entourage, which included Department Commander Terry and his staff and the Department of Dakota quartermaster, Major Benjamin C. Card. After the Fifth Infantry band had played a rousing air of welcome for the general, the party proceeded to the cantonment, where Miles greeted his wife, whom he had not seen for more than a year. The next day Sherman toured the military reservation and the site of the new post.[10]

On Tuesday, Sherman notified the secretary of war that, in his opinion, the Sioux War was over:

> I now regard the Sioux Indian problem, as a war question, as solved by the operations of General Miles last winter and by the establishment of the two new posts on the Yellowstone, now assured this summer. Boats come and go now, where a year ago none would venture except with strong guards. Wood-yards are being established to facilitate navigation, and the great mass of the hostiles have been forced to go to the agencies for food and protection, or have fled across the border to the British territory.

That night Sherman formally received the officers of Miles's command and the next evening attended a parade of the Fifth Infantry. Before reviewing the troops, however, a ceremony occurred during which the general pinned Medals of Honor on the dress coats of thirty-one enlisted men who had displayed exceptional bravery in one or more of the engagements from Cedar Creek to Wolf Mountains. (Five more would receive medals later for their performance in the Lame Deer Fight.) After the dress review, Generals Sherman and Terry departed upstream for the Bighorn Post.[11]

There they met Generals Sheridan and Crook and their staffs who had reached the Bighorn by traveling from the south. At the Bighorn Post the officers deliberated over the status of the forts and what to name them. Sherman's report to Secretary of War George W. McCrary regarding this matter stated:

> We have discussed the subject of names for the new post[s]. I suggested the names of Custer and Keogh, both killed last summer. I find General Terry indisposed thus to honor Genl. Custer, as he thinks he drew on

himself the terrible calamity which involved the lives of 250 good soldiers, by disregarding his instructions and by pushing his command so
rapidly as to ignore the cooperating force. Still, death generally ends
all controversy, and I think General Sheridan agrees with me, still we
dislike to act without General Terry's consent. I wish you would take
the matter in consideration and give names to these two new posts, now
among the most important of all.

Hence, late in 1877, the Bighorn Post became Fort Custer and
the new post at Tongue River became Fort Keogh.[12]

Following this meeting, Sherman proceeded west while Sheridan, Crook, and their staffs traveled down the Yellowstone to
Tongue River for a brief inspection before going on to Fort
Buford. Two days later, Terry came through on his way back
down the Yellowstone. Sherman's visit to the war zone symbolized an official end of hostilities with the Sioux and Cheyennes
in the region. Although Miles continued to send out scouting
detachments over the next few weeks, the reality was that there
remained no one left to chase, much less fight.[13]

On August 10, Miles was alerted to an Indian outbreak involving the Nez Perces of Idaho Territory and eastern Oregon.
For reasons historically grounded in the loss of their Wallowa
Valley lands to whites, a few of these people provoked an incident that resulted in conflict with U.S. soldiers, with the army
sustaining severe losses. Through early July, the Indians evaded
the troops, but following a battlefield setback at the Clearwater
River, the warriors struck east cross-country with their women
and children—roughly eight hundred people. Military authorities throughout the region converged on the Indians, and Miles
readied his Yellowstone troops for an immediate role in this
new action. On the tenth, he ordered six companies of the Seventh Cavalry under Colonel Sturgis to take a station opposite
the mouth of Tongue River, and on the twelfth he sent them
west to Clark's Fork on the upper Yellowstone to help head off
the Nez Perces. These troops were unable to halt the Indians,
however. On September 18, Miles led forth a command that
included his mounted infantrymen and moved diagonally
northwest in an effort to prevent the Nez Perces from joining
the Tetons near the Canadian line. These troops dealt the Nez
Perces a demoralizing loss on September 30 at Snake Creek.
Miles continued to play a major part in the campaign to subjugate these Indians after their epic flight of seventeen hundred

miles. On October 5, 1877, he accepted the surrender of the Nez Perce leader, Joseph, at Bear Paw Mountains, Montana.[14]

Miles's involvement in the Nez Perce War coincided with the beginning of a peace initiative to Sitting Bull, led by General Terry and diplomat Albert Gallatin Lawrence. The "Sitting Bull Commission," as it was called, responded to a request from the Privy Council of Canada that the Indians now ensconced on British soil be induced "to return to their reserves in the United States territory." President Hayes approved the joint War–Interior Department overture and troops from the cantonment were ordered to join Terry's party en route to the British line. On September 24, Miles wrote Terry, expressing concern over reports that the Sioux had received new arms and ammunition since taking refuge. "I hope your Commission may be successful, but should it not, the available force in this District is not strong enough to encounter Sitting Bull's force after having been strengthened by nearly a year's rest."[15]

Terry's party crossed the border and met the refugee Hunkpapas in council on October 17. In the course of the proceeding, Sitting Bull declined peace proposals extended by Terry, declaring the intention of his people to remain in Canada. The objective of the Sitting Bull Commission thus frustrated, its members returned to the United States with only an understanding that future boundary crossings by the Sioux in Canada would be viewed by both governments as hostile demonstrations. Over the next few months, Sitting Bull's people were joined by small groups from the Red Cloud and Spotted Tail agencies, who fled after the killing of Crazy Horse and the implementation of a government decision to move the tribes to new agencies along the Missouri River. Similar migrations occurred over the next several years.[16]

Although the Sioux War was over, mostly because the Indians had withdrawn from the theatre of war—either to give themselves up at the agencies or to seek refuge in the British Possessions—a potential for isolated hostilities existed for several years. Miles continued to press for a sustained military presence north of the Missouri River, preferably by a command headed by himself as brigadier general. But General Sherman sternly rejected that proposal, especially after the British authorities agreed to try and stem future crossings. As long as white settlements remained unmolested and navigation of the

Missouri proceeded without disruption, Sherman's policy henceforth would oppose military operations against Indians north of that stream. While Miles did not gain the promotion he coveted, he did achieve his long-held command objective on September 4, 1877, when the District of the Yellowstone was formally created. The district, headquartered at the new Fort Keogh, embraced the country guarded by that post, Fort Custer, and the subpost of Fort Peck.[17]

Regardless of Sitting Bull's absence from the immediate region, a paranoia existed that he might somehow incite other tribes to warfare. In 1878, tribes such as the Blackfeet, Gros Ventres, and Assiniboines were faced with starvation because of dwindling numbers of bison in their region. To prevent their succumbing to Sioux pressure to take action against the whites, Colonel Gibbon advised giving these tribes provisions. To further counter the prospect of fighting returning Tetons, General Terry recommended the establishment of two more military posts to act in concert with Forts Keogh and Custer. He thought one should be built in north-central Montana to serve as a barrier between the Sioux and the "friendly" tribes in the western part of the territory. Because the agency Sioux still constituted a threat as they moved north to join the Canadian refugees, Terry urged construction of a fort near the Black Hills to protect the mining centers. Finally, he called for the establishment of a telegraph line to link the Dakota forts on the Missouri River with Forts Buford, Keogh, and Custer. This combination of troop concentration and quick communication would ensure the demise of the unsurrendered Sioux. Within a year, all of these recommendations were enacted; construction was begun on Fort Meade at the northeast edge of the Black Hills and on Fort Assinniboine above the Bear Paw Mountains in northern Montana Territory.[18]

By and large, this means of averting future Indian conflicts succeeded, and there occurred no major outbreaks involving the Sioux in Canada. During the years between 1877 and 1881, however, the Indians randomly came into the United States, confounding Miles and his subordinates in the Yellowstone District. Many of them, facing starvation above the boundary, journeyed to the vicinity of Fort Peck to reside with the Yanktonais and other agency tribes. In April 1878, not far from Fort Peck, Lieutenant Baldwin met with nearly one hundred of the

Sioux and, at Miles's direction, offered terms under which they and their Canadian kin might return and remain in the United States. One of Baldwin's leading converts was Gall, who had played an instrumental role in the destruction of Custer's command. Through Gall's intercession, a camp of Hunkpapas under No Neck, numbering more than one hundred lodges, agreed to come in during the summer. Baldwin also followed orders to abandon Fort Peck. Subjected to repeated incidents of flooding that threatened its buildings, the popular agency formally closed in May 1878, and the small body of troops stationed there marched to Fort Buford.[19]

Soon after, when large numbers of Tetons from Canada were reported hunting below the international boundary on grounds reserved for the Assiniboines, Colonel Miles won permission to force them back across the border. The Indians reportedly numbered two thousand. Miles's command consisted of seven companies of the Fifth Infantry, two of the Sixth, seven companies of the Second Cavalry, and an artillery unit—in all nearly seven hundred officers and men, plus Crow and Cheyenne scouts. On July 17, the scouts happened upon a party of Sioux hunters and chased them across the Milk River before the tribesmen countered and surrounded the scouts. Miles finally arrived and extricated them, driving the Indians north of the border and arresting several hundred mixed-bloods who had given the Sioux ammunition. These Miles expelled into Canada before at last turning south, much to Sherman's and Sheridan's relief. En route, a part of Miles's command intercepted fifty-seven Sioux going from the Rosebud Agency to join Sitting Bull.[20]

The following year brought repeated military actions with the Sioux. In February a detachment of Second Cavalrymen under Sergeant Thaddeus B. Glover, sent to subdue a party of Indians that had reportedly attacked some citizens on the Powder River, surrounded a camp near Pumpkin Creek and held it until the arrival of Captain Snyder's mounted infantrymen from Fort Keogh. The Indians surrendered. Early the next month, units of the Fifth cornered a party of Sioux north of the Yellowstone, capturing their livestock, while west of Rosebud Creek another detachment killed several warriors and destroyed their camp. Captain Baldwin pursued others across the Yellowstone and on March 9 seized many Sioux ponies after a prolonged engagement on Little Porcupine Creek. Yet sporadic raiding parties continued to sweep through the Yellowstone region, striking civilian targets along the trail between Bismarck and Fort Keogh and making off with horses, mules, and cattle. Detachments of troops went out repeatedly from Forts Keogh and Custer, variously striking the warrior camps and regaining lost livestock. Military patrols increased in the spring and summer of 1880, when more than five hundred of the former so-called hostiles came in to Fort Keogh and laid down their arms. Two hundred fifty more gave up there in September.[21]

By autumn, 1880, the Tetons were returning from Canada in droves, partly in response to the work of emissaries sent by the commanding officer of Fort Buford, Major David H. Brotherton, but mostly out of hunger. Several hundred of these Indians camped near the agency established at Poplar River on the Missouri, downstream from the site of Fort Peck. Miles directed Major Guido Ilges and 180 men to reinforce that station, two hundred miles northeast of Fort Keogh and guarded by units of the Seventh Infantry and Seventh Cavalry. Ilges's command, consisting of five mounted companies of the Fifth Infantry and two artillery pieces, marched through deep snows and subfreezing temperatures to reach the agency. On January 2, 1881, the soldiers, assisted by one company of the Seventh Cavalry and units of the Eleventh and Seventh Infantry Regiments, attacked 400 Sioux camped nearby, forcing the surrender of more than 300. Ten days later, Ilges effected the capitulation of 185 more Indians who had taken refuge with the Yanktonais.

Ilges's actions prompted similar surrenders elsewhere, particularly one on February 26, when 325 Indians from Canada came in to Fort Buford, and another on April 11, when 135 more yielded. Finally, on July 19, 1881, the weary Hunkpapa Sitting Bull, accompanied by 45 men, 67 women, and 73 children, rode into Fort Buford, virtually ending further Teton resistance. Imprisoned at Fort Randall, Dakota Territory, for two years, Sitting Bull eventually settled near the Standing Rock Agency, where he largely stayed until his murder in December 1890, during the height of the messianic movement that preceded the Wounded Knee massacre.[22]

For all intents and purposes, the surrender of Sitting Bull symbolized the conclusion of three decades of confrontation between the government and the Sioux. The Great Sioux War

44. Major Guido Ilges (center), who conducted the last important
field operations against the Sioux before Sitting Bull's surrender. A
native of Prussia, Ilges served during the Civil War and Indian wars,
but was dismissed from the army in 1883 for duplicating pay accounts.
He is shown here surrounded by subordinate officers and civilians.
The man at Ilges's left is Joseph Culbertson, who scouted for Miles in
1876–77, and the civilian seated in front is photographer L. A. Huffman of Miles City. (Montana Historical Society, Helena)

however, had ended four years earlier, in 1877, with the massive
surrenders at the Dakota and Nebraska agencies and to Miles
at the cantonment, as well as with Sitting Bull's withdrawal from
United States soil. All had occurred in the wake of Colonel

45. The Hunkpapa chief Gall, as photographed in 1880 by David
F. Barry. Gall played an important part in the Battle of the Little
Bighorn and went into Canada with Sitting Bull in 1877. He later
helped induce the surrender of a large body of his tribesmen, pres-
aging Sitting Bull's surrender in 1881. (Paul Harbaugh and the Denver
Public Library)

Miles's appearance in the Yellowstone Valley. Whereas the first phase of General Sheridan's 1876 strategy failed when, because of logistics and extended marches, great numbers of troops in the field had been unable to contend with their more mobile foe, phase two—the creation of a stationary presence in the heart of the Indian country—proved immensely successful. This objective, long advocated by Sheridan, came only with congressional action following the Little Bighorn defeat.[23]

But most of the positive military results were due to the man chosen to implement Sheridan's strategy. Although it is clear that the consensus among his seniors in the fall of 1876 was that he should build the cantonment and occupy it through the winter, Colonel Miles had another agenda. Guided by ambition, intelligence, imagination, and a proclivity for hard work, Miles evolved his own strategy to deal with the Sioux and Cheyennes and labored industriously for eight months to make it succeed. When the tribes placed themselves on opposite sides of the Yellowstone, he used the river as a barrier to prevent their reunion. Then he went after each group separately.

Miles's procedures were methodical, yet inspired. An eminently competent field commander, he brought all of his carefully honed beliefs to bear: a determination to lead only well-trained troops, the use of both white and Indian scouts, a commitment to the practice of mounting infantry in a manner reminiscent of its use during the Civil War, and the regular employment of artillery. Most important, Miles possessed a firm resolve to pursue his quarry to the last—and he kept after the Indians in all kinds of weather. Adopting clothing and gear to accommodate his men during the coldest of winters, Miles led them on taxing campaigns that often involved clashes with the Indians under the worst possible conditions.

In all such confrontations, Miles properly claimed victory. At Cedar Creek he forcibly rejected Sitting Bull's demands that the troops leave the region, significantly lowering the Hunkpapa leader's prestige before his people and garnering the surrender of some of the Indians. Following up the events at Cedar Creek with the expedition to Fort Peck, Miles reasserted his presence and finished Sitting Bull as a serious foe after Lieutenant Baldwin's attack on his camp along Ash Creek in December 1876. The Battle of Wolf Mountains had a similar effect on the Sioux and Cheyennes south of the Yellowstone, and most of

46. Gall's village at Poplar Creek, Montana, as photographed by David F. Barry in 1881. The camp approximated in appearance those attacked by Miles's command a few years earlier, although by that time the tipis were fashioned more often from government-furnished canvas than from hides. (Paul Harbaugh and the Denver Public Library)

them, including Crazy Horse, soon surrendered at the agencies. And when small numbers of Indians under Lame Deer presented a final challenge, Miles showed them no mercy.

Besides defeating the Indians, Miles's campaigns drew media notice that promoted the development of eastern Montana by cattlemen and sheepherders. Over the next few years the presence of Forts Keogh and Custer opened the Yellowstone to regular steamboat and railroad transit, encouraging settlement throughout the river valley and along its tributaries. The removal of the Sioux and Cheyennes from the region thus coincided with the objectives of the federal government in fostering westward migration by the white population.

Because of the Custer disaster, the Great Sioux War produced inordinate casualty figures for the army, compared with those estimated for the Indians. Total losses during the period of February 1876, through December 1877 numbered 283 men killed (16 officers, 267 enlisted men) and 125 wounded (2 officers, 123 enlisted), for an aggregate of 408 killed or wounded. Indian losses have been much harder to determine, but a reasonable estimate, partly based on the testimony of warrior participants, places them at approximately 150 killed and 90 wounded, including the noncombatant elderly and women and children (although many other noncombatants died of starvation or exposure). Total government cost for prosecuting the conflict with the Sioux and Cheyennes, as calculated in the offices of the Military Division of the Missouri, was $2,312,531.24. In 1990 dollars the amount equals approximately $27,663,242.[24]

Colonel Nelson A. Miles's army career was improved by his performance in 1876 and 1877 and in the following years that he spent at Fort Keogh overseeing the District of the Yellowstone. Now widely acknowledged as one of the country's premier Indian fighters, Miles finally attained the promotion he so diligently sought. In 1880 he won the star of a Regular Army brigadier general, departing Fort Keogh to become commander of the Department of the Columbia, which comprised Washington, Idaho, and Alaska territories and the state of Oregon. In 1885 he was assigned to the Department of the Missouri, and less than a year later he replaced General Crook as commander of the Department of Arizona, in time to receive the final surrender of the Chiricahua Apache leader, Geronimo. His role in the Geronimo Campaign was marred by controversy leading to protracted public disagreements with Crook over the conduct of that campaign and the treatment of the Apache prisoners. Ironically, Crook's death in March 1890 prompted Miles's promotion to major general, commanding the Military Division of the Missouri. Perhaps fittingly, he oversaw operations at Pine Ridge and the other Sioux reservations in 1890–91 before and after the Wounded Knee tragedy, which proved to be the last major armed encounter with those Indians.

In 1895, on the basis of seniority, Miles became commanding general of the United States Army. His tenure was stormy and marked by contention, stemming partly from his past perceived transgressions against fellow officers and from the fact that he lacked the normally prerequisite West Point training. When the Spanish-American War broke out in 1898, Miles presided over an army that was unprepared and ill-equipped. He developed policy differences with President William McKinley and quickly lost favor as an advisor. While most fighting in the brief conflict occurred in Cuba and the Philippines, Miles led an expedition to Puerto Rico that met little resistance. Later he became embroiled in a controversy over beef supplies for the army that further compromised his effectiveness.

Miles's increasing propensity for altercation made him a political liability after Theodore Roosevelt became president. Although he had been promoted to lieutenant general, he was not happy in his office and welcomed retirement in 1903. Despite his long and distinguished military career, Miles was largely forgotten by the public. Indications that he regarded his Indian wars service as perhaps his most significant can be seen in his membership in the Order of Indian Wars, a fraternal body composed of officers of the western campaigns, and in his enthusiastic support for pensions for retired enlisted men, many of whom had logged months under his command during the Great Sioux War. In the end, Miles outlived most of the veterans of his campaigns. On May 15, 1925, he died in Washington, D.C., at age eighty-five, among the last to have engaged Crazy Horse and Sitting Bull on the stark Montana plains.

Appendix

Colonel Miles's Congratulatory Order to His Troops, Tongue River Cantonment, January 31, 1877. (Source: Miles Collection, U.S. Army Military History Institute.)

General Orders No. 2.

The Commanding Officer takes pleasure in expressing to his Regiment his full acknowledgement of the laborious and dangerous service it has performed and his congratulation on the enviable record it has made and valuable results achieved.

The record of the Fifth Infantry in the Seminole War in Florida, in the Mexican War, and against the Navajo Indians in New Mexico, and the Cheyennes, Kiowas and Comanches in the Indian Territory, has gained for it an honored name. Its service during the past three months has been one of continued and gratifying success. Taking advantage of a division of the enemy, it fell suddenly upon the main portion of the hostile Sioux Indians under Sitting Bull, and in a fair and open contest against superior numbers it defeated and routed the entire body, and by its rapid pursuit compelled the surrender of the main portion, double its number, and, it is believed, the largest body of Indians ever surrendered to troops in the field. Receiving as hostages the principal Chiefs as a guarantee of their good faith, the Regiment turned to pursue those still hostile. If a series of unfortunate circumstances shall to any extent impair the full consummation of that important work, the responsibility rests not with the Regiment. Its work was well done.

Having followed the retreating remnant, thoroughly examined and cleaned a wide section of country and divided into small columns, one of which defeated and utterly routed the remainder of Sitting Bull's band, then it was that the Command turned its face southward to cope with the best armed and most noted warriors of the Sioux Nation, the confederated tribes of the Ogalallas and Cheyennes, the followers of Crazy Horse. Though wearied by long marches and blinding storms, it cheerfully responded to the summons. Leaving a small portion replaced by two companies of the 22nd Infantry, the Command marched out in mid winter to contend not only against the threatening elements, but against a formidable foe, and with undaunted courage it defeated, on ground of their own choosing, thrice its numbers in the fastnesses of the Wolf Mountains.

Here in the home of the hostile Sioux this command during the past three months has marched twelve hundred miles, fought three engagements, besides affairs of less importance, has cleared a vast section of country, and demonstrated the fact that the American Soldier hesitates not at any undertaking however hazardous, and can overcome obstacles apparently insurmountable. Fortunate indeed is the officer who commands men who will improvise boats of wagon beds, and fearlessly dash out into the cold and turbid waters and amid the treacherous current and floating ice, cross and recross the Great Missouri; who will defy the elements on these bleak plains in a Montana winter, and who have on every field defeated superior numbers. The Commanding Officer would especially congratulate those officers who, setting a soldierly example, have marched at the head of their commands and have led them in battle, and who have shared the hardships as well as honors of the Regiment, and trusts that to the officers this valuable experience will be beneficial in after years, and to the soldier, the record he has made cannot but be exceedingly gratifying.

While he would congratulate the living, he could not fail to pay a tribute to the few honored dead who have laid down their lives in this remote region, battling against a savage foe for the advancement of civilization.

By Command of Colonel N. A. Miles,
J. W. Pope
2d Lieut. 5th Infantry
Act'g Adjutant

Notes

NOTES TO CHAPTER ONE

1. *Leavenworth Daily Times*, July 13, 1876; Simon Snyder, "Diary of Simon Snyder, Captain, Co. F, 5th U.S. Infantry for 1876," July 12, 1876, Custer Battlefield National Monument, Crow Agency, Montana (hereinafter cited as Snyder, Diary); Samuel J. Ovenshine Diary (hereinafter cited as Ovenshine, Diary), July 12, 1876, Ovenshine Family Papers, Army War College, U.S. Army Military History Institute, Carlisle, Pennsylvania (hereinafter cited as Ovenshine Family Papers); Nelson A. Miles, *Personal Recollections and Observations of General Nelson A. Miles*, p. 213. For a description of Fort Leavenworth at the approximate time, see John S. Billings, War Department, U.S. Surgeon General's Office, Circular no. 8. *A Report on the Hygiene of the United States Army, with Descriptions of Posts*, pp. 273–78.

2. *Leavenworth Daily Times*, July 7, 1876.

3. Ibid.; *Leavenworth Daily Times*, July 11 and 18, 1876; *New York Herald*, July 9 and 29, 1876; Miles, *Personal Recollections*, p. 212. Miles's immediate command leaving Fort Leavenworth numbered 17 officers, 212 enlisted men, and 17 civilian employees, plus 7 horses, 12 six-mule teams, and 2 ambulances. Nelson A. Miles, "Diary—July & Aug. 1876," July 7 and 12, 1876, Nelson Miles Papers, folder, Indian Campaigns, 1869–1876, inclusive, Army War College, U.S. Army Military History Institute, Carlisle, Pennsylvania (hereinafter cited as Miles, Diary).

4. *Leavenworth Daily Times*, July 12, 1876.

5. Factors bearing on the westward migration of the Teton Sioux and its impact on adjacent tribes and the United States are in Richard White, "The Winning of the West: The Expansion of the Western Sioux in the Eighteenth and Nineteenth Centuries," pp. 319–43.

6. Robert M. Utley, "War Houses in the Sioux Country," p. 22. Detailed discussion of the specific features of the 1868 treaty is in Paul L. Hedren, *Fort Laramie in 1876: Chronicle of a Frontier Post at War*, pp. 3–6.

7. Robert M. Utley, *The Indian Frontier of the American West, 1846–1890*, pp. 164–65, and 170; Henry E. Fritz, *The Movement for Indian Assimilation, 1860–1890*, pp. 126–27. Details of the Peace Policy are discussed in several works. See, particularly, Robert M. Utley, "The Celebrated Peace Policy of General Grant," pp.

121–42; Henry E. Fritz, "The Making of Grant's Peace Policy," pp. 411–32; Henry Waltmann, "Circumstantial Reformer: President Grant and the Indian Problem," pp. 323–42; and Richard R. Levine, "Indian Fighters and Indian Reformers: Grant's Indian Peace Policy and the Conservative Consensus," pp. 329–52. A nineteenth-century appraisal is in Lawrie Tatum, *Our Red Brothers and the Peace Policy of President Ulysses S. Grant.* For broad views of federal Indian policy of the period, see Fritz, *Indian Assimilation*; Francis Paul Prucha, *American Indian Policy in Crisis: Christian Reformers and the Indian, 1865–1900*; Loring Benson Priest, *Uncle Sam's Stepchildren: The Reformation of U.S. Indian Policy, 1865–1887*; Robert W. Mardock, *The Reformers and the American Indian*; Richard N. Ellis, *General Pope and U.S. Indian Policy*; and Robert Wooster, *The Military and United States Indian Policy, 1865–1903.*

8. Paul A. Hutton, *Phil Sheridan and His Army*, p. 292; Wooster, *United States Indian Policy*, p. 161; Hedren, *Fort Laramie in 1876*, pp. 11–12.

9. A standard ethnological treatment of the Teton Sioux appears in Royall B. Hassrick, *The Sioux: Life and Customs of a Warrior Society*, while their history is perhaps best recounted in the trilogy by George E. Hyde, *Red Cloud's Folk: A History of the Oglala Sioux Indians, Spotted Tail's Folk: A History of the Brule Sioux*, and *A Sioux Chronicle.* For the Northern

Cheyennes' association with the Teton Sioux during the period of the 1850s to the 1880s, see the Hyde books and also George Bird Grinnell, *The Fighting Cheyennes.* Grinnell treats Cheyenne culture and history in several works, but notably in *The Cheyenne Indians: Their History and Ways of Life.* For the Northern Arapahoes, see Virginia Cole Trenholm, *The Arapahoes, Our People.*

10. Utley, *Indian Frontier*, pp. 178–80. The best modern overview of northern plains ethnohistory, to include intertribal and intratribal dynamics respecting treaty making and treaty stipulations and Teton-U.S. Army relations during the 1850s through 1880s is in Raymond J. DeMallie, "The Sioux in Dakota and Montana Territories: Cultural and Historical Background of the Ogden B. Read Collection," in *Vestiges of a Proud Nation: The Ogden B. Read Northern Plains Indian Collection*, pp. 19–69. *Annual Report of the Commissioner of Indian Affairs, to the Secretary of the Interior for the Year 1876*, p. xiv (hereinafter cited as *Report of the Commissioner of Indian Affairs, 1876*).

11. Utley, "War Houses," pp. 20, 21, and 24.

12. Ibid., pp. 24–25; William E. Lass, "Steamboats on the Yellowstone," p. 29; Maurice Frink and Casey Barthelmess, *Photographer on an Army Mule*, pp. 71 and 73.

13. Hutton, *Phil Sheridan and His Army*, p. 299; Wooster, *United States Indian Policy*, p. 162; Hed-

i
ii
ei
m
15.
late
rec
mer
chap
Cust
Cente
War of 1876.

16. Hutton, *Phil Sheridan and His Army*, pp. 301–2. For Sheridan's role in the post–Civil War army, and especially during the Sioux and Cheyenne troubles of the 1870s, see also Paul Andrew Hutton, "Philip H. Sheridan," in *Soldiers West: Biographies from the Military Frontier*, ed., Paul Andrew Hutton, pp. 78–99.

17. An alternative explanation of the origin and development of total war as applied in Indian combat is in Wooster, *United States Indian Policy*, pp. 135–42.

18. Utley, *Indian Frontier*, pp. 166–67, and 169.

19. The most thorough account of the Powder River campaign and the Reynolds fight is in Jesse W. Vaughn, *The Reynolds Campaign on Powder River*.

20. For the Rosebud encounter, see Neil C. Mangum, *Battle of the Rosebud: Prelude to the Little Bighorn*; Jesse W. Vaughn, *With Crook at the Rosebud*; and Jesse W. Vaughn, *Indian Fights: New Facts on Seven Encounters*, pp. 117–44. A biographical essay of Crook appears in Jerome A. Greene, "George Crook," in Hutton, *Soldiers West*, pp. 115–36.

21. The Custer fight on the Little Bighorn River dominated the campaign news in the summer of 1876; it continues to dominate the historical record of the army's actions against the Sioux and Northern Cheyennes as well as the entire spectrum of the Indian wars between 1865 and 1890. The literature on the event is extensive. For a sampling, see the following works and their bibliographies: Stewart, *Custer's Luck*; Jerome A. Greene, *Evidence and the Custer Enigma: A Reconstruction of Indian-Military History*; William A. Graham, comp., *The Custer Myth: A Source Book of Custeriana*; Douglas D. Scott, Richard A. Fox, Jr., Melissa A. Connor, and Dick Harmon, *Archaeological Perspectives on the Battle of the Little Bighorn*; and Robert M. Utley, *Cavalier in Buckskin: George Armstrong Custer and the Western Military Frontier*.

22. *New York Herald*, July 21, 1876; Hutton, *Phil Sheridan and His Army*, pp. 318–19; Henry Romeyn, "The First March of the Fifth Infantry in Montana," p. 113.

23. "Report of Lieut. Gen. P. H. Sheridan," Nov. 25, 1876, in *Re-*

port of the Secretary of War, 1876, p. 445; Annual Report of the Commissioner of Indian Affairs, to the Secretary of the Interior for the Year 1877, p. 14 (hereinafter cited as Report of the Commissioner of Indian Affairs, 1877); Utley, "War Houses," p. 25; Hutton, Phil Sheridan and His Army, p. 319; Hedren, Fort Laramie in 1876, p. 154; Robert A. Murray, Military Posts in the Powder River Country of Wyoming, 1865–1894, p. 109.
24. New York Herald, July 23, 1876. For the Warbonnet Creek encounter, see, particularly, Paul L. Hedren, First Scalp for Custer: The Skirmish at Warbonnet Creek, Nebraska, July 17, 1876, with a Short History of the Warbonnet Battlefield.
25. "The Fifth Regiment of Infantry," in Theophilus F. Rodenbough and William L. Haskin, eds., The Army of the United States: Historical Sketches of Staff and Line, with Portraits of Generals-in-Chief, pp. 466–75; Nelson A. Miles, Serving the Republic: Memoirs of the Civil and Military Life of Nelson A. Miles, Lieutenant-General, United States Army, pp. 143–44; Kenneth S. Gallagher and Robert L. Pigeon, eds., Infantry Regiments of the United States Army: A Complete Guide to the History, Decorations, Honors, and Colors of each Infantry Regiment in the Regular Army, pp. 35–39. For the campaigns of the Fifth Infantry in 1874–75, see James L. Haley, The Buffalo War: The History of the Red River Indian Uprising of 1874.
26. Francis B. Heitman, comp., Historical Register and Dictionary

of the United States Army, from Its Organization, September 29, 1789, to March 2, 1903, 1:709.
27. This biographical sketch of Miles is drawn from Peter R. DeMontravel, "The Career of Lieutenant General Nelson A. Miles from the Civil War through the Indian Wars," pp. 1–7; Robert M. Utley, "Nelson A. Miles," in Hutton, Soldiers West, pp. 213–27; Charles D. Rhodes, "Nelson Appleton Miles," in Dictionary of American Biography, ed. Dumas Malone, 6:614–16; Heitman, Historical Register, 1:708–9; George E. Pond, "Major-General Nelson A. Miles," pp. 562–74; and Mark Mayo Boatner III, The Civil War Dictionary, p. 550; For other background information on Miles, see Virginia W. Johnson, The Unregimented General: A Biography of Nelson A. Miles; Newton F. Tolman, The Search for General Miles; Brian C. Pohanka, ed., Nelson A. Miles: A Documentary Biography of His Military Career, 1861–1903; and two autobiographical efforts, Personal Recollections and Serving the Republic. In addition to the biographies, discussion of specific aspects of Miles's later career is in Peter R. DeMontravel, "General Nelson A. Miles and the Wounded Knee Controversy," pp. 23–44, and Edward Ranson, "Nelson A. Miles as Commanding General," pp. 179–200. Quote is from Harry H. Anderson, "Nelson A. Miles and the Sioux War of 1876–77," p. 25.

NOTES TO CHAPTER TWO

1. Miles, *Personal Recollections*, p. 213.

2. Ibid.; Miles, Diary, July 12, 14, and 20, 1876; *Leavenworth Daily Times*, July 27, 1876; Ovenshine, Diary, July 14, 16, and 17, 1876; Regimental Returns of Companies B, E, F, G, H, and K, Regimental Returns of the Fifth Infantry, 1870–79, Record of Events. National Archives (NA) Microfilm Publications M665, Roll 58 (hereinafter cited as Regimental Returns of the Fifth Infantry); and Miles to wife, Mary, July 16, 1876, in Johnson, *Unregimented General*, p. 85.

3. Miles, Diary, July 22, 1876; Miles to Mary, July 22, 1876, in Johnson, *Unregimented General*, p. 86; Ovenshine, Diary, July 22, 1876.

4. Snyder, Diary, July 23, 1876; Ovenshine, Diary, July 23, 1876; *Leavenworth Daily Times*, Feb. 4, 1877; Miles, *Personal Recollections*, pp. 213–14; Regimental Returns of the Fifth Infantry, July 1876, Record of Events. Quote is from Miles to Mary, July 23, 1876, in Johnson, *Unregimented General*, p. 87. See also Miles, Diary, July 23, 1876.

5. Snyder, Diary, July 24, 1876.

6. Quotes are from Miles, *Personal Recollections*, pp. 214–15. See also Miles, *Serving the Republic*, p. 141.

7. Ovenshine to wife, July 27, 1876, in letter no. 6, folder, Samuel J. Ovenshine Personal Correspondence, 1874 and 1876, Ovenshine Family Papers. See also, Miles, Diary, July 27, 1876.

8. Snyder, Diary, July 26, 27, and 28, 1876; Ovenshine, Diary, July 26, 27, and 28, 1876; Miles to Mary, July 29, 1876, in Johnson, *Unregimented General*, p. 88; Miles, *Serving the Republic*, pp. 142–43.

9. Miles, *Serving the Republic*, p. 144; Miles to Mary, July 29, 1876, in Johnson, *Unregimented General*, pp. 89–90; George M. Miles, "Notes of a Trip made by G. M. Miles from Westminster Mass to Montana 1876," entry for July 31, 1876, George M. Miles Papers, folder 1, Montana Historical Society, Helena, Montana (hereinafter cited as G. M. Miles, "Notes of a Trip").

10. Thomson P. McElrath, *The Yellowstone Valley: What It Is, Where It Is, and How to Get to It: A Handbook for Tourists and Settlers*, pp. 19–24.

11. Mark H. Brown, *The Plainsmen of the Yellowstone: A History of the Yellowstone Basin*, pp. 110–24 and 138–39. A synopsis of military exploration on the northern plains, and particularly in the area of the Yellowstone River and its tributaries, is in Thomas W. Symons, "The Army and the Exploration of the West," pp. 205–49.

12. *New York Times*, Sept. 12, 1876 (The *Times* dispatches have been compiled in Cuthbert Mills, *The Cuthbert Mills Letters to the New York Times during the Indian War of 1876*. Compiled and edited by James Willert); Brown, *Plainsmen*, pp. 195–203; McElrath, *Yellowstone Valley*, pp. 31–33. For the Yellowstone expedition of *1873*,

see John M. Carroll, ed., *The Yellowstone Expedition of 1873*, and Lawrence A. Frost, *Custer's 7th Cav. and the Campaign of 1873*.
13. Edgar I. Stewart, ed., *Pennyan-Acre Empire in the West*, pp. 180–83; Marvin E. Kroeker, "William B. Hazen," in Hutton, *Soldiers West*, pp. 204–5. Quote is from "Report of General Gibbon," Oct. 17, 1876, in *Report of the Secretary of War, 1876*, p. 476.
14. *Chicago Daily Tribune*, Sept. 9, 1876.
15. Robert Bruce, "Alfred Howe Terry," in *Dictionary of American Biography*, ed. Dumas Malone, 9:378–79; Boatner, *Civil War Dictionary*, p. 831; Hutton, *Phil Sheridan and His Army*, pp. 130–31. For Terry's western service, see John W. Bailey, *Pacifying the Plains: General Alfred Terry and the Decline of the Sioux, 1866–1890*.
16. John G. Bourke, *Bourke's Diary, from Journals of 1st Lt. John Gregory Bourke, June 27–Sept. 15, 1876. Chronicle of the 1876 Indian War*, compiled by James Willert, pp. 107–8.
17. George W. Cullum, *Biographical Register of the Officers and Graduates of the U.S. Military Academy, at West Point, N.Y. . . .*, 2:192–93 ; Boatner, *Civil War Dictionary*, pp. 340–41.
18. "Report of Lieut. Gen. P. H. Sheridan," Nov. 25, 1876, in *Report of the Secretary of War, 1876*, p. 445; "Report of General Terry," Nov. 21, 1876, in *Report of the Secretary of War, 1876*, p. 465; "Report of General Gibbon," Oct. 17, 1876, in *Report of the Sec-*

retary of War, 1876, p. 474; John Gibbon, *Gibbon on the Sioux Campaign of 1876*, p. 49; Samuel L. Meddaugh, "Diary of S. L. Meddaugh, 6th U.S. Infantry, Covering the Indian Campaign along the Yellowstone River, from May to September, 1876," typescript copy in the Newberry Library, Chicago, p. 5 (hereinafter cited as Meddaugh, Diary); "Annual Report of Lieutenant Edward Maguire, Corps of Engineers, for the Fiscal Year Ending June 30, 1877," in *Annual Report of the Chief of Engineers to the Secretary of War for the Year 1877*, part 2, p. 1349, (hereinafter cited as Maguire report). Lisle G. Brown, "The Yellowstone Supply Depot," pp. 27–28. The supply depot had earlier been established near the mouth of Glendive Creek, downstream on the Yellowstone, and had been relocated at the mouth of the Powder River in early June at Terry's direction. Terry utilized the mobility afforded by steamers on the Yellowstone throughout his operation to relocate his supplies in accordance with the movements of his command. Ibid., pp. 25 and 26–27.
19. First quote is from Gibbon, *Sioux Campaign*, p. 49. Brown, "Yellowstone Supply Depot"; Henry B. Freeman, *The Freeman Journal: The Infantry in the Sioux Campaign of 1876*, edited by George A. Schneider, p. 72. Second quote is from John S. Gray, "Captain Clifford's Story—Part III," p. 42.

20. Gray, "Captain Clifford's Story," pp. 42–43; Freeman, *Journal*, p. 72; Maguire report, p. 1349; Gibbon, *Sioux Campaign*, p. 50; "Journal of the Marches made by the Forces under Colonel John Gibbon, Commanding the Expedition down the Yellowstone, between the 1st Day of April, and the 29th Day of September, 1876, by Lieutenant E. J. M'Clernand, Second Cavalry, Acting Engineer Officer," in Maguire report, p. 1372 (hereinafter cited as McClernand, *Journal*); John S. Gray, "Sutler on Custer's Last Campaign," p. 20. For the movement of the Sixth Infantry companies from the Powder River to Rosebud Creek, see Meddaugh, Diary, pp. 5–7.

21. Ovenshine, Diary, July 31, 1876; Miles, Diary, July 31, 1876; *New York Herald*, Aug. 7, 1876; Oskaloosa M. Smith, "Twenty-second Regiment of Infantry," in Rodenbough and Haskins, *Army of the United States*, pp. 685–86; George W. Webb, comp., *Chronological List of Engagements between the Regular Army of the United States and Various Tribes of Hostile Indians, which Occurred during the Years 1790 to 1898, Inclusive*, p. 77; Gray, *Centennial Campaign*, pp. 210–11; Miles to Mary, Aug. 2, 1876, in Johnson, *Unregimented General*, p. 90; Regimental Returns of the Twenty-second Infantry, 1876–77. NA Microfilm Publications M665, roll no. 228 (hereinafter cited as Regimental Returns of the Twenty-second Infantry); *Leavenworth Daily Times*, July 21, 1876; *History*

of the Twenty-second United States Infantry, 1866–1922, p. 7. The wounded soldier was Private John Donahoe, Company G, Twenty-second Infantry. "List of Wounded." NA, RG 94, Records of the Adjutant General's Department, entry 624, box 1.

22. For the movement of the Indians after the Little Bighorn fight, see Doane Robinson, *A History of the Dakota or Sioux Indians*, p. 437; Stanley Vestal, *Sitting Bull, Champion of the Sioux*, p. 183; Thomas B. Marquis, *A Warrior Who Fought Custer*, pp. 275–80; Peter J. Powell, *People of the Sacred Mountain: A History of the Northern Cheyenne Chiefs and Warrior Societies, 1830–1879, with an Epilogue, 1969–1974*, 2:1045–47; Hyde, *Red Cloud's Folk*, pp. 274–76; Hyde, *Spotted Tail's Folk*, p. 383; John G. Neihardt, *Black Elk Speaks: Being the Life Story of a Holy Man of the Oglala Sioux*, pp. 135–37; and Grinnell, *Fighting Cheyennes*, p. 383. For the military view of the fires set by the Indians, see telegram, Lieutenant Colonel James W. Forsyth to Sheridan, Aug. 6, 1876, NA, RG 393, Records of United States Army Continental Commands (hereinafter cited as NA, RG 393), Records of the Military Division of the Missouri, item 5287.

23. Regimental Returns of the Twenty-second Infantry, Return for August 1876; Gibbon, *Sioux Campaign*, p. 50; Gray, "Captain Clifford's Story," p. 43; Joseph Mills Hanson, *The Conquest of the Missouri: Being the Story of the Life and Exploits of Captain Grant*

Marsh, p. 323; Edward S. Godfrey, *The Field Diary of Lt. Edward Settle Godfrey*, edited by Edgar I. and Jane R. Stewart, p. 30.

24. Meddaugh, Diary, p. 8. The warrior killed was apparently an Oglala named Yellow Shirt. Raymond J. DeMallie, ed., *The Sixth Grandfather: Black Elk's Teachings Given to John G. Neihardt*, p. 199.

25. For accounts of Moore's encounter with the Indians at the mouth of the Powder, see DeMallie, *Sixth Grandfather*, pp. 7–8; *New York Herald*, Aug. 8 and 11, 1876; Michael D. Hill and Ben Innis, eds., "The Fort Buford Diary of Private Sanford, 1876–1877," p. 19; "Report of Maj. Orlando H. Moore," Aug. 4, 1876, in *Report of the Secretary of War, 1876*, pp. 480–81; Hanson, *Conquest of the Missouri*, pp. 325–30; *Record of Engagements with Hostile Indians within the Military Division of the Missouri, from 1868 to 1882, Lieutenant-General P. H. Sheridan, Commanding*, p. 60; Webb, *Chronological List*, p. 77; Gray, "Captain Clifford's Story," p. 43; Smith, "The Twenty-second Regiment of Infantry," in Rodenbough and Haskin, *Army of the United States*, pp. 685–86; Gray, *Centennial Campaign*, pp. 210–11; and Brown, "Yellowstone Supply Depot," pp. 29–30. Scout Thomas H. Leforge stated that the Indians emptied the grain because they wanted the sacks, which they carried off. Thomas B. Marquis, *Memoirs of a White Crow Indian*, p. 263. Certain press accounts of the fight at the mouth of the Powder River cast

Moore's performance negatively. It was said that when Moore refused to send troops in relief of the scouts, eight soldiers disobeyed him and accompanied the steamer's captain, Grant Marsh, in the attempt, for which action Moore threatened their courts-martial. "Steamboat men do not hesitate to pronounce Col. Moore's conduct cowardly in the extreme." *Leavenworth Daily Times*, Aug. 8, 1876. The location of Moore's defense site was described years later: "This high ground commanding was a kind of half & 1/4 circle sand dune. . . . We used to find pieces of shell & some that did not explode in the vicinity. The landing could be located by rubbish &c. long afterward." Daniel H. Bowman to William Carey Brown, Mar. 17, 1932. William Carey Brown Collection, box 21, folder 36, Western History Collections, University of Colorado Library, Boulder.

26. *New York Herald*, July 21, 1876; Alfred H. Terry: *The Field Diary of General Alfred H. Terry: The Yellowstone Expedition, 1876*, p. 12; Hutton, *Phil Sheridan and His Army*, p. 319; quote is from Assistant Adjutant General (AAG), Division of the Missouri, to Terry, July 20, 1876, NA, RG 393, Records of the Military Division of the Missouri, item 1981; telegram, Forsyth to Sheridan, Aug. 6, 1876, ibid., item 5287; Gray, *Centennial Campaign*, pp. 209–10.

27. Miles, Diary, Aug. 1, 1876; G. M. Miles, "Notes of a Trip," pp. 18, and 20; Ovenshine, Diary,

Aug. 1 and 2, 1876; Ovenshine to wife, Aug. 1, 1876, in letter no. 8, Ovenshine Family Papers; Gray, "Captain Clifford's Story," p. 43; "Report of General Terry," Nov. 21, 1876, in *Report of the Secretary of War*, 1876, p. 465; Terry, *Field Diary*, p. 12; Snyder, Diary, Aug. 2, 1876; Godfrey, *Field Diary*, pp. 30–31; Gray, *Centennial Campaign*, p. 210.

28. Terry, *Field Diary*, p. 12; "Report of General Terry," Nov. 21, 1876, in *Report of the Secretary of War, 1876*, p. 465; "Report of General Gibbon," Oct. 17, 1876, in *Report of the Secretary of War, 1876*, p. 474; McClernand, Journal, p. 1372; Gibbon, *Sioux Campaign*, pp. 50–51; Snyder, Diary, Aug. 3, 1876; Gray, "Captain Clifford's Story," p. 43; Godfrey, *Field Diary*, p. 31; Ovenshine to wife, Aug. 3, 1876, in letter no. 9, Ovenshine Family Papers.

29. Telegram, Forsyth to Sheridan, Aug. 6, 1876, NA, RG 393, item 5287; Miles to Mary, Aug. 2, 1876, in Johnson, *Unregimented General*, pp. 90–91.

30. Quotes of Miles are from Miles to Mary, Aug. 4, 1876, in Johnson, *Unregimented General*, pp. 93–95. Baldwin to wife Alice, Aug. 4, 1876, Frank D. Baldwin Papers, Henry H. Huntington Library, San Marino, California (hereinafter cited as Baldwin Papers), quoted in Robert C. Carriker, "Frank D. Baldwin," in Hutton, *Soldiers West*, p. 241. As early as August 1, Captain Ovenshine heard from other officers that "we are to build the new post." Ovenshine to wife, Aug. 1, 1876,

in letter no. 8, Ovenshine Family Papers.

31. Quoted in Gray, "Captain Clifford's Story," p. 43. For activities of August 4, see Terry, *Field Diary*, p. 12; Snyder, Diary, Aug. 4, 1876; Freeman, *Freeman Journal*, p. 73; Hill and Innis, "Fort Buford Diary," p. 19; and William H. White, *Custer, Cavalry, and Crows: The Story of William White as told to Thomas Marquis*, pp. 89–90.

32. White, *Custer, Cavalry, and Crows*, 89–90. G. M. Miles, "Notes of a Trip," pp. 22–24; Terry, *Field Diary*, pp. 12–13; Godfrey, *Field Diary*, pp. 31–32; Ovenshine to wife, Aug. 3, 1876, in letter no. 9, Ovenshine Family Papers; Ovenshine, Diary, Aug. 5, 1876; Maguire report, p. 1349; "Report of General Terry," Nov. 21, 1876, in *Report of the Secretary of War, 1876*, p. 466; Meddaugh, Diary, p. 8; *New York Herald*, Aug. 15, 1876; Brown, "Yellowstone Supply Depot," p. 30. George Miles described the fortification of the depot on the north side of the Yellowstone opposite the mouth of Rosebud Creek. The entrenchments were composed of "grain[,] earth works & timber," and were "nearly square with one side on the river over 100 yds square with a gatling gun at 2 corners[,] a trench on the other side & a row of bush & limbs about 30 ft. in front of trench." On August 12, George Miles noted, "The soldiers are still at work building breastworks[,] putting another layer of logs round & banking up with earth." "Notes of a Trip," pp. 26 and 29.

33. Maguire report, p. 1349; Freeman, *Freeman Journal*, p. 73; Godfrey, *Field Diary*, p. 32.

34. Miles to Mary, Aug. 7, 1876, in Johnson, *Unregimented General*, p. 95; Journal of Frank D. Baldwin, Aug. 2, 1876, Baldwin Papers, box 1, folder A3f (hereinafter cited as Journal of Baldwin). See also Baldwin to wife, Aug. 4, 6, and 7, 1876. Baldwin Papers, box 11.

35. *New York Herald*, Aug. 15, 1876; Freeman, *Freeman Journal*, p. 73; Hanson, *Conquest of the Missouri*, pp. 331–32; Terry, *Field Diary*, p. 13; Gibbon, *Sioux Campaign*, p. 51; G. M. Miles, "Notes of a Trip," pp. 24–25; "Report of General Terry," Nov. 21, 1876, in *Report of the Secretary of War, 1876*, pp. 465–66.

36. McClernand, Journal, p. 1372; Maguire report, p. 1350.

37. Freeman, *Freeman Journal*, p. 73; *New York Herald*, Aug. 24, 1876; G. M. Miles, "Notes of a Trip," p. 25; Terry, *Field Diary*, p. 13; Snyder, Diary, Aug. 8, 1876; McClernand, Journal, p. 1372; Godfrey, *Field Diary*, p. 32; Ovenshine, Diary, Aug. 8, 1876; Ovenshine to wife, Aug. 8, 1876, in letter no. 11, Ovenshine Family Papers; Meddaugh, Diary, p. 8; "Report of General Gibbon," Oct. 17, 1876, in *Report of the Secretary of War, 1876*, p. 474; "Report of General Terry," Nov. 21, 1876, in ibid.; Gibbon, *Sioux Campaign*, p. 51; Hill and Innis, "Fort Buford Diary," p. 19; Gray, "Captain Clifford's Story," pp.

43 and 48; Journal of Baldwin, Aug. 8, 1876; Smith, "Twenty-second Regiment of Infantry," p. 686; Johnson, *Unregimented General*, p. 97; Gray, *Centennial Campaign*, p. 214. John F. Finerty placed Terry's command strength at 83 officers and 1,536 enlisted men, besides the scouts, broken down as follows: infantry, 55 officers and 922 men; cavalry, 26 officers and 574 men; artillery complement, 2 officers and 40 men. *War-Path and Bivouac; or, The Conquest of the Sioux*, p. 355.

38. Romeyn, "First March of the Fifth Infantry," pp. 113–16; Hill and Innis, "Fort Buford Diary," p. 19; Ovenshine, Diary, Aug. 9, 1876; Ovenshine to wife, Aug. 9, 1876, in letter no. 11, Ovenshine Family Papers; Godfrey, *Field Diary*, p. 33; Freeman, *Freeman Journal*, p. 74; Meddaugh, Diary, p. 9; McClernand, Journal, p. 1372; Terry, *Field Diary*, p. 13; Snyder, Diary, Aug. 9, 1876; "Report of General Terry," Nov. 21, 1876, in *Report of the Secretary of War, 1876*, p. 466; Gibbon, *Sioux Campaign*, p. 51. Quoted material is from Gray, "Captain Clifford's Story," p. 48.

39. Quoted in Gray, "Captain Clifford's Story," p. 48. For the disposition of Terry's troops, see also the accounts of James J. O'Kelly of the *New York Herald*, Aug. 24, 1876, and James W. Howard of the *Chicago Daily Tribune*, Sept. 9, 1876, included in Bourke, *Bourke's Diary*, pp. 108–12.

40. Bourke, *Bourke's Diary*, pp. 108–12; Freeman, *Freeman Jour-*

nal, p. 74; McClernand, Journal, p. 1372; Maguire report, p. 1350; Terry, *Field Diary*, p. 13; *New York Herald*, Aug. 21 and 24, 1876; *Cheyenne Daily Leader*, Aug. 27, 1876; Charles King, *Campaigning with Crook and Stories of Army Life*, pp. 78–79; Gibbon, *Sioux Campaign*, pp. 51–52; Ovenshine, Diary, Aug. 10, 1876; Ovenshine to wife, Aug. 11, 1876, in letter no. 11, Ovenshine Family Papers; Godfrey, *Field Diary*, pp. 33–34; White, *Custer, Cavalry, and Crows*, pp. 91–92; Romeyn, "First March of the Fifth Infantry," pp. 113–16; Meddaugh, Diary, p. 9; Thaddeus H. Capron, *Marching with General Crook; or, The Bighorn and Yellowstone Expedition against Hostile Indians in the Summer of 1876, . . . Being the Diary of Lieutenant Thaddeus Hurlbut Capron, Company C, Ninth Infantry*, ed. by Ray Meketa, pp. 43–44; John G. Bourke, *On the Border with Crook*, p. 351; William F. Cody, *An Autobiography of Buffalo Bill*, pp. 270–71.

41. King, *Campaigning with Crook*, pp. 81–82.

42. Cody, *Autobiography*, pp. 271–72.

43. See General Field Orders no. 8, Headquarters Department of Dakota, Camp on Rosebud Creek, August 10, 1876, NA, RG 393, Records of the Military Division of the Missouri. item 3945.

44. Romeyn, "First March of the Fifth Infantry," pp. 113–16; Freeman, *Freeman Journal*, p. 74; McClernand, Journal, p. 1372; Terry, *Field Diary*, p. 13; "Report of General Terry," Nov. 21, 1876,

in *Report of the Secretary of War, 1876*, p. 466; "Report of General Gibbon," Oct. 17, 1876, in ibid., p. 474; Bourke, *On the Border with Crook*, p. 352; Cody, *Autobiography*, p. 272; Hill and Innis, "Fort Buford Diary," p. 19; Gibbon, *Sioux Campaign*, pp. 52–53; King, *Campaigning with Crook*, pp. 80–81; Finerty, *War-Path and Bivouac*, pp. 165 and 244; Regimental Returns of the Fifth Infantry; Gray, *Centennial Campaign*, pp. 216 and 221. Miles told his wife that he had suggested to Terry "that the fords of the Yellowstone be guarded to prevent the Indians [from] going north," also writing, "[Terry] gave me the order to 'go.' " Miles to Mary Aug. 12, 1876, in Johnson, *Unregimented General*, p. 101.

45. Miles to Mary, Aug. 12, 1876, in Johnson, *Unregimented General*, p. 101; Romeyn, "First March of the Fifth Infantry," pp. 115–16; Edwin M. Brown, "Terror of the Bad Lands. Sioux Expedition, M.T., 1876 & 1877. Written for John L. Penwell," p. 3, manuscript in Edwin M. Brown Diaries, folder 1, Montana Historical Society, Helena, Montana (hereinafter cited as Brown, "Terror of the Bad Lands"). Brown stated that Miles reached the Yellowstone at about 4 P.M. Ibid. George Miles noted that the infantrymen arrived on the south bank "just at eve[ning]." "Notes of a Trip," p. 28. See also, Ovenshine to wife, Aug. 11, 1876, in letter no. 11, Ovenshine Family Papers; Ovenshine, Diary, Aug. 11,

1876; and *New York Herald*, Aug. 22, 1876.

46. Miles to Mary, Aug. 12, 1876, in Johnson, *Unregimented General*, p. 102.

47. G. M. Miles, "Notes of a Trip," p. 28. Ovenshine, Diary, Aug. 12 and 13, 1876; Ovenshine to wife, Aug. 11, 1876, in letter no. 11, Ovenshine Family Papers; "Report of General Terry," Nov. 21, 1876, in *Report of the Secretary of War, 1876*, p. 466; Miles to Assistant Adjutant General, Department of Dakota (AAGDD), Aug. 14, 1876, NA, RG 393, Records of the Military Division of the Missouri, item 3945; Gray, *Centennial Campaign*, pp. 221–23; Hanson, *Conquest of the Missouri*, pp. 335, 337, 339, and 340; Brown, "Terror of the Bad Lands," pp. 3–4; Edwin M. Brown, "Diary, 1876–77," p. 3. Edwin M. Brown Diaries, folder 1, Montana Historical Society (hereinafter cited as Brown, Diary). This document parallels but does not altogether duplicate material in Brown, "Terror of the Bad Lands." The diary and manuscript narrative surfaced in an eastern Montana ranch house in the 1890s. See *Stockgrower's Journal*, October 9, 1907.

NOTES TO CHAPTER THREE

1. Quote is from King, *Campaigning with Crook*. Gray, "Captain Clifford's Story," p. 48; McClernand, Journal, pp. 1372–73; White, *Custer, Cavalry, and Crows*, p. 93; King, *Campaigning with Crook*, pp. 83–85; Freeman, *Freeman Journal*, p. 74; Terry, *Field*

Diary, p. 14; Maguire report, p. 1350; Hill and Innis, "Fort Buford Diary," p. 19; "Report of General Gibbon," Oct. 17, 1876, in *Report of the Secretary of War, 1876*, pp. 474–75; Godfrey, *Field Diary*, p. 34; Capron, *Marching with General Crook*, pp. 44–45; Meddaugh, Diary, p. 9; Bourke, *Bourke's Diary*, pp. 113 and 115; Bourke, *On the Border with Crook*, pp. 353–55; Smith, "Twenty-second Regiment of Infantry," p. 686; Alfred E. Bates, "The Second Regiment of Cavalry," in Rodenbaugh and Haskin, *Army of thee United States*, p. 188; "Subreport of General Crook," Sept. 25, 1876, in *Report of the Secretary of War, 1876*, p. 508; Hutton, *Phil Sheridan and His Army*, p. 320. During the march that day, Private John Walton of the Twenty-second Infantry fell out of ranks and became lost; it was later determined that Walton died from exhaustion trying to reach the camp opposite Rosebud Creek. Regimental Returns of the Twenty-second Infantry. Nearly fifty years later a veteran soldier of the Twenty-second Infantry stated that the Indian village site had in fact been but very recently abandoned and that they "took [the Indians'] stock of sun-cured horseflesh and dried buffalo meat. . . . It was disgusting stuff to eat." Anthony Gavin, "Campaigning against the Hostile Sioux," *National Tribune*, Apr. 22, 1926 (hereinafter cited as Gavin, "Campaigning against the Hostile Sioux").

2. Gibbon, *Sioux Campaign*, p. 54; Freeman, *Freeman Journal*, p. 74; McClernand, Journal, p. 1373; Terry, *Field Diary*, p. 14; King, *Campaigning with Crook*, pp. 85–86; Maguire report, pp. 1350–51; Hill and Innis, "Fort Buford Diary," pp. 19–20; Godfrey, *Field Diary*, pp. 34–35; Capron, *Marching with General Crook*, p. 47; Meddaugh, Diary, p. 9; Bourke, *Bourke's Diary*, p. 117; *Chicago Daily Tribune*, Sept. 9, 1876, as quoted in ibid.; Valentine T. McGillycuddy, "Dr. McGillycuddy's Diary," in *Denver Westerners' 1953 Brand Book*, ed. Agnes Wright Spring, p. 289; Hanson, *Conquest of the Missouri*, pp. 339–40.

3. Freeman, *Freeman Journal*, p. 75; Terry, *Field Diary*, p. 14; G. M. Miles, "Notes of a Trip," p. 31; Godfrey, *Field Diary*, pp. 35–36; Maguire report, p. 1351; McClernand, Journal, p. 1373; Capron, *Marching with General Crook*, pp. 47–48; McGillycuddy, "Dr. McGillycuddy's Diary," p. 290; King, *Campaigning with Crook*, p. 88.

4. Godfrey, *Field Diary*, p. 36; Freeman, *Freeman Journal*, p. 75; Hill and Innis, "Fort Buford Diary," p. 20; Terry, *Field Diary*, p. 14; Maguire report, p. 1351; Meddaugh, Diary, p. 10; McClernand, Journal, p. 1373; McGillycuddy, "Dr. McGillycuddy's Diary," p. 290; White, *Custer, Cavalry, and Crows*, p. 93; Bourke, *On the Border with Crook*, p. 355; King, *Campaigning with Crook*, p. 89; "Report of General Terry," Nov. 21, 1876, in *Report of the Secretary of War, 1876*, p. 466; Gibbon, *Sioux Campaign*, p. 54; Capron, *Marching with General Crook*, p. 48; Bourke, *Bourke's Diary*, pp. 125–26.

5. Gibbon, *Sioux Campaign*, pp. 54–55; King, *Campaigning with Crook*, pp. 90–91; Maguire report, p. 1351; Godfrey, *Field Diary*, p. 37; Meddaugh, Diary, p. 10; Hill and Innis, "Fort Buford Diary," p. 20; Freeman, *Freeman Journal*, p. 75; McClernand, Journal, p. 1373; Terry, *Field Diary*, p. 14. Lieutenant Capron of the Ninth Infantry, with Crook, noted on the sixteenth: "All kinds of rumors afloat as to the whereabouts of the Indians." *Marching with General Crook*, p. 49.

6. Terry, *Field Diary*, p. 14; Ovenshine, Diary, Aug. 17, 1876; King, *Campaigning with Crook*, p. 90; Hill and Innis, "Fort Buford Diary," p. 20; Gibbon, *Sioux Campaign*, p. 55; Freeman, *Freeman Journal*, p. 75; Godfrey, *Field Diary*, pp. 37–38; Journal of Baldwin, Aug. 17, 1876; Bourke, *Bourke's Diary*, p. 133; McClernand, Journal, p. 1373; "Report of General Terry," Nov. 21, 1876, in *Report of the Secretary of War, 1876*, p. 466; Hanson, *Conquest of the Missouri*, pp. 340–41. Lieutenant Capron reported that two Mackinaw boats loaded with sutler goods arrived on the seventeenth and that "the rush for them was immense." *Marching with General Crook*, p. 49.

7. Terry, *Field Diary*, p. 14; Maguire report, p. 1373; G. M. Miles, "Notes of a Trip," pp. 32–

36; McGillycuddy, "Dr. Mc-
Gillycuddy's Diary," p. 290; Miles
to Terry, Aug. 14, 1876, NA, RG
393, Records of the Military Division of the Missouri, item 3945;
Miles to AAGDD, Aug. 14, 1876,
ibid.; AAGDD to Adjutant General
(AG), Division of the Missouri,
Sept. 2, 1876, NA, RG 393, Rec-
ords of the Military Division of
the Missouri; Bourke, *Bourke's
Diary*, pp. 131–32; Finerty, *War-
Path and Bivouac*, p. 168; Webb,
Chronological List, p. 77; Gray,
Centennial Campaign, p. 224.
8. Terry, *Field Diary*, p. 15; Ovenshine, Diary, Aug. 18 and 19,
1876; Freeman, *Freeman Journal*,
p. 75; King, *Campaigning with
Crook*, pp. 90–93 and 95; *New
York Herald*, Aug. 24, 1876, and
Oct. 2, 1876, quoted in Bourke,
Bourke's Diary, pp. 132 and 143;
Godfrey, *Field Diary*, p. 38; Hill
and Innis, "Fort Buford Diary,"
p. 20; Matthew Carroll, "Diary,"
in *Montana Historical Society Contributions*, 2 (1896): 229, as cited in
Gray, "Sutler on Custer's Last
Campaign," p. 21; Meddaugh, Diary, p. 10; *New York Times*, Sept.
12, 1876; Hanson, *Conquest of the
Missouri*, pp. 340–41; Brown,
"Yellowstone Supply Depot," p.
32; Gray, *Centennial Campaign*, p.
226; Cody, *Autobiography*, p. 274.
9. Godfrey, *Field Diary*, pp. 38–
39; Hill and Innis, "Fort Buford
Diary," p. 20; Freeman, *Freeman
Journal*, p. 75; Terry, *Field Diary*,
p. 15; *New York Times*, Sept. 12,
1876; King, *Campaigning with
Crook*, pp. 95–96; Bourke, *On the
Border with Crook*, pp. 356–57;
Bourke, *Bourke's Diary*, p. 145;

Gray, *Centennial Campaign*, p.
227; Brown, "Yellowstone Supply
Depot," p. 32.
10. Miles to Mary, Aug. 20, 1876,
quoted in Johnson, *Unregimented
General*, p. 103.
11. King, *Campaigning with Crook*,
pp. 93–94 and 96; Ovenshine,
Diary, Aug. 21, 1876; Terry, *Field
Diary*, p. 15; Hill and Innis, "Fort
Buford Diary," p. 20; Meddaugh,
Diary, p. 10; Godfrey, *Field Diary*,
p. 39; *New York Times*, Sept. 12,
1876; Bourke, *On the Border with
Crook*, pp. 358–59; Gray, *Centennial Campaign*, p. 227. Quote is
from King, *Campaigning with
Crook*, pp. 93–94. See also
Bourke, *Bourke's Diary*, pp. 149–
50.
12. Bourke, *Bourke's Diary*, pp.
149–50 and 154; Terry, *Field Diary*, p. 15; Freeman, *Freeman Journal*, p. 75; Godfrey, *Field Diary*,
pp. 39–40; *New York Times*, Sept.
12, 1876. For the daily activities of
the wagon train as it proceeded
to the Powder River, see G. M.
Miles, "Notes of a Trip," pp. 36–
41.
13. Freeman, *Freeman Journal*,
p. 76; G. M. Miles, "Notes of
a Trip," pp. 42–43; Bourke,
Bourke's Diary, pp. 155 and 163;
Godfrey, *Field Diary*, p. 40;
Ovenshine, Diary, Aug. 23, 1876;
Record of Engagements, p. 60;
Capron, *Marching with General
Crook*, p. 50; *New York Times*,
Sept. 5 and 12, 1876; "Report of
General Terry," Nov. 21, 1876,
in *Report of the Secretary of War,
1876*, p. 467; Gray, *Centennial
Campaign*, pp. 228 and 231–32;
Charles Byrne, "The Sixth Regi-

ment of Infantry," in Roden-bough and Haskin, *Army of the United States*, p. 496. The soldier killed was Private Dennis Shields of Company G, Sixth Infantry. Ibid.

14. Quote is from Miles to Mary, Aug. 24, 1876, in Johnson, *Unregimented General*, p. 105. For accounts of the activities of August 24, see McClernand, Journal, p. 1373; Gibbon, *Sioux Campaign*, p. 56; King, *Campaigning with Crook*, p. 96; Hill and Innis, "Fort Buford Diary," p. 21; McGillycuddy, "Dr. McGillycuddy's Diary," p. 290; G. M. Miles, "Notes of a Trip," pp. 44–45; Godfrey, *Field Diary*, pp. 40–41; Capron, *Marching with General Crook*, p. 51; Bourke, *Bourke's Diary*, p. 159; "Report of General Terry," Nov. 21, 1876, in *Report of the Secretary of War, 1876*, p. 467; and Gray, *Centennial Campaign*, p. 229.

15. McClernand, Journal, pp. 1373–74; Gibbon, *Sioux Campaign*, p. 56; Pocket Diary of Frank D. Baldwin, Aug. 25, 1876, Frank D. Baldwin diaries, 1860–90, Baldwin Papers (hereinafter cited as Pocket Diary of Baldwin); Capron, *Marching with General Crook*, p. 52; Meddaugh, Diary, p. 11; William L. English, "With Gibbon against the Sioux in 1876: The Field Diary of Lt. William L. English," ed. by Barry C. Johnson, p. 8; "Subreport of General Crook," Sept. 25, 1876, in *Report of the Secretary of War, 1876*, p. 508; Hill and Innis, "Fort Buford Diary," p. 21; Snyder, Diary, Aug. 25, 1876; Ovenshine, Diary, Aug. 25, 1876; G. M. Miles, "Notes of

a Trip," pp. 45–46; Freeman, *Freeman Journal*, p. 76; Godfrey, *Field Diary*, p. 41; King, *Campaigning with Crook*, pp. 96–97; Maguire report, p. 1351; "Report of General Gibbon," Oct. 17, 1876, in *Report of the Secretary of War, 1876*, p. 475; Gray, *Centennial Campaign*, p. 232; Don Russell, *The Lives and Legends of Buffalo Bill*, p. 248. Correspondence from Rice to Terry is reproduced in Bourke, *Bourke's Diary*, pp. 156–57.

For details on Terry's decision to return to the Yellowstone, see "Report of General Terry," Nov. 21, 1876, in *Report of the Secretary of War, 1876*, p. 467. There was logic in Terry's reasoning, and the fear that the Indians would escape into Canada was pervasive, even among the British. On August 23, British Minister Sir Edward Thornton had registered his government's concern with the State Department over the possibility of "Indians escaping from the United States into the Territory of Canada," and indicated the Canadian government's intention to strengthen its frontier posts "north of the scene of the present disturbance with the Sioux Indians." See Thornton to Acting Secretary of State John L. Cadwalader, NA, RG 393, Records of the Military Division of the Missouri, item 6579, and Cadwalader to Secretary of War James D. Cameron, Aug. 30, 1876, enclosed in ibid. Officers with Crook did not share Terry's belief that the Indians would head north, pronouncing the idea that they had forded the Yellowstone "insane." "It is useless to try to combat such notions. . . . Not a single officer of our column but has thrown discredit, and even ridicule upon the subject." Bourke, *Bourke's Diary*, pp. 155–56.

16. This exchange is quoted in Bourke, *Bourke's Diary*, pp. 171–72 and 173–74, and in Gray, *Centennial Campaign*, pp. 233–34. Although it is clear that Crook and Terry were going their separate ways, apparently an illusion of potential mutual support persisted for several days after the parting of the commands. Officers in Crook's force held out hope for some kind of converging action against the Indians, and so, seemingly, did Terry. Despite his assurances to the contrary, it is obvious that Crook did not share these sentiments and wanted to steer his own course. See, for example, Capron, *Marching with General Crook*, p. 53.

17. For Crook's expedition, see King, *Campaigning with Crook*, Bourke, *On the Border with Crook*, and Jerome A. Greene, *Slim Buttes, 1876: An Episode of the Great Sioux War*.

18. Telegram, Headquarters, Department of Dakota, to Commanding Officer, Fort Lincoln, Aug. 18, 1876, NA, RG 393, records of the Military Division of the Missouri, item 3945; "Report of Lieut. Gen. P. H. Sheridan," Nov. 25, 1876, in *Report of the Secretary of War, 1876*, p. 445; "Report of General Terry," Nov. 21, 1876, in

Report of the Secretary of War, 1876, p. 468; Gibbon, *Sioux Campaign*, p. 56; Gray, *Centennial Campaign*, pp. 234–35. In his annual report for 1877, Terry stated that he did not receive Sheridan's directive until August 28, although at least two contemporary diaries stated that positive word about the Fifth's wintering in Montana circulated among the troops on the twenty-seventh. See "Report of Brigadier-General Terry," Nov. 12, 1877, in *Report of the Secretary of War, 1877*, p. 487; Snyder, *Diary*, Aug. 27, 1876; Godfrey, *Field Diary*, p. 42.

19. Sherman to Sheridan, Aug. 25, 1876, NA, RG 393, Records of the Military Division of the Missouri, item 6053.

20. Maguire report, p. 1351; Gibbon, *Sioux Campaign*, p. 56; "Report of General Terry," Nov. 21, 1876, in *Report of the Secretary of War, 1876*, pp. 467–68; "Report of General Gibbon," Oct. 17, 1876, in *Report of the Secretary of War, 1876*, p. 475; Godfrey, *Field Diary*, pp. 41–42; Snyder, *Diary*, Aug. 26, 1876; McClernand, *Journal*, p. 1374; Hill and Innis, "Fort Buford Diary" p. 21; G. M. Miles, "Notes of a Trip," pp. 46–48; Hanson, *Conquest of the Missouri*, pp. 350–51; Gray, *Centennial Campaign*, pp. 234–35.

21. Company C had departed Fort Gibson, Indian Territory, on August 7, while Company I left Fort Leavenworth on August 9. Regimental Returns of the Fifth Infantry, Return for August 1876. See also "Report of Brigadier-General Terry," Nov. 12,

1877, in *Report of the Secretary of War, 1877*, p. 488; Major George Gibson to AAGDD, Oct. 1, 1877, in *Report of the Secretary of War, 1877*, p. 540; G. M. Miles, "Notes of a Trip," p. 48; AAGDD George Ruggles to Miles, Aug. 25, 1876, NA, RG 393, Records of the Military Divison of the Missouri, item 6171; Whistler to AAGDD, Aug. 28, 1876, ibid., item 6485; and AAGDD to AGDM, Sept. 2, 1876, ibid., item 6365. Frink and Barthelmess, *Photographer on an Army Mule*, pp. 76–77.

22. Maguire report, p. 1351; Freeman, *Journal*, p. 76; "Report of General Gibbon," Oct. 17, 1876, in *Report of the Secretary of War, 1876*, p. 475; McClernand, Journal, p. 1374; Meddaugh, Diary, p. 11; Pocket Diary of Baldwin, Aug. 27, 1876; Gibbon, *Sioux Campaign*, p. 56; Snyder, Diary, Aug. 27, 1876; Godfrey, *Field Diary*, p. 42; Hanson, *Conquest of the Missouri*, pp. 349–50; Gray, *Centennial Campaign*, p. 235. Quote is from Gavin, "Campaigning Against the Hostile Sioux."

23. Gibbon, *Sioux Campaign*, pp. 56–57; Meddaugh, Diary, p. 11; Maguire report, p. 1351; Snyder, Diary, Aug. 28, 1876; Freeman, *Freeman Journal*, p. 77; Pocket Diary of Baldwin, Aug. 28, 1876; Godfrey, *Field Diary*, pp. 42–43; Gray, *Centennial Campaign*, p. 236. Cody, possibly embellishing his account with personal derring-do, reported seeing Indians hunting buffalo during his ride to Glendive. *Autobiography*, pp. 277–78.

24. "Report of General Terry," Nov. 21, 1876, in *Report of the Secretary of War, 1876*, p. 467; Maguire report, pp. 1351–52; McClernand, Journal, p. 1374; White, *Custer, Cavalry, and Crows*, p. 94; Pocket Diary of Baldwin, Aug. 29, 1876; Gibbon, *Sioux Campaign*, pp. 57–59; Freeman, *Freeman Journal*, p. 77; Snyder, Diary, Aug. 29, 1876; Godfrey, *Field Diary*, pp. 43–44; *New York Herald*, Sept. 7, 1876; Gray, *Centennial Campaign*, p. 236.

25. McClernand, Journal, p. 1374; "Report of General Terry," Nov. 21, 1876, in *Report of the Secretary of War, 1876*, p. 467; Maguire's report, p. 1352; Freeman, *Freeman Journal*, p. 77; Snyder, Diary, Aug. 30, 1876; Godfrey, *Field Diary*, p. 44; Gibbon, *Sioux Campaign*, p. 59; Russell, *Buffalo Bill*, p. 250; Gray, *Centennial Campaign*, p. 236.

26. "Report of General Terry," Nov. 21, 1876, in *Report of the Secretary of War, 1876*, pp. 467–68; Gibbon, *Sioux Campaign*, p. 59; Freeman, *Freeman Journal*, p. 77; English, "Field Diary," p. 9; Snyder, Diary, Aug. 31, 1876; Godfrey, *Field Diary*, pp. 44–45; McClernand, Journal, p. 1374; Gray, *Centennial Campaign*, pp. 236–37.

27. "Report of General Terry," Nov. 21, 1876, in *Report of the Secretary of War, 1876*, p. 468; G. M. Miles, "Notes of a Trip," pp. 50–52; McClernand, Journal, p. 1374; *Cheyenne Daily Leader*, Sept. 5–7 and 13, 1876; Hanson, *Conquest of the Missouri*, p. 352; Gray, *Centennial Campaign*, pp. 235 and

236–37; Russell, *Buffalo Bill*, p. 250; Robert G. Athearn, ed., "A Winter Campaign against the Sioux," p. 273; Brown, "Yellowstone Supply Depot," p. 32.

28. McClernand, *Journal*, p. 1374; Snyder, *Diary*, Aug. 31, 1876; Gray, *Centennial Campaign*, p. 237. Quote is from Miles to AAGDD (in the field), Aug. 31, 1876, NA, RG 393, Records of the Military Division of the Missouri, item 3945. See also the *Cheyenne Daily Leader*, Sept. 16, 1876.

29. Snyder, *Diary*, Sept. 1 and 2, 1876; Freeman, *Freeman Journal*, p. 77; Gray, *Centennial Campaign*, p. 237. Companies A and D had been en route from Fort Reno, Indian Territory, since August 4 and traveled north via Fort Leavenworth, St. Paul, and Bismarck. *Leavenworth Daily Times*, Aug. 13, 1876; Regimental Returns of the Fifth Infantry, Return for September 1876. Miles now had in Montana Companies A, B, C, D, E, F, G, H, I, and K of the Fifth Infantry. Quote is from Hill and Innis, "Fort Buford Diary," p. 22.

30. Godfrey, *Field Diary*, pp. 45–46.

31. Regimental Returns of the Fifth Infantry, Return for September 1876; Snyder, *Diary*, Sept. 3, 1876; "Report of Brigadier-General Terry," Nov. 12, 1877, in *Report of the Secretary of War, 1877*, p. 487; Hill and Innis, "Fort Buford Diary," p. 22.

32. Godfrey, *Field Diary*, p. 46; telegram, Terry to AAGDD, Sept. 5, 1876, NA, RG 393, Records of the Military Division of the Mis-

souri, item 6675; Snyder, *Diary*, Sept. 5, 1876.

33. Telegram, Terry to AAGDD, Sept, 5, 1876, NA, RG 393, Records of the Military Division of the Missouri, item 6675; telegram, Terry to Sheridan, Sept. 22, 1876, ibid., item 6987; "Report of General Terry," Nov. 21, 1876, in *Report of the Secretary of War, 1876*, pp. 468–69; "Report of Brigadier-General Terry," Nov. 12, 1877, in *Report of the Secretary of War, 1877*, p. 487; A. B. Johnson, "The Seventh Regiment of Infantry," in Rodenbough and Haskin, *Army of the United States*, p. 508; Hanson, *Conquest of the Missouri*, p. 358; Freeman, *Freeman Journal*, pp. 77–78; Godfrey, *Field Diary*, pp. 46–50; "Report of General Gibbon," Oct. 17, 1876, in *Report of the Secretary of War, 1876*, p. 475; Gibbon, *Sioux Campaign*, pp. 59–60; Snyder, *Diary*, Sept. 6 and 7, 1876; Hill and Innis, "Fort Buford Diary," p. 22; Maguire report, p. 1352; Melbourne C. Chandler, *Of Garryowen in Glory: The History of the Seventh United States Cavalry Regiment*, p. 73; Gray, *Centennial Campaign*, pp. 241–42. The march of the Sixth Infantry soldiers from Glendive to Fort Buford is described in Meddaugh, *Diary*, pp. 12–13.

34. Gibbon, *Sioux Campaign*, p. 59. For the reaction to the failed campaign, see Athearn, "Winter Campaign against the Sioux," p. 274.

NOTES TO CHAPTER FOUR

1. Military correspondence revealed that Crook's army had earlier passed close to a large "hostile" camp on Buffalo Creek, in present North Dakota, some forty miles north of Slim Buttes, but that bad weather had prevented its detection. Telegram, Lieutenant Colonel George P. Buell to AAGDD, Sept. 19, 1876, NA, RG 393, Records of the Military Division of the Missouri, item 6905. For early details of the Slim Buttes fight, see Buell to AAGDD, Sept. 19, 1876, ibid., item 7215. A number of the Indians who proposed to surrender sent word of their intention to the officer in charge at the Cheyenne River Agency. Lieutenant Colonel George P. Buell notified Terry on September 9 that these Indians, "then near Sentinel Buttes south of the South Fork of Grand River [were] out of rations and short of ammunition." He added, "They seem anxious to come in and surrender, but express themselves as determined to remain where they are unless evicted by you, until they learn the best terms to be granted them." The leaders reportedly included Spotted Eagle, Red Bear, Black Moon, Crazy Horse, and Sitting Bull. Buell to AAGDD, Sept. 9, 1876, ibid., item 7029.

2. Lieutenant Colonel George P. Buell to AAGDD, Feb. 19, 1877, NA, RG 393. Records of the Military Division of the Missouri, item 1249; Stanley Vestal, *Warpath, The True Story of the Fighting Sioux in a Biography of Chief White Bull*, pp. 208 and 217; Vestal, *Sitting Bull*, p. 184; Hyde, *Red Cloud's Folk*, p. 275; Hyde, *Spotted Tail's*

Folk, p. 238; Neihardt, *Black Elk Speaks*, pp. 137–38; Marquis, *Warrior Who Fought Custer*, pp. 281–82; Powell, *People of the Sacred Mountain*, 2:1049–50; *Army and Navy Journal*, Feb. 10, 1877; Hanson, *Conquest of the Missouri*, pp. 358–59; and telegram, Major Guido Ilges to AAGDD, Sept. 20, 1876, NA, RG 393, Records of the Military Division of the Missouri. For Sitting Bull's movements, see "Map—Showing Tral [*sic*] of Sitting Bull From Custer Battlefield till he reached Canada. As gathered from Sitting Bull at Ft. Randall, D.T. Dec. 12, 1881," NA, RG 94, Records of the Adjutant General's Office, miscellaneous file, no. 105.

3. Robert W. Mardock, "The Plains Frontier and the Indian Peace Policy, 1865–1880," pp. 198–99. Quote is from *Report of the Commissioner of Indian Affairs, 1876*, p. vi.

4. *Report of the Commissioner of Indian Affairs, 1876*, p. xv; *Report of the Commissioner of Indian Affairs, 1877*, p. 17; *New York Herald*, Sept. 22 and 27, 1876; Robinson, *History of the Dakota*, pp. 439 and 441–42; Hyde, *Spotted Tail's Folk*, pp. 226–29; Hedren, *Fort Laramie in 1876*, p. 178; DeMallie, "Sioux in Dakota and Montana," p. 39.

5. However, the agent at Cheyenne River reported a reduction in the number of Indians there, prompted by rumors that the soldiers were coming to punish them. Between August and November nearly thirteen hundred Indians reportedly left the agency, presumably to join the

others who had already left. J. F. Cravens to Commissioner of Indian Affairs, Aug. 18, 1877, *Report of the Commissioner of Indian Affairs, 1877*, p. 52.
6. "Report of Lieut. Gen. P. H. Sheridan," Nov. 25, 1876, in *Report of the Secretary of War, 1876*, pp. 445–46; "Report of General Terry," Nov. 21, 1876, in ibid., p. 469; Lieutenant Colonel William P. Carlin to AAGDD, Sept. 12, 1876, NA, RG 393, item 6887; *New York Herald*, Oct. 27, 1876; C. St. J. Chubb, "The Seventeenth Regiment of Infantry," in Rodenbough and Haskins, *Army of the United States*, p. 640; Chandler, *Of Garryowen in Glory*, pp. 73–74; Robinson, *History of the Dakota*, p. 437; Hyde, *Spotted Tail's Folk*, p. 227; Hutton, *Phil Sheridan and His Army*, pp. 321–22 and 325. Crook carried out Sheridan's dictum only partially, taking the guns and mounts of two bands of peaceably inclined Sioux and ignoring the rest at Red Cloud, thereby drawing Sheridan's wrath for his disobedience. Ibid., pp. 325–26. For contemporary questions over the legal propriety of disarming the Sioux, see George W. Manypenny, *Our Indian Wards*, pp. 314–15. Miles disagreed with the disarming, partly because Crook was involved, but mostly because he believed that the decision to confiscate firearms in fact would have the effect of driving the Indians and their weapons back into the field. Johnson, *Unregimented General*, p. 111.

7. Godfrey, *Field Diary*, p. 48; G. M. Miles, "Notes of a Trip," pp. 56–57; *Army and Navy Journal*, Feb. 10, 1877; Brown, Diary, p. 3; Regimental Returns of the Fifth Infantry, Return for September 1876; Snyder, Diary, Sept. 12, 1876; telegram, Pope to Sheridan, Sept. 5, 1876, NA, RG 393, Records of the Military Division of the Missouri, item 6369; telegram, Terry to Sheridan, Sept. 22, 1876, ibid., item 6987; *Leavenworth Daily Times*, Sept. 7, 1876; Hill and Innis, "Fort Buford Diary," p. 24; Miles, *Personal Recollections*, p. 222; Miles, *Serving the Republic*, pp. 144–46; Johnson, *Unregimented General*, p. 109; Athearn, "Winter Campaign against the Sioux," p. 279; George W. Baird, "General Miles's Indian Campaigns," p. 354.
8. Miles to AAGDD, Oct. 24, 1877, NA, RG 393, Records of the Military Division of the Missouri, item 5074; Miles, *Serving the Republic*, p. 147; Miles, *Personal Recollections*, p. 216.
9. Miles, *Personal Recollections*, p. 218.
10. Gibbon, *Sioux Campaign*, p. 64. See also Baird, "General Miles's Indian Campaigns," p. 354; Miles, *Personal Recollections*, p. 216; Miles, *Serving the Republic*, pp. 146–47; Johnson, *Unregimented General*, pp. 109–10.
11. McElrath, *Yellowstone Valley*, p. 95; *Winners of the West*, Aug. 30, 1932; John S. Gray, "Sitting Bull Strikes the Glendive Supply Trains," pp. 26–27; Cody, *Autobiography*, p. 275; "Map of the

Yellowstone River from Fort Keogh to Fort Buford, from Surveys made under the direction of Lieut. Edw. Maguire, Corps of Engineers, U.S.A., by Asst. Engineers F. M. Tower & W. H. Lightner," 1878, NA, RG 77, Records of the Office of the Chief of Engineers, file Q–356, Cartographic Archives Division; *Records of Living Officers of the United States Army*, p. 325; Boatner, *Civil War Dictionary*, p. 614; Timothy K. Nenninger, *The Leavenworth Schools and the Old Army: Education, Professionalism, and the Officer Corps of the United States Army, 1881–1918*, pp. 24–27. Otis authored *The Indian Question*, a treatise in which, among other things, he lamented an anticipated racial amalgamation of Indians and whites that would produce "an inferior being, both in mind and morals." Ibid., p. 282.

12. Smith, "Twenty-second Regiment of Infantry," p. 685; Chubb, "Seventeenth Regiment of Infantry," p. 640; James Willert, comp., *After Little Bighorn: 1876 Campaign Rosters*, pp. 19–20 and 41–46; Gray, "Sitting Bull," p. 26; Athearn, "Winter Campaign against the Sioux," p. 281; Regimental Returns of the Twenty-second Infantry. Return for September 1876. Spring Creek, also known in 1876 as Deadwood Creek and Whoop-Up Creek, is presently called Sand Creek. Enterprising contract freighters reported that the journey from Glendive to Tongue River was 110 miles long, a measurement at least partially justi-

fied by the circuitous nature of the terrain being traversed. Gray, "Sitting Bull," p. 26. Quote is from Athearn, "Winter Campaign against the Sioux," p. 281.

13. AAGDD to Miles, Oct. 7, 1876, NA, RG 393, Records of the Military Division of the Missouri, item 3945.

14. Quotes are from Miles to AAGDD, Sept. 11, 1876, NA, RG 393, Records of the Military Division of the Missouri, items 2717 and 7113. See also G. M. Miles, "Notes of a Trip," p. 57; Snyder, Diary, Sept. 13 and 15, 1876; Brown, "Terror of the Badlands," p. 5; Miles, *Personal Recollections*, p. 218; Johnson, *Unregimented General*, pp. 110–11; Frink and Barthelmess, *Photographer on an Army Mule*, p. 77.

15. Miles's scouts at the Tongue River Cantonment as of late September were: Victor Smith, William Sellew, John "Liver-Eating" Johnson, George Johnson, Albert F. Gaeheder, George W. Morgan, Luther S. "Yellowstone" Kelly, Edwin G. Fountain, Albert Scotney, James Parker, James M. Turner, and William Cross. An Indian named Lone Bull was hired at the cantonment on October 1, 1876. See Gray, "Sitting Bull," p. 26. For information about Yellowstone Kelly, see Miles to Terry, Sept. 19, 1876, NA, RG 393, Records of the Military Division of the Missouri, item 2928; Luther S. Kelly, *"Yellowstone Kelly": The Memoirs of Luther S. Kelly*, ed. by Milo Milton Quaife, pp. 146–48; Fred W. Shipman, "Luther Sage Kelly,"

in Malone, *Dictionary of American Biography*, 5:309.
16. Quotes are from Kelly, *"Yellowstone Kelly,"* pp. 149 and Miles, *Personal Recollections*, p. 217. See also, *Cheyenne Daily Leader*, Nov. 28, 1877; and Johnson, *Unregimented General*, p. 112.
17. AAGDM to Terry, Sept. 29, 1876, NA, RG 393, Records of the Military Division of the Missouri, item 2763; Regimental Returns of the Fifth Infantry. Return for September 1876; Thomas B. Marquis, *Memoirs*, pp. 265–66; AAGDD to Miles, Oct. 7, 1876, NA, RG 393, Records of the Military Division of the Missouri, item 3945; AAGDD to Miles, Oct. 7, 1876, NA, RG 393, Records of the Department of Dakota, item 3073. While Sheridan wanted cavalry at the new post, Terry clearly did not feel that companies of the Seventh regiment should be assigned there. On September 22 he wired the division commander: "[The regiment] is greatly in need of refitting, and I therefore concluded to let it come on to [Fort] Lincoln. I will immediately designate at least three companies and direct them to be prepared to return to the Tongue, and as soon as possible I will determine whether they can be wintered there. I shall make every effort to carry your wishes into effect." Telegram, Terry to Sheridan, Sept. 22, 1876, NA, RG 393, Records of the Military Division of the Missouri, item 6987. Terry evidently persuaded Sheridan that cavalry would not be effective at the cantonment over

the winter. For reference to his opposition to the plan, see Captain Frederick W. Benteen to his wife, Sept. 26, 1876, in Frederick W. Benteen, *Camp Talk, The Very Private Letters of Frederick W. Benteen of the 7th U.S. Cavalry to His Wife, 1871 to 1888*, edited by John M. Carroll, p. 54.
18. "Report of the Chief of Ordnance," Oct. 10, 1878, in *Report of the Secretary of War, 1878*, 3:xiii; Miles to AAGDD, Sept. 16, 1876, NA, RG 393, Records of the Military Division of the Missouri, item 2055. Terry endorsed Miles's request, but Sheridan concluded that "for aggressive warfare against the Indians, artillery is of very little practical use." Ibid.
19. John Gibbon, *The Artillerist's Manual, Compiled from Various Sources, and Adapted to the Service of the United States*, p. 455; *The Ordnance Manual for the Use of the Officers of the United States Army*, pp. 18 and 384–85; Warren Ripley, *Artillery and Ammunition of the Civil War*, pp. 26–29 and 162–63.
20. Miles to AAGDD, Sept. 19, 1876, NA, RG 393, Records of the Department of Dakota, item 3072. See also Major George Gibson to AAGDD, Oct. 1, 1877 (Report on Cantonment at Tongue River, Montana), in *Report of the Secretary of War, 1877*, pp. 540–41.
21. Miles to Terry, Sept. 19, 1876, NA, RG 393, Records of the Military Division of the Missouri, item 2928.

22. Gibson to AAGDD, Oct. 1, 1877, in *Report of the Secretary of War, 1877*, p. 541; G. M. Miles, "Notes of a Trip," p. 57; Snyder, Diary, Sept. 25, 1876; Hill and Innis, "Fort Buford Diary," p. 24.

23. John S. Billings, War Department, U.S. Surgeon General's Office, Circular no. 4. *A Report on Barracks and Hospitals, with Descriptions of Military Posts*, pp. 400–405; Billings, *Report on the Hygiene of the United States Army, with Descriptions of Posts*, pp. 399–402; Ronald Phil Warner, "A History of Fort Buford, 1866–1895," in *Fort Buford and the Military Frontier on the Northern Plains, 1850–1900*, pp. 41–55 and 59–63; Robert W. Frazer, *Forts of the West*, pp. 110–11; Robert G. Athearn, *Forts of the Upper Missouri*, pp. 259 and 268; Herbert M. Hart, *Old Forts of the Northwest*, p. 61.

24. George W. Cullum, *Biographical Register*, 2:413–15; Marvin E. Kroeker, *Great Plains Command: William B. Hazen in the Frontier West*, pp. 113–17, 119–21, 143 and 152–55. A concise essay on Hazen's life is in Kroeker, "William B. Hazen," pp.193–212. Hazen's books were: *The School and the Army in Germany and France* (New York: Harper and Brothers, 1872); *Our Barren Lands: The Interior of the United States West of the One Hundredth Meridian and East of the Sierra Nevadas* (Cincinnati: Robert Clarke, 1875); and *A Narrative of Military Service* (Boston: Ticknor, 1885). He authored many articles published in leisure and professional journals of his

time. Hazen's debate with Custer and others over the utility of the lands of the Upper Missouri and Yellowstone drainage is recounted in Stewart, *Penny-an-Acre Empire in the West.*

25. This brief engagement is mentioned in the *Army and Navy Journal*, Feb. 10, 1877. See also, Miles, *Personal Recollections*, pp. 221–22; and Miles, *Serving the Republic*, pp. 147–48.

26. Kelly, "*Yellowstone Kelly,*" pp. 149–53; telegram, Terry to Sheridan, Oct. 7, 1876, NA, RG 393, Records of the Military Division of the Missouri, item 7451; G. M. Miles, "Notes of a Trip," p. 57; Gibson to AAGDD, Oct. 1, 1876, in *Report of the Secretary of War, 1877*, p. 541; Regimental Returns of the Twenty-second Infantry, Return for October 1876.

27. Gibson to AAGDD, Oct. 1, 1877, in *Report of the Secretary of War, 1877*, p. 541; Hill and Innis, "Fort Buford Diary," p. 25.

28. Miner's Report, Oct. 12, 1876, contained in "Report of Lieut. Col. E. S. Otis," Oct. 13, 1876, in *Report of the Secretary of War, 1876*, p. 486.

29. Ibid.

30. In addition to material in Miner's report, this account of the October 10 combat is drawn from Regimental Returns of the Twenty-second Infantry. Return for October 1876; *Record of Engagements*, p. 61; Smith, "Twenty-second Regiment of Infantry," p. 686; *History of the Twenty-second*, p. 8; Webb, *Chronological List*, p. 78; Vestal, *Warpath*, p. 219; Gray, "Sitting Bull," pp. 27 and 31; Ves-

tal, *Sitting Bull*, p. 190; and Miles, *Personal Recollections*, p. 222.

31. Vestal, *Warpath*, p. 219; Gray, "Sitting Bull," pp. 31–32; Robert M. Utley, *Frontier Regulars: The United States Army and the Indian, 1866–1890*, p. 273.

32. "Report of Lieut. Col. E. S. Otis," Oct. 13, 1876, in *Report of the Secretary of War, 1876*, p. 485. With word of the attack on Miner's train, Hazen left Buford with three companies of the Sixth Infantry and proceeded to Glendive. Hazen's movement is referenced in Athearn, "Winter Campaign against the Sioux," p. 277.

33. The dead scout was Albert F. Gaeheder. Gray, "Sitting Bull," p. 27. Lieutenant Smith estimated the number of Indians surrounding the train at four hundred to five hundred. Ibid.

34. Quoted in Gray, "Sitting Bull," p. 32. The sergeant hit by the spent bullet was either George Hathaway or Michael Hyland. Willert, *After Little Bighorn*, p. 44.

35. Quoted in Gray, "Sitting Bull Strikes," p. 32.

36. "Report of Lieut. Col. E. S. Otis," Oct. 27, 1876, in *Report of the Secretary of War, 1876*, p. 516.

37. Quoted in ibid. The verbatim translation of Sitting Bull's message given to Bruguier, according to Sioux informants of Stanley Vestal (Walter S. Campbell), was: "Friend: I am coming up here to hunt. Ever since I was grown I have been unwilling to fight with soldiers or white men. But wherever I camp, you come

and begin shooting at me. Now again you are shooting at me, but still I have come only for hunting. Therefore, when you see my letter, move away. I am coming there to hunt. I am Sitting Bull." *Warpath*, p. 222. The Lakota text of this message appears in ibid., fn. 1. A slight variant of the English text is in Baird, "General Miles's Indian Campaigns," p. 354. The specification of this event as occurring on Cedar Creek is given in Snyder, *Diary*, Oct. 18, 1876.

38. "Report of Lieut. Col. E. S. Otis," Oct. 27, 1876, in *Report of the Secretary of War, 1876*, p. 516.

39. One of the three Sioux, Kills-Enemy, supposedly posed as Sitting Bull during the meeting, this according to sources of Stanley Vestal. *Sitting Bull*, p. 192. Although Otis did not indicate in his official report that such a ruse occurred, Lieutenant Sharpe's account implied that "Sitting Bull" was present. See Gray, "Sitting Bull," p. 32. According to a Sioux witness named Spotted Elk, Sitting Bull declined to meet with Otis, against the advice of other chiefs present, because "he was in mourning for the loss of a child who had just died. He said he was ashamed to go in the condition he was in to shake hands with any one." When the lesser chiefs returned from meeting Otis they "abused Sitting Bull for not going to meet the officer when he was sent for." Colonel William H. Wood to AAGDD, Mar. 1, 1877, NA, RG 393, Records of the Military Division of the Missouri, item 1385.

Years later, Private Anthony Gavin of Company G, Twenty-second Infantry, recollected that before the chiefs were allowed to leave the meeting, Otis inspected and unloaded their carbines and rifles and confiscated their knives and small arms. Gavin also asserted that Otis told them they could consider themselves prisoners of war. "Campaigning against the Hostile Sioux."

40. In addition to the material cited in the above notes, this account of the actions of October 15 and 16 is drawn from "Report of Lieut. Col. E. S. Otis," Oct. 27, 1876, in *Report of the Secretary of War, 1876*, pp. 515–18; *Record of Engagements*, pp. 61–62; Gray, "Sitting Bull," pp. 26 and 27–32; Smith, "Twenty-second Regiment of Infantry," pp. 686–87; *Army and Navy Journal*, Dec. 16, 1876 and Feb. 10, 1877; *History of the Twenty-second*, p. 8; telegram, AAGDD to Sheridan, Nov. 18, 1876, NA, RG 393, Records of the Military Division of the Missouri, item 8099; Regimental Returns of the Twenty-second Infantry; W. F. Beyer and O. F. Keydel, eds., *Deeds of Valor*, 2:227; Vestal, *Sitting Bull*, p. 192; Vestal, *Warpath*, pp. 220–21; Stanley Vestal, *New Sources of Indian History, 1850–1891*, p. 136; DeLand, "The Sioux Wars," p. 198; Athearn, "Winter Campaign against the Sioux," pp. 277–78; Cyrus Townsend Brady, *Indian Fights and Fighters*, pp. 321–22; Webb, *Chronological List*, p. 78; *Chrono-*

logical List of Actions, &c., with Indians, from January 15, 1837 to January, 1891, p. 63. One of the Indians wounded was Sitting Bull's nephew, White Bull. Vestal, *Sitting Bull*, p. 191; James H. Howard, *The Warrior Who Killed Custer: The Personal Narrative of Chief Joseph White Bull*, p. 51. Names of soldiers injured in the Spring Creek encounters appear in the "List of Wounded" for that affair. NA, RG 94, entry 624, box 1. In 1890 Captains Conway, Miner, and Hooton, and Lieutenants Sharpe, Smith, and Kell received brevets for "gallant services in action against Indians at Spring Creek, Montana, October 15 and 16, 1876." Lieutenant Nickerson likewise received a brevet, but declined it for unspecified reasons. *Official Army Register for 1901*, pp. 357, 359, 376, and 381. In 1890 Private John Moloney, Company I, Twenty-second Infantry, received a certificate of merit based on his conduct at Spring Creek. *U.S. Army Gallantry and Meritorious Conduct, 1866–1891*, p. 67.

41. Gibson to AAGDD, Oct. 1, 1877, in *Report of the Secretary of War, 1877*, p. 541; Moore to AAGDD, Oct. 1, 1877, in ibid., p. 558.

42. Quote is from Brown, "Terror of the Bad Lands," pp. 5–6. Miles's movement from Tongue River is discussed in ibid.; Gibson to AAGDD, Oct. 1, 1877, NA, RG 393, Records of the Military Division of the Missouri; Miles to AAGDD, Dec. 27, 1877 (Report on the District of the Yellowstone), in *Report of the Secretary of War,*

1877, p. 523; Miles to AAGDD, Oct. 25, 1876, in *Report of the Secretary of War, 1876*, p. 482; *Record of Engagements*, p. 62; Snyder, Diary, Oct. 17 and 18, 1876; *Army and Navy Journal*, Dec. 16, 1876 and Feb. 10, 1877; *Leavenworth Daily Times*, Dec. 7, 1876 and Feb. 4, 1877; Miles, *Personal Recollections*, pp. 222 and 225; Miles, *Serving the Republic*, p. 148; Regimental Returns of the Twenty-second Infantry. Return for Oct. 1876; Gray, "Sitting Bull," p. 31; Johnson, *Unregimented General*, pp. 113–14 and Athearn, "Winter Campaign against the Sioux," p. 278. Both Brown and Kelly stated that Miles was notified of the distress of the train by a courier sent by Otis. Brown, "Terror of the Bad Lands," p. 5; Kelly, *"Yellowstone Kelly,"* p. 153–54. Otis reported that he came upon Miles during the evening of the eighteenth and found him "encamped with his entire regiment on Custer Creek." "Report of Lieut. Col. E. S. Otis," Oct. 27, 1876, in *Report of the Secretary of War, 1876*, p. 517.

NOTES TO CHAPTER FIVE

1. Snyder, Diary, Oct. 19, 1876; Brown, Diary, p. 5; "Report of Lieut. Col. E. S. Otis," Oct. 27, 1876, in *Report of the Secretary of War, 1876*, p. 517; Kelly, *"Yellowstone Kelly,"* pp. 154–55; Vestal, *Sitting Bull*, p. 193.

2. The decision of Sitting Bull to meet with Miles and discuss surrendering resulted from an early morning council in the Sioux village held in response to the mis-

sion of the two emissaries from the agency. Vestal reported that Long Feather alone approached the command with the white flag. *Sitting Bull*, p. 193. Another Indian source identified Bear's Face, accompanied by Crow Feather (Long Feather?) and Charging Thunder, as the one who brought the flag forward. Josephine Waggoner, "Mato Ite, or Bear Face," unpublished manuscript, n.d., copy provided by Robert G. Palmer, Denver.

3. Lieutenant Bailey, according to Vestal, shook hands with Sitting Bull and advised him that Miles wanted to speak to him. The Hunkpapa leader proposed that the meeting occur between the lines, reportedly telling Miles, through Bailey, "If you will leave your guns and ammunition behind, I will." *Sitting Bull*, p. 194.

4. Miles wrote his wife of thinking that he might be assassinated, as Canby had been, should Sitting Bull "become desperate." "But I had been forewarned the night before. I can not explain the very singular dream that I had, but I woke up with a shock as I seemed to have been struck directly in the forehead by a ball or some powerful instrument. . . . [I took] it as a warning from my guardian angel to avoid unnecessary danger. Therefore I took every precaution to have the ground covered by the guns and rifles of the command, and to show the Indians that any act of violence would result in their destruction." Miles to Mary, Dec. 15, 1876, in John-

son, *Unregimented General*, pp. 118–19.

White Bull stated that Miles refused to sit on the robe, but instead knelt upon it. Interview with White Bull, July 23, 1910, Walter M. Camp Papers, interviews, group 1, box 2, Archives and Manuscripts, Special Collections, Harold B. Lee Library, Brigham Young University, Provo, Utah (hereinafter cited as White Bull interview). Spotted Elk similarly reported that "Sitting Bull . . . took a robe, spread it on the ground and invited the officer to sit down on it. He refused to do so and they stood up and talked with the robe spread out between them." Wood to AAGDD, Mar. 1, 1877, NA, RG 393, Records of the Military Division of the Missouri, item 1385.

The Indian accounts differ as to the identities of the chiefs who accompanied Sitting Bull to the October 20 council with Miles. The names presented here are as told to Stanley Vestal (*Sitting Bull*, p. 195) and are probably close to being accurate. However, White Bull told Walter M. Camp that the Indian participants besides Sitting Bull were Lazy White Bull, High Bear, and Small Bear. White Bull interview. The Sioux Spotted Elk maintained that he shook hands with Miles and participated in the conference. Wood to AAGDD, Mar. 1, 1877, NA, RG 393, Records of the Military Division of the Missouri, item 1385. A nephew of John Bruguier who was not present stated that the other chiefs were

Gall, Pretty Bear, Bull Eagle, John Sans Arc, Standing Bear, and White Bull—all representing the three tribes present, the Hunkpapas, Minneconjous, and Sans Arcs. *Winners of the West*, Aug. 30, 1932. Miles recalled that Sitting Bull brought six Indians into the council circle. He implied that three of them were Gall, Low Neck, and Pretty Bear. *Personal Recollections*, pp. 225–26.

5. "Report of General Gibbon," Oct. 17, 1876, in *Report of the Secretary of War, 1876*, p. 475. For biographical treatments of Sitting Bull, see W. J. Ghent, "Sitting Bull," in Malone, *Dictionary of American Biography*, 9:192–93; Herbert T. Hoover, "Sitting Bull," in *American Indian Leaders: Studies in Diversity*, ed. R. David Edmunds, pp. 152–74; Vestal, *Sitting Bull*; and Alexander B. Adams, *Sitting Bull: An Epic of the Plains*.

6. Miles, *Personal Recollections*, p. 226.

7. Miles to AAGDD, Oct. 25, 1876, in "Report of Brigadier-General Terry," Nov. 12, 1877, in *Report of the Secretary of War, 1877*, p. 492.

8. Miles, *Personal Recollections*, p. 226. White Bull maintained that Miles also insisted on the return of the mules stampeded the night of October 10 during the attack on Captain Miner's wagon train, whereupon Sitting Bull demanded the return of the "buffalo your soldiers scared away from us." White Bull interview.

Miles to Mary, Dec. 15, 1876, in Johnson, *Unregimented General*, p. 119. See also Miles, *Personal*

Recollections, p. 227. Interestingly, this incident is recorded from the Sioux perspective in Waggoner, "Mato Ite, or Bear Face": "While Sitting Bull and General Miles were having a conference it was discovered . . . that the soldiers who were armed with pistols had broken the straight line ranks and were gradually forming a skirmish line in a half circle around the Indians. When this was reported to Sitting Bull, he ordered the Indians to form a skirmish line the same as the soldiers were doing, which order was obeyed at once. General Miles ordered Sitting Bull to call his men back. Sitting Bull replied by telling General Miles to call his own men back; that the soldiers had been the first to break their lines, and that as soon as he called his men back, the Indians would be called back also. General Miles was not in a very good humor after this." Spotted Elk's statement further verifies this event: "The Commander desired us to leave our young men behind, at a reasonable distance, and meet him in the center. We told him we would consent to that provided he would send back his troops. It was done." Wood to AAGDD, Mar. 1, 1877, NA. RG 393, Records of the Military Division of the Missouri, item 1385.

9. Miles to Mary, Nov. 6, 1876, in Johnson, *Unregimented General*, p. 129.

10. Miles, *Personal Recollections*, p. 226. Stanley Vestal (Walter S. Campbell) presented a transcript of the council dialogue with Miles, evidently reconstructed from information provided him by his several Sioux informants but largely derived from a report of one of the council members, White Bull. Although the transcript makes it clear that Sitting Bull was the principal spokesman for the Indians, the account suffers from one-sidedness and, likely because of memory lapses and difficulties in language translation, is probably inaccurate in places. See *Sitting Bull*, pp. 195–98. Miles to Mary, October 25, 1876, in Johnson, *Unregimented General*, p. 118. See "Statement of 'Long Feather' and 'Bear's Face,' " undated (ca. Nov., 1876), NA, RG 393, Records of the Military Division of the Missouri, item 3394. See also, Wood to AAGDD, Mar. 1, 1877, enclosing Spotted Elk's statement, NA, RG 393, Records of the Military Division of the Missouri, item 1385.

11. Miles, *Personal Recollections*, p. 226. Miles to Mary, Oct. 25, 1876, in Johnson, *Unregimented General*, p. 118. In addition to the sources given above, this account of the October 20 council is based on material found in Snyder, Diary, Oct. 20, 1876; Brown, "Terror of the Bad Lands," pp. 6–8; Brown, Diary, pp. 5–6; *Army and Navy Journal*, Nov.18, 1876, Dec. 16, 1876, and Feb. 10, 1877; *Leavenworth Daily Times*, Dec. 7, 1876, and Feb. 4, 1877; Miles, *Personal Recollections*, pp. 225–26; Miles, *Serving the Republic*, pp. 148–50; James Willard Schultz, *William Jackson, Indian Scout*, pp. 177–78; Baird, "General Miles's

Indian Campaigns," p. 354; Johnson, *Unregimented General,* pp. 116–17; and Vestal, *Sitting Bull,* pp. 194–95.
12. Vestal, *Sitting Bull,* p. 198; Wood to AAGDD, Mar. 1, 1877, NA, RG 393, Records of the Military Division of the Missouri, item 1385.
13. Brown, "Terror of the Bad Lands," p. 8.
14. Vestal stated that there were but five or six participants on each side at the second day's council. He gave the Indians as Old Bull, Good Crow, One Bull, Good Bear, and Crazy Bull. *Sitting Bull,* p. 199. However, Miles's letter to AAGDD, Oct. 25, 1876, gave the names of most of the Sioux attendees. "Report of Brigadier-General Terry," Nov. 12, 1877, in *Report of the Secretary of War, 1877,* p. 492. Also, Miles's letter to his wife of October 25, quoted in Johnson, *Unregimented General,* p. 119, supports the assertion of Spotted Elk as to the presence of Bull Eagle and Red Skirt, although Miles referred to the former as "Bald Eagle." Spotted Elk's account is in Wood to AAGDD, Mar. 1, 1877, NA, RG 393, Records of the Military Division of the Missouri, item 1385.
15. Baird, "General Miles's Indian Campaigns," p. 355.
16. White Bull's recollection of the exchange between Sitting Bull and Miles just before the Indian left the meeting is in Vestal, *Sitting Bull,* pp. 200–201. See also Snyder, Diary, Oct. 21, 1876; *Leavenworth Daily Times,* Dec. 7, 1876, and Feb. 4, 1877; *Army and*

Navy Journal, Feb. 10, 1877; *Record of Engagements,* p. 63. Miles to George W. Baird, Feb. 28, 1890, George W. Baird Papers, Manuscripts Department, Kansas State Historical Society, Topeka. Miles stated that he gave Sitting Bull fifteen minutes to accept his terms before "we would open fire and hostilities would commence." *Personal Recollections,* p. 227; Miles, *Serving the Republic,* p. 151. Vestal suggested that the remark was probably not translated by Bruguier, for it likely would have precipitated a confrontation at the meeting. *Sitting Bull,* p. 201. However, Long Feather and Bear's Face reported that "at this council the officer told the Indians that he would open hostilities against them." "Statement of 'Long Feather' and 'Bear's Face,' " undated (ca. Nov. 1876), NA, RG 393, Records of the Military Division of the Missouri, item 3394. Details of the October 21 conference have been assembled from the sources cited above, as well as from the following: Miles to Mary, Dec. 15, 1876, in Johnson, *Unregimented General,* p. 119; Miles to AAGDD, Oct. 25, 1876, in "Report of Brigadier-General Terry," Nov. 12, 1877, in *Report of the Secretary of War, 1877,* p. 492; Miles to Terry, Sept. 24, 1877, NA, RG 393, Records of the Military Division of the Missouri, item 4043; *Army and Navy Journal,* Dec. 16, 1876, and Feb. 10, 1877; and *Leavenworth Daily Times,* Dec. 7, 1876, and Feb. 4, 1877. Indian accounts appear in Wood to AAGDD, Mar.

1, 1877, enclosing Spotted Elk's statement, NA, RG 393, Records of the Military Division of the Missouri, item 1385; White Bull interview; Waggoner, "Mato Ite, or Bear Face"; and Vestal, *Sitting Bull*, pp. 198–200.

17. *Army and Navy Journal*, Feb. 10, 1877. This is the most comprehensive account of the affair at Cedar Creek yet to surface. The writer was Second Lieutenant James W. Pope, commanding Company E, Fifth Infantry. Miles to Mary, Oct. 25, 1876, in Johnson, *Unregimented General*, p. 122.

18. White Bull told Stanley Vestal that Miles's treachery in initiating the attack so infuriated him that he started to charge the troops by himself, but, having been wounded in the attack on Otis's train, he was restrained by Sitting Bull and sent to join the noncombatants far to the rear. *Warpath*, p. 223. For the formation and movement of the troops, see *Army and Navy Journal*, Feb. 10, 1877; and *Leavenworth Daily Times*, Dec. 7, 1876. In a biographical sketch recounting his military service, Captain Edmond Butler stated that he "commanded centre—six companies" during the Cedar Creek engagement. *Records of Living Officers*, p. 253.

19. *Army and Navy Journal*, Feb. 10, 1877.

20. Brown, Diary, p. 7; *Leavenworth Daily Times*, Dec. 7, 1876; and Brown, "Terror of the Bad Lands," pp. 9–10.

21. Snyder, Diary, Oct. 21, 1876; Brown, Diary, p. 7. It is clear that Miles's artillery performed valuable service at Cedar Creek, despite the misgivings of his superiors over the value of such ordnance in Indian campaigning. Miles recalled that the action of the gun surprised the warriors. *Serving the Republic*, pp. 151–52. Another participant observed that "the presence of the Rodman gun may have had something to do with helping the Sioux to a determination [to withdraw], as we believe it was the first time in which artillery has been brought to bear upon them during the year." *Army and Navy Journal*, Nov. 18, 1876. See also, Larry Don Roberts, "The Artillery with the Regular Army in the West, from 1866 to 1890," (Ph. D. diss., Oklahoma State University, 1981), p. 70.

22. Smith letter, 1897, in *Recreation*, p. 44. For Kelly's version of this incident, see *"Yellowstone Kelly,"* pp. 155–56.

23. Snyder, Diary, Oct. 21, 1876. For the casualty count, see *Army and Navy Journal*, Feb. 10, 1877. The army wounded were Private John Geyer of Company I, lower thigh wound, and Sergeant Robert W. McPhelan, Company E, bullet in upper thigh. "List of Wounded," NA. RG 94, entry 624, box 1; Regimental Returns of the Fifth Infantry. McPhelan was cited for "gallantry in charging with three privates and driving from hills a larger number of Indians, and for meritorious conduct in the performance of his duty as file closer in the execution of which he was severely wounded." NA, RG 94, Letters Received by the Enlisted Branch, box 224, item 11524B. He received a Medal of Honor specifically for his role at Cedar Creek. *U.S. Army Gallantry*, p. 56. Vestal accounted for only one Indian wounded, Iron Wing (Iron Ribs), who was shot in the side and died later from his injury. *Sitting Bull*, p. 202. Spotted Elk's statement confirmed that only one warrior died. Wood to AAGDD, Mar. 1, 1877, NA, RG 393, Records of the Military Division of the Missouri, item 1385. On the other hand, Vestal's talley in *New Sources of Indian History*, p. 136, indicates that no Indians were killed. The medical officer accompanying the command at Cedar Creek was Assistant Surgeon (First Lieutenant) Louis S. Tesson.

Quote of Miles is from Miles to Mary, Oct. 25, 1876, in Johnson, *Unregimented General*, p. 123. In addition to the specific references cited in the notes above, material on the Cedar Creek engagement has been drawn from: Snyder, Diary, Oct. 21, 1876; Brown, Diary, pp. 6–7; Brown, "Terror of the Bad Lands," pp. 8–11; *New York Herald*, Nov. 6, 1876 (also in *Cheyenne Daily Leader*, Nov. 12, 1876); Wood to AAGDD, enclosing Spotted Elk's statement, Mar. 1, 1877, NA, RG 393, Records of the Military Division of the Missouri, item 1385; Miles to AAGDD, Dec. 27, 1877, in *Report of the Secretary of War, 1877*, pp. 523–24; *Record of Engagements*, p. 63; *Leavenworth Daily Times*, Dec. 7, 1876, and Feb. 4,

1877; *Army and Navy Journal*, Dec. 16, 1876, and Feb. 10, 1877; Miles, *Personal Recollections*, pp. 227–28; Baird, "General Miles's Indian Campaigns," p. 355; Webb, *Chronological List*, p. 78; *Chronological List of Actions*, p. 63; and Brady, *Indian Fights and Fighters*, p. 325. The site of the Cedar Creek battleground straddles either side of the East Fork Cedar Creek Road in Prairie County, about twenty-one miles northwest of the modern community of Terry, Montana. It encompasses the land in Sections 4, 5, 6, 7, 8, and 9, T. 15 N., R. 49 E., Prime Montana Meridian. The encounter was evidently initiated in Section 7 and probably terminated in Sections 4 and 9. These conclusions are based on lengthy field reconnaissances by the author in 1981–88. See also, Prairie County Surveyor Roy L. Stith to Brigadier General William C. Brown, Jan. 25, 1932, William Carey Brown Collection, box 21, folder 32, University of Colorado Library.

24. Brown, "Terror of the Bad Lands," p. 11; Kelly, "*Yellowstone Kelly*," p. 157. Brown reported that the Sioux delivered a volley into the camp and that two men were wounded, a statement unsupported by the official documents. Brown, "Terror of the Badlands," pp. 11–12.

25. *Army and Navy Journal*, Feb. 10, 1877. Regarding the use of the hollow, or, as it was sometimes known, British, square in combat situations with American Indians, one observer wrote:

"The advantages of the square in fighting . . . [is] as a means of protecting the supplies, ammunition, and *impedimenta* generally. No one who has fought our indigenous enemy—the Indian—can fail to understand how valuable this formation in square would be in a campaign against a numerous enemy which has no particular base and as many lines of retreat as there are points in the compass." "The British Square," p. 90. In *Personal Recollections*, p. 228, Miles, writing nearly twenty years after the event, gave the impression that the hollow square formation had been used during the initial fighting at Cedar Creek. His recollection is not borne out by the more contemporary accounts, which maintain that the formation was adopted only afterwards, in the march down Bad Route Creek.
26. The post-Cedar Creek pursuit of the Indians is treated in most of the material cited above, but see especially Miles to AAGDD, Oct. 25, 1876, in "Report of Brigadier-General Terry," Nov. 12, 1877, in *Report of the Secretary of War, 1877*, p. 492; *Army and Navy Journal*, Dec. 16, 1876, and Feb. 10, 1877; *Leavenworth Daily Times*, Feb. 4, 1877; Snyder, Diary, Oct. 22, 1876; Brown, Diary, pp. 8–9; and Brown, "Terror of the Bad Lands," pp. 11–12. Brown identified the attacked person as the wagonmaster rather than a herder and indicated that Miles had already entered into communication with the Indians when the attack occurred. Ibid., pp. 13–14.

27. Miles to AAGDD, Oct. 25, 1876, in "Report of Brigadier-General Terry," Nov. 12, 1877, in *Report of the Secretary of War, 1877*, p. 492.
28. Kelly, *"Yellowstone Kelly,"* p. 158.
29. Miles to Mary, Oct. 25, 1876, in Johnson, *Unregimented General*, p. 124.
30. Forbes to AAGDD, Nov. 17, 1876, Miles Papers, folder, Indian Campaigns, 1869–1876, inc, U.S. Army Military History Institute; Special Field Orders, Headquarters, Yellowstone Command, Camp Opposite Cabin Creek, Yellowstone River, Oct. 27, 1876, NA, RG 393, Records of the Military Division of the Missouri, item 8081; *Leavenworth Daily Times*, Dec. 7, 1876; George W. Baird, "Memoranda of Movements of, and Events in, Yellowstone Command, from October 1876, to October 1878." Baird Papers, Kansas State Historical Society (hereinafter cited as Baird, "Memoranda").
31. Miles to AAGDD, Oct. 27, 1876, NA, RG 393, Records of the Military Division of the Missouri, item 8079. A certificate of protection issued by Miles to the Indians going to Cheyenne River Agency is enclosed in Miles to AAGDD, Oct. 27, 1876, NA, RG 393, Records of the Military Division of the Missouri, item 8079. Miles to Terry, Oct. 28, 1876, NA, RG 393, Records of the Military Division of the Missouri, item 8083; Miles to Terry, Oct. 26, 1876, in "Report of General Nelson A. Miles," Oct. 25, 26, 27, and 28,

1876, in *Report of the Secretary of War, 1876*, p. 484.

32. Miles to Terry, Oct. 26, 1876, in "Report of General Nelson A. Miles," Oct. 25, 26, 27, and 28, 1876, in *Report of the Secretary of War, 1876*, p. 483.

33. Spotted Elk's statement, enclosed in Wood to AAGDD, Mar. 1, 1877, NA, RG 393, Records of the Military Division of the Missouri, item 1385.

34. Anderson, "Miles and the Sioux War," pp. 25–26; Miles to AAGDD, Dec. 17, 1876, NA, RG 393, Records of the Military Division of the Missouri, item 569; Hyde, *Spotted Tail's Folk*, p. 226. See also, Manypenny, *Our Indian Wards*, pp. 312–13. The escape of Red Skirt is detailed in Forbes to CO, Cheyenne River Agency, Nov. 13, 1876, NA, RG 393, Records of the Department of Dakota, item 3546. See also Forbes to AAGDD, Nov. 17, 1876, Miles Papers, folder, Indian Campaigns, 1869–1876, inc., U.S. Army Military History Institute. On December 2, Lieutenant Colonel Buell at Cheyenne River Agency reported: "It will be seen that but thirty seven (37) men, thirty five (35) women, ninety two (92) children of the indians reported captured by General Miles, have come in, the rest, as per report, are with hostiles' camp." Buell to AGDM, Dec. 2, 1876, NA, RG 92, Records of the Office of the Quartermaster General, Consolidated Correspondence Files, Division of the Missouri, item 8729. Quote is

from *Report of the Commissioner of Indian Affairs, 1877*, pp. 15–16.

35. Hyde, *Spotted Tail's Folk*, pp. 237–38; Anderson, "Miles and the Sioux War," p. 26.

36. Miles to Terry, Oct. 28, 1876, NA, RG 393, Records of the Military Division of the Missouri, item 8083.

37. Mitchell to Hazen, October 23, 1876, enclosed in AAGDD to AGDM, Nov. 1, 1876, NA, RG 393, Records of the Military Division of the Missouri, item 7889. Hazen to Commanding Officer, Fort Lincoln, Oct. 31, 1876, enclosed in AAGDD to AGDM, Nov. 1, 1876, NA, RG 393, Records of the Military Division of the Missouri, item 7889; Moore to AAGDD, Oct. 1, *1877*, in *Report of the Secretary of War, 1877*, p. 558; Hill and Innis, "Fort Buford Diary," pp. 27–28; Manypenny, *Our Indian Wards*, p. 313.

This account of the chase and surrender of the Minneconjous and Sans Arcs is based on information contained in the above sources as well as in Snyder, Diary, Oct. 23, 1876; Brown, Diary, pp. 9–10; *Record of Engagements*, p. 63; Kelly, *"Yellowstone Kelly,"* pp. 157–58; Baird, "General Miles's Indian Campaigns," p. 355; Miles, *Personal Recollections*, p. 228; Miles, *Serving the Republic*, p. 152; "Statement of 'Long Feather' and 'Bear's Face,'" undated (ca. November, 1876), NA, RG 393, Records of the Military Division of the Missouri, item 3394; Wood to AAGDD, Mar. 1, 1877, enclosing Spotted Elk's statement, ibid., item 1385; Miles

to AAGDD, Oct. 26, 1876, ibid., item 3283; Regimental Returns of the Fifth Infantry, Return for October 1876; Major George Gibson to AAGDD, Oct. 1, 1877, in *Report of the Secretary of War, 1877*, p. 541; Miles's statement, Oct. 27, 1876, Miles to AAGDD, Oct. 27, 1876, and Miles to Terry, Oct. 27, 1876, in "Report of General Nelson A. Miles," Oct. 25, 26, 27, and 28, 1876, in *Report of the Secretary of War, 1876*, pp. 483–85; "Report of General W. B. Hazen," Nov. 2 and 9, 1876, in ibid., pp. 481–82; *Army and Navy Journal*, Dec. 16, 1876, Feb. 3 and 10, 1877; *Leavenworth Daily Times*, Feb. 4, 1877; Vestal, *Sitting Bull*, pp. 203–4; Vestal, *Warpath*, p. 223; Hyde, *Red Cloud's Folk*, p. 276; Brady, *Indian Fights and Fighters*, p. 325; Webb, *Chronological List*, p. 78; and *Chronological List of Actions*, p. 63.
38. Miles to Mary, Oct. 25, 1876, in Johnson, *Unregimented General*, p. 125.

NOTES TO CHAPTER SIX

1. Gibson to AAGDD, Oct. 1, 1877, in *Report of the Secretary of War, 1877*, p. 541. Snyder, Diary, Nov. 1, 1876; Brown, Diary, p. 10.
2. Regimental Returns of the Fifth Infantry, Returns for July, August, September, October, and November 1876; *Leavenworth Daily Times*, Sept. 30, 1876; Athearn, "Winter Campaign against the Sioux," p. 275.
3. "Report of Lieut. Gen. P. H. Sheridan," Nov. 25, 1876, in *Report of the Secretary of War, 1876*, pp. 446–47; telegram, Sherman

to Sheridan, Nov. 10, 1876, NA, RG 393, Records of the Military Division of the Missouri, item 8161; *Army and Navy Journal*, Nov. 18, 1876. See also Manypenny, *Our Indian Wards*, p. 312.
4. Spotted Elk's statement, NA, RG 393, Records of the Military Division of the Missouri, item 1385; Neihardt, *Black Elk Speaks*, p. 138; Day to Hazen, Dec. 1, 1876, NA, RG 393, Records of the Military Division of the Missouri, item 3840.
5. Hazen to Miles, Nov. 2, 1876, in "Report of General W. B. Hazen," Nov. 2 and 9, 1876, in *Report of the Secretary of War, 1876*, pp. 481–82. See also "Journal of the Marches Made by the Forces under the Command of Colonel Nelson A. Miles," *Report of the Secretary of War, 1878*, p. 1688 (hereinafter cited as "Journal of the Marches").
6. Gibson to AAGDD, Oct. 1, 1877, in *Report of the Secretary of War, 1877*, p. 541; Regimental Returns of the Twenty-second Infantry; Frink and Barthelmess, *Photographer on an Army Mule*, p. 96. Quote is from Miles to AAGDD, Oct. 28, 1876, NA, RG 393, Records of the Department of Dakota, item 3298.
7. Quoted in Athearn, "Winter Campaign against the Sioux," p. 275.
8. Ibid., pp. 279 and 280–81.
9. Walter M. Camp interview with Frank D. Baldwin, June 16, 1919, Interviews, group 1, box 2, folder 28, Camp Papers, BYU (hereinafter cited as Baldwin interview); Baird, "General Miles's Indian

Campaigns," p. 356. Quote is from Miles, *Personal Recollections*, p. 217.

10. Meigs to Sherman, Oct. 9, 1876, NA, RG 393, Records of the Department of Dakota, item 3082.

11. Quoted in Hill and Innis, "Fort Buford Diary," p. 28, fn 137. See also ibid., pp. 29 and 32.

12. Buffalo overshoes had been standard issue since the early 1870s, although a new pattern was adopted in 1873 and distributed on the northern plains the following year. The rubber arctic overshoes, called "snow-excluders," were adopted by the army in 1876, along with the sealskin gauntlets and caps and the woolen mittens. See Sidney B. Brinckerhoff, *Boots and Shoes of the Frontier Soldier, 1865–1893*, pp. 9–10; Edgar M. Howell, *United States Army Headgear, 1855–1902: Catalog of United States Army Uniforms in the Collections of the Smithsonian Institution*, 2:pp. 76–78; "Report of the Quartermaster-General," Oct. 10, 1877, in *Report of the Secretary of War, 1877*, pp. 265, 268 and 269; "Report of the Quartermaster-General," Sept. 30, 1880, in *Report of the Secretary of War, 1880*, p. 403; and Gavin, "Campaigning against the Hostile Sioux." Major Orlando Moore reported that the troops of the Sixth Infantry at Fort Buford "were generally supplied with buffalo overcoats, overshoes, and the seal-skin cap and gloves." Moore to AAGDD, Oct. 1, 1877, in *Report of the Secretary of War, 1877*, p. 558. Quote is from

Miles, *Personal Recollections*, p. 219.

13. Miles, *Personal Recollections*, pp. 218–19. Data on determining wind chill and wind velocity is readily available from the Environmental Science Services Administration and the U.S. Weather Bureau. Accounts that provide information about the temperature and wind during the Fort Peck Expedition in November and December 1876 include *Leavenworth Daily Times*, Feb. 18, 1877; Brown, "Terror of the Badlands"; Snyder, Diary; "Journal of the Marches"; Frank D. Baldwin, "Diary, 1st Lieut. Frank D. Baldwin, 5th U.S. Infantry, Nov. 6–Dec. 21, 1876," transcribed copy, William Carey Brown Collection, box 21, folder 21, University of Colorado Library (hereinafter cited as Baldwin, Diary).

14. Baldwin, Diary Nov. 6, 1876; Johnson, *Unregimented General*, p. 127.

15. Miles to Mary, Nov. 6, 1876, in Johnson, *Unregimented General*, pp. 128–29.

16. *Leavenworth Daily Times*, Feb. 18, 1877.

17. The quote is from Ibid. The march is described in Gibson to AAGDD, Oct. 1, 1877, in *Report of the Secretary of War, 1877*, p. 541; "Report of Brigadier-General Terry," Nov. 12, 1877, in ibid., p. 493; Miles to AAGDD, Dec. 27, 1877, in ibid., p. 524; Regimental Returns of the Fifth Infantry, Return for November 1876; Snyder, Diary, Nov. 6–11, 1876; Baldwin, Diary, Nov. 6–11, 1876; "Journal of the Marches," pp.

1688–89; Miles, *Personal Recollections*, pp. 228, 229, and 231; Miles, *Serving the Republic*, p. 152; Brown, Diary, pp. 10–11; and Brown, "Terror of the Bad Lands," pp. 15 and 16.

18. "Journal of the Marches," p. 1689.

19. This portion of the march is described in Snyder, Diary, Nov. 12–15, 1876; Baldwin, Diary, Nov. 12–15, 1876; "Journal of the Marches," p. 1689; Walter Camp, Notes of Interview with Joseph Culbertson, Camp Papers, BYU (hereinafter cited as Camp, Notes of Interview with Culbertson); and Miles to Mary, Nov. 13, 1876, in Johnson, *Unregimented General*, p. 130. Brown, in "Terror of the Badlands," p. 16, stated that as the command approached the Missouri near Fort Peck, "the mounted party came back and reported Indians on the bluffs in the front; skirmish lines were deployed and the scouts sent out; presently they came back and reported that it was only two miles to Ft. Peck, [and that] the Indians were friendly." The quote about the Missouri River is from the *Leavenworth Daily Times*, Feb. 18, 1877.

20. Baldwin, Diary, Nov. 15 and 16, 1876; Snyder, Diary, Nov. 16, 1876; "Journal of the Marches," p. 1689; *New York Herald*, Nov. 30, 1876; *Leavenworth Daily Times*, Feb. 18, 1877; Miles to AAGDD, Dec. 27, 1877, in *Report of the Secretary of War, 1877*, p. 524; *Report of the Commissioner of Indian Affairs, 1876*, p. 90; *Report of the Commissioner of Indian Affairs,*

1877, p. 137; Don C. Miller and Stan B. Cohen, *Military and Trading Posts of Montana*, p. 71. For the intertribal relationships among the various Indian groups that occupied the country north of the Missouri River, see DeMallie, "Sioux in Dakota and Montana," pp. 28–30.

21. Snyder, Diary, Nov. 17, 1876; Baldwin, Diary, Nov. 17, 1876; "Journal of the Marches," p. 1689.

22. For accounts of Miles's meeting with the agency Indians, see Snyder, Diary, Nov. 18, 1876, and Baldwin, Diary, Nov. 18, 1876. Miles to Sherman, Nov. 18, 1876, quoted in Johnson, *Unregimented General*, pp. 125 and 131.

23. Snyder, Diary, Nov. 19, 1876; Baldwin, Diary, Nov. 19, 1876; "Journal of the Marches," p. 1689; Brown, "Terror of the Bad Lands," p. 17; Regimental Returns of the Fifth Infantry, Return for November 1876. Originally, Baldwin was to lead four companies up the Missouri, "west to the mouth of Squaw Cr., within 6 miles of the Mussel Shell, then South to Black Buttes." Miles was to go with the remainder of the regiment back up the Big Dry and around to Black Buttes. New information about the location of Sitting Bull's village, plus knowledge of the ammunition at Carroll City, changed Miles's mind, sending him with Baldwin and putting Snyder in charge of the movement up the Big Dry. Baldwin, Diary, Nov. 19, 1876.

24. Baldwin, Diary, Nov. 21, 1876; "Journal of the Marches," p. 1690.
25. "Journal of the Marches," p. 1690; Baldwin, Diary, Nov. 20–26, 1876; Regimental Returns of the Fifth Infantry, Return for November 1876.
26. *Leavenworth Daily Times*, Feb. 18, 1877.
27. Brown, "Terror of the Bad Lands," p. 21. The incident of the pickets firing and Miles yelling orders is also described in *Leavenworth Daily Times*, Feb. 18, 1877.
28. Baldwin, Diary, Nov. 27, 1876.
29. Baldwin, Diary, Nov. 28 and 29, 1876.
30. Baldwin, Diary, Nov. 30, 1876. "Journal of the Marches," p. 1690; and *Leavenworth Daily Times*, Feb. 18, 1877. The side trip of Captain Bennett to Carroll City met delay because that officer ignored directions of his guide and led his command on a sixteen–mile odyssey into and out of a dead-end canyon. When the infantrymen finally reached the Missouri, across from the trading post, on the evening of the fourth day, it was too dark to cross on the ice with the mule teams and wagons and they were compelled to wait until morning. Brown, "Terror of the Bad Lands," pp. 17–19.
31. Regimental Returns of the Fifth Infantry, Return for November 1876; Snyder, Diary, Nov. 20–30, 1876; Kelly, *"Yellowstone Kelly,"* pp. 161–62. The Black Buttes are located approx-

imately fifteen miles south of the present community of Jordan, Garfield County, Montana.
32. Snyder, Diary, Dec. 1–10, 1876; Regimental Returns of the Fifth Infantry, Return for December 1876; G. M. Miles, "Notes of a Trip," p. 61; Gibson to AAGDD, Oct. 1, *1877*, in *Report of the Secretary of War, 1877*, p. 493. In his memoirs, Kelly stated that he went out to find Miles only after Snyder's troops had reached the Tongue River Cantonment. *"Yellowstone Kelly,"* p. 165. Snyder's diary entry for December 9, however, states that the scouts, including Kelly, left to find Miles on that date and before the soldiers reached the cantonment on the tenth.
33. "Journal of the Marches," p. 1691; Baldwin, Diary, Dec. 1, 1876. See also, Day to Hazen, Nov. 25, 1876. NA, RG 92, Records of the Office of the Quartermaster General, Consolidated Correspondence Files, Military Division of the Missouri, item 8881, in which Day reported, "Sitting Bull has declared his intention of moving east to Red Water [River], of coming in here [to Fort Peck] when the soldiers leave and everything is quiet, and of then going to the Rosebud, thence up that stream and across to the main camp [of Crazy Horse] on Powder River." See also Day to Hazen, Dec. 1, 1876, NA, RG 393, Records of the Military Division of the Missouri, item 3840; Miles to AAGDD, Dec. 27, *1877*, in *Report of the Secretary of War, 1877*, p. 524.

34. "Journal of the Marches," p. 1691. The site of Fort Hawley lies today beneath the Fort Peck Reservoir. Miller and Cohen, *Military and Trading Posts of Montana*, p. 39.

35. Miller and Cohen, *Military and Trading Posts of Montana*, p. 39; "Journal of the Marches," p. 1691–92.

36. "Journal of the Marches," p. 1692; Kelly, *"Yellowstone Kelly,"* pp. 165–66; Regimental Returns of the Fifth Infantry, Return for December 1876. The text of Miles's dispatch to Baldwin, Dec. 11, 1876, is in the William Carey Brown Collection, box 21, folder 27, University of Colorado Library.

37. Brown, "Terror of the Bad Lands," pp. 22–23. Brown reported that the night march lasted until after 11 P.M. Ibid. Miles, *Personal Recollections*, pp. 219–20. See also ibid., pp. 228 and 231; "Journal of the Marches," p. 1692; and Miles, *Serving the Republic*, pp. 152–53.

38. Brown, "Terror of the Bad Lands," p. 23. For other accounts of the journey back to the Tongue River, see "Journal of the Marches," p. 1692; Snyder, Diary, Dec. 12–14, 1876; Regimental Returns of the Fifth Infantry, Return for December 1876; G. M. Miles, "Notes of a Trip," p. 61; Gibson to AAGDD, Oct. 1, 1877, in *Report of the Secretary of War, 1877*, p. 541; Baird, "Memoranda." See also Miles to AAGDD, Dec. 21, 1876, enclosed in "Report of Brigadier-General

Terry," Nov. 12, 1877, in *Report of the Secretary of War, 1877*, p. 493.

39. Snyder, Diary, Dec. 15, 1876; Day to Post Adjutant, Fort Buford, Dec. 8, 1876, NA, RG 393, Records of the Military Division of the Missouri, item 3880; Day to Post Adjutant, Fort Buford, Dec. 17, 1876, ibid., item 3945.

40. Baldwin, Diary, Dec. 1, 1876; Baldwin interview; Regimental Returns of the Fifth Infantry, Return for December 1876; Brady, *Indian Fights and Fighters*, p. 326. Captain Wyllys Lyman, who normally commanded Company I, had taken sick while the troops were previously at Fort Peck. *Leavenworth Daily Times*, Feb. 18, 1877.

41. For Baldwin's background and military record, see Robert C. Carriker, "Frank D. Baldwin," in Hutton, *Soldiers West*, pp. 228–42; Heitman, *Historical Register*, 1:185–56; Guy V. Henry, comp., *Military Record of Civilian Appointments in the United States Army*, 1:242; Alice Blackwood Baldwin, *Memoirs of the Late Frank D. Baldwin, Major General, U.S.A.*; and Robert H. Steinbach, *A Long March: The Lives of Frank and Alice Baldwin*.

42. Baldwin to Miles, Dec. 6, 1876. William Carey Brown Collection, box 21, folder 27, University of Colorado Library.

43. Baldwin, Diary, Dec. 2–6, 1876; Day to Post Adjutant, Fort Buford, Dec. 8, 1876, NA, RG 393, Records of the Military Division of the Missouri; Special Orders no. 1, Headquarters, Battalion 5th Infantry, Fort Peck, M.T.,

Dec. 6, 1876, William Carey Brown Collection, box 21, folder 27, University of Colorado Library.

44. Frank D. Baldwin, Narrative of the Sioux Campaign of December, 1876, William Carey Brown Collection, box 21, folder 27, University of Colorado Library (hereinafter cited as Baldwin, Narrative). Culbertson's recollection of this incident is in Joseph Culbertson, *Joseph Culbertson: Famous Indian Scout Who Served under General Miles in 1876–1895*, pp. 41–42. For Culbertson's history and family background, see Jack Holterman, *King of the High Missouri: The Saga of the Culbertsons*, pp. 185–99.

45. Baldwin, Narrative.

46. Baldwin, Diary, Dec. 7, 1876.

47. Ibid.; William Carey Brown's notes on Baldwin's diary, in Brown Collection, box 21, folder 21, University of Colorado Library (hereinafter cited as Brown, notes on Baldwin's diary); Baldwin, Narrative; Baldwin to Miles, Dec. 8, 1876, William Carey Brown Collection, box 21, folder 27, University of Colorado Library; Walter M. Camp Field Notes, Camp Papers, folder 28, BYU, (hereinafter cited as Camp Field Notes); Baldwin interview; Special Orders no. 3, Headquarters, Battalion Fifth Infantry, Dec. 8, 1876, copy in William Carey Brown Collection, box 21, folder 27, University of Colorado Library; Baldwin to wife, Dec. 8, 1876, Baldwin Papers, box 11, Huntington Library; Baird,

"General Miles's Indian Campaigns," p. 355; Vestal, *Sitting Bull*, pp. 206–7; Johnson, *Unregimented General*, p. 134; Webb, *Chronological List*, p. 78; *Chronological List of Actions*, p. 63. Joseph Culbertson told Walter Camp that Bark Creek was also known as Hell Creek. Camp, Notes of Interview.

48. Baldwin interview. Brown, "Terror of the Bad Lands," p. 25. Ibid.

49. Baldwin, Diary, Dec, 8, 1876; Brown, notes on Baldwin's diary; Baldwin, Narrative; Baldwin to AAGDD, Dec. 8, 1876. William Carey Brown Collection, box 21, folder 27, University of Colorado Library; Baldwin to Miles, Dec. 8, 1876, in ibid.

50. Baldwin, Narrative; Baldwin to Miles, Dec. 9, 1876, copy in Brown Collection, box 21, folder 27, University of Colorado Library; Baldwin, Diary, Dec. 9 and 10, 1876; Baldwin interview; Baldwin to Miles, Dec. 10, 1876, copy in William Carey Brown Collection, box 21, folder 27, University of Colorado Library.

51. Baldwin, Diary, Dec. 11–13, 1876; Day to Post Adjutant, Fort Buford, Dec. 17, 1876, NA, RG 393, Records of the Military Division of the Missouri, item 3945; Baldwin interview.

52. Quote is from Baldwin, Diary, Dec. 16, 1876. Ibid., Dec. 14–17, 1876; Baldwin, Narrative.

53. Baldwin interview.

54. This description of the Ash Creek action and its preliminaries has been prepared from the following sources: Baldwin, Nar-

rative; Baldwin, Diary, Dec. 16–
19, 1876; Baldwin interview; Culbertson to Camp, May 2, 1919,
Camp Papers, BYU; "Journal of
the Marches," pp. 1692–93; Gibson to AAGDD, Oct. 1, 1877, in *Report of the Secretary of War, 1877*,
pp. 541–42; Miles to AAGDD, Dec.
24, 1876, in "Report of Brigadier-General Terry," Nov. 12,
1877, in ibid., pp. 493–94; telegram, Miles to Terry, Dec. 29,
1876, NA, RG 393, Records of the
Department of Dakota, item 886;
New York Herald, Feb. 19, 1877;
Miles, *Personal Recollections*, p.
230; Culbertson, *Joseph Culbertson*, p.74; *Record of Engagements*,
p. 65; *Chronological List of Actions*,
p. 63; Webb, *Chronological List*, p.
78. In 1890 Baldwin received the
brevet of major, partly for his
"gallant and successful attack on
Sitting Bull's camp." *Official
Army Register for 1901*, p. 358. In
his rambling, often inaccurate,
and more often fictitious mem-
oir, scout Joseph Culbertson
maintained that it was he who discovered the Ash Creek village
and notified Baldwin, who "had
the bugle call sounded to get
ready"—a most unlikely occurrence. *Joseph Culbertson*, pp. 42–
43. The site of Baldwin's fight is
located in Prairie County, Montana, almost exactly four miles
northwest of the site of Miles's
Cedar Creek engagement. The
encounter took place in T. 16 N.,
R. 48 E., Prime Montana Meridian, on Sections 16, 17, 21, and 28.
During the early 1930s, retired
Brigadier General William Carey
Brown, himself a former Indian

fighter, succeeded in finding the
December 18, 1876, battleground, aided by the correspondence of the then-deceased Baldwin (who had searched for the
site with Joseph Culbertson in
1920) and Prairie County Surveyor Roy L. Stith. In June 1932,
a marker containing a bronze
tablet was placed on the site. For
the search and designation of the
site, see Camp to L. R. McLean,
Jan. 9, 1921, William Carey
Brown Collection, box 21, folder
37; Stith to Brown, Jan. 4, 1931,
ibid., box 21, folder 32; C. A. Ras-
musson to Brown, Oct. 1, 1931,
ibid., box 21, folder 37; undated
clipping from the *Terry* (Montana) *Tribune*, ca. April 1932, in
ibid., box 21, folder 32; *Terry*
(Montana) *Tribune*, June 16, 1932;
and Culbertson, *Joseph Culbertson*, p. 103.

55. Baldwin, Diary, Dec. 19–21,
1876; Baldwin interview; Notes of
Interview with Culbertson; Baldwin, Narrative; Baldwin to Camp,
Apr. 14, 1919, box 2, folder 4,
Camp Papers, BYU; Camp Field
Notes; Culbertson, *Joseph Culbertson*, pp. 74–75 and 44–45.
Baldwin praised the performance
of Hinkle, "for the gallant and
skillful manner in which he handled his company during the
fight," and also those of First
Sergeant Henry Hogan, Company G; Corporal George Miller,
Company H; and Private Charles
H. Montrose, Company I, for
their gallantry in action. Baldwin
to Miles, Dec. 23, 1876, copy in
William Carey Brown Collection,
box 21, folder 36, University of

Colorado Library. In addition, Montrose and Private Joseph A. Cable earned Medals of Honor specifically for their performances at Ash Creek. *U.S. Army Gallantry*, p. 56.

56. Miles to Baldwin, Dec. 20, 1876. Copy in William Carey Brown Collection, box 21, folder 36, University of Colorado Library; Baldwin, Narrative; Kelly, "*Yellowstone Kelly,*" p. 180.

NOTES TO CHAPTER SEVEN

1. Sources for the Dull Knife fight—actually one of the largest battles between the soldiers and Indians in 1876—include the following: "Report of Brigadier General Crook," Aug. 1, 1877, in *Report of the Secretary of War, 1877*, p. 84; *Record of Engagements*, pp. 64–65; *New York Herald*, Dec. 1, 1876, Dec. 11, 1876, and Jan. 14, 1877; John G. Bourke, *Mackenzie's Last Fight with the Cheyennes: A Winter Campaign in Wyoming and Montana*; Homer W. Wheeler, *The Frontier Trail*, pp. 167–90; Homer W. Wheeler, *Buffalo Days*, pp. 130–47; Luther North, *Man of the Plains: Recollections of Luther North, 1856–1882*, ed. by Donald F. Danker, pp. 210–18; George Bird Grinnell, *Two Great Scouts and Their Pawnee Battalion*, pp. 253–81; Grinnell, *Fighting Cheyennes*, pp. 359–82; Brady, *Indian Fights and Fighters*, pp. 312–318; Utley, *Frontier Regulars*, pp. 275–76; and Lessing H. Nohl, Jr., "Mackenzie against Dull Knife: Breaking the Northern Cheyennes in 1876," in *Probing the American West: Papers from*

the *Santa Fe Conference*, edited by K. Ross Toole, et al, pp. 86–92. Indian recollections are contained in Peter J. Powell, *Sweet Medicine: The Continuing Role of the Sacred Arrows, the Sun Dance, and the Sacred Buffalo Hat in Northern Cheyenne History*, 1:143–69. Casualty figures are from *Record of Engagements*, p. 65; *Chronological List of Actions*, p. 63; and Webb, *Chronological List*, p. 78. See also Hedren, *Fort Laramie in 1876*, pp. 196 and 202–4. On the Yellowstone there was some thought that Crook would march to the Tongue River Cantonment for supplies. "That is why so much hauling is being done," wrote Major Hough from Glendive. Athearn, "Winter Campaign against the Sioux," p. 281.

2. Hyde, *Red Cloud's Folk*, p. 288; Wood to AAGDD, Dec. 28, 1876, NA, RG 393, Records of the Military Division of the Missouri, item 217; Marquis, *Warrior Who Fought Custer*, pp. 286–89; Neihardt, *Black Elk Speaks*, pp. 139–40; Powell, *Sweet Medicine*, 1:169 and 170; Powell, *People of the Sacred Mountain*, 2:1070–72; Paul D. Riley, ed., "Oglala Sources on the Life of Crazy Horse," p. 37.

3. First Lieutenant William P. Clark to AG, Department of the Platte, Sept. 14, 1877, NA, RG 393, Records of the Military Division of the Missouri, item 5839; *Leavenworth Daily Times*, Apr. 19, 1877. For a discussion of the schism that developed between Crazy Horse and some of the Cheyenne bands, particularly that of Little Wolf, see Harry H.

Anderson, "Indian Peace-Talkers and the Conclusion of the Sioux War of 1876," pp. 245–46. See also Hyde, *Spotted Tail's Folk*, pp. 238–39.

4. Mari Sandoz, *Crazy Horse, the Strange Man of the Oglalas*, p. 348; Spotted Elk's statement, in NA, RG 393, Records of the Military Division of the Missouri, item 1385.

5. Spotted Elk's statement, in NA, RG 393, Records of the Military Division of the Missouri, item 1385. This account of the killing of the chiefs is drawn from *New York Herald*, Feb. 19, 1877; *Cheyenne Daily Leader*, Apr. 27, 1877; Powell, *Sweet Medicine*, 1:170–71; Powell, *People of the Sacred Mountain*, 2:1072–73; Sandoz, *Crazy Horse*, pp. 348–49; Marquis, *Memoirs*, pp. 269–71; Miles to AAGDD, Dec. 17, 1876, NA, RG 393, Records of the Military Division of the Missouri, item 569; Snyder, Diary, Dec. 16 and 18, 1876; G. M. Miles, "Notes of a Trip," pp. 60–62; Brown, Diary, pp. 17–18; Baldwin to Camp, Nov. 10 and 11, 1912, box 1, folder 22, Camp Papers, BYU; Kelly, "*Yellowstone Kelly*," p. 166; Anderson, "Miles and the Sioux War," p. 27; Anderson, "Indian Peace-Talkers," pp. 235–36. Vestal, through his Indian sources, maintained that another Sioux, Hollow Horns, escaped the initial Crow attack, but was pursued and killed, too. *New Sources of Indian History*, pp. 182–83. See also DeMallie, *Sixth Grandfather*, pp. 199–200.

6. Miles to AAGDD, Dec. 17, 1876, NA, RG 393, Records of the Mili-

tary Division of the Missouri, item 569. For Bull Eagle's visit of November 7, see G. M. Miles, "Notes of a Trip," p. 60.

7. Miles to AAGDD, Dec. 17, 1876, NA, RG 393, Records of the Military Division of the Missouri, item 569. See also Miles to Indian Agent L. H. Carpenter, Dec. 23, 1876, NA, RG 393, Records of the Department of Dakota, item 886; Brown, Diary, p. 18; Snyder, Diary, Dec. 17 and 21, 1876; Anderson, "Indian Peace-Talkers," pp. 236–37; Powell, *Sweet Medicine*, 1:173; Powell, *People of the Sacred Mountain*, 2:1074; Sandoz, *Crazy Horse*, pp. 350–51; Johnson, *Unregimented General*, p. 136; Anderson, "Miles and the Sioux War," p. 27.

8. Marquis, *Warrior Who Fought Custer*, pp. 289–90; Grinnell, *Fighting Cheyennes*, pp. 383–84; Hyde, *Red Cloud's Folk*, pp. 288–89; Powell, *Sweet Medicine*, 1: 172–73; Powell, *People of the Sacred Mountain*, 2:1074; Anderson, "Miles and the Sioux War," p. 27.

9. "Map—Showing Tral [*sic*] of Sitting Bull From Custer Battlefield till he reached Canada," NA, RG 94; Miles to AAGDD, Dec. 24, 1876, copy in William Carey Brown Collection, box 21, folder 27, University of Colorado Library; Miles to AAGDD, Dec. 27, 1877, in *Report of the Secretary of War, 1877*, p. 521; Wood to AAGDD, Dec. 28, 1876, NA, RG 393, Records of the Military Division of the Missouri; Wood to AAGDD, Feb. 16, 1877, ibid., item 1169; *Report of the Commissioner of Indian Affairs, 1877*, pp. 15–16; First

Lieutenant William P. Clark, Report on the Sioux War, September 14, 1877, NA, RG 393, Records of the Military Division of the Missouri, item 5839; Miles to AAGDD, Mar. 24, 1877, in *Leavenworth Daily Times*, Apr. 18, 1877; Hyde, *Red Cloud's Folk*, p. 276; Vestal, *Sitting Bull*, p. 207; Hyde, *Spotted Tail's Folk*, p. 242; Anderson, "Miles and the Sioux War," p. 32. Yellowstone Kelly reported early in April that Sitting Bull's people had crossed the Missouri above Fort Peck after the ice broke up, sustaining in their passage "a considerable loss of lodges and equipage from the high water." Kelly to unidentified recipient (Miles?), Apr. 9, 1877, NA, RG 94, Appointments, Commissions, and Personal File, Luther S. Kelly.

10. Miles to Agent L. H. Carpenter, Dec. 23, 1876, NA, RG 393, Records of the Department of Dakota, item 886; Snyder, Diary, Dec. 17, 1876; Regimental Returns of the Twenty-second Infantry, Return for December 1876; Gibbon to AAGDD, Oct. 18, 1877, in *Report of the Secretary of War, 1877*, p. 520; G. M. Miles, "Notes of a Trip," pp. 60 and 61; Hill and Innis, "Fort Buford Diary," p. 31.

11. For details about the shop, see McElrath, *Yellowstone Valley*, pp. 65–66. Quote is from Athearn, "Winter Campaign against the Sioux," p. 282.

12. G. M. Miles, "Notes of a Trip," p. 64.

13. Snyder, Diary, Dec. 19, 1876; G. M. Miles, "Notes of a Trip," p.

64; Miles, *Personal Recollections*, p. 232; McElrath, *Yellowstone Valley*, pp. 34–35; Clyde McLemore, "The Keogh-Bismarck Stage Route," p. 141; Frink and Barthelmess, *Photographer on an Army Mule*, pp. 82–83.

14. Miles to Terry, Dec. 20, 1876, NA, RG 393, Records of the Military Division of the Missouri, item 319; Baldwin interview.

15. Tilton to Surgeon General, Jan. 24, 1877, titled "Report of an Expedition against Hostile Indians, Which Left Tongue River December 27th 1876, and Returned Jan'y 18th 1877," NA, RG 94, entry 624, box 1 (hereinafter cited as Tilton, "Report of an Expedition"). Baird, "General Miles's Indian Campaigns," p. 356.

16. G. M. Miles, "Notes of a Trip," pp. 62 and 63; Snyder, Diary, Dec. 17, 21, 28 and 29, 1876; Tilton, "Report of an Expedition"; *Harper's Weekly*, Mar. 10, 1877; Baldwin, *Memoirs*, p. 79; Miles to AAGDD, Jan. 23, 1877, in *Report of the Secretary of War, 1877*, p. 495; *Army and Navy Journal*, Mar. 31, 1877, and May 5, 1877; Gibson to AAGDD, Oct. 1, 1877, in *Report of the Secretary of War, 1877*, p. 542; *Leavenworth Daily Times*, Mar. 24, 1877; Miles, *Personal Recollections*, p. 236; Miles, *Serving the Republic*, pp. 153–54; Powell, *Sweet Medicine*, 1:173–74; Powell, *People of the Sacred Mountain*, 2:1074; Brady, *Indian Fights and Fighters*, p. 326; Don Rickey, Jr., "The Battle of Wolf Mountain," pp. 47–48; Anderson, "Miles and the Sioux War," p. 27.

Interestingly, Lieutenant Cusick was a hereditary sachem of the Six Nations of Indians in New York State, having been installed in 1860. *Records of Living Officers,* p. 338. Surgeon Tilton reported that six Indian scouts went along. "Report of an Expedition." Quote is from Miles to Mary, Dec. 27, 1876, in Johnson, *Unregimented General,* pp. 137–38.

17. Hough to Mary Hough, Jan. 11, 1877, quoted in Athearn, "Winter Campaign against the Sioux," p. 283; Baird, "General Miles's Indian Campaigns," p. 356.

18. "Journal of the Marches," p. 1693.

19. Gibson to AAGDD, Oct. 1, 1877, in *Report of the Secretary of War, 1877,* p. 542; "Journal of the Marches," p. 1693; Tilton, "Report of an Expedition"; Regimental Returns of the Fifth Infantry.

20. "Journal of the Marches," p. 1693; Miles to Mary, Jan. 19 and 25, 1877, in Johnson, *Unregimented General,* pp. 141 and 150; *Army and Navy Journal,* Mar. 31, 1876; *Leavenworth Daily Times,* Mar. 24, 1877. Quote is from "Journal of the Marches," p. 1693. Tilton placed the location of this encounter about fifty-five miles from the cantonment. Tilton, "Report of an Expedition."

21. "Journal of the Marches," p. 1693; *Leavenworth Daily Times,* Mar. 24, 1877; Kelly, "*Yellowstone Kelly,*" p. 167.

22. Tilton, "Report of an Expedition." See also "List of Wounded in the Forces of the Upper Yellow-stone Dept of Dakota, at the Battle of Wolf Mountains on the 8th day of January, 1877," NA, RG 94, entry 624, box 1.

23. Ibid. Quote of Long is from "Journal of the Marches," pp. 1693–94. See also Regimental Returns of the Fifth Infantry, Return for January 1877; *Leavenworth Daily Times,* Mar. 24, 1877; *Army and Navy Journal,* Mar. 31, 1877; Kelly, "*Yellowstone Kelly,*" pp. 167–68; Rickey, "Battle of Wolf Mountain," p. 48; Powell, *Sweet Medicine,* 1:174; Powell, *People of the Sacred Mountain,* 2:1074.

24. Kelly, "*Yellowstone Kelly,*" p. 168; Tilton, "Report of an Expedition"; *Leavenworth Daily Times,* Mar. 24, 1877; *Army and Navy Journal,* Mar. 31, 1877.

25. "Journal of the Marches," p. 1694. See also Tilton, "Report of an Expedition"; *Leavenworth Daily Times,* Mar. 24, 1877; *Army and Navy Journal,* Mar. 31, 1877; Kelly, "*Yellowstone Kelly,*" p. 167. Characteristics of the Wolf Mountains are addressed in B. Coleman Renick, *Geology and Ground-Water Resources of Central and Southern Rosebud County, Montana,* pp. 3–4 and 21–24.

26. Kelly stated that the Indian scouts had a brief, inconsequential clash with the Sioux earlier in the day. "*Yellowstone Kelly,*" pp. 168–69.

27. Ibid. p. 170.

28. Ibid., pp. 169–70; Miles to AAGDD, Oct. 24, 1877, NA, RG 393, Records of the Military Division of the Missouri, item 5074; Miles to AAGDD, Jan. 23, 1877, in *Report of the Secretary of War, 1877,* p.

495; "Journal of the Marches," p. 1694; Luther S. Kelly, "Memoranda on the Wolf Mountain Campaign, Montana, 1877," in *Northwestern Fights and Fighters*, ed. Cyrus Townsend Brady, pp. 360–61; Tilton, "Report of an Expedition"; Miles to Mary, Jan. 19, 1877, in Johnson, *Unregimented General*, p. 150; *Leavenworth Daily Times*, Feb. 24, 1877, and Mar. 24, 1877; *Army and Navy Journal*, Mar. 31, 1877; Baird, "General Miles's Indian Campaigns," p. 356; Miles, *Personal Recollections*, p. 236; Miles, *Serving the Republic*, p. 154; Marquis, *Warrior Who Fought Custer*, p. 293; Powell, *Sweet Medicine*, 1:174–75; Powell, *People of the Sacred Mountain*, 2:1074; Rickey, "Battle of Wolf Mountain," p. 48; Charles B. Erlanson, *Battle of the Butte: General Miles' Fight with the Indians on Tongue River, January 8, 1877*, p. 12; Anderson, "Miles and the Sioux War," p. 27. For details of the movements of the party of Cheyennes, see Powell, *Sweet Medicine*, 1:175–76; and John Stands in Timber and Margot Liberty, *Cheyenne Memories*, pp. 219–20. A divergent view critical of Kelly's role in the affair is in Marquis, *Memoirs*, pp. 271–72.

29. Kelly, "*Yellowstone Kelly*," p. 170.

30. Quote is from Brown, Diary, p. 23. See also "Journal of the Marches," p. 1694; Tilton, "Report of an Expedition"; Miles to Mary, Jan. 19, 1877, in Johnson, *Unregimented General*, p. 150; Miles to AAGDD, Jan. 23, 1877, in *Report of the Secretary of War, 1877*,

p. 495; *Leavenworth Daily Times*, Feb. 24, 1877, and Mar. 24, 1877; *Army and Navy Journal*, Mar. 31, 1877; Baird, "General Miles's Indian Campaigns," p. 356; Kelly, "*Yellowstone Kelly*," pp. 170–72; Kelly, "Memoranda," pp. 360–61; Marquis, *Memoirs*, pp. 272–73; Grinnell, *Fighting Cheyennes*, p. 384; Powell, *Sweet Medicine*, 1:176.

31. Powell, *People of the Sacred Mountain*, 2:1075; Kelly, "*Yellowstone Kelly*," p. 172; Rickey, "Battle of Wolf Mountain," pp. 48–49.

32. Miles to Mary, Jan. 21, 1877, in Johnson, *Unregimented General*, p. 150; Miles to AAGDD, Jan. 23, 1877, in *Report of the Secretary of War, 1877*, p. 495.

33. Baldwin to Camp, Mar. 19, 1913, Camp Papers, BYU. A large number of expended cartridge casings found in the area occupied by Ewers testified to the importance of his position on the ridge throughout the course of the fighting. See Erlanson, *Battle of the Butte*, p. 16. Quote is from Baird, "General Miles's Indian Campaigns," p. 357.

34. Miles to AAGDD, Jan. 23, 1877, in *Report of the Secretary of War, 1877*, p. 495; Leopold Holiman to Brown, May 21, 1932, William Carey Brown Collection, box 21, folder 36, University of Colorado Library.

35. *Army and Navy Journal*, Mar. 31, 1877. Butler's purpose in submitting this account for publication was, according to Baldwin, self-serving. Baldwin felt that Butler had held back during the assault up the bluffs and that his

own leadership had helped compensate for Butler's failures under fire. Frank D. Baldwin, "Statement of Captain Frank D. Baldwin, 5th Infantry, regarding the Battle of Wolf Mountain," ca. 1891, William Carey Brown Collection, box 21, folder 24, University of Colorado Library (hereinafter cited as Baldwin, "Statement"). The feud lasted for years, with Butler, in return, discounting altogether Baldwin's role in the fight. In 1891, reacting to George Baird's article, "General Miles's Indian Campaigns," which favorably related Baldwin's performance, Butler enlisted the help of former Private Patton G. Whited, who authored a letter testifying that Baldwin had not accompanied the assault on the hill. "He never went within a quarter mile of the crest, never crossed the ravine at the base of the hill." Baird responded that he had testimony from officers who praised Baldwin's action, including one who described it as "the most conspicuous act of dashing gallantry I ever witnessed." "Notes on 'General Miles's Indian Campaigns,' " p. 478. Butler died in 1895.
36. Butler to Baird, Apr. 26, 1878, and Butler to Baird, ca. Apr. 1878, NA, RG 94, Letters Received, box 78; Baldwin, "Statement"; Tilton, "Report of an Expedition."
37. *Leavenworth Daily Times*, Feb. 24, 1877. Sources for the Wolf Mountains battle are as follows: Miles to AAGDD, Jan. 20, 1877, in *Report of the Secretary of War, 1877*,

p. 494; Miles to AAGDD, Jan. 23, 1877, in ibid., p. 495; Regimental Returns of the Fifth Infantry, Return for January 1877; Regimental Returns of the Twenty-second Infantry, Return for January 1877; "Journal of the Marches," pp. 1694–95; Baldwin, "Statement"; Miles to Mary, Jan. 21, 1877, and Mar. 15, 1877, in Johnson, *Unregimented General*, pp. 150–51; Baird, "General Miles's Indian Campaigns," pp. 356–57; idem., "Notes on 'General Miles's Indian Campaigns,' " p. 478; Tilton, "Report of an Expedition"; Brown, Diary, pp. 23–24; *Army and Navy Journal*, Mar. 31, 1877, and May 5, 1877; *Leavenworth Daily Times*, Feb. 24, 1877, and Mar. 24, 1877; *New York Herald*, Feb. 6, 1877; *Record of Engagements*, p. 66; Frank D. Baldwin, "Battle of Wolf Mts.," ca. 1890, Baird Papers, Kansas State Historical Society; Long to Baird, Mar. 14, 1890, ibid.; Butler to Baird, July 6, 1891, ibid.; Statements of Privates Henry Rodenburg and John McHugh, Aug. 4, 1891, ibid. (hereinafter cited as Statements of Rodenburg and McHugh); Pope to Butler, Aug. 21, 1891, ibid.; Private John McHugh, sketch map, 1891, ibid. (hereinafter cited as McHugh, sketch map); Lieutenant Oscar F. Long, map, "Battle of 'Wolf Mts.' between Gen. Miles' command and Crazy Horse's Oglallallas and Cheyennes, Jan. 8, 1877," loaned by Robert C. Carriker; Miles, *Personal Recollections*, pp. 237–38; Miles, *Serving the Republic*, pp. 154–55; Kelly, "*Yellowstone*

Kelly," pp. 172–75; Lou F. Grill, "Crazy Horse's Last Stand; or, The Battle of Wolf Mountains," *Miles City Daily Star,* June 1926 (four installments); P. L. Peterson to Camp, July 13, 1926, Walter M. Camp Collection, folder 82, Custer Battlefield National Monument, Crow Agency, Montana; Brady, *Indian Fights and Fighters,* pp. 327–30; Rickey, "Battle of Wolf Mountain," pp. 49–52; Erlanson, *Battle of the Butte,* pp. 16 and 21; and Anderson, "Miles and the Sioux War," p. 27. Quote of Miles is from Miles to Mary, Mar. 15, 1877, in Johnson, *Unregimented General,* p. 151. The Indians' withdrawal, as well as Miles's line of pursuit, is shown on Long, map, "Battle of 'Wolf Mts.' "

38. Marquis, *Warrior Who Fought Custer,* p. 290.

39. Quoted in DeMallie, *Sixth Grandfather,* p. 202.

40. Marquis, *Warrior Who Fought Custer,* pp. 290–91.

41. Powell, *Sweet Medicine,* 1:177–79; Powell, *People of the Sacred Mountain,* 2:1075–77; Eagle Shield's statement in Buell to AAGDD, Feb. 19, 1877, NA, RG 393, Records of the Military Division of the Missouri, item 1249; Marquis, *Warrior Who Fought Custer,* pp. 290–92; Neihardt, *Black Elk Speaks,* pp. 141–42; Sandoz, *Crazy Horse,* p. 353; Riley, "Oglala Sources on the Life of Crazy Horse," pp. 36–37; Stands in Timber and Liberty, *Cheyenne Memories,* pp. 220–21.

42. The wounded men were: Private Henry Rodenburgh, Company A, Fifth Infantry, flesh wound to the face, "accompanied by very free hemorrhage"; Private George Danha, Company H, Fifth Infantry (attached to Company A), flesh wound to the breast; Private Bernard McCann, Company F, Twenty-second Infantry, severe fracture of right thigh (died January 12, 1877); Corporal Emil Rocheu, Company F, Fifth Infantry (attached to Company D), slightly wounded; Private John Duiroud (Diamond?), Company D, Fifth Infantry, slightly wounded; Private William Daily, Company D, Fifth Infantry, slightly wounded; Sergeant Hiram Spangenberg, Company F, Twenty-second Infantry, slightly wounded; Private John McHugh, Company H, Fifth Infantry, slightly wounded; and Corporal Thomas Boehm, Company F, Fifth Infantry, slightly wounded. List compiled from "List of Wounded in the Forces of the Upper Yellowstone Dept of Dakota, at the Battle of Wolf Mountains on the 8th day of January, 1877," NA, RG 94, entry 624, box 1; Miles to AAGDD, Jan. 23, 1877, NA, RG 393, Records of the Military Division of the Missouri, item 629; Regimental Returns of the Fifth Infantry, Return for January 1877; Regimental Returns of the Twenty-second Infantry, Return for January 1877; Tilton, "Report of an Expedition." Brown reported that fourteen men had been wounded, seven seriously. Diary, p. 25. Quote is from Holiman to Brown, May 21, 1932, William

Carey Brown Collection, box 21, folder 36, University of Colorado Library.

43. Miles to Mary, Mar. 15, 1877, in Johnson, *Unregimented General*, p. 152. Miles later wrote of the Indians, "Some of them admit that they lost fifteen killed and forty-five wounded." Ibid., p. 161. See also Marquis, *Warrior Who Fought Custer*, pp. 292–93; *Leavenworth Daily Times*, Mar. 24, 1877; Rickey, "Battle of Wolf Mountain," p. 52, citing an Indian account published in the Missouri *Republican*, Feb. 14, 1877; Eagle Shield's statement in Buell to AAGDD, Feb. 19, 1877, NA, RG 393, Records of the Military Division of the Missouri, item 1249. The Wolf Mountains battlefield is in T. 6 S., R. 42 E., Sections 21, 22, 27, and 28.

44. "Journal of the Marches," p. 1695, and Rickey, "Battle of Wolf Mountain," p. 52; Miles to Mary, Jan. 21, 1877, in Johnson, *Unregimented General*, p. 151.

45. Miles to AAGDD, Dec. 27, 1877, in *Report of the Secretary of War, 1877*, p. 525; *Medal of Honor, 1863–1968*, pp. 281, 283, and 308; Beyer and Keydel, *Deeds of Valor*, 2:232. In addition, Miles recommended brevet promotions for Casey, Butler, Hargous, and Baldwin, and in 1890 McDonald and Captain Ewers won brevets of captain and major, respectively, for their performances at Wolf Mountains. Miles to the Adjutant General, Feb. 9, 1877, Miles Papers, folder, Indian Campaigns, 1877, U.S. Army Military History Institute; *U.S. Army*

Gallantry, p. 73; *Official Army Register for 1901*, pp. 357 and 379.

46. "Journal of the Marches," p. 1695; Tilton, "Report of an Expedition"; Brown, Diary, pp. 24–25; Miles to Mary, Mar. 15, 1877, in Johnson, *Unregimented General*, p. 152.

47. Marquis, *Warrior Who Fought Custer*, pp. 292 and 293–94; Powell, *Sweet Medicine*, 1:180–81; Powell, *People of the Sacred Mountain*, 2:1077–78; Grinnell, *Fighting Cheyennes*, p. 384; Sandoz, *Crazy Horse*, p. 354; Hyde, *Red Cloud's Folk*, p. 289; James C. Olson, *Red Cloud and the Sioux Problem*, pp. 236–37; Hyde, *Spotted Tail's Folk*, p. 242; Neihardt, *Black Elk Speaks*, pp. 141–42.

48. "Journal of the Marches," p. 1695; Tilton, "Report of an Expedition"; Brown, Diary, pp. 25–26. For the quote about frequent crossings of the Tongue, see *Leavenworth Daily Times*, Mar. 24, 1877.

49. Tilton, "Report of an Expedition." Similarly, an account in *Leavenworth Daily Times*, Mar. 24, 1877, reported that "it was not an uncommon sight—that of a soldier sitting in the snow and rubbing with it a naked foot that was as white—and looked cold and marble-like as the foot of a statue."

50. Tilton, "Report of an Expedition."

51. Ibid. Trumpeter Brown wrote: "Melting of snow in the men's shoes causing wet feet was the cause of many frozen feet, when the march was delayed and the water [would] freeze in the shoes." Diary, pp. 27–28.

52. Tilton, "Report of an expedition."

53. Quotes are from Brown, Diary, pp. 26 and 27. See also "Journal of the Marches," p. 1695; Snyder, "Diary of Simon Snyder, Captain, Co. F, 5th U.S. Infantry for 1877," Jan. 18, 1877, Custer Battlefield National Monument, (hereinafter cited as Snyder, Diary); *Leavenworth Daily Times*, Feb. 24, 1877; Gibson to AAGDD, Oct. 1, 1877, in *Report of the Secretary of War, 1877*, p. 542; Baird, "General Miles's Indian Campaigns," p. 357; Miles to Mary, Jan. 19, 1877, in Johnson, *Unregimented General*, p. 156.

54. Brown, Diary, p. 28; Snyder, Diary, Jan. 22, 23, and 29, 1877.

55. Quotes are from Miles to Mary, Jan. 19, 1877, in Johnson, *Unregimented General*, p. 155–56. See also Snyder, Diary, Jan. 25, 1877.

56. Miles to Sherman, Jan. 20, 1877, in *Unregimented General*, p. 154.

57. Miles to AAGDD, Jan. 23, 1877, NA, RG 393, Records of the Military Division of the Missouri, entry 886 (part 3).

58. General Orders no. 2, Headquarters Fifth Infantry, Jan. 31, 1877, Miles Papers, folder, Indian Campaigns, 1877, U.S. Army Military History Institute. The full text of this order appears in the Appendix.

59. Miles to Mary, Mar. 15, 1877, in Johnson, *Unregimented General*, p. 152.

NOTES TO CHAPTER EIGHT

1. Telegram, Sherman to Sheridan, Feb. 6, 1877, NA, RG 393. Records of the Military Division of the Missouri, item 715. Miles registered his disdain for Crook's recent operations in a letter to his wife: "I am surprised to learn that he turned his back on that very large Indian camp [Crazy Horse's assemblage in the upper Tongue region]; it must have been within forty miles of his camp [after Crook moved north, following Mackenzie's strike], and had been there for weeks. I think his official annual report is the most extraordinary document ever signed by a Brigadier General." Miles to Mary, Feb. 5, 1877, in Johnson, *Unregimented General*, p. 158. Quotes are from Sherman to Sheridan, Feb. 2, 1877, NA, RG 92, CCF, Military Division of the Missouri, item 937.

2. Miles to Mary, Mar. 22, 1877, in Johnson, *Unregimented General*, p. 164. See also, *Cheyenne Daily Leader*, Mar. 15, 1877. For details of the lack of provisions, see Miles to AAGDD, Feb. 23, 1877, NA, RG 393, Records of the Military Division of the Missouri, item 1529; Miles to Mary, Feb. 19, 1877, Mar. 22, 1877, and Apr. 15, 1877, in Johnson, *Unregimented General*, pp. 159, 164, and 170; *Leavenworth Daily Times*, Mar. 16, 1877.

3. Regimental Returns of the Second Cavalry, 1877–1878, NA Microfilm Publications M744, roll no. 19 (hereinafter cited as Regimental Returns of the Second Cavalry), Return for April

1877; Gibbon to AAGDD, Oct. 18, 1877, in *Report of the Secretary of War, 1877*, pp. 520–21; "Report of Brigadier-General Terry," Nov. 12, 1877, in ibid., p. 497; Regimental Returns of the Twenty-second Infantry, Return for March 1877; Snyder, Diary, Mar. 11, 1877; Athearn, "Winter Campaign against the Sioux," pp. 279 and 283; Smith, "Twenty-second Regiment of Infantry," p. 687; Baird, "General Miles's Indian Campaigns," p. 358.

4. Quote is from Miles to Mary, Apr. 5, 1877, in Johnson, *Unregimented General*, pp. 168–69. Miles to AAGDD, Dec. 27, 1877, in *Report of the Secretary of War, 1877*, pp. 526–27; Major James Brisbin to AAGDD, Feb. 26, 1877, NA, RG 393, Records of the Military Division of the Missouri, item 1006.

5. Buell to AAGDD, Oct. 24, 1877, in *Report of the Secretary of War, 1877*, p. 550; R.J.C. Irvine, "The Eleventh Regiment of Infantry," in Rodenbough and Haskin, *Army of the United States*, p. 554; Baldwin interview; Tongue River settlers to Hon. Martin McGinnis, Delegate from Montana, Mar. 19, 1877, NA, RG 393, Records of the Military Division of the Missouri, item 1846; McGinnis to Terry, Apr. 24, 1877, in ibid.; Colonel Richard C. Drum, AAGDM, to Terry, Mar. 27, 1877, NA, RG 393, Records of the Military Division of the Missouri, item 1196.

6. Snyder, Diary, Jan. 3–12, 1877; Baird, "General Miles's Indian Campaigns," pp. 357; Miles to

Mary, Feb. 5, 1877, in Johnson, *Unregimented General*, p. 157.

7. Details of these activities are in Gibson to AAGDD, Oct. 1, 1877, in *Report of the Secretary of War, 1877*, p. 542; Regimental Returns of the Twenty-second Infantry, Return for February 1877; Regimental Returns of the Fifth Infantry, Return for February 1877; Snyder, Diary, various entries for February, March, and April 1877; Miles to Mary, Apr. 5, 1877, in Johnson, *Unregimented General*, p. 169.

8. Snyder, Diary, Feb. 13–18, 1877; Gibson to AAGDD, Oct. 1, 1877, in *Report of the Secretary of War, 1877*, p. 542.

9. General Orders no. 8, Headquarters Battalion 22nd Infantry, Camp near Glendive Creek, Feb. 9, 1877, NA, RG 391, Records of the U.S. Regular Army Mobile Units, 1821–1942, entry 1726, "General and Special Orders Issued by a Battalion of the 22nd Infantry Stationed near Glendive Creek, Montana Territory, Feb.–Oct. 1877." See also General Orders No. 12, ibid. On the ice jam and flooding, see Athearn, "Winter Campaign against the Sioux," pp. 282–83.

10. Anderson, "Indian Peace-Talkers," pp. 238–39; Powell, *Sweet Medicine*, 1:181; Hyde, *Spotted Tail's Folk*, p. 241.

11. Anderson, "Indian Peace-Talkers," pp. 234–35 and 239–46; Anderson, "Miles and the Sioux War," p. 27; Sandoz, *Crazy Horse*, pp. 354–55; Olson, *Red Cloud*, p. 237; Oliver Knight, "War or

Peace: The Anxious Wait for Crazy Horse," p. 523.

12. *New York Herald*, Feb. 23, 1877; Anderson, "Indian Peace-Talkers," pp. 247–48 and 250; *Report of the Commissioner of Indian Affairs, 1877*, pp. 17 and 66; Hyde, *Spotted Tail's Folk*, pp. 240 and 243–44; Hyde, *Red Cloud's Folk*, p. 289; Knight, "War or Peace," pp. 530 and 531; Neihardt, *Black Elk Speaks*, p. 142; Robinson, *History of the Dakota*, p. 443; Sandoz, *Crazy Horse*, p. 358; Riley, "Oglala Sources," p. 37.

13. U.S. Marshal J. H. Burdick to Sheridan, Mar. 6, 1877, NA, RG 393, Records of the Military Division of the Missouri, item 1339; John E. Bruguier to Brown, Oct. 4, 1932, William Carey Brown Collection, box 21, folder 40, University of Colorado Library; Josephine Waggoner, "Tahunska Tanka: John Bruguier," unpublished manuscript, n.d., provided by Robert G. Palmer, Denver; Culbertson, *Joseph Culbertson*, p. 90; Kelly, *"Yellowstone Kelly,"* pp. 175–76; Vestal, *Sitting Bull*, p. 183; John S. Gray, "What Made Johnnie Bruguier Run?," p. 34.

14. Peace and goodwill was exactly what Miles had wanted to instill in the Cheyenne prisoners and, through them, the other Indians. "We have shown them our strength, and we will now show them our kindness. That is one reason for keeping the women and children captured by the scouts [on January 7]. They seem quite contented and pleased with the ways of the white people." Miles to Mary, Mar. 15, 1877, in

Johnson, *Unregimented General*, p. 152. For accounts of Bruguier's meeting with the Indians, see Miles to AAGDD, Dec. 27, 1877, in *Report of the Secretary of War, 1877*, p. 525 (in which Miles reported that he had sent two captives instead of one); Miles, *Personal Recollections*, pp. 239 and 240; Miles, *Serving the Republic*, p. 157; Baird, "General Miles's Indian Campaigns," pp. 357–58; Stands in Timber and Liberty, *Cheyenne Memories*, pp. 222–23; Riley, "Oglala Sources," p. 37; Powell, *People of the Sacred Mountain*, 2:1089, 1090, and 1124; Powell, *Sweet Medicine*, 1:182–87; Sandoz, *Crazy Horse*, pp. 357–58; and Anderson, "Indian Peace-Talkers," pp. 246–47. Kelly wrote that three Cheyenne women prisoners accompanied Bruguier. *"Yellowstone Kelly,"* pp. 175–76. Wooden Leg noted that only Bruguier and Sweet Taste Woman came into the camp. Marquis, *Warrior Who Fought Custer*, p. 295.

15. Baird, "General Miles's Indian Campaigns," p. 358; Miles to Mary, Feb. 19, 1877, in Johnson, *Unregimented General*, p. 158.

16. Quoted in Grinnell, *Fighting Cheyennes*, p. 385. Quoted in Powell, *Sweet Medicine*, 1:189. See also Snyder, Diary, Feb. 19–23, 1877; "Report of Brigadier-General Terry," Nov. 12, 1877, in *Report of the Secretary of War, 1877*, p. 496; Baird, "Memoranda"; Powell, *People of the Sacred Mountain*, 2:1090 and 1193; Powell, *Sweet Medicine*, 1:187–89; Stands in Timber and Liberty, *Cheyenne*

Memories, pp. 223–25; Baird, "General Miles's Indian Campaigns," p. 358.
17. Miles to AAGDD, Feb. 23, 1877, NA, RG 393, Records of the Military Division of the Missouri, item 1105; Miles to Mary, Feb. 19, 1877, in Johnson, *Unregimented General*, pp. 158 and 159. See also Miles, *Serving the Republic*, pp. 159–60, and Grinnell, *Fighting Cheyennes*, pp. 384–86.
18. Snyder, Diary, Feb. 24, 1877; *Cheyenne Daily Leader*, Apr. 12, 1877; Miles to AAGDD, Mar. 24, 1877, in *Report of the Secretary of War, 1877*, pp. 496–97 (also in *Leavenworth Daily Times*, Apr. 18, 1877); Miles to Mary, Mar. 17, 1877, in Johnson, *Unregimented General*, p. 161; Stands in Timber and Liberty, *Cheyenne Memories*, p. 225; Miles, *Personal Recollections*, pp. 240–41. Wooden Leg described the finding of Big Crow's body in Marquis, *Warrior Who Fought Custer*, p. 296.
19. Miles to Mary, Mar. 22, 1877, in Johnson, *Unregimented General*, p. 163; Ibid.; Miles to Mary, Mar. 20, 1877, in ibid., pp. 162–63. Snyder, Diary, Mar. 17–21, 1877.
20. Miles to Mary, Mar. 22, 1877, in Johnson, *Unregimented General*, pp. 163–64; Miles to Mary, Mar. 17, 1877, in ibid., p. 162; *Record of Engagements*, p. 67; Miles to AAGDD, Mar. 24, 1877, in *Leavenworth Daily Times*, Apr. 18, 1877; Miles to Mary, Mar. 24, 1877, in Johnson, *Unregimented General*, p. 165; Snyder, Diary, Mar. 22, 1877.

21. *Serving the Republic*, pp. 158–59. For Little Chief's performance, see also Miles, *Personal Recollections*, pp. 241–43.
22. Miles to Mary, Mar. 31, 1877, in Johnson, *Unregimented General*, p. 168. See also Miles, *Personal Recollections*, pp. 243–44. The Indians who remained at the cantonment as hostages were: Hump (Minneconjou), Horse Road (Oglala), and White Bull, Little Chief, Crazy Mule, Magpie Eagle, Old Wolf, Little Creek, and Fast Whirl (Cheyennes). Miles to AAGDD, Mar. 24, 1877, in *Leavenworth Daily Times*, Apr. 18, 1877. Baird stated that Miles kept the hostages to guarantee the surrender of the others in thirty days. "General Miles's Indian Campaigns," p. 358.
23. *Cheyenne Daily Leader*, Apr. 12, 1877; Anderson, "Indian Peace-Talkers," pp. 248–50; Stands in Timber and Liberty, *Cheyenne Memories*, p. 223; Knight, "War or Peace," pp. 530 and 531; Powell, *People of the Sacred Mountain*, 2:1124–25; Marquis, *Warrior Who Fought Custer*, pp. 297–303; Powell, *Sweet Medicine*, 1:190–91. There are slight variances among some of these accounts as to where the great fragmentation occurred and where exactly the Cheyennes decided their various destinies.
24. DeMallie, "Sioux in Dakota and Montana," pp. 41–42. The standard, albeit novelized, treatment of the Cheyenne flight across Kansas and Nebraska is in Mari Sandoz, *Cheyenne Autumn*.

25. Miles to Mary, Mar. 17, 1877, in Johnson, *Unregimented General*, p. 161; Miles to AAGDD, Dec. 27, 1877, in *Report of the Secretary of War, 1877*, p. 525; *Record of Engagements*, p. 67; Snyder, Diary, Apr. 15, 20, and 22, 1877; Baird, "Memoranda"; Thomas W. Dunlay, *Wolves for the Blue Soldiers: Indian Scouts and Auxiliaries with the United States Army, 1860–90*, pp. 143–44; Powell, *People of the Sacred Mountain*, 2:1125–26; Knight, "War or Peace," p. 531; Grinnell, *Fighting Cheyennes*, p. 387. Most of the earliest surrendered guns were Spencer and Springfield carbines, along with numerous Sharp's rifles. Miles to AAGDD, Apr. 22, 1877, in *Report of the Secretary of War, 1877*, p. 497; "List of Indians, Ponies and Arms surr'd," Miles Papers, folder, Indian Campaigns, 1877, U.S. Army Military History Institute.

26. *New York Herald*, May 7, 1877; Olson, *Red Cloud*, pp. 237–38; Knight, "War or Peace," pp. 521–23, 531–32, and 540; Anderson, "Indian Peace-Talkers," p. 250; Hyde, *Spotted Tail's Folk*, pp. 244–45; Powell, *Sweet Medicine*, 1:192 and 194; Sandoz, *Crazy Horse*, pp. 363–64; Robinson, *History of the Dakota*, p. 443.

27. Hyde, *Red Cloud's Folk*, pp. 289–90; Hyde, *Spotted Tail's Folk*, pp. 245–46; Anderson, "Indian Peace-Talkers," p. 252; Anderson, "Miles and the Sioux War," p. 32; Knight, "War or Peace," p. 531.

NOTES TO CHAPTER NINE

1. Statement of Iron Shield, Apr. 7, 1877, NA, RG 393, Records of the Military Division of the Missouri, item 2871, (hereinafter cited as Statement of Iron Shield); Powell, *Sweet Medicine*, 1:191; Powell, *People of the Sacred Mountain*, 2:1129; Marquis, *Warrior Who Fought Custer*, p. 299; Anderson, "Indian Peace-Talkers," p. 252.

2. Miles, *Personal Recollections*, pp. 244 and 248; Statement of Iron Shield; *Army and Navy Journal*, June 16, 1877; Miles to Camp, Apr. 14, 1912, Camp Collection, Custer Battlefield National Monument.

3. Regimental Returns of the Twenty-second Infantry, Return for May 1877; Regimental Returns of the Second Cavalry, Return for May 1877; Regimental Returns of the Fifth Infantry, Return for May 1877; Miles to AAGDD, May 16, 1877, in *Report of the Secretary of War, 1877*, pp. 497–98; Miles to AAGDD, Dec. 27, 1877, in ibid., p. 525; Snyder, Diary, Apr. 29 and May 1, 1877; Gibson to AAGDD, Oct. 1, 1877, in *Report of the Secretary of War, 1877*, p. 542; *Army and Navy Journal*, June 16, 1877; Smith, "Twenty-second Regiment of Infantry," p. 687; *History of the Twenty-second*, p. 9; *Record of Engagements*, p. 68; David L. Brainard, "Notes on the Lame Deer Fight," in Brady, *Indian Fights and Fighters*, pp. 335–36. Still conscious of possible activity north of the Yellowstone, Miles dispatched two companies of the Fifth Infantry under Lieutenant Bailey north of that river to scout the area above Sunday Creek. These soldiers returned to the cantonment on May 6. Regimental Returns of the Fifth Infantry, Return for May 1877; Gibson to AAGDD, Oct. 1, 1877, in *Report of the Secretary of War, 1877*, p. 543. Also on May 1, Major James S. Brisbin and Dr. Holmes O. Paulding, who had accompanied the Second Cavalry battalion from Fort Ellis, started back to that post after having become ill at the cantonment. Regimental Returns of the Second Cavalry, Return for May 1877; Snyder, Diary, Apr. 29, 1877.

4. "Journal of the Marches," p. 1695; Brainard, "Notes on the Lame Deer Fight," p. 336; David L. Brainard, account of the Lame Deer fight in Grinnell, *Fighting Cheyennes*, p. 394; Miles to AAGDD, Dec. 27, 1877, in *Report of the Secretary of War, 1877*, p. 525; Regimental Returns of the Twenty-second Infantry, Return for May 1877; Smith, "Twenty-second Regiment of Infantry," pp. 687–88. As was his wont, Miles embellished on the record in his account in *Personal Recollections*, writing (pp. 248–49): "Foreseeing that some of their men [the Sioux] would be watching our command, we passed on as if apparently not seeking their camp, or noticing their trail. After a short march beyond the trail, the command went into camp apparently for the night, on the Tongue River. Then after dark, leaving our wagon-train with an escort of three infantry companies, we marched directly west under cover of the darkness with the remainder of the command." No

other accounts mention this ruse. Moreover, as indicated, the march across the divide began in daylight.

5. Miles, *Personal Recollections*, p. 249.

6. Baird, "General Miles's Indian Campaigns," p. 359; Miles to AAGDD, May 16, 1877, in *Report of the Secretary of War, 1877*, p. 498; Regimental Returns of the Twenty-second Infantry; *Army and Navy Journal*, June 16, 1877; Miles, *Personal Recollections*, p. 249; Smith, "Twenty-second Regiment of Infantry," p. 688; "Journal of the Marches," p. 1696; Brainard, "Notes on the Lame Deer Fight," p. 336; Grinnell, *Fighting Cheyennes*, pp. 388–89; Brainard account in ibid., pp. 394 and 396; Powell, *People of the Sacred Mountain*, 2:1129–30.

7. Baird, "General Miles's Indian Campaigns," p. 359.

8. Ibid.; "Journal of the Marches," p. 1696; Havilah Carpenter, "Account of His Army Service," compiled by James Havilah Gordon, unpublished, ca. 1937, unpaginated typescript copy provided by James H. Gordon; Grinnell, *Fighting Cheyennes*, p. 389; Brainard account in ibid., p. 394; *Army and Navy Journal*, June 16, 1877; Miles, *Personal Recollections*, p. 249. While Miles and White Bull surveyed the village, they saw an Indian on horseback, who appeared to discover them. Instead of alarming the village occupants, however, this person packed up his family and quickly departed. Grinnell, *Fighting Cheyennes*, p. 390; Pow-

ell, *People of the Sacred Mountain,*
2:1130. Quote is from Miles to
AAGDD, May 16, 1877, in *Report of
the Secretary of War, 1877,* p. 498.
See also Brainard, "Notes on the
Lame Deer Fight," p. 336; *Army
and Navy Journal,* June 2 and 16,
1877; Smith, "Twenty-second
Regiment of Infantry," pp. 687–
88; Grinnell, *Fighting Cheyennes,*
p. 393; Powell, *People of the Sacred
Mountain,* 2:1134.

9. Quotes are from the Brainard
account in Grinnell, *Fighting
Cheyennes,* pp. 391 and 395. Elsewhere, Robert Jackson is credited with having killed Iron Star
by shooting him in the head.
Ibid., pp. 391–92. Brainard later
received a commission in the Second Cavalry and became a noted
explorer, serving in the Arctic
with Adolphus Greely. Bates,
"The Second Regiment of Cavalry," p. 188.

This version of the Miles–
Lame Deer incident presents a
synthesis of information drawn
from a variety of sources. See,
particularly, Powell, *People of the
Sacred Mountain,* 2:1132–33; and
Don Rickey, Jr., *Forty Miles a Day
on Beans and Hay; The Enlisted
Soldier Fighting the Indian Wars,*
p. 229, for Indian recollections
that identify the agitated nephew
with Lame Deer as Big Ankles or
Bad Ankle instead of Iron Star.
See also Grinnell, *Fighting Cheyennes,* pp. 390–92, 396, and 397
(wherein Brave Wolf identified
the man with Lame Deer as
Flying); Brainard's account in
ibid., pp. 394–95; John F. Mc-
Blain, "The Last Fight of the

Sioux War of 1876–77," p. 125;
Interview with F. E. Server (soldier participant), August 1906,
tablet no. 2, Eli S. Ricker Collection, Nebraska State Historical
Society (hereinafter cited as
Server interview); Baird, "General Miles's Indian Campaigns,"
p. 359; Fred A. Hunt, "The Fight
on the Little Muddy," pp. 596–
98; Brainard, "Notes on the
Lame Deer Fight," pp. 337–38;
Cheyenne Daily Leader, June 3,
1877; Regimental Returns of the
Second Cavalry, Return for May
1877; *Army and Navy Journal,*
June 2 and 16, 1877; David L.
Brainard, interview notes, Oct.
14, 1912, Camp Papers, BYU (hereinafter cited as Brainard, Interview notes). Miles blamed the incident on an overzealous scout,
presumably Robert Jackson. See
Miles's description of the affair in
Personal Recollections, pp. 250–51.
See also *Serving the Republic,* p.
162. Joseph Culbertson, who was
not present, maintained that
Lame Deer was killed by a shot
from Jackson. *Joseph Culbertson,*
p. 45. A contemporary account in
the *New York Herald,* June 11,
1877, ascribed Lame Deer's killing to Private Henry L. Davis of
Company L, Second Cavalry,
who later presented the chief's
headdress to Miles. Private Anthony Gavin, who was present,
remembered that it was Jackson—not White Bull—who
scalped Lame Deer, and that
Jackson took "ears and all" and
kept the scalp on his bridle "for
over a week after the fight."
Gavin to Camp, ca. Apr. 15, 1914,

Camp Papers, Robert S. Ellison Collection, Denver Public Library. Lame Deer's remains were later interred in a sandstone cave on the heights overlooking the village site, near the point where he fell.

10. John F. McBlain, "Last Fight of the Sioux War," p. 125. A somewhat variant deployment of the three companies was remembered by McBlain. Ibid.

11. *New York Herald*, June 11, 1877. White, *Custer, Cavalry, and Crows*, p. 124. This account of the fighting at Lame Deer's village is prepared from the following sources: "Journal of the Marches," p. 1696; Miles to AAGDD, May 16, 1877, in *Report of the Secretary of War, 1877*, p. 498; Miles to AAGDD, Dec. 27, 1877, in ibid., pp. 525–26; Regimental Returns of the Second Cavalry, Return for May 1877, and Field Return, Battalion Companies F, G, H, and L, May 1877; *Cheyenne Daily Leader*, May 29, 1877; Smith, "Twenty-second Regiment of Infantry," pp. 687–88; *New York Herald*, June 11, 1877; *Army and Navy Journal*, June 2, 1877, and June 16, 1877; Interview with Lovell H. Jerome, Sept. 1914, item 78, Camp Papers, Ellison Collection, Denver Public Library (hereinafter cited as Jerome interview); Carpenter, "Account of His Army Service"; Brainard, "Notes on the Lame Deer Fight," pp. 336–37; Brainard account in Grinnell, *Fighting Cheyennes*, pp. 394 and 396; McBlain, "Last Fight of the Sioux War," pp. 125–26; Grinnell,

Fighting Cheyennes, pp. 390 and 397; Miles, *Personal Recollections*, p. 250; Miles, *Serving the Republic*, p. 162; Edward J. McClernand, "Second Regiment of Cavalry," in Rodenbough and Haskins, *Army of the United States*, p. 188; Smith, "Twenty-second Regiment of Infantry," p. 688; Baird, "General Miles's Indian Campaigns," p. 359; Hunt, "Fight on the Little Muddy," pp. 598, 600; John S. Gray, "The Lame Deer Fight Ends the Sioux War," pp. 17–19 and 23–24; Jerome A. Greene, "The Lame Deer Fight: Last Drama of the Sioux War of 1876–1877," pp. 11–21. A valuable source for the May 7 engagement is the manuscript map drawn the next day by Sergeant Charles Grillon, Company H, Second Cavalry, who served as battalion topographer. Grillon's map shows much detail, including the route of the troops' advance up Muddy Creek to initiate the attack, the spots where two of the soldiers were killed, the point where the pony herd was finally halted and where it was corraled, and the dispositions of the cavalry units in the pursuit of the Indians to Rosebud Creek. The map (hereinafter cited as Grillon map) turned up among the papers of Major General Frank D. Baldwin, and can be found today with the William Carey Brown Collection, University of Colorado Library. Brown to Montana Governor John E. Erickson, Dec. 29, 1932, William Carey Brown Collection. The battle site is located in present Rosebud County on Sec. 3, T. 3 S., R. 41 E., at the south edge of the modern community of Lame Deer and along Montana Highway 315. At a point west of where Lame Deer was killed is a sandstone rock formation locally referred to as "Lame Deer's Tomb." Superintendent W. R. Centerwall to W. C. Brown, Apr. 29, 1932, ibid., box 21, folder 36.

12. Miles to AAGDD, May 16, 1877, in *Report of the Secretary of War, 1877*, p. 498. Miles's description of the horses is in his *Personal Recollections*, p. 252.

13. White Bull's recollections of Sioux casualties appear in his interview with Walter Camp. White Bull interview. Some Indian casualties are mentioned in Powell, *People of the Sacred Mountain*, 2:1134. Grinnell noted that only six Sioux were killed. *Fighting Cheyennes*, p. 397. Soldiers wounded in the fight were Lieutenant Fuller, F (right shoulder); Trumpeter William C. Osmer, F; and Privates Samuel Freyer, F (left arm); Andrew Jeffers, G (head); Patrick Ryan, G (right arm); Thomas B. Gilmore, H (neck); Brainard, L (right cheek); William Leonard, L (chin); and Frederick Wilks, L (left hand). Miles to AAGDD, May 16, 1877. Sioux War Papers, NA Microfilm Publications M666, roll 281, 4163 AGO 1876; Lieutenant Colonel Albert G. Brackett to Second Lieutenant Henry Tiffany, Oct. 15, 1877, in *Report of the Secretary of War, 1877*, p. 551; Regimental Returns of the Second Cavalry, Return for May 1877; "List of

Wounded." NA, RG 94, entry 624, box 1; *Army and Navy Journal*, June 2 and 16, 1877 (which, citing General Order no. 3, Headquarters, Second Cavalry, June 6, 1877, includes Privates John O'Flynn and John W. Jones, Company F, among the wounded); *Record of Engagements*, p. 68; "Journal of the Marches," p. 1696; Brainard, "Notes on the Lame Deer Fight," p. 337; Miles, *Personal Recollections*, pp. 251–52. Later, Miles would commend several of the cavalry and infantry officers, particularly Captains Wheelan, Ball, Norwood, Tyler, Dickey, and Poole, and Lieutenants Fuller, Jerome, Casey, and Cusick, all of whom subsequently received brevets for their performance. *U.S. Army Gallantry*, p. 74; *Official Army Register for 1901*, pp. 353 and 354. Five enlisted men won Medals of Honor for their conduct in the Lame Deer Fight: Corporal Harry Garland, Farrier William H. Jones, Private William Leonard, and First Sergeant Henry Wilkens, all of Company L, Second Cavalry; and Private Samuel D. Phillips, Company H, Second Cavalry. *The Medal of Honor of the United States Army*, pp. 229–30; *Medal of Honor*, pp. 291, 301, 304, 316, and 330; *U.S. Army Gallantry*, p. 74.

14. Miles to AAGDD, May 16, 1877, in *Report of the Secretary of War, 1877*, p. 498; Brainard account in Grinnell, *Fighting Cheyennes*, pp. 395–96; ibid., p. 393; Baird, "General Miles's Indian Campaigns," p. 359; Smith, "Twenty-second Regiment of Infantry," pp. 687–88. Powell identified Brave Eagle as the Sioux who attacked the pack train. *People of the Sacred Mountain*, 2:1134. The stranded Second Cavalry soldier was Private William Leonard of Company L, who was listed as one of the wounded. Brainard, "Notes on the Lame Deer Fight," p. 338.

15. Grillon map; "Journal of the Marches," p. 1696; Regimental Returns of the Second Cavalry, Return for May 1877; Regimental Returns of the Twenty-second Infantry, Return for May 1877; Smith, "Twenty-second Regiment of Infantry," p. 688; McBlain, "Last Fight of the Sioux War," p. 126.

16. Carpenter, "Account of His Army Service." Regarding this incident, Lieutenant Jerome recalled how he had "told Miles that they [the horses] were mostly squaw ponies and that squaws mounted from [the] right side and that if the men would try to mount in the same way they would have less trouble. They did this and got along with them all right." Jerome interview. See also Miles, *Personal Recollections*, pp. 252–53, and Baird, "General Miles's Indian Campaigns," p. 359. Many of the ponies were later used to mount members of the Fifth Infantry in a unit that was humorously referred to as "The Eleventh Cavalry" (there being only ten regiments in the service at the time). Ibid.

17. Miles to AAGDD, May 16, 1877, in *Report of the Secretary of War, 1877*, p. 498; "Journal of the

Marches," p. 1696; Smith, "Twenty-second Regiment of Infantry," p. 688; McBlain, "Last Fight of the Sioux War," p. 126. In August 1878, Miles's wife, Mary, in company with other officers' ladies, visited the Lame Deer battlefield during an outing that also included a journey to Custer Battlefield. At the Lame Deer site, wrote a member of the entourage, "we . . . found the rifle pits, empty cartridge shells, bones, clothing, ornaments and clothing of several Indians. . . . [One member] was particularly fortunate in finding the breastplate worn by Lame Deer himself, and in having it identified by some of the Sioux Indians in the party who knew that warrior. To the ladies of the party this little excursion was exceedingly interesting, as it was where nearly all their husbands had risked their lives and the first battle ground they had visited." *New York Herald*, Sept. 15, 1878.

18. General Orders no. 1, Headquarters Battalion 2d Cavalry, in Camp on the Rosebud, May 10, 1877, in *New York Herald*, June 11, 1877; "Journal of the Marches," p. 1696; Snyder, Diary, May 14, 1877; Gibson to AAGDD, Oct. 1, 1877, in *Report of the Secretary of War, 1877*, p. 543.

19. Terry to AG, Military Division of the Missouri, May 31, 1877, NA, RG 393, Records of the Military Division of the Missouri, item 3039; Crook to Sheridan, May 30, 1877, ibid., item 3021; DeMontravel, "Career of Lieutenant General Nelson A. Miles," pp. 207–8.

20. Regimental Returns of the Fifth Infantry, Return for May 1877; Regimental Returns of the Second Cavalry, Return for May 1877; *Army and Navy Journal*, June 16, 1877; Snyder, Diary, May 16 and 17, 1877; Miles to AAGDD, May 16, 1877, in *Report of the Secretary of War, 1877*, p. 498; Miles to AAGDD, May 16, 1877, NA, RG 393, Records of the Military Division of the Missouri, item 31251; Gibson to AAGDD, Oct. 1, 1877, in *Report of the Secretary of War, 1877*, p. 543; Smith, "Twenty-second Regiment of Infantry," p. 488.

21. Snyder, Diary, May 23, 1877; Regimental Returns of the First Infantry, 1877, NA Microfilm Publications M665, roll 7 (hereinafter cited as Regimental Returns of the First Infantry), Return for May 1877; Gibson to AAGDD, Oct. 1, 1877, in *Report of the Secretary of War, 1877*, p. 543. Quote is from the *Leavenworth Daily Times*, June 5, 1877.

22. Regimental Returns of the Twenty-second Infantry, Return for May 1877; Gibson to AAGDD, Oct. 1, 1877, in *Report of the Secretary of War, 1877*, p. 543; Athearn, "Winter Campaign against the Sioux," pp. 283–84. Quote is from ibid., p. 284.

23. Regimental Returns of the First Infantry, Return for May 1877; Gibson to AAGDD, Oct. 1, 1877, in *Report of the Secretary of War, 1877*, p. 543; Ami Frank Mulford, *Fighting Indians! In the Seventh United States Cavalry, Custer's Favorite Regiment*, pp. 73–74,

76, 79–84, and 87; Benteen, *Camp Talk*, pp. 64–65; *Cheyenne Daily Leader*, May 11, 1877; "Report of Lieut. L. R. Hare," Jan. 24, 1878, in *Annual Report of the Chief of Engineers to the Secretary of War for the Year 1878*, vol. 2, part 3, p. 1674. For a topographical description of the terrain traversed during the cavalry march from Fort Lincoln, see also "Botanical Outlines of the Country Marched over by the Seventh United States Cavalry," in ibid., pp. 1681–87.

24. Miles to AAGDD, May 30, 1877, NA, RG 393, Records of the Military Division of the Missouri, item 3217. See also Miles to AAGDD, Dec. 27, 1877, in *Report of the Secretary of War, 1877*, p. 526.

NOTES TO CHAPTER TEN

1. "Report of Brigadier-General Terry," Nov. 12, 1877, in *Report of the Secretary of War, 1877*, p. 499; *Cheyenne Daily Leader*, Aug. 7, 1877; First Lieutenant William P. Clark to AG, Department of the Platte, Sept. 14, 1877, NA, RG 393, Records of the Military Division of the Missouri, item 5839.

2. Miles to AAGDD, June 10, 1877, NA, RG 393, Records of the Military Division of the Missouri, item 3439; "Report of Brigadier-General Terry," Nov. 12, 1877, in *Report of the Secretary of War, 1877*, p. 499. The following appear in NA, RG 393, Records of the Military Division of the Missouri: Terry to Sheridan, June 9, 1877, item 3247; AAGDD to Hazen, June 10, 1877, item 3297; Miles to AAGDD, June 19, 1877, item 2636;

Terry to Sheridan, June 23, 1877, item 3545; Terry to Miles, June 26, 1877, item 3635; Sheridan to Sherman, June 16, 1877, item 2596; AAG to Sheridan, June 20, 1877, item 2596; Hazen to AAGDD, June 26, 1877, item 2869. See also *Report of the Commissioner of Indian Affairs, 1877*, pp. 16–17; *New York Herald*, June 15, 1877.

3. Gibson to AAGDD, Oct. 1, 1877, in *Report of the Secretary of War, 1877*, p. 544. For details of the construction of the Bighorn post, see Buell to AAGDD, Oct. 24, 1877, NA, RG 393, Records of the Military Division of the Missouri, item 4606. (Also in *Report of the Secretary of War, 1877*, p. 550.) For construction and occupation of this post, see also Richard Upton, comp., ed., *Fort Custer on the Big Horn, 1877–1898*. For the new post at Tongue River, see "Report of the Quartermaster-General," Oct. 10, 1877, in *Report of the Secretary of War, 1877*, p. 213; "Report of Brigadier-General Terry," Nov. 12, 1877, in *Report of the Secretary of War, 1877*, pp. 517–18; *Cheyenne Daily Leader*, Nov. 28, 1877. This post was known as Tongue River Barracks until designated Fort Keogh. It remained active until 1900 and served as an army remount station until 1908. During World War I the fort was a depot for quartermaster stores. Frazer, *Forts of the West*, p. 82.

4. Regimental Returns of the Second Cavalry; Gibson to AAGDD, Oct. 1, 1877, in *Report of the Secretary of War, 1877*, p. 543; Snyder, Diary, June 4 and 8,

1877; Mulford, *Fighting Indians*, pp. 88–92; Benteen, *Camp Talk*, p. 67.

5. Benteen, *Camp Talk*, p. 69; Gibson to AAGDD, Oct. 1, 1877, in *Report of the Secretary of War, 1877*, pp. 543–44; Snyder, Diary, June 17 and 18, 1877; Gibson to AAGDD, Oct. 1, 1877, in *Report of the Secretary of War, 1877*, pp. 544–45.

6. Lazelle to AAG, Headquarters, Yellowstone Command, Sept. 5, 1877, in *Report of the Secretary of War, 1877*, pp. 574–75; Miles to AAGDD, Dec. 27, 1877, in *Report of the Secretary of War, 1877*, p. 526; *Cheyenne Daily Leader*, Aug. 4 and 29, 1877; Regimental Returns of the First Infantry, Battalion Field Return for July 1877, and Return for August 1877; Regimental Returns of the Second Cavalry, Return for July, 1877; Baird, "Memoranda"; Smith, "Twenty-second Regiment of Infantry," pp. 688–89; *Record of Engagements*, pp. 68–69; Gibson to AAGDD, Oct. 1, 1877, in *Report of the Secretary of War, 1877*, pp. 543–44; John E. Cox, *Five Years in the United States Army: Reminiscences and Records of an Ex-Regular*, pp. 119–28; David D. Laudenschlager, "In Pursuit: The 1877 Summer Campaign against the Sioux, according to the Letters of Lt. [Frank H.] Edmunds," in *Karl Mundt Historical and Education Foundation Series No. 13, Sixteenth Dakota History Conference, April 12–14, 1984*, comp. H. W. Blakely, pp. 359–69; Benteen, *Camp Talk*, pp. 81–82; Captain Daniel W. Burke to AAG, Department of the Platte, July 23, 1877, NA, RG 393, Rec-

ords of the Military Division of the Missouri, item 3155. See also Marquis, *Memoirs*, pp. 267–68.

7. Terry to Miles, June 4, 1877, Miles Papers, folder, Indian Campaigns, 1877, U.S. Army Military History Institute. See also Gibson to AAGDD, Oct. 1, 1877, in *Report of the Secretary of War, 1877*, p. 544; Benteen, *Camp Talk*, p. 76.

8. Gibson to AAGDD, Oct. 1, 1877, in *Report of the Secretary of War, 1877*, p. 544. For details of this march, see "Report of Lieut. L. R. Hare," in "Report of the Chief of Engineers, 1878, in *Report of the Secretary of War, 1878*, vol. 2, part 3, pp. 1675–76; Miles to AAGDD, Dec. 27, 1877, in *Report of the Secretary of War, 1877*, p. 527; Mulford, *Fighting Indians*, pp. 100–13; Snyder, Diary, July 4–14, 1877; Hanson, *Conquest of the Missouri*, pp. 369–71; De-Montravel, "Career of Lieutenant General Nelson A. Miles," p. 211.

9. *Leavenworth Daily Times*, May 11, 1877; Gibson to AAGDD, Oct. 1, 1877, in *Report of the Secretary of War, 1877*, p. 545; Miles, *Personal Recollections*, p. 256; Hanson, *Conquest of the Missouri*, p. 369; Johnson, *Unregimented General*, p. 178.

10. Snyder, Diary, July 16, 1877; Gibson to AAGDD, Oct. 1, 1877, in *Report of the Secretary of War, 1877*, p. 545; Hanson, *Conquest of the Missouri*, pp. 372–73.

11. Quoted in Finerty, *War-Path and Bivouac*, p. 343, and in Miles, *Serving the Republic*, pp. 165–66. Gibson to AAGDD, Oct. 1, 1877, in

Report of the Secretary of War, 1877, p. 545; Snyder, Diary, July 17 and 18, 1877; Hanson, *Conquest of the Missouri*, pp. 373–74; Beyer and Keydel, *Deeds of Valor*, 2:233 and 234. For information about these medal of honor recipients, see *Medal of Honor*, passim.

12. Sherman to McCrary, July 25, 1877, Miles Papers, folder, Indian Campaigns, 1877, U.S. Army Military History Institute. Frazer, *Forts of the West*, pp. 79–80 and 82.

13. Gibson to AAGDD, Oct. 1, 1877, in *Report of the Secretary of War, 1877*, p. 545; Snyder, Diary, July 24, 1877; Hutton, *Phil Sheridan and His Army*, p. 329; Hanson, *Conquest of the Missouri*, p. 381. For examples of the scouting parties, see Gibson to AAGDD, Oct. 1, 1877, in *Report of the Secretary of War, 1877*, p. 545; Miles to Mary, July 25, 1877, in Johnson, *Unregimented General*, p. 181; Hugh Lenox Scott, *Some Memories of a Soldier*, pp. 49–52.

14. "Report of Lieut. L. R. Hare," in "Report of the Chief of Engineers," 1878, in *Report of the Secretary of War, 1878*, vol. 3, part 3, p. 1676; Gibson to AAGDD, Oct. 1, 1877, in *Report of the Secretary of War, 1877*, pp. 546–47; Miles to Terry, Sept. 24, 1877, NA, RG 393, Records of the Military Division of the Missouri, item 4043; Miles to AAGDD, Dec. 27, 1877, in *Report of the Secretary of War, 1877*, p. 527; Regimental Returns of the Second Cavalry, Return for September 1877; Snyder, Diary, Sept. 17, 1877. For the Nez Perce conflict, see Mark H.

Brown, *The Flight of the Nez Perce;* Merrill D. Beal, *"I Will Fight No More Forever"*: *Chief Joseph and the Nez Perce War;* Helen Addison Howard and Dan L. McGrath, *War Chief Joseph;* and Utley, *Frontier Regulars,* pp. 296–321. For Miles's account of his participation, see *Personal Recollections,* pp. 259–80. See also Miles's August 16, 1877, instructions to Sturgis in light of unconfirmed reports that Sitting Bull had moved back into U.S. territory and was headed toward the Yellowstone. On August 19, Miles told Sturgis, "At least keep your force between the Nez Perces and Sitting Bull, if possible." Baird Papers, Kansas State Historical Society.

15. Quoted in *Report of the Commissioner of Indian Affairs, 1877,* p. 17. Miles to Terry, Sept. 24, 1877, NA, RG 393, Records of the Military Division of the Missouri, item 4043.

16. *Report of the Commissioner of Indian Affairs, 1877,* p. 17; Scout John Howard to Miles, Nov. 3, 1877, NA, RG 393, Records of the Military Division of the Missouri, item 4806; "Report of the Commanding General of the Department of Dakota, General Gibbon Commanding," Oct. 4, 1878, in *Report of the Secretary of War, 1878,* p. 65; Christopher C. Joyner, "The Hegira of Sitting Bull to Canada: Diplomatic Realpolitik, 1876–1881," pp. 10, and 12–13; William P. Clark, *The Indian Sign Language,* p. 382; Neihardt, *Black Elk Speaks,* p. 150.

17. DeMontravel, "Career of Lieutenant General Nelson A. Miles," pp. 269–71; "Report of the Commanding General of the Department of Dakota, General Gibbon Commanding," Oct. 4, 1878, in *Report of the Secretary of War, 1878,* p. 66; Utley, *Frontier Regulars,* p. 286. For the creation of the District of the Yellowstone, see "Report of Brigadier-General Terry," Nov. 12, 1877, in *Report of the Secretary of War, 1877,* pp. 484–85; General Orders no. 1, Headquarters, District of the Yellowstone, Sept. 4, 1877, NA, RG 393, entry 903, General orders and circulars, September 1877–June 1881, District of the Yellowstone; Baird, "Memoranda."

18. "Report of Brigadier-General Terry," Nov. 12, 1877, in *Report of the Secretary of War, 1877,* pp. 519–20; Miles to AAGDD, Dec. 27, 1877, in *Report of the Secretary of War, 1877,* pp. 529–30; "Report of the Commanding General of the Department of Dakota, General Gibbon Commanding," Oct. 4, 1878, in *Report of the Secretary of War, 1878,* pp. 66 and 70. For Forts Meade and Assinniboine, see Frazer, *Forts of the West,* pp. 79 and 136; and Miller and Cohen, *Military and Trading Posts of Montana,* pp. 3–9.

19. Baldwin to Miles, May 20, 1878, William Carey Brown Collection, box 21, folder 30; DeMallie, "Sioux in Dakota and Montana," p. 42.

20. *Record of Engagements,* pp. 87–88; "Fifth Regiment of Infantry," p. 478; Utley, *Frontier Regulars,* pp. 286–87. An extensive account of the 1879 campaign is in Finerty, *War-Path and Bivouac*, pp. 236–300.

21. *Record of Engagements*, pp. 93–97; Rickey, *Forty Miles a Day on Beans and Hay*, pp. 307–8; *Medal of Honor*, p. 292; "Fifth Regiment of Infantry," p. 478; Baldwin interview; McLemore, "Keogh-Bismarck Stage Route," pp. 145–46; Gary S. Freedom, "Moving Men and Supplies: Military Transportation on the Northern Great Plains, 1866–1891," pp. 119–20.

22. "Report of Brigadier-General Terry," Oct. 9, 1881, in *Report of the Secretary of War, 1881*, p. 100; Ilges to AAGDD, Jan. 31, 1881, and Feb. 12, 1881, in ibid., pp. 101–6; *Record of Engagements*, pp. 98–99; "Fifth Regiment of Infantry," pp. 478–79; Irvine, "The Eleventh Regiment of Infantry," p. 554; Robinson, *History of the Dakota*, pp. 447 and 449–50; Vestal, *Sitting Bull*, pp. 232 and 299–300; *The Last Years of Sitting Bull*, pp. 15, 17, and 49. For a contemporary account of the campaigning by Miles's troops in 1879–80, see Francis Haines, "Letters of an Army Captain [Eli L. Huggins, Second Cavalry] on the Sioux Campaign of 1879–1880," pp. 39–64. An enumeration of the events leading to Sitting Bull's surrender is in DeMallie, "Sioux in Dakota and Montana," pp. 47–54. For the frustrating reservation experience that typified the existence of many of the Tetons following the 1876–77 con-

flict with the army, see Ernest L. Schusky, *The Forgotten Sioux: An Ethnohistory of the Lower Brule Reservation*, pp. 97–140; and Robert M. Utley, *The Last Days of the Sioux Nation*, pp. 18–39.

23. Hutton, *Phil Sheridan and His Army*, p. 327.

24. "Statement of casualties among rank and file, United States Army, during the late war with Sioux Indians, Commencing in February 1876," NA, RG 92, Consolidated Correspondence File, Special File, entry 225, "Sioux." This estimate of Indian casualties has been consolidated from information contained in the several documented accounts of engagements mentioned herein, but see also Vestal, *New Sources of Indian History*, pp. 136–37. On the cost of the campaign, see U.S. Congress, Senate, "Message from the President of the United States, Communicating, in Answer to a Senate Resolution of December 7, 1877, Further Information in relation to the Cost of the Sioux War." 45th Cong. 2d. sess. S. Ex. Doc. no. 33, part 2, March 26, 1878, p. 5. The 1990 figure is calculated from data in *The Statistical History of the United States from Colonial Times to the Present*, pp. 210–11; and U.S. Bureau of the Census, *Statistical Abstract of the United States, 1987*, table no. 764, "Annual Percent Change in Selected Price Indexes: 1960 to 1985," p. 455.

Bibliography

Manuscript Material, Theses, and Dissertations

Boulder, Colorado. University of Colorado Library. Western History Collections.

William Carey Brown Collection.

Campbell, Donald B. "The Indian Campaigns of General Nelson A. Miles in Eastern Montana and the Political Organization and Settlement of that Region." Master's thesis, Montana State University, 1941.

Carlisle, Pennsylvania. Army War College. U.S. Army Military History Institute. Manuscript Division.

Nelson A. Miles Papers.

Ovenshine Family Papers.

Carpenter, Havilah. "Account of His Army Service." Unpublished manuscript, dated ca. 1937. Copy provided by James H. Gordon, Post Falls, Idaho.

Cheyenne, Wyoming. Wyoming State Archives and Historical Department. Wyoming Works Projects Administration.

Federal Writers Project Collection.

Chicago, Illinois. The Newberry Library.

Meddaugh, Samuel L., "Diary of S. L. Meddaugh, 6th U.S. Infantry, Covering the Indian Campaign along the Yellowstone River, from May to September, 1876."

Crow Agency, Montana. Custer Battlefield National Monument.

Walter M. Camp Collection.

"Diary of Simon Snyder, Captain, Co. F, 5th U.S. Infantry for 1876."

"Diary of Simon Snyder, Captain, Co. F, 5th U.S. Infantry for 1877."

DeMontravel, Peter R. "The Career of Lieutenant General Nelson A. Miles from the Civil War through the Indian Wars." Ph.D. diss., St. John's University, 1982.

Denver, Colorado. Denver Public Library. Western History Collections.

Robert S. Ellison Collection.

Denver, Colorado. Waggoner, Josephine. "Mato Ite, or Bear Face." Unpublished manuscript, n.d. Copy provided by Robert G. Palmer.

Denver, Colorado. Waggoner, Josephine. "Tahunska Tanka: John Bruguier." Unpublished manuscript, n.d. Copy provided by Robert G. Palmer.
Helena, Montana. Montana Historical Society.
Edwin M. Brown Diaries.
George M. Miles Papers.
Lincoln, Nebraska. Nebraska State Historical Society.
Eli S. Ricker Collection.
Provo, Utah. Brigham Young University. Harold B. Lee Library. Special Collections. Archives and Manuscripts.
Walter M. Camp Papers.
Roberts, Larry Don. "The Artillery with the Regular Army in the West, from 1866 to 1890." Ph.D. diss., Oklahoma State University, 1981.
San Marino, California. Henry E. Huntington Library.
Frank D. Baldwin Papers.
Topeka, Kansas. Kansas State Historical Society. Manuscripts Department.
George W. Baird Papers.
Washington, D.C. National Archives.
Luther S. Kelly, Appointments, Commissions, and Personal File.
Record Group 77. Records of the Office of the Chief of Engineers.
Record Group 92. Records of the Office of the Quartermaster General.
Record Group 94. Records of the Adjutant General's Department.
Record Group 391. Records of the U.S. Regular Army Mobile Units, 1821–1942.
Record Group 393. Records of United States Army Continental Commands.
Regimental Returns of the Fifth Infantry, 1870–79. Microfilm.
Regimental Returns of the First Infantry, 1877. Microfilm.
Regimental Returns of the Second Cavalry, 1877–78. Microfilm.
Regimental Returns of the Twenty-second Infantry, 1876–77. Microfilm.
Sioux War Papers. Microfilm.

Government Publications

Annual Report of the Chief of Engineers to the Secretary of War for the Year 1877. Washington: Government Printing Office, 1877.
Annual Report of the Chief of Engineers to the Secretary of War for the Year 1878. Washington: Government Printing Office, 1877.
Annual Report of the Commissioner of Indian Affairs, to the Secretary of the Interior for the Year 1876. Washington: Government Printing Office, 1876.

Annual Report of the Commissioner of Indian Affairs, to the Secretary of the Interior for the Year 1877. Washington: Government Printing Office, 1877.

Billings, John S. War Department. U.S. Surgeon General's Office. Circular no. 4. *A Report on Barracks and Hospitals, with Descriptions of Military Posts.* Washington: Government Printing Office, 1870. Reprint. New York: Sol Lewis, 1974.

———. War Department. U.S. Surgeon General's Office. Circular no. 8. *A Report on the Hygiene of the United States Army, with Descriptions of Posts.* Washington: Government Printing Office, 1875. Reprint. New York: Sol Lewis, 1974.

Heitman, Francis B., comp. *Historical Register and Dictionary of the United States Army, from Its Organization, September 29, 1789, to March 2, 1903.* 2 vols. Washington: Government Printing Office, 1903.

Howell, Edgar M. *United States Army Headgear, 1855–1902: Catalog of United States Army Uniforms in the Collections of the Smithsonian Institution.* Vol. 2. Washington: Smithsonian Institution Press, 1975.

Medal of Honor, 1863–1968. Washington: Government Printing Office, 1969.

The Medal of Honor of the United States Army. Washington: Government Printing Office, 1948.

Official Army Register for 1901. Washington: Adjutant General's Office, 1900.

Record of Engagements with Hostile Indians within the Military Division of the Missouri, from 1868 to 1882, Lieutenant-General P. H. Sheridan, Commanding. Washington: Government Printing Office, 1882. Reprint. Bellevue, Nebr.: Old Army Press, 1969.

Renick, B. Coleman. *Geology and Ground-Water Resources of Central and Southern Rosebud County, Montana.* Washington: Government Printing Office, 1929.

Report of the Secretary of War, 1876. Washington: Government Printing Office, 1876.

Report of the Secretary of War, 1877. Washington: Government Printing Office, 1877.

Report of the Secretary of War, 1878. Washington: Government Printing Office, 1878.

Report of the Secretary of War, 1880. Washington: Government Printing Office, 1880.

Report of the Secretary of War, 1881. Washington: Government Printing Office, 1881.

Thian, Raphael P., comp. *Notes Illustrating the Military Geography of the United States, 1813–1880.* Washington: Adjutant General's Office, 1881. Reprint. Austin: University of Texas Press, 1979.

U.S. Bureau of the Census. *Statistical Abstract of the United States, 1987.* Washington: Government Printing Office, 1987.

U.S. Congress. Senate. "Message from the President of the United
States, Communicating, in Answer to a Senate Resolution of December 7, 1877, Further Information in relation to the Cost of the
Sioux War." 45th Cong., 2d sess. S. Ex. Doc. no. 33, part 2, March
26, 1878.

Books

Adams, Alexander B. *Sitting Bull: An Epic of the Plains.* New York:
G. P. Putnam's Sons, 1973.
Athearn, Robert G. *Forts of the Upper Missouri.* Englewood Cliffs, N.J.:
Prentice-Hall, 1967.
Bailey, John W. *Pacifying the Plains: General Alfred Terry and the Decline
of the Sioux, 1866–1890.* Westport, Conn.: Greenwood Press, 1979.
Baldwin, Alice Blackwood. *Memoirs of the Late Frank D. Baldwin, Major
General, U.S.A.* Los Angeles: Wetzel, 1929.
Beal, Merrill D. *"I Will Fight No More Forever": Chief Joseph and the Nez
Perce War.* Seattle: University of Washington Press, 1963.
Benteen, Frederick W. *Camp Talk: The Very Private Letters of Frederick
W. Benteen of the 7th U.S. Cavalry to His Wife, 1871 to 1888.* Edited by
John M. Carroll. Mattituck, N.Y.: J. M. Carroll and Co., 1983.
Beyer, W. F., and O. F. Keydel, eds. *Deeds of Valor.* 2 vols. Detroit:
Perrien-Keydel Co., 1907.
Boatner, Mark Mayo III. *The Civil War Dictionary.* New York: David
McKay Co., 1959.
Bourke, John G. *Bourke's Diary, from Journals of 1st Lt. John Gregory
Bourke, June 27–Sept. 15, 1876. Chronicle of the 1876 Indian War.*
Compiled by James Willert. La Mirada, Calif.: James Willert, 1986.
————. *Mackenzie's Last Fight with the Cheyennes: A Winter Campaign
in Wyoming and Montana.* Governor's Island, New York Harbor:
Military Service Institution, 1890. Reprint. Bellevue, Nebr.: Old
Army Press, 1970.
————. *On the Border with Crook.* New York: Charles Scribner's Sons,
1891.
Brady, Cyrus Townsend. *Indian Fights and Fighters.* Garden City, N.Y.:
Doubleday, Page and Co., 1909.
Brinckerhoff, Sidney B. *Boots and Shoes of the Frontier Soldier, 1865–
1893.* Tucson: Arizona Historical Society, 1976.
Brown, Mark H. *The Flight of the Nez Perce.* New York: G. P. Putnam's
Sons, 1967.
————. *The Plainsmen of the Yellowstone: A History of the Yellowstone
Basin.* New York: G. P. Putnam's Sons, 1961.
Brown, Mark H., and W. R. Felton. *The Frontier Years: L. A. Huffman,
Photographer of the Plains.* New York: Bramhall House, 1955.

Capron, Thaddeus H. *Marching with General Crook; or, The Big Horn and Yellowstone Expedition against Hostile Indians in the Summer of 1876, . . . Being the Diary of Lieutenant Thaddeus Hurlbut Capron, Company C, Ninth Infantry.* Edited by Ray Meketa. Douglas, Alaska: Cheechako Press, 1983.

Carroll, John M., ed. *The Yellowstone Expedition of 1873.* Mattituck, N.Y.: J. M. Carroll & Co., 1986.

Chandler, Melbourne C. *Of Garryowen in Glory: The History of the Seventh United States Cavalry Regiment.* Annandale, Va.: Turnpike Press, 1960.

Chronological List of Actions, &c., with Indians, from January 15, 1837 to January, 1891. Fort Collins, Colo.: Old Army Press, 1979.

Clark, William P. *The Indian Sign Language.* Philadelphia: L. R. Hamersley and Co., 1885.

Cody, William F. *An Autobiography of Buffalo Bill.* New York: Cosmopolitan Book Corporation, 1920.

Cox, John E. *Five Years in the United States Army: Reminiscences and Records of an Ex-Regular.* Owensville, Ind.: General Baptist Publishing House, 1892. Reprint. New York: Sol Lewis, 1973.

Culbertson, Joseph. *Joseph Culbertson: Famous Indian Scout Who Served under General Miles in 1876–1895.* Wolf Point, Mont.: Privately published, 1958.

Cullum, George W. *Biographical Register of the Officers and Graduates of the U.S. Military Academy, at West Point, N.Y. . . .* 2 vols. New York: D. Van Nostrand, 1868.

DeMallie, Raymond J., ed. *The Sixth Grandfather: Black Elk's Teachings Given to John G. Neihardt.* Lincoln: University of Nebraska Press, 1984.

Dunlay, Thomas W. *Wolves for the Blue Soldiers: Indian Scouts and Auxiliaries with the United States Army, 1860–90.* Lincoln: University of Nebraska Press, 1982.

Ellis, Richard N. *General Pope and U.S. Indian Policy.* Albuquerque: University of New Mexico Press, 1970.

Erlanson, Charles B. *Battle of the Butte: General Miles' Fight with the Indians on Tongue River, January 8, 1877.* Privately published, 1963.

———. *General Miles, the Red Man's Conqueror and Champion: General Miles' Campaign against Lame Deer.* Privately published, 1969.

Finerty, John F. *War-Path and Bivouac; or, The Conquest of the Sioux.* Norman: University of Oklahoma Press, 1961.

Frazer, Robert W. *Forts of the West.* Norman: University of Oklahoma Press, 1965.

Freeman, Henry B. *The Freeman Journal: The Infantry in the Sioux Campaign of 1876.* Edited by George A. Schneider. San Rafael, Calif.: Presidio Press, 1977.

Frink, Maurice, and Casey Barthelmess, *Photographer on an Army Mule.*
Norman: University of Oklahoma Press, 1965.
Fritz, Henry E. *The Movement for Indian Assimilation, 1860–1890.* Phil-
adelphia: University of Pennsylvania Press, 1963.
Frost, Lawrence A. *Custer's 7th Cav. and the Campaign of 1873.* El Se-
gundo, Calif.: Upton and Sons, 1986.
Gallagher, Kenneth S., and Robert L. Pigeon, eds. *Infantry Regiments
of the United States Army: A Complete Guide to the History, Decorations,
Honors, and Colors of Each Infantry Regiment in the Regular Army.*
New York: Military Press, 1986.
Gibbon, John. *The Artillerist's Manual, Compiled from Various Sources,
and Adapted to the Service of the United States.* New York: D. Van Nos-
trand, 1863.
_____. *Gibbon on the Sioux Campaign of 1876.* Bellevue, Nebr.: Old
Army Press, 1970.
Godfrey, Edward S. *The Field Diary of Lt. Edward Settle Godfrey.* Edited
by Edgar I. Stewart and Jane R. Stewart. Portland, Oreg.: Cham-
poeg Press, 1957.
Graham, William A., comp. *The Custer Myth: A Source Book of Custer-
iana.* Harrisburg: Stackpole Co., 1953.
Gray, John S. *Centennial Campaign: The Sioux War of 1876.* Fort Col-
lins, Colo.: Old Army Press, 1976.
Greene, Jerome A. *Evidence and the Custer Enigma: A Reconstruction of
Indian-Military History.* 1973. Rev. ed. Golden, Colo.: Outbooks,
1986.
_____. *Slim Buttes, 1876: An Episode of the Great Sioux War.* Norman:
University of Oklahoma Press, 1982.
Grinnell, George Bird. *The Cheyenne Indians: Their History and Ways of
Life.* 2 vols. New Haven: Yale University Press, 1923.
_____. *The Fighting Cheyennes.* Norman: University of Oklahoma
Press, 1956.
_____. *Two Great Scouts and Their Pawnee Battalion.* Cleveland: Arthur
H. Clark Co., 1928.
Haley, James L. *The Buffalo War: The History of the Red River Indian
Uprising of 1874.* Garden City, N.Y.: Doubleday and Co., 1976.
Hanson, Joseph Mills. *The Conquest of the Missouri: Being the Story of
the Life and Exploits of Captain Grant Marsh.* Chicago: A. C. McClurg
and Co., 1909.
Hart, Herbert M. *Old Forts of the Northwest.* Seattle: Superior, 1963.
Hassrick, Royal B. *The Sioux: Life and Customs of a Warrior Society.*
Norman: University of Oklahoma Press, 1964.
Hedren, Paul L. *First Scalp for Custer: The Skirmish at Warbonnet Creek,
Nebraska, July 17, 1876, with a Short History of the Warbonnet Battle-
field.* Glendale, Calif.: Arthur H. Clark Co., 1980.

————. *Fort Laramie in 1876: Chronicle of a Frontier Post at War*. Lincoln: University of Nebraska Press, 1988.

Henry, Guy V., comp. *Military Record of Civilian Appointments in the United States Army*. 2 vols. New York: Carleton, 1869.

History of the Twenty-second United States Infantry, 1866–1922. N.p., n.d.

Holterman, Jack. *King of the High Missouri: The Saga of the Culbertsons*. Billings, Mont.: Falcon Press, 1987.

Howard, Helen Addison, and Dan L. McGrath, *War Chief Joseph*. Caldwell, Idaho: Caxton Printers, 1941.

Howard, James H. *The Warrior Who Killed Custer: The Personal Narrative of Chief Joseph White Bull*. Lincoln: University of Nebraska Press, 1968.

Hutton, Paul A. *Phil Sheridan and His Army*. Lincoln: University of Nebraska Press, 1985.

————, ed. *Soldiers West: Biographies from the Military Frontier*. Lincoln: University of Nebraska Press, 1987.

Hyde, George E. *Red Cloud's Folk: A History of the Oglala Sioux Indians*. Norman: University of Oklahoma Press, 1937.

————. *A Sioux Chronicle*. Norman: University of Oklahoma Press, 1956.

————. *Spotted Tail's Folk: A History of the Brule Sioux*. Norman: University of Oklahoma Press, 1961.

Johnson, Virginia W. *The Unregimented General: A Biography of Nelson A. Miles*. Boston: Houghton Mifflin Co., 1962.

Kelly, Luther S. *"Yellowstone Kelly": The Memoirs of Luther S. Kelly*. Edited by Milo Milton Quaife. New Haven: Yale University Press, 1926.

King, Charles. *Campaigning with Crook and Stories of Army Life*. New York: Harper and Brothers, 1890.

Kroeker, Marvin E. *Great Plains Command: William B. Hazen in the Frontier West*. Norman: University of Oklahoma Press, 1976.

The Last Years of Sitting Bull. Bismarck: State Historical Society of North Dakota, 1984.

McElrath, Thomson P. *The Yellowstone Valley: What It Is, Where It Is, and How to Get to It: A Handbook for Tourists and Settlers*. St. Paul: Pioneer Press Co., 1880.

Malone, Dumas, ed. *Dictionary of American Biography*. 11 vols. New York: Charles Scribner's Sons, 1933.

Mangum, Neil C. *Battle of the Rosebud: Prelude to the Little Bighorn*. El Segundo, Calif.: Upton and Sons, 1987.

Manypenny, George W. *Our Indian Wards*. Cincinnati: Robert Clarke and Co., 1880.

Mardock, Robert W. *The Reformers and the American Indian*. Columbia: University of Missouri Press, 1971.

Marquis, Thomas B. *Memoirs of a White Crow Indian*. New York: Century Co., 1928.
———. *A Warrior Who Fought Custer*. Minneapolis: Midwest Co., 1931.
Miles, Nelson A. *Personal Recollections and Observations of General Nelson A. Miles*. Chicago: Werner and Co., 1896.
———. *Serving the Republic: Memoirs of the Civil and Military Life of Nelson A. Miles, Lieutenant-General, United States Army*. New York: Harper and Brothers, 1911.
Miller, Don C., and Stan B. Cohen. *Military and Trading Posts of Montana*. Missoula: Pictorial Histories, 1978.
Mills, Cuthbert. *The Cuthbert Mills Letters to the New York Times during the Indian War of 1876*. Compiled and edited by James Willert. La Mirada, Calif.: James Willert, 1984.
Mulford, Ami Frank. *Fighting Indians! In the Seventh United States Cavalry, Custer's Favorite Regiment*. 1925. Reprint. Fairfield, Wash.: Ye Galleon Press, 1972.
Murray, Robert A. *Military Posts in the Powder River Country of Wyoming, 1865–1894*. Lincoln: University of Nebraska Press, 1968.
Neihardt, John G. *Black Elk Speaks: Being the Life Story of a Holy Man of the Oglala Sioux*. New York: William Morrow and Co., 1932. Reprint. Lincoln: University of Nebraska Press, 1961.
Nenninger, Timothy K. *The Leavenworth Schools and the Old Army: Education, Professionalism, and the Officer Corps of the United States Army, 1881–1918*. Westport, Conn.: Greenwood Press, 1978.
North, Luther. *Man of the Plains: Recollections of Luther North, 1856–1882*. Edited by Donald F. Danker. Lincoln: University of Nebraska Press, 1961.
Olson, James C. *Red Cloud and the Sioux Problem*. Lincoln: University of Nebraska Press, 1965.
The Ordnance Manual for the Use of the Officers of the United States Army. Philadelphia: J. B. Lippincott, 1862.
Otis, Elwell S. *The Indian Question*. New York: Sheldon and Co., 1878.
Pohanka, Brian C., ed. *Nelson A. Miles: A Documentary Biography of His Military Career, 1861–1903*. Glendale: Arthur H. Clark Co., 1985.
Powell, Peter J. *People of the Sacred Mountain: A History of the Northern Cheyenne Chiefs and Warrior Societies, 1830–1979, with an Epilogue, 1969–1974*. 2 vols. San Francisco: Harper and Row, 1981.
———. *Sweet Medicine: The Continuing Role of the Sacred Arrows, the Sun Dance, and the Sacred Buffalo Hat in Northern Cheyenne History*. 2 vols. Norman: University of Oklahoma Press, 1969.
Priest, Loring Benson. *Uncle Sam's Stepchildren: The Reformation of U.S. Indian Policy, 1865–1887*. New Brunswick, N.J.: Rutgers University Press, 1942.
Prucha, Francis Paul. *American Indian Policy in Crisis: Christian Reformers and the Indian, 1865–1900*. Norman: University of Oklahoma Press, 1976.

Records of Living Officers of the United States Army. Philadelphia: L. R. Hamersly and Co., 1884.

Rickey, Don, Jr. *Forty Miles a Day on Beans and Hay: The Enlisted Soldier Fighting the Indian Wars.* Norman: University of Oklahoma Press, 1963.

Ripley, Warren. *Artillery and Ammunition of the Civil War.* New York: Promontory Press, 1970.

Robinson, Doane. *A History of the Dakota or Sioux Indians.* Pierre: South Dakota State Historical Society, 1904. Reprint. Minneapolis: Ross and Haines, 1967.

Rodenbough, Theophilus F., and William L. Haskin, eds. *The Army of the United States: Historical Sketches of Staff and Line, with Portraits of Generals-in-Chief.* New York: Maynard, Merrill, and Co., 1896.

Russell, Don. *The Lives and Legends of Buffalo Bill.* Norman: University of Oklahoma Press, 1960.

Sandoz, Mari. *Cheyenne Autumn.* New York: Hastings House, 1953.

———. *Crazy Horse, the Strange Man of the Oglalas.* New York: Hastings House, 1942.

Schultz, James Willard. *William Jackson, Indian Scout.* Boston: Houghton Mifflin, 1926.

Schusky, Ernest L. *The Forgotten Sioux: An Ethnohistory of the Lower Brule Reservation.* Chicago: Nelson-Hall, 1975.

Scott, Douglas D., Richard A. Fox, Jr., Melissa A. Connor, and Dick Harmon. *Archaeological Perspectives on the Battle of the Little Bighorn.* Norman: University of Oklahoma Press, 1989.

Scott, Hugh Lennox. *Some Memories of a Soldier.* New York: Century Co., 1928.

Stands in Timber, John, and Margot Liberty. *Cheyenne Memories.* New Haven: Yale University Press, 1967.

The Statistical History of the United States from Colonial Times to the Present. New York: Basic Books, 1976.

Steinbach, Robert H. *A Long March: The Lives of Frank and Alice Baldwin.* Austin: University of Texas Press, 1989.

Stewart, Edgar I. *Custer's Luck.* Norman: University of Oklahoma Press, 1955.

———, ed. *Penny-an-Acre Empire in the West.* Norman: University of Oklahoma Press, 1968.

Tatum, Lawrie. *Our Red Brothers and the Peace Policy of President Ulysses S. Grant.* 1899. Reprint. Lincoln: University of Nebraska Press, 1970.

Terry, Alfred H. *The Field Diary of General Alfred H. Terry: The Yellowstone Expedition, 1876.* Bellevue, Nebr.: Old Army Press, n.d.

Tolman, Newton F. *The Search for General Miles.* New York: G. P. Putnam's Sons, 1968.

Trenholm, Virginia Cole. *The Arapahoes, Our People*. Norman: University of Oklahoma Press, 1970.

Upton, Richard, comp. *Fort Custer on the Big Horn, 1877–1898*. Glendale, Calif.: Arthur H. Clark Co., 1973.

U.S. Army Gallantry and Meritorious Conduct, 1866–1891. Alexandria, Va.: Planchet Press, 1986.

Utley, Robert M. *Cavalier in Buckskin: George Armstrong Custer and the Western Military Frontier*. Norman: University of Oklahoma Press, 1988.

_____. *Frontier Regulars: The United States Army and the Indian, 1866–1890*. New York: Macmillan Co., 1973.

_____. *The Indian Frontier of the American West, 1846–1890*. Albuquerque: University of New Mexico Press, 1984.

_____. *The Last Days of the Sioux Nation*. New Haven: Yale University Press, 1963.

Vaughn, Jesse W. *Indian Fights: New Facts on Seven Encounters*. Norman: University of Oklahoma Press, 1966.

_____. *The Reynolds Campaign on Powder River*. Norman: University of Oklahoma Press, 1961.

_____. *With Crook at the Rosebud*. Harrisburg: Stackpole Co., 1956.

Vestal, Stanley. *New Sources of Indian History*. Norman: University of Oklahoma Press, 1934.

_____. *Sitting Bull: Champion of the Sioux*. Norman: University of Oklahoma Press, 1957.

_____. *Warpath: The True Story of the Fighting Sioux in a Biography of Chief White Bull*. Boston: Houghton Mifflin, 1934.

Webb, George W., comp. *Chronological List of Engagements between the Regular Army of the United States and Various Tribes of Hostile Indians, which Occurred during the Years 1790 to 1898, Inclusive*. St. Joseph, Mo.: Wing Printing Co., 1939. Reprint. New York: AMS Press, 1976.

Wheeler, Homer W. *Buffalo Days*. Indianapolis: Bobbs-Merrill Co., 1923.

_____. *The Frontier Trail*. Los Angeles: Times-Mirror Press, 1923.

White, William H. *Custer, Cavalry, and Crows: The Story of William White, as told to Thomas Marquis*. Fort Collins, Colo.: Old Army Press, 1975.

Willert, James, comp. *After Little Bighorn: 1876 Campaign Rosters*. La Mirada, Calif.: James Willert, 1985.

Wooster, Robert. *The Military and United States Indian Policy, 1865–1903*. New Haven: Yale University Press, 1988.

Articles

Anderson, Harry H. "Indian Peace-Talkers and the Conclusion of the Sioux War of 1876." *Nebraska History* 44 (December 1963): 233–55.

———. "Nelson A. Miles and the Sioux War of 1876–77." *Chicago Westerners Brand Book* 16 (June 1959): 25–27 and 32.
Athearn, Robert G. "A Winter Campaign against the Sioux." *Mississippi Valley Historical Review* 35 (September 1948): 272–84.
Baird, George W. "General Miles's Indian Campaigns." *Century Magazine* 42 (July 1891): 351–70.
"The British Square." *Journal of the Military Institution of the United States* 6 (March 1885): 90.
Brown, Lisle G. "The Yellowstone Supply Depot." *North Dakota History: Journal of the Northern Plains* 40 (Winter 1973): 24–33.
DeLand, Charles E. "The Sioux Wars." *South Dakota Historical Collections* 17 (1934): 177–551.
DeMallie, Raymond J. "The Sioux in Dakota and Montana Territories: Cultural and Historical Background of the Ogden B. Read Collection." In *Vestiges of a Proud Nation: The Ogden B. Read Northern Plains Indian Collection*, 19–69. Burlington, Vt.: Robert Hull Fleming Museum, 1986.
DeMontravel, Peter R. "General Nelson A. Miles and the Wounded Knee Controversy." *Arizona and the West* 28 (Spring 1986): 23–44.
English, William L. "With Gibbon against the Sioux in 1876: The Field Diary of Lt. William L. English." Edited by Barry C. Johnson. *English Westerners' Brand Book* 8 (October 1966): 1–10.
Freedom, Gary S. "Moving Men and Supplies: Military Transportation on the Northern Great Plains, 1866–1891." *South Dakota History* 14 (Summer 1984): 114–33.
Fritz, Henry E. "The Making of Grant's Peace Policy." *Chronicles of Oklahoma* 34 (Winter 1959): 411–32.
Gray, John S. "Captain Clifford's Story—Part III." *Westerners Brand Book* 29 (August 1972): 41–43 and 48.
———. "The Lame Deer Fight Ends the Sioux War." *Westerners Brand Book* 31 (May 1974): 17–19 and 23–24.
———. "Sitting Bull Strikes the Glendive Supply Trains." *Westerners Brand Book* 28 (June 1971): 25–27 and 31–32.
———. "Sutler on Custer's Last Campaign." *North Dakota History: Journal of the Northern Plains* 43 (Summer 1976): 14–21.
———. "What Made Johnnie Bruguier Run?" *Montana: Magazine of Western History* 14 (April 1964): 32–37.
Greene, Jerome A. "The Lame Deer Fight: Last Drama of the Sioux War of 1876–1877." *By Valor and Arms: Journal of American Military History* 3, no. 3 (1979): 11–21.
Haines, Francis, ed. "Letters of an Army Captain [Eli L. Huggins, Second Cavalry] on the Sioux Campaign of 1879–1880." *Pacific Northwest Quarterly* 39 (January 1948): 39–64.
Hill, Michael D., and Ben Innis, eds. "The Fort Buford Diary of Private Sanford, 1876–1877." *North Dakota History: Journal of the Northern Plains* 52 (Summer 1986): 2–40.

Hoover, Herbert. "Sitting Bull." In *American Indian Leaders: Studies in Diversity*, edited by R. David Edmunds, 152–74. Lincoln: University of Nebraska Press, 1980.

Hunt, Fred A. "The Fight on the Little Muddy." *Pacific Monthly* 18 (November 1907): 594–601.

Joyner, Christopher C. "The Hegira of Sitting Bull to Canada: Diplomatic Realpolitik, 1876–1881." *Journal of the West* 13 (April 1974): 6–18.

Kelly, Luther S. "Memoranda on the Wolf Mountain Campaign, Montana, 1877." In *Northwestern Fights and Fighters*, Cyrus Townsend Brady, 360–61. Garden City, N.Y.: Doubleday, Page and Co., 1913.

Knight, Oliver. "War or Peace: The Anxious Wait for Crazy Horse." *Nebraska History* 54 (Winter 1973): 521–44.

Lass, William E. "Steamboats on the Yellowstone." *Montana: Magazine of Western History* 35 (Autumn 1985): 26–41.

Laudenschlager, David D. "In Pursuit: The 1877 Summer Campaign against the Sioux, according to the Letters of Lt. [Frank H.] Edmunds." In *Karl Mundt Historical and Education Foundation Series No. 13, Sixteenth Dakota History Conference, April 12–14, 1984*, compiled by H. W. Blakely, 359–69. Madison, S.D.: Dakota State College, 1985.

Levine, Richard R. "Indian Fighters and Indian Reformers: Grant's Indian Peace Policy and the Conservative Consensus." *Civil War History: Journal of the Middle Period* 31 (December 1985): 329–52.

McBlain, John F. "The Last Fight of the Sioux War of 1876–77." *Journal of the United States Cavalry Association* 10 (June 1897): 122–27.

———. "With Gibbon on the Sioux Campaign of 1876." *Journal of the United States Cavalry Association* 9 (June 1896): 139–48.

McGillycuddy, Valentine T. "Dr. McGillycuddy's Diary." Edited by Agnes Wright Spring. *Denver Westerners' 1953 Brand Book*. Boulder, Colo.: Johnson Co., 1954, pp. 277–307.

McLemore, Clyde. "The Keogh-Bismarck Stage Route." *Frontier* 13 (January 1933): 140–47.

Mardock, Robert W. "The Plains Frontier and the Indian Peace Policy, 1865–1880." *Nebraska History* 49 (Summer 1968): 187–201.

Nohl, Lessing H., Jr. "Mackenzie against Dull Knife: Breaking the Northern Cheyennes in 1876." In *Probing the American West: Papers from the Santa Fe Conference*, edited by K. Ross Toole, A. R. Mortensen, John Alexander Carroll, and Robert M. Utley, et al., 86–92. Santa Fe: Museum of New Mexico Press, 1962.

"Notes on 'General Miles's Indian Campaigns.' " *Century Magazine* 43 (January 1892): 478.

Pond, George E. "Major-General Nelson A. Miles." *McClure's Magazine* 5 (October 1895): 562–74.

Ranson, Edward. "Nelson A. Miles as Commanding General." *Military Affairs* 29 (Winter 1965–66): 179–200.

Rickey, Don, Jr. "The Battle of Wolf Mountain." *Montana: Magazine of Western History* 13 (Spring 1963): 44–54.

Riley, Paul D., ed. "Oglala Sources on the Life of Crazy Horse." *Nebraska History* 57 (Spring 1976): 1–51.

Romeyn, Henry. "The First March of the Fifth Infantry in Montana." *United Service*. Third series, 8 (August 1905): 113–16.

Smith, Vic. Letter. *Recreation* 7 (July 1897): 44.

Symons, Thomas W. "The Army and the Exploration of the West." *Journal of the Military Service Institution of the United States* 4 (September 1883): 205–49.

Utley, Robert M. "The Celebrated Peace Policy of General Grant." *North Dakota History* 20 (July 1953): 121–42.

———. "War Houses in the Sioux Country." *Montana: Magazine of Western History* 35 (Autumn 1985): 18–25.

Wade, Arthur P. "The Military Command Structure: The Great Plains, 1853–1891." *Journal of the West* 15 (July 1976): 5–22.

Waltmann, Henry. "Circumstantial Reformer: President Grant and the Indian Problem." *Arizona and the West* 13 (Winter 1971): 323–42.

Warner, Ronald Phil. "A History of Fort Buford, 1866–1895." In *Fort Buford and the Military Frontier on the Northern Plains, 1850–1900*, 41–56 and 59–63. Bismarck: State Historical Society of North Dakota, 1987.

White, Richard. "The Winning of the West: The Expansion of the Western Sioux in the Eighteenth and Nineteenth Centuries." *Journal of American History* 65 (September 1978): 319–43.

Newspapers

Army and Navy Journal, 1876–77.
Cheyenne Daily Leader, 1876–77.
Chicago Daily Tribune, 1876.
Frank Leslie's Illustrated Newspaper, 1877.
Harper's Weekly, 1877.
Leavenworth Daily Times, 1876–77.
Miles City Daily Star, 1926.
National Tribune, 1926.
New York Herald, 1876–78.
New York Times, 1876.
Stockgrower's Journal, 1907.
Winners of the West, 1932.

Index

Belknap, William W.: 80
Belle Fourche River: 111, 164
Bellows, Richard: 126
Bennett, Andrew S.: 45, 54, 102,
202; marches to Carroll City,
124–25, 127, 132, 273n30
Benton: 60, 61
Big Ankles: 291n9
Big Crow: 168–71, 173, 175,
176, 195
Big Dry River: 81, 97, 115, 121,
124, 127, 131, 132, 133, 134,
135, 222, 272n23
Big Dry Valley: 122
Bighorn and Yellowstone
Expedition: 55
Big Horn Mountains: 3, 4, 31,
33, 37, 43, 67, 69, 149, 197
Bighorn Post, Mont. Terr.: 223,
224; construction of, 185,
220; *see also* Fort Custer
Bighorn River: 5, 16, 25, 36, 69,
77, 109, 116, 178, 185, 215,
220, 223
Bighorn River Valley: 31
Big Horse: 197
Big Porcupine Creek (near
Yellowstone River): 25, 186
Bismarck, Dak.: 23, 32, 39, 182,
202, 223, 228, 254n29
Black Buttes: 123, 124, 127,
131, 132, 272n23, 273n31
Black Eagle: 99, 108
Black Elk: 175
Blackfeet Indians: 226
Blackfeet Sioux: 5, 68; *see also*
Sioux Indians (Lakotas)
Black Hairy Dog: 197
Black Hawk War: 18
Black Hills: 5, 8, 33, 55, 69, 106,
115, 154, 178, 187, 188, 219,
221, 226; gold discovered in,
5; Crook marches to, 55; and
government purchase of, 68,
151

Black Hills Agreement of 1876:
68
Black Hills Expedition of 1874:
5, 8
Black Horse: 164
Black Moccasin: 149
Black Moon: 111, 134, 255n1
Boehm, Thomas: 283n42
Boston, Mass.: 19
Bowen, William H. C.: 102
Bozeman, Mont.: 25, 155, 182
Bozeman Trail: 7
Brainard, David L.: 210, 291n9,
293n13
Brave Eagle: 294n14
Brave Wolf: 194, 203
Bridger, Jim: 25
Brisbin, James S.: 39, 290n3
Bristol, Henry B.: 61
British Possessions: 154, 223,
225
British square: 267n25
Brockmeyer, Wesley ("Yank"):
35
Brotherton, David H.: 228
Brown, Edwin M.: 45, 46, 91,
103, 104, 178, 180, 262n42,
267n24, 283n42
Brown, Paul R.: 202
Brown, William C.: 276n54
Bruguier, John: 89, 93, 94, 96,
100, 133, 135, 158, 195, 198,
202, 203, 260n37, 263n4,
265n16, 287n14;
background, 123, 188–92;
and mission to Crazy Horse,
192–93
Brule Sioux: 5, 6, 68, 94, 115,
187, 188, 195, 200; *see also*
Sioux Indians (Lakotas)
Buell, George P.: 109, 185, 220,
255n1, 269n34
Buffalo Creek: 254n1
Buffalo Horn: 158, 164